D1402928

THE
ENCYCLOPEDIA
— OF —
GAMES

MetroBooks

MetroBooks

This edition published by MetroBooks, an imprint
of Friedman/Fairfax Publishers, by arrangement with
Amber Books Ltd

2000 MetroBooks

M 10 9 8 7 6 5 4 3 2

ISBN: 15866 30962

Editorial and design by
Amber Books Ltd
Bradley's Close
74-77 White Lion Street
London N1 9PF

Contributors: Nina Hathway, Byron Jacobs, Andrew
Kinsman, Nigel Perryman, Jenny Sutcliffe
Additional material: Molly Perham, Jason Beckford-Ball
Project Editor: Brian Burns
Editor: Molly Perham
Editorial consultant: Jim Glenn
Design: Colin Hawes

Printed in the Slovak Republic

Picture Acknowledgements
Jacket design: Wilson Design Associates
Jacket photographs: Andrew Kolesnikow
All step-by-step illustrations: Colin Hawes
Chapter opener illustrations: Mike Fuller
The Publisher would like to thank the following for supplying
the equipment photographed on the jacket:
Frederick Beck Ltd
Gerry's of Wimbledon
Donay Antiques
Hamleys
Wembley Sports

CONTENTS

INTRODUCTION   6

Chapter 1

CARD GAMES   10
• PATIENCE GAMES • GAMBLING GAMES •
• NON-TRICK GAMES • TRICK GAMES • CHILDREN'S GAMES •

Chapter 2

BOARD GAMES   100
• FAMILY BOARD GAMES • RACE GAMES • WAR GAMES •
• TERRITORIAL GAMES •

Chapter 3

DOMINO & DICE GAMES   178
• DOMINO GAMES • DICE GAMES •

Chapter 4

FAMILY GAMES   202
• PARLOR GAMES • PAPER & PENCIL GAMES •
• WORD GAMES & SPOKEN GAMES • WRITTEN GAMES •

Chapter 5

SPORTING & ACTIVE GAMES   254
• GAMES OF SKILL • OUTDOOR GAMES •

RESOURCES & REFERENCES   290
• GAMES ASSOCIATIONS • READING LIST •

INDEX   294
TRADE MARK ACKNOWLEDGMENTS   304

INTRODUCTION

For thousands of years history has recorded that man has been a keen games player. The earliest recorded writings from ancient civilizations frequently refer to simple games such as Tic-Tac-Toe. As civilization has progressed so has the complexity of its games. The earliest games played were probably of the simple race variety, but many of these have developed and matured through the centuries to become sophisticated modern games such as Chess and Shogi. References to games and game boards have frequently been found etched onto classical remains, such as Hadrian's Wall.

Further evidence of the antiquity of game-playing was unearthed in early 1997 when the remains of a game and board were found at an archaeological site in Colchester – a town situated on the east coast of England and used by the Romans as a garrison town 2000 years ago. This was the first time that a gaming board of such antiquity, with the pieces set out in what appeared to be the starting position, had been found. The board measured 55 x 35cm (22 x 14in) and appeared to be checkered. The playing pieces, neatly lined up in their initial array, were blue and white glass beads, similar in size to children's marbles. One can only speculate at the rules by which play in this game was conducted.

Mental and Physical Games

It has often been thought that mental games would never achieve the prominence of their physical counterparts. Events such as the Olympic Games and the soccer World Cup have caught the public imagination in ways that never seemed possible for games such as Chess and Shogi. Historically this is probably due to the fact that a sporting event played in a large stadium can be witnessed by many thousands of people, whereas a board game would seem to restrict the possibilities for spectators. These days, however, this is no longer the case. Although television can transmit the excitement of an event such as the Olympic Games to more than a billion people, it also has the facility to home in on a small-scale game. This was apparent in 1991 when the Icelandic Bridge team won the Bermuda Bowl (the World Championship of Bridge), the first time that this small country had won any world title. The crucial final ten hands of the match concluded around 5:00 am Icelandic time. Nevertheless, 50 percent of the population stayed up to watch the conclusion on television. It is difficult to imagine any sporting event exceeding this level of spectator interest.

It has often been suggested that board games are simply not as popular as physical ones and that people much prefer an activity involving kicking or hitting a ball to one that involves a mental battle. However, the incredible popularity of board games offers compelling evidence to the contrary. Many top football players, golfers, and tennis players can command substantial fees for playing their games and also for endorsing products. However, top players in games of mental skill are also very well rewarded. For example, recent Chess matches for the World Championship have all had prize funds in excess of $1.5 million, while in Japan, top Shogi professionals can earn in excess of $1 million per season. Ely Culbertson, an erstwhile revolutionary in Russia, Mexico, and Spain, turned his hand to card-playing activities when the family fortune was wiped out in the Russian revolution in 1917. The new game of Contract Bridge provided him with the opportunity he had been looking for. After winning a prolonged match against his main rival, Sidney Lenz, in 1931, he received in excess of US$3 million for a series of short movies.

Games and Technology

The Internet provides the perfect medium for the relaying of board games to the masses. This was spectacularly demonstrated during the clash in 1997 between world Chess champion Garry Kasparov and IBM's Deep Blue computer. The games were shown live on IBM's World Wide Web site and the final game generated more "hits" than the whole of the 1996 Atlanta Olympics.

The Internet also enables players located in geographically distant locations to compete together in games. Almost all well-known board games are represented on web sites that have facilities for the games to be played in real time. This is a tremendous development, allowing enthusiasts of the more obscure games to find regular opponents.

The Strategy of Games

Expertise in games is not seen as a purely esoteric ability; it is also recognized as a manifestation of intellectual prowess. The game most frequently used as an intellectual metaphor in literature is that of Chess; many writers have expanded on this theme and incorporated it into their work. Goethe, for example, described Chess as "the touchstone of the intellect," while Lenin called it "the gymnasium of the mind." This perception of an ability at games as being evidence of an agile mind is not limited to literature. In 1990 Bankers Trust, a leading US financial institution, ran a series of advertisements in Chess Life, *the world's widest-read Chess magazine, seeking applicants for their trading division. They received over 1000 responses, eventually hiring five chessplayers, two of whom were grandmasters.*

As this example shows, games are not always merely viewed as entertaining diversions. The strategies employed to achieve success over the gaming board can also be applied in many real life situations. In fact a whole branch of study, game theory, has built up around this idea. Game theory is the abstract study of games and becomes relevant to the more serious aspects of life when the results are applied in situations such as warfare, political conflict, and economic competition. A game theorist will study the strategies that players in such "games" adopt. In 1993 the Nobel prize in economics was shared between John Harsanyi, Reinhard Selten, and John Nash. Nash's contribution was the development of his idea which has now become known as the Nash Equilibrium, a key component in the study of game theory.

Whether you wish to play games in order to improve your career prospects, or whether they simply act as an entertaining diversion, The Encyclopedia of Games *will furnish you with fascinating material on the history, rules, and basic strategies of all well-known games.*

Chapter 1
CARD
GAMES

P laying cards originated in the Far East, dating back to the tenth century. Early "cards" were made from other materials as well as card – thin strips of wood, metal, ivory, or tortoise shell. Initially cards were used in religious ceremonies, before they were used for playing games.

Cards reached Europe from the Far East in the fourteenth century, brought across by traders and gypsies in traveling caravans. At first, they were hand-painted; then, in the early fifteenth century, the first mass-produced cards appeared in Germany, followed by the rest of Europe. Christopher Columbus took a pack with him on his voyage in 1492 and introduced playing cards to America.

The early European packs had 78 cards, comprising the four standard suits each containing 14 cards, 21 tarot cards which made a fifth suit, and a joker. The fifth suit of 21 tarot cards became known as "triumphs," from which the current word "trumps" emerged. The four standard suits originally represented four classes of people: a cup for the clergy; a sword for knights; a coin for merchants; and a stave for peasants. In France, these eventually became hearts, spades, diamonds, and clubs, and Britain adopted the same symbols. Elsewhere in Europe, the suits retained their original identities.

In time, the 78-card pack split into two: the 21 tarot cards were used for fortune telling, leaving 56 playing cards. The 14 playing cards in each suit were the numbers 1–10 and four court cards – the king, queen, knight, and jack. The number of cards in each suit was then reduced to 13 by dropping the knight, and to keep the number of court cards at four, the one was promoted above the king and became the ace. This explains why the ace is sometimes high and sometimes low in different card games. In other parts of Europe, the packs were reduced still further. In Spain, the eights, nines, and tens were dropped, leaving a 40-card pack. In Germany, the twos to sixes were dropped, leaving a 32-card pack. These reduced packs are still used in games such as Piquet, which is one of the earliest games and is still popular today.

SOLITAIRE GAMES

Few activities can while away idle hours as effectively as one of the Solitaire-style card games. They can be positively mesmerizing, filling the player with a determination to reach a successful outcome.

Solitaire games are intended to be played by one person, to while away the time – as Napoleon did during his exile at St Helena after the Battle of Waterloo in 1815. The exact origin of card games for one player is obscure, but the name "Patience" (the European name for Solitaire) originated in France. One of the classical French games, La Belle Lucie, survives to this day under various names, including Lovely Lucie (a close translation of the original French) as well as The Fan – because the pack of cards is spread out on the table in 17 fans of three cards each.

The word "patience" has an identical meaning in French as in English. The craze for one-player card games was brought to Britain from mainland Europe in the 1870s. Queen Victoria's husband, Prince Albert, was an avid player and solitaire games soon became popular in drawing rooms throughout Victorian Britain.

Klondike, one of the most popular games devised in America and said to have originated during the Alaskan goldrush of 1897, is now familiar to computer games players all over the world under the name of Solitaire. It owes its popularity to an unbeatable combination of judgement, luck, attractive layout and fast-moving tempo – all of which are vital ingredients of a good solitaire game.

The number of different solitaire games runs into many hundreds. Most are played with one or two packs of cards, some with three packs and just a few with four. Special solitaire cards, which are smaller than ordinary cards, are especially useful when playing in a confined space, and are often included in specially designed travel sets for use to while away the hours on long journeys by train, bus, or plane.

At the start of most solitaire games, the cards are laid out in a prescribed formation that varies from game to game. This formation , or "tableau," together with any other cards dealt out at the beginning of play, forms the "layout." Foundation cards are the first cards of certain piles onto which sequences of cards are built – the objective of most solitaire games. In some games they form part of the layout and are set out at the beginning of the game. More often, they are not included in the layout, but are put out as they come into play.

Sometimes, as in Clock Solitaire, success depends solely on the lie of the cards and the chances of winning are slight. In other solitaire- style games, a skilled player can manipulate the cards to reach a successful conclusion. Generally, double-pack solitaire games depend more on skill than one-pack games.

CLOCK SOLITAIRE

Also known as Four of a Kind, Hidden Cards, Sundial or Travelers, this is a game that depends entirely on chance and demands no skill from the player.

Players: *one*
Equipment: *a pack of playing cards with jokers removed*
Difficulty: *no skill required*
Duration: *about five minutes for adults; children, 15 minutes or more*

The aim of the game

To arrange the cards in 13 piles, each containing four cards of the same rank, as though on the face of a clock – starting with aces at one o'clock and ending with kings in the center.

Laying out the game

Shuffle the cards and deal them into 13 piles of four cards each. The first 12 piles should be laid out in the shape of a clock-face, with each pile representing one of the numerals on the dial. The thirteenth pile is placed in the center of the circle.

Playing the game

Take the top card from the pile in the center of the clock-face (the king pile). Place it on or under the pile at the corresponding "hour" on the dial – if it is a seven, for example, place it where the hour hand would be pointing at seven o'clock. Jacks and queens should be placed at eleven and twelve o'clock respectively. Note that the king pile, because the first card is taken from it, only ever has three cards in it.

Next, pick up a facedown card from the pile that you have just added to, and place this in turn in its appropriate place on the clock-face. Take the card from the bottom if you are playing with exposed cards at the top of the pile, and from the top if you are putting the exposed cards underneath the pile. If you turn up the last face-down card of any pile and find that it belongs to that pile, take the first available face-down card from the sequence of piles going clockwise. Continue playing until you have four of a kind on each number on the dial, or until you can play no longer because you have turned up a king when the other three are already exposed.

VARIATION

One variation of Clock Solitaire is designed to overcome the obvious drawback that the game comes to a complete halt once the fourth king is turned up. This version is known as Watch Solitaire and is played in exactly the same way as Clock Solitaire with a single exception. If the fourth king is turned up before the end of the game, the player is allowed to return it facedown to any other pile in which there are unexposed cards, and to take a replacement card from the same pile. Only one replacement is allowed, but the chances of completing the game are increased fivefold.

***Diagram 1** Layout for a game of Clock Solitaire*

Diagram 2 Playing a game of Clock Solitaire

GRANDFATHER'S CLOCK

This game also involves laying out the cards as though on the dial of a clock, and the aim is to end up with the top card on each pile representing the correct number on the dial.

Players: *one*
Equipment: *a pack of playing cards with the jokers removed*

Difficulty: *no skill required*
Duration: *about 5 minutes*

The aim of the game

To build an ascending sequence of cards of the same suit on each pile or foundation.

Laying out the game

Shuffle the cards and remove 12 from the pack. These should be in sequence from the two to the king, and should follow a strict rotation of suits: for example, 2♣, 3♦, 4♥, 5♠, 6♣, 7♦, and so on. Place these in a circle, with the nine at twelve

Diagram 3 *Layout for a game of Grandfather's Clock*

o'clock, and the remainder following in clockwise sequence. Shuffle the remaining cards thoroughly and arrange them in five overlapping rows of eight cards each, with the cards facing up. This is the tableau from which cards will be taken to build up the foundations.

***Diagram 4** Playing a game of Grandfather's Clock*

Playing the game

The play is straightforward. Any card may be taken from the top row of the tableau and placed on the preceding card in the same suit on the clock-face. For example, if the 5♠ is uppermost on the clock-face, and the 6♠ is in the top row of the tableau, the six can simply be placed on top of the five, and the card underneath the six comes into play. To be placed on the clock-face, cards must be in sequence and of the same suit.

There are, however, some additional moves that can be made within the tableau itself. Any card in the top row of the pool can be moved to another column, providing that it forms a descending sequence with the top card in that column. For example, the 6♠ can be placed on the seven of any other suit. If a column becomes empty, it can be replaced by any card from the top row of the seven remaining columns.

Play continues until each of the piles on the clock-face has the correct card at the top – an ace at one o'clock, a two at two o'clock, and a queen at twelve o'clock.

KLONDIKE

Said to have originated in Alaska during the goldrush of 1897, this game will be familiar to many computer users because of its similarity to the Windows game of Solitaire.

Players: one
Equipment: a pack of playing cards with jokers removed
Difficulty: a little strategy helps
Duration: five to ten minutes

The aim of the game

To build four ascending sequences of cards of the same suit, from aces to kings.

Laying out the game

Shuffle the cards and deal out a row of seven cards, with the first card in the row faceup and the remainder facedown. Then deal a row of six cards on top of the facedown cards in the first row, again with the first card in the row faceup and the remainder facedown. Follow this in similar fashion with rows of five, four, three, two, and finally one card, until you end up with seven faceup cards in seven piles containing from one to seven cards each. This is the tableau. You should have 24 cards left in your hand to form the reserve.

Playing the game

Any exposed aces should be removed from the top row of cards and placed to one side, where they form the foundations. The card beneath the ace is then turned up – there should always be a card faceup at the top of each of the seven columns. If another ace, or a two of a suit in which the ace has already been exposed, is turned up, this can also be added to the foundations. If there are no aces showing, as is often the case, there are two further possibilities.

You may move any card in the top row to any other column provided that it forms a descending sequence with the top card of that column and is of a different color (you can move the 5♦ onto the 6♠ or 6♣, but not the 6♥). Eventually, this will mean that there is a sequence or build of several cards at the top of a column and you may move the entire sequence, or just the top

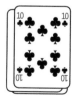

Diagram 5 Layout for a game of Klondike

Diagram 6 *Playing a game of Klondike*

part of it if you wish, to another column provided that the sequence is maintained.

If you cannot move any of the cards in the top row, you need to use the cards remaining in your hand – the reserve. There are two different ways of doing this. In the first method, cards in the reserve are turned up one at a time and you may only go through the pack once. When played this way, the game very seldom comes out. In the second method, cards are turned up three at a time, and you may go through the pack three times (or more if you don't want to observe strict rules). In the second method, you may only play the top card of the three you turn up, but once you have played the top card you can play the card beneath it, and then the ones below that, for as long as you can find somewhere to put them. Cards may be placed either directly onto a foundation, providing that they are in ascending sequence and in the same suit, or onto a card in the top row of the tableau if they are in descending sequence and of a different color.

Once a card has been played on the foundation, it cannot be returned to the tableau.

If any column becomes empty, you may fill the vacant space with a king, but not with any other card. You may move any sequence of cards built on the king at the same time.

Play continues until you have four piles, each of the same suit, in ascending order, or you cannot move a card and have been through the cards in your hand as many times as permitted.

Hints and tips

The opportunities for strategic play are greatly enhanced if you play the version in which three cards are turned up at a time. This enables you to get to know the pack and note the positions of any key cards, and plan your play accordingly. Say, for example, that the middle card of a triplet turned up from the reserve is an ace. It would obviously be beneficial to uncover it so that it can be laid in the foundation. Say the card above the ace is a 4♦, and you subsequently turn up a 5♣ in the tableau. You may decide to leave the

Diagram 7 *A completed game of Klondike*

5♣ exposed, even though you may be able to move the 4♥ to it from another column in the tableau, or you may be able to lay it onto the 4♣ in the foundation. Similarly, you may want to delay moving a king to a vacant space in the tableau if you know that you are going to turn up another, perhaps more useful king, from the reserve. And there is quite a lot that can be done by judicious moving of blocks of cards from one column to another to free cards that can then be transferred to the foundation, and perhaps to enable facedown cards to be turned up.

VARIATIONS

There are several variations on the basic game of Klondike, some involving two or more players, and others involving different layouts of the tableau. A few of these are described here.

Klondike for two or more players

In the two-player version, each player plays their own hand but to common foundations. The player with the lowest card in the left-hand, single-card, column in the tableau plays first. If these are of equal rank, the card in the second column is taken into account. A turn comes to an end when a player turns up a card or cards from the reserve.

If a player is able to move an ace to a foundation and does not do so, the second player may call the end of the turn, provided that he or she does so before the first player has made another move.

Diagram 8 *Layout of the cards for Agnes (see page 20)*

Diagram 9 Playing a game of Agnes

If the game is blocked, the winner is the player who has managed to move most cards to the foundation.

Multiple Klondike is very similar to Klondike, except that the players do not take turns: instead, all play simultaneously at their own rate from their own tableaux, and to common foundations. If more than one player is able to play to the same foundation, only the one who gets the card down first is allowed to make the play – the other player must return the card to its original position before continuing play.

Joker Klondike

This is played in exactly the same way as Klondike, but with a single joker included in the pack. When a joker is turned up, it must be played onto a foundation as a wild card. When the natural card for that foundation becomes available, it is substituted for the joker, which must then be placed on top of any of the foundation piles. If no ace has yet been played, the joker must remain where it is until one turns up.

Agnes

Play is the same as in Klondike, but with the following modifications. After dealing out the tableau, card 29 should be dealt faceup above the tableau to form the first foundation. All the other foundations must start with a card of the same value – if card 29 is a queen, then all foundations must start with a queen and all will end with a jack. The ace falls between the king and the two. After dealing card 29, lay out a row of seven cards below the tableau. These act as the reserve. Cards are played from the tableau and the reserve in exactly the same way, and according to the same rules, as in standard klondike. However, vacant columns in the tableau are filled not by kings but by cards of the next lowest value to the cards at the base of the foundations – jacks in the case of foundations that start with a queen, for example.

When it is no longer possible to play from either the tableau or the reserve, another row of seven cards is dealt to the reserve. Only the top row of the reserve can be used, and vacant spaces in the reserve must be left empty until a new row is dealt. Turn up the last two cards alongside the final row of seven.

THE FOUR CORNERS

Also known as "The Four Winds," this interesting variety of Double-pack Solitaire is difficult to complete, mainly because success relies largely on luck.

Players: *one*
Equipment: *two packs of playing cards with jokers removed*
Difficulty: *little skill involved*
Duration: *about 15 minutes*

The aim of the game
To build four ascending sequences of cards from aces, according to suit, and four descending sequences of cards from kings, also according to suit.

Laying out the game
Shuffle the two packs of cards together thoroughly. Lay out 12 cards, following the arrangement shown in diagram 10. Start at the top left-hand corner and lay a card down, faceup, at an angle of 45° to a column of four cards below it, finishing with a card at the same angle at the bottom left-hand corner. Leave sufficient space to the right of this column to accommodate a separate pile for the aces and kings of each suit – you will need to allow for four piles, two abreast. Then lay a card at 45° at the top of a right-hand column, finishing off with a card at the same angle at the bottom right-hand corner.

Move any king or ace that comes up during this stage and use it to form the base of a pile in the area that you have left in the middle, and

replace it in the outer columns or corners by another card from the pack. The kings occupy the top two rows, with two kings to each row, and the aces the bottom two. You cannot, however, move any cards from the columns other than kings and aces at this stage. If, for example, you have moved the A♣ into the middle, you cannot build on its pile with a 2♣, should you deal one (see diagram 11), until the whole game is laid out. If you find a 2♣ at a corner, though, you may move it into the centre now.

Each card in a column forms the base of a "depot," while the cards at the corners are known as "corner cards."

Playing the game
First, look at the cards that you have laid out: the idea is to build up from any ace in the center of the arrangement – first a two of the same suit, then a three and so on – and to build down from any king – a queen first, then a jack and so on. The

Diagram 10 *Layout for a game of Four Corners*

Diagram 11 *Playing a game of Four Corners*

catch is that while you can move any corner card to a central pile, as long as the suit and the sequence are correct, you can only move a card from a depot to a central pile if it is in the same row as that pile. You do not replace any cards that may have been moved from the original layout at this stage.

Next, you repeat the layout sequence, in exactly the same order, placing cards as they come from the top of the deck – again, if an ace or king are revealed, they should be moved into the central area immediately and replaced from the deck. Again, any appropriate corner cards can be moved

to the central piles, but cards from the depots can only be moved if they are in the same row as the central pile to which they are appropriate.

Continue to deal out the cards, moving them to the central pile if this is permissible, until your stock of cards is exhausted. At this point, the rules change and the real interest of the game becomes apparent. You are now allowed to move a top card from any depot onto an appropriate central pile; you can also move any of the depot cards or the corner cards to any other depot or corner, in either ascending or descend-

ing order in the same suit. However, it is as well to think carefully about the consequences before you move a card: you may be able to move more cards if you move one way rather than another.

If you come to a stop once more, you have a further option, which gives you two more chances to complete the game. Pick up the corner cards and depot cards in the order in which you first laid them down, and form a pack – but do not shuffle them. You can then deal them round the layout to see if you can improve your situation. The rules of the game allow you to do this twice, but no more.

Hints and tips

To a large extent, success in this game depends on the fall of the cards. However, it is possible to improve the chances that you will play the game out if you pay particular attention to your tactics during the stage when you have exhausted your stock of cards and the rules of the game are relaxed. Think about the consequences of any move, paying particular attention to what further opportunities any move can give you. Remember, too, that if you build up an ascending sequence in a depot at this stage, it will turn into a descending sequence when you pick up all the outer cards and deal them once more: if you have a 7♥ in a central pile, for example, an 8♥, 9♥, 10♥ sequence in a depot can be moved onto the central pile after they have been turned over to be dealt once more.

LOVELY LUCY

Originally a French game called La Belle Lucie, this is a surprisingly subtle and flexible form of Solitaire.

Players: one
Equipment: a pack of playing cards with jokers removed
Difficulty: a little strategy helps
Duration: about 15 minutes

Diagram 12 *Layout for a game of Lovely Lucy*

The aim of the game

To build four ascending sequences of cards of the same suit, from aces to kings.

Laying out the game

Shuffle the cards thoroughly, then deal three at a time, faceup, into 17 piles or "fans" of three cards each and one singleton (the only card from one suit). They can be arranged in any convenient fashion. This forms the tableau.

Playing the game

The top card of any fan, including the singleton, is available for play. Those beneath it are blocked until the top card is moved. Move any aces to one side where they form the foundations.

The remaining cards can be moved in one of two ways. They can be added to the foundations provided they are in ascending sequence and in the same suit; or they may be moved to any other fan provided they form a descending sequence in the same suit as the top card of that fan. No more than one card can be moved at a

Diagram 13 *Vacant spaces*

time. Once a card has been placed on a foundation, it cannot be moved back to the tableau. When all the cards in a fan have been used, the vacant space is not filled by moving any other card – it remains empty. When there are no further moves you can make, the remaining cards in the tableau should be picked up, shuffled thoroughly, and re-dealt in threes as before. Two re-

deals are allowed, making three deals in all.

Finally, when you have dealt three times and run out of cards that you can play, one further move is allowed. You may take any card that is blocked by the card or cards on top of it and move it anywhere appropriate on the tableau or foundations. This is known as the "merci" – the French for "thank you."

Hints and tips

It is important to remember that each card has only one other card to which it can be moved in a tableau. Once you have moved a card, therefore, it will block the cards beneath it, unless it is subsequently moved to a foundation. Not only will you not be able to move these cards to a foundation, but you will not be able to build on them, either. So take care before you bury cards

that might be valuable to you – there may be alternatives that provide a better outcome. A king at the top of a fan also renders the cards beneath it inaccessible. Remember that cards that are next lowest in sequence to cards that are blocked are effectively blocked themselves, so you can build on these with impunity. Also, you should always move any card to a foundation as soon as possible: if it can be moved to a

Diagram 14 *A re-deal*

Diagram 15 *The 5♠ is blocked by the K♣*

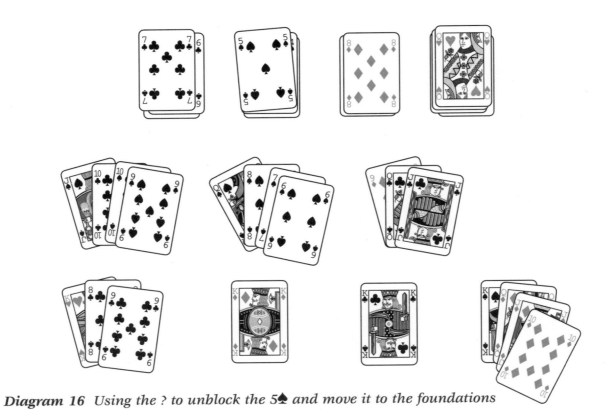

Diagram 16 *Using the ? to unblock the 5♠ and move it to the foundations*

foundation, there is nowhere it can go on the tableau, and it is merely trapping the card beneath it.

VARIATIONS
Trefoil

In a variation of the game known as Trefoil, play is exactly the same, but the four aces are taken from the pack before dealing and put on one side to form the foundations. The first tableau, therefore, consists of 16 fans of three cards each.

Shamrocks

A slightly more complex variation is known as Shamrocks. The layout of the game is identical to that of Lovely Lucy. However, after the deal, any king found above another card of the same suit is transferred beneath the lower card. Building on the tableau also follows different rules. You may build either up or down on any fan, and you need not follow suit. The catch is that no fan may contain more than three cards – a card can only be placed on top of a fan when one has already been removed from it. Empty fans are not replaced and only one deal is allowed, rather than three.

The trick in Shamrocks is to maintain as much flexibility and choice as possible for building on the tableau. The last card in a fan should not be moved until you are sure that you have no further need for it, and cards should not be transferred automatically to the foundations because they may be more useful in the short-term for building on the tableau. As a general rule, the foundations should be kept more or less level.

MONTE CARLO

Despite its name, this simple, straightforward game of chance is unlikely to have been played at the famous casino. It is also known as Double or Quits, or Weddings.

Players: one
Equipment: a pack of playing cards with the jokers removed
Difficulty: no skill involved
Duration: five to ten minutes

The aim of the game

To arrange the pack into 26 pairs of cards of equal rank.

Laying out the game

Shuffle the cards thoroughly, then deal them face-up in five rows each containing five cards. Put the remainder of the pack to one side.

Playing the game

Cards may be picked up from the tableau and discarded if they form adjoining pairs of equal rank. They may be adjoining horizontally, vertically, or diagonally. Any card is thus considered to have eight adjoining neighbors.

Once all the adjoining pairs have been removed, there will be gaps in the tableau. Fill these by moving cards to the left, or to the end of the row above, so that they still fall in the order in which they were dealt. When the tableau has been consolidated in this way, use some of the remaining cards from the pack to build up the array to 25 cards again, and discard any adjoining pairs as before. Once again, fill any gaps and rebuild the tableau with further cards from the pack.

When the pack is exhausted, continue to play, consolidating the tableau each time all pairs have been discarded. The game ends when you have 26 pairs of cards in the discard pile, or when you are faced with the final cards in an unhappy and frustrating combination such as 2-4-2-4.

Hints and tips

The only time you have a chance to influence the course of the game in Monte Carlo is when a card is paired with more than one adjoining card. In this case, you should discard the pair that will create a further pair or pairs when the tableau is consolidated.

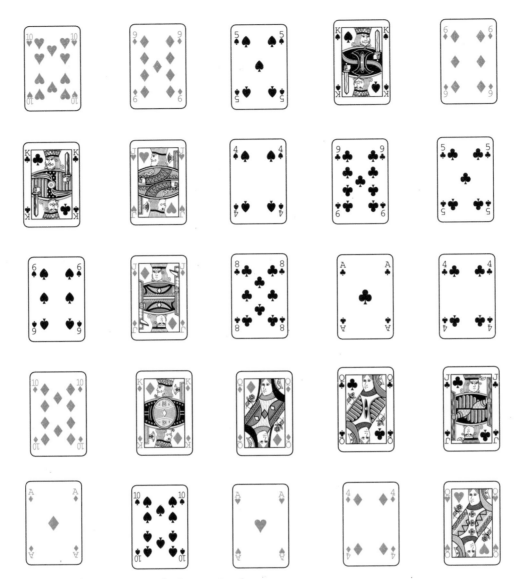

Diagram 17 *Layout for a game of Monte Carlo*

NINETY-ONE

This unusual game requires a certain amount of mental arithmetic from the player.

Players: *one*
Equipment: *a pack of playing cards with the jokers removed*
Difficulty: *a good grasp of mental arithmetic is required*
Duration: *until your patience runs out*

The aim of the game
To achieve a total score of 91 on the tableau after assigning each card its appropriate numerical value.

Laying out the game
Shuffle and deal the cards faceup into 13 piles of four cards each.

Playing the game
Each card is assigned its usual numeric value: the ace is one (not 11); two to 10 are the same as their face value; the jack is 11, the queen 12, and

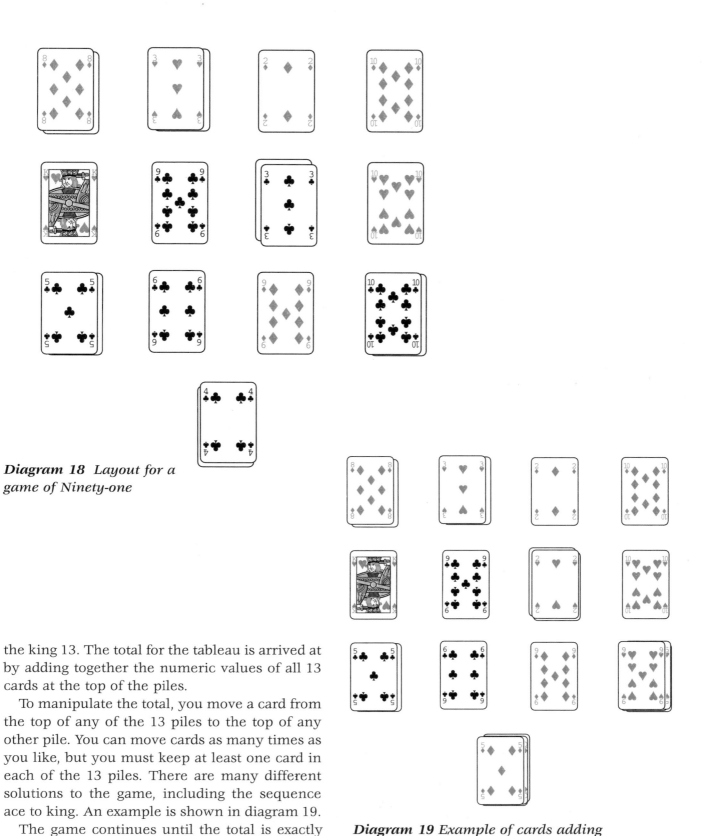

Diagram 18 *Layout for a game of Ninety-one*

the king 13. The total for the tableau is arrived at by adding together the numeric values of all 13 cards at the top of the piles.

To manipulate the total, you move a card from the top of any of the 13 piles to the top of any other pile. You can move cards as many times as you like, but you must keep at least one card in each of the 13 piles. There are many different solutions to the game, including the sequence ace to king. An example is shown in diagram 19.

The game continues until the total is exactly 91, or until your patience finally runs out.

Diagram 19 *Example of cards adding up to 91*

GAMBLING GAMES

Throughout Europe and the USA, Baccarat and related games are the mainstay of the casinos, where many a fortune has been won or lost. But there are variations of the casino games that can easily be played in less formal surroundings and can provide excellent family entertainment.

Gambling and betting date back to ancient Egyptian times, but cards were first used for gambling in the late fourteenth century. For hundreds of years, gambling games were illegal in both Britain and the USA and were played illicitly in unauthorized gambling clubs. It became a massive underground industry, with many links to organized crime. Nowadays there is a more liberal attitude to gambling and casinos are commonplace.

Games of the Baccarat and Chemin de Fer family originated in the form of Baccarat that became popular in French casinos in the 1830s. During the twentieth century, they have traveled from Europe to the USA, back to Europe again, and from both points to casinos throughout the world. This has resulted in wide variations in playing rules, and what is known as Baccarat in one casino more nearly resembles the Chemin de Fer of another. Both are games of chance with no skill involved, and the only decision the players have to make is how much to bet. A distinctive feature of Chemin de Fer is that the role of banker rotates rapidly amongst the players, whereas in Baccarat it is usually held permanently by the casino or concessionaires.

Gambling games such as Pontoon provide good family entertainment, with buttons or matchsticks as stakes and a changing banker. In the USA, the word Blackjack is often used for the domestic game, while the casino version is called Twenty-one. Confusingly, in many other countries the casino version is called Blackjack and the casino is the permanent banker.

Poker has been called the national card game of the USA, where it developed the form in which it is now known. It is the most widely played card game and the most heavily betted on. In casinos around the world, millions of dollars change hands over the Poker table. Although Poker is often said to be a game of bluffing, good play is more a question of knowing the probabilities of improving a hand, assessing whether the stake required to stay in the game is worth risking in relation to the pot and the probability of winning it, and assessing the possible value of opposing hands by the play of other players. A good player will try to work out the habits of the other players at the table, which may call for detailed assessment of the other players. The game has many variations, far more than any other card game, but a player who knows the values of the Poker hands and the principles of betting can play any variation without difficulty.

CHEMIN DE FER

This popular casino game can be played with a group of friends at home. In casinos, at least three packs of cards are used, and the cards are dispensed one at a time from a wooden box or tray called a "shoe."

Players: any number, but at least 10
Equipment: one or more identical packs of cards with the jokers removed; gambling chips or tokens
Difficulty: strategic play helps
Duration: an hour to a whole evening

The aim of the game

The object is to acquire a hand of two or three cards whose face values total nine, or as near to nine as possible; and to win a bet against the bank by having a higher total than the dealer. To arrive at the total for a hand, the cards are given values as follows:

aces = 1
twos to nines = 2 to 9 (the pip count)
tens, jacks, queens and kings = 0
In adding up the score, the 10s are ignored, so that 8 + 3 = 1 (not 11)

Beginning to play

The cards are split into smaller packs for shuffling, and passed backwards and forwards among the players until they are thoroughly shuffled. Play begins with an auction to determine who will be the first banker. The player willing to put up the highest amount to be the "bank" wins. The banker then normally deals three or four cards from the top of the pack, displays them to the players, and throws them on the discard pile. Betting then begins – the first to bet is the player to the dealer's right.

Playing the game: betting

The first player may bet up to the maximum value of the bank – if the bank is worth 50 chips, the bet can be from nothing to 50 chips against the bank. The second player to the right then bets in the same way, except that the bet may now only be as high as the value of the remaining "uncovered" chips in the bank. For example, if the first player bets 20 against a bank of 50, the second player can bet no more than 30. Play continues in this way until all players have bet, or until the total value of bets is equal to the bank's resources. The bank can never lose more than there is in the bank.

Any player is entitled to bet against the entire bank by calling "Banco," whether it is their turn or not. However, if more than one player wishes

Diagram 1 *Chemin de Fer hands with natural eights and nines*

to call "Banco," the player nearest to the dealer's right has precedence, and sitting players have preference over standing players.

Dealing the cards

When all bets have been made, the deal commences. Only two hands are dealt, one to the banker and the other to the player who holds the highest bet against the bank. This second hand represents all those who have bet against the bank: if it beats the bank, all those who have bet win; if it loses they all lose.

Cards are dealt one at a time facedown, starting with the bank's opponent, with two cards in each hand. The players examine their cards. If the bank's opponent has a "natural" eight or nine, the hand must be shown immediately (see diagram 1). If the total is anything less than five, a third card must be requested. If the total is five, the player has the option of asking for a third card, but is not obliged to do so. If the total is six or seven, the player must "stand." The additional card is always given faceup.

It is now the banker's turn. Depending on what is in the banker's hand, and on any third card given to the opponent, the banker must decide whether to take a third card. If the hand is a natural 8 or 9 the banker will always stand. The bank will also, in practice, always stand on seven, and will always draw to a zero, one, two, or three. In the case of any other total, the decision will be determined by whether the opponent took a third card or not, and if so, what its value was. Usually, decisions are made as follows:

Additional card	Banker draws to
none (opponent stands)	5, 4, 3, 2, 1, 0
ace	3, 2, 1, 0
two or three	4, 3, 2, 1, 0
four or five	5, 4, 3, 2, 1, 0
six or seven	6, 5, 4, 3, 2, 1, 0
eight	2, 1, 0
nine	(3), 2, 1, 0
ten and court cards	3, 2, 1, 0

When the banker has finished the play, both hands are shown. If the totals are equal, all bets are off and may be reclaimed from the table, and a new round of betting commences. If they are not equal, and the banker's opponent has the higher hand, all those who bet can now collect an amount equal to their bet from the bank. The bank then passes to the next player on the right, who may accept it or pass it on to the next player. There is no further auction. The new banker announces the amount they are prepared to stake, and this becomes the new bank.

If the banker wins, all bets are collected and the winnings are added to the bank, increasing the amount that can be staked in subsequent rounds. Alternatively, the banker can decide to retire, and pass the bank to the right. Until the bank has been passed on, the banker is not allowed to remove any winnings.

VARIATIONS
Baccarat

The game of Baccarat, or Baccarat banque, is one of the oldest European gambling games. It varies in two main respects from the game of Chemin de Fer described above. First, the bank does not rotate in the same way as in Chemin de Fer. The banker does not automatically lose the bank after losing a hand – it stays where it is until it is literally "bankrupt," or until the banker withdraws. When this happens, the bank is put up for auction once again. In casinos, this provides the opportunity for the casino to take a commission (usually 2%) to cover the cost of providing tables, cards, and a croupier to deal the cards. In some casinos, the bank does not change hands at all, but is held by the casino throughout. In this case, the limit is usually not the value of a specific bank, but the casino's house limit for an individual bet.

Second, the banker plays against two hands rather than one. One hand is dealt to the banker's left, the other to the right. Each hand is independent, and players may bet against the bank on either of the hands or on both. Priority in betting on the left hand circulates clockwise to the left, while betting on the right hand passes anticlockwise to the right. Betting on both hands is known as betting "à cheval," meaning "in the saddle:" these bets win only if the bank loses both hands and lose only if the bank wins both hands; otherwise they are returned.

Baccarat–Chemin de Fer

Las Vegas is the home of a further variation on the Baccarat theme. The major difference between this variation and either Baccarat or Chemin de Fer is that players can bet both for and against the bank, rather than simply against it. They can also often bet on the bank being dealt a natural eight or a natural nine, at odds of nine to one. The game is played with eight or nine packs of cards, and only two hands are dealt. The bank is usually held by the casino, and there is no banco bet.

In the Las Vegas game, the small element of discretion allowed to both player and banker is removed entirely. The question of whether to stand or draw is governed entirely by the rules.

PONTOON

Known to many as Vingt-et-un, this is an old family favorite, often played on rainy afternoons for matchsticks. It is related to the well-known casino game, Blackjack.

Players: any number
Equipment: one or more packs of cards, with jokers removed; gambling chips or tokens
Difficulty: suitable for adults and children; some strategy helps
Duration: an hour to a whole afternoon

The aim of the game

To achieve a score of 21, or as near to it as possible, and at the same time to get a higher score than the bank. To arrive at the total for a hand, the cards are given values as follows:

aces = 1 or 11
2s to 9s = two to nine (the pip count)
tens, jacks, queens and kings = 10

Players are allowed to use their discretion as to which value they attach to the ace, and can actually use both values if they have more than one ace in their hand.

Playing the game

One player is chosen as banker, usually by cutting the pack to see who draws the highest card. The banker then deals a single card facedown to each player, including the bank, starting with the player to the left. Each player then places a bet on the table. It is usual to place a limit on the bets that are allowed – no less than one token and no more than eight, for example. Once the bets are placed, the dealer, having considered their card, may double the bets. Players may then each redouble their own bets. No further doubling is allowed.

Each player then receives a second card facedown. If the second card gives any player a "pontoon" – an ace with a 10, jack, queen, or king – they immediately put the cards down on the table, with the ace facing up and the court card or 10 facing down. If the dealer also has a pontoon, the round comes to an end. The dealer collects all bets, except those belonging to other players with pontoons who are allowed to retrieve their stakes.

If the dealer does not have a pontoon, the remaining players, beginning with the player to the dealer's left, are offered more cards. A player has two options: to take the card face-up, in which case the player says "twist" or "draw," or to take the card facedown, in which case the player has to "buy" it by putting further tokens on the table – thus increasing the stake. Players cannot buy for more than their original stake, nor for less than the minimum bet.

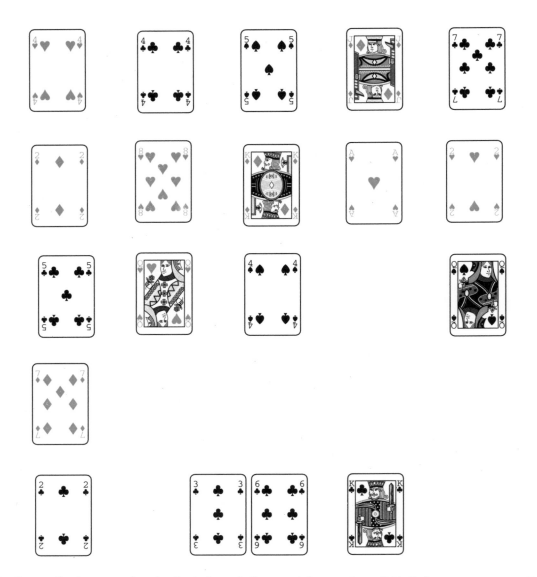

Diagram 2 *The end of a round – dealer's hand (bottom) beats C and E; D has a pontoon; B is bust*

If a player wants no more cards, they say "Stand" or "Stick," and play passes to the next player to the left. If, however, the score is still well short of 21, most players will want further cards. If they bought the previous card, they have the choice of buying or twisting the next one, otherwise they must twist – players cannot buy once they have twisted. The player continues to receive cards until they want no more, or until the total in the hand exceeds 21, at which point the player declares "Bust." A bust hand is thrown onto the table, and added face-up to the bottom of the pack. The loser's stake is taken by the bank.

The game then passes to the next player to the left, and the whole process is repeated, until all players have had their turn, and play has returned to the dealer. The dealer may stick, or may draw as many additional cards as they want, until the hand goes bust or the risk of drawing further cards seems too high. Bets are then settled (see below), and the next round begins. If any player has shown a pontoon, the bank automatically passes to them, unless they refuse it or the current dealer has also shown a pontoon. If more than one player has shown a pontoon, the player nearest the dealer's left has precedence.

Splits and five-card tricks

Pontoon is usually played with two additional features. A player who receives a pair in the first two cards of the hand may split them to make two hands. The two cards are put side by side, and the player receives a second card on each from the dealer, and matches the stake on the first hand with a similar stake on the second. This is done when the player's turn comes, and each hand is played independently.

In the five-card trick, the bank pays higher odds for hands that contain five or more cards and still totals 21 or less.

Paying up

If the dealer goes bust, the bank pays out to all players who have not also gone bust. If the dealer has not gone bust, the bank pays out to all players who have higher hands, but wins against all players with equal or lower hands. The exception is the five-card trick: this wins even when its score is beaten by the the bank. The bank pays out according to the following odds:

for a pontoon	*three times the stake*
for a score of 21	*two times the stake*
for a five-card trick	*two times the stake*
any other winner	*the value of the stake*

In addition, in some versions of the game, the bank pays higher odds for hands that total 21 through the combinations 7, 7, 7 (three times the stake) or 8, 7, 6 (two times the stake).

Hints and tips

The bank has a natural advantage in pontoon because it beats any other hand of the same value, so don't refuse it if you are entitled to claim it. Otherwise, you should be careful with your initial bet – remember that the bank can double it. An ace is obviously worth a strong bet because there are four cards that will give you a pontoon, and a second low card gives you the chance of a five-card trick. Two very low cards are worth backing for the same reason. Two aces are also worth splitting.

If your first two cards add up to 11, or are both very low in value, it is worth buying the next card – there is no further risk of the bank doubling the stakes. It can also pay off to keep an eye on the cards as they are played. If very few court cards have appeared, the odds that they will turn up are increased. You may want to think twice before drawing to 16 or 15 – or even less.

VARIATIONS
Blackjack

This is the variation of Pontoon most commonly found in European casinos. In America, where the "domestic" game more closely resembles casino practice, the term "Blackjack" is often used for the domestic game, while the casino version is called Twenty-one. Whichever of these forms it takes, Blackjack differs in several respects from Pontoon.

Most importantly, in casino Blackjack, the bank remains permanently in the hands of the casino, and the croupier deals all the hands. Bets are placed before the first card is dealt, and then two rounds are dealt, either faceup or facedown or one-up, one-down, depending on the rules of the casino. The dealer always has one card facedown. Players cannot buy cards, and there is usually no premium for five-card tricks. Splitting is usually allowed. Buying is not permitted, but players may be allowed to increase their initial stakes by "doubling down." This involves turning both cards faceup, while doubling the stake, and receiving a third card facedown. Players may not look at this third card until all other players, including the dealer, have played their hands, when it is turned up by the dealer. In some places, players may only double down if their first two cards total 10 or 11. Doubling down is a common feature of American Blackjack.

The dealer has no options in drawing cards. The bank must stand on 17 or better and must draw on 16 or lower. The bank must also accept the value of an ace as 11 unless it busts the hand.

Finally, the odds paid for a natural are three to two rather than two to one, and every other winning hand, including five-card tricks, is paid at evens.

POKER GAMES

Poker is the archetypal gambling game. The combination of card-playing skills, luck, intuition, and psychology that poker requires make it one of the most fascinating and difficult of all card games.

Players: *ideally five, six, or seven*
Equipment: *one pack of playing cards, with jokers removed (jokers may be included as wild cards); gambling chips or tokens*
Difficulty: *requires skill to play well, but can be played at a simple level*
Duration: *an hour to a whole evening*

Brief history

Poker has its roots in medieval Europe, but the modern form developed in nineteenth-century America and was spread westwards by pioneer settlers and gold prospectors. The game is so deeply ingrained in American culture that many Poker terms have passed into the language – everyone knows the meaning of "a busted flush," "when the chips are down," "an ace in the hole," or "calling someone's bluff." Famous gamblers, saloons, and even particular games have passed into American folklore. Today, Poker is far from being an exclusively American game: it is played throughout the world and there are hundreds, if not thousands, of variations on the basic game.

The aim of the game

Players bet against each other that theirs is the best hand. All bets go into a pile at the center of the table known as the "pot," and the object of the game is to win the pot.

Cards and hands

The cards are ranked in the usual order, from king down to two. Aces count high except in the sequence ace, 2, 3, 4, 5. However, in "high-low" games the ace can be either high or low and sometimes both (see below). Suit is immaterial – the ace of spades is exactly equal to any other ace.

In standard Poker games, the ranking of winning combinations of cards follows the same sequence:

Royal straight flush: *A, K, Q, J, 10 of the same suit. This is the highest possible hand in Poker; it is only beaten in single-joker games (using a 53-card pack), when "five-of-a-kind" takes precedence.*
Straight flush: *any five cards in sequence of the same suit; a 9-high straight flush beats an 8-high straight flush. This is beaten by "five-of-a-kind."*
Four-of-a-kind: *any four cards of the same rank; the fifth card is irrelevant unless it is a wild card, or there is more than one four-of-a-kind of the same rank (as can happen in some "hold 'em" variations).*
Full house: *three of a kind and a pair; the winner between two full houses is the one with the higher ranking three; thus Q, Q, Q, 2, 2 ("queens full" or "queens full of twos") beats J, J, J, 10, 10 ("jacks full" or "jacks full of tens").*
Flush: *any five cards in the same suit; the winner of two flushes is determined by the highest card or, if these are the same, by the second highest and so on; thus Q, 10, 8, 6, 5 beats Q, 10, 8, 6, 4.*
Straight: *any five cards in sequence of whatever suit; the winner of two straights is determined in the same way as for flushes.*
Two pairs: *the lower pair is only used to determine the winner if two hands have the same high pair; if both pairs are the same, the one with the higher fifth card is the winner.*
Pair: *two cards of the same rank and three unmatched cards, which are used to determine the winner if two hands have the same pair.*

High card: *if two hands match the same high card, the highest unmatched card wins.*

In low-ball (Misère) games (see page 41), including high-low games, this order is exactly reversed, and there are a few variations such as Three-card Brag and point-count games that have rules of their own. Otherwise, in virtually every form of Poker, this hierarchy is used to decide the winning hand.

Dealing

The dealer is chosen by dealing cards to each player in turn until a jack appears. The player who receives the jack becomes the first dealer. The dealer shuffles the cards, and the player on the right cuts them. The dealer then deals the cards, one at a time, starting with the player to the left, and continuing clockwise round the table. In most types of poker, each player receives five cards. These may be all facedown, or there may be a combination of faceup and facedown cards. Where there is a mixture of face-up and face-down cards, the facedown cards are referred to as "hole" cards, or simply "the hole." There may or may not be rounds of betting between cards. At the end of a "hand" (the term given to each individual game in a Poker session), the deal passes to the next player to the left, and the cards are shuffled, cut and dealt once again.

Many informal Poker schools operate on the principle of "dealer's choice," in which the dealer can nominate the particular game to be played in the next hand, leading to much variety in the course of the evening. In more formal games, for example in clubs, the same game is usually played throughout.

Betting

Betting is the essence of Poker. While the game can be played for mere tokens, Poker becomes very sedate and loses its edge if it is not played for at least a small sum of money. It is important to establish the scale of the betting (the value of the chips) at the outset – you should never play in a game where you simply cannot afford the possible losses. The maximum bet allowable should also be set. In some games, the maximum is set at "pot limit" or "half pot limit," which means that no bet can exceed the amount, or half the amount, already on the table. However, the size of the pot can escalate very quickly in

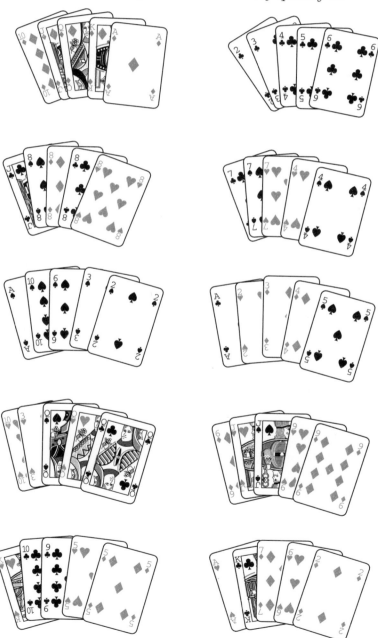

Diagram 3 *Some possible Poker hands*

a hotly contested hand, and many Poker schools prefer to set a fixed limit, for example 20 chips, on any single bet. One player is selected to keep the bank and all players then buy chips whenever they need them from the banker.

Once these preliminaries have been sorted out, and before the first hand is dealt, all players are required to "ante." This means putting an agreed initial stake, the "ante," into the pot. No hand can commence until all players have put in their ante.

Betting commences after each player has received two or more cards, depending on the variation being played. As with all other procedures in Poker, the first to bet is the player to the dealer's left, with the betting passing clockwise around the table. The first player has three options: to make no bet (check); to place a bet of any size up to the maximum allowable; or to throw in the cards (drop or fold) and take no further part in the hand. Throwing in the cards would be an unlikely choice at this stage because checking is a better option – if all the other players do the same, then the next card is free.

If the first player checks, then the second player can do the same. However, if the first player makes a bet, the second player can do one of three things: "see" or "call" the bet by putting exactly the same number of chips into the pot as the first player; "raise" it by putting in more than the bet; or fold and drop out of the hand. Players must announce clearly what they are doing as they play – for example "see your four and raise four," while putting eight chips into the pot. Play continues in this way, rotating in a clockwise direction, until all bets are equalized – that is, every player still in the game has put exactly the same amount into the pot. No player may check once the betting has opened, and no player may raise if the bets are equalized.

A typical round of betting in a hand with five players (A, B, C, D, and E) might go as follows. A, on the dealer's left, announces "check." B follows with "I'll bet two," and places two chips in the pot. C announces "raise you two," or "your two and up two," and places four chips in the

pot. D decides that the hand is getting too expensive, says "fold" and throws the cards on the table (without exposing any facedown cards), where they remain until the end of the hand. E, the dealer, announces "call" and places four chips in the pot. Play now returns to A, who must put in four chips to stay in the game. A decides to call. B then raises again with "raise you four." This means putting six chips into the pot, two to meet the earlier raise from C and four for the raise. C calls and puts in four chips. D is out of the hand. E folds and A calls again by putting four chips into the pot. At this stage, the pot contains 28 chips, plus the ante, and the three remaining players, A, B, and C, have each put in eight chips during the betting. The betting interval comes to an end. The final round of betting is followed by the "showdown," in which all players remaining in the game turn their cards faceup on the table. The best hand takes the pot.

Sometimes a situation occurs in which two players will gang up to force a third player out of the game by repeatedly raising each other – this is particularly the case in high-low games (see below). For this reason, many Poker schools place a limit on the number of raises allowed – say three or four within any one betting interval. Limits can also be set on the size of a raise: for example, no raise can more than double the current bet, and raises are limited to, say, five chips once the bet has been doubled three times. All these limits should be set before the game begins.

Hints and tips

Perhaps the best advice ever given to a budding Poker player was "Never raise a man who beats you on top." But this, very sound though it is, hardly scratches the surface of the stratagems and devices that have to be employed by a successful Poker player.

The first thing to realize is that Poker is not a game for the softhearted. The point of the game is to win, and to win as much as possible. Sympathy for your opponents – allowing them to call you cheaply rather than raising them, for example – because they have been losing all evening, has no place at the Poker table, however admirable it might be in the world outside.

Apart from this, there are two attributes that go into the making of a successful Poker player: an ability to calculate, or at least sense, the odds, and a perception of the psychology of the other players. Any hand of poker involves evaluation of your own cards. You need to be aware of the chances of improving your hand by exchanging cards, or by drawing new ones. But winning depends on the hands that the other players hold, and you can only guess what is in other people's hands by watching how they play and how they behave – do they behave in a suspiciously confident manner when they have a bad hand and go very quiet when they have a good one, for example? Some of the thinking involved in playing is illustrated in the descriptions of the different types of Poker games that follow.

DRAW POKER

One of the simplest forms of Poker, Draw Poker is easy to learn and can be more or less guaranteed to produce some good hands and exciting play.

Players: seven maximum
Equipment: one pack of playing cards; gambling chips or tokens
Difficulty: a simple form of Poker
Duration: an hour to a whole evening

Playing the game

Players ante up (put an agreed intial stake into the pot), and five cards are dealt facedown, one at a time, to each player. There is then a round of betting. Bets are placed in the usual way until all bets are equalized. Then each remaining player in turn, starting with the player to the dealer's left, may exchange any of the cards in their hand for new cards dealt from the top of the pack. Any number of cards may be exchanged.

When all players have examined their revised hands, there is a second round of betting, which continues until the bets are equalized and no further raises are possible. All players left in the game then turn up their cards – the showdown – and the best hand takes the pot. The hand comes to an end, dealership rotates to the left, and the cards are shuffled and dealt as before.

A sample game

There are five players, A, B, C, D, and E, and the hands they have been dealt are shown in diagram 4.

E was the dealer, so A is the first to bet. With A, K, Q, 10, 4, player A has the chance to make a straight if the 4 is exchanged for a jack. However, the odds against drawing to an inside straight are not good, and player A therefore decides to check. Player B has a pair of 8s. This is more promising, and B duly bets two chips. Player C has three 7s. This is a good hand, and has a reasonable chance of winning, but C has something of a dilemma: a maximum bet could frighten off the other players if they have weak hands. Merely calling the bet might encourage the other players to stay in, but the pot is still going to be relatively small. C decides to raise the bet by two chips. D also has a good hand, with four cards to a flush and a pair of jacks. However, D suspects that the hand cannot win unless it improves with the draw. C has just raised and probably has two pairs or three of a kind – unless it is a bluff, and D rather thinks that it is not. So D merely calls and puts four chips into the pot. E, with only a king high, has a decidedly mediocre hand and folds. The betting is now back to A who, wisely, decides to fold. B only needs to put in two chips to stay in the game, and decides to call. This is the wrong thing to do. B is chasing the two chips already put in: the fact that C has raised and D called should lead B to suspect that both have something better than a pair of eights. The draw will

Diagram 4 *The five hands*

have to produce something spectacular if B is to stand a chance of winning. All bets are now equalized, so C cannot raise again and the draw takes place.

Since A has folded, the first to draw is B, who draws three cards. This gives B two pairs – 8s and 6s: not a bad hand, but unlikely to win in these circumstances (see diagram 5). C draws two cards and fails to improve. D draws three cards, hoping to improve on the jacks rather than discarding a jack and drawing to the flush. D is probably making a mistake: the odds of making the flush are better than those

Diagram 5 *Three players are left in the game*

of making three of a kind. Nevertheless, D draws a third jack.

The second round of betting now commences. B decides to test the water with two chips – another mistake, but B knows that if C and D both bet, then a hand with two low pairs will have to fold. B is trying a weak preemptive bid in the vain hope that C and D both had poor hands and failed to improve. C, having only drawn two, still considers the position reasonably strong and decides to raise four, putting in six chips. D calls. D wins in the showdown and takes the pot.

The hand could have been played in a number of different ways. B should have folded in the first round of betting; D should have drawn to the flush rather than the pair. C could have tried a maximum raise at the beginning to try to force the other players out and ensure at least a meager profit from the hand.

VARIATIONS
Jacks-or-better and Aces-or-better

All these variations are dealt and bet on in the same way as straight Draw Poker. Where they differ is in the requirements for opening the betting. In Jacks-or-better the player to the dealer's left is, as usual, the first to bet. However, no player may open without a pair of Jacks or better, and in Aces-or-better the opening hand must have a minimum of a pair of aces. If the player to the dealer's left cannot open, the privilege passes to the next player to the left, and so on. If no player opens, the cards are reshuffled and redealt, and each player is required to "sweeten" the pot with a further ante. The opening player must retain their hand until the end of the game in order to display the "openers" – that is, the pair of jacks or aces or higher that qualified them to open the betting.

Wild cards

Wild card variations are common in dealer's choice games. The number of wild cards can vary considerably. In one popular variation, a single joker is used, giving a 53-card pack. The joker may be used simply as a wild card, or it may be a "bug" that can only be used to complete a flush or straight and cannot be used to duplicate a card already in the player's hand. In another popular variation, only one-eyed jacks are wild. Often, however, several wild cards are specified – twos and jacks, or both, are common choices.

The introduction of wild cards considerably changes the odds. The holder of three sevens in the example above might reasonably expect to win a hand of straight draw poker but would stand little chance of winning with wild cards involved. Wild cards also make possible the combination of "five-of-a-kind," which is normally assumed to beat any other hand except a royal straight flush.

Low-ball or Misère

This differs from standard Draw Poker in that the hierarchy of winning hands is reversed, and the lowest hand wins. Usually, the best possible hand is taken to be A, 2, 3, 4, 6, not of the same suit, and the next best is A, 2, 3, 5, 6. However, many Poker schools, and most American casinos, ignore straights and flushes in Low-ball games,

which means that the ideal hand is A, 2, 3, 4, 5 of any suit. Dealing, betting, and drawing take place in exactly the same way as in standard Draw Poker.

Low-ball hands require a rather different strategic approach. A player with a 7 or 8 high hand stands a very good chance of winning, and should not draw. But a 10-high, say, is more problematic. If several other players have stayed in the game, there is a good chance that 10-high will not win. However, drawing to four low cards, for example A, 2, 3, 4, is fraught with danger. Any A, 2, 3, 4, or 5 will ruin the hand, and a court card will not help much either. Players therefore have to remain particularly alert to what other players are doing, and improvise their strategy accordingly.

STUD POKER

For many Poker players, this is the purest form of the game, demanding all the strategic and psychological skills that the player can muster.

Players: up to 10, but no more than seven is best
Equipment: one pack of playing cards; gambling chips or tokens
Difficulty: requires a great deal of strategic skill
Duration: an hour to a whole evening

Playing the game

Players ante up (put the initial stake in the pot), and the dealer then deals one facedown card (the "hole" card) to each player, followed by one card faceup. There is then a betting interval. The player with the highest hand "on the table" – that is, the highest card showing – is the first to bet. The dealer will normally announce "ace to bet" or "king to bet." If two hands have cards showing of the same rank, the player nearest the dealer's left has priority, and the dealer announces "first ace to bet." Players are not allowed to check in the first round, although they may do so in subsequent rounds, and they may fold at any stage.

After the betting interval, a third card is dealt faceup, and another betting interval ensues. As before, the player with the highest Poker combination showing is the first to bet. Play continues in this way until all players who have not dropped or folded have received five cards – four faceup and one down – and there is a showdown. Players who have folded should turn all their cards facedown on the table; the hole card should never be revealed except in a showdown.

A sample game

There are five players, A, B, C, D, and E, with E acting as the dealer. After the ante, players are dealt one card facedown and one faceup, and the first round of betting commences. B, with an ace showing, has the highest hand, and the dealer announces "ace to bet."

B only has a two "in the hole." This is not particularly good. On the other hand, there are two sevens and two kings showing, which reduces the likelihood of the opposing players being paired. B decides that it is worth staying in for at least an initial bet and places a cautious two chips in the pot. C has ♦7 showing and ♣J in the hole. With an ace and two kings on the table, this is far from promising, so C folds. D has ♣9 in the hole to match the king. Again, this is not a particularly promising start, but it is early in the game and not yet expensive to stay, so D calls B's two chips. E has ♦Q in the hole, with ♥7 faceup.

This doesn't seem to merit even a two-chip bet, so E folds. A is showing ♠K and has ♦6 in the hole. This is not really a hand worth staying in on, but A is either feeling very lucky or very foolhardy and decides to call. At this stage there are a modest six chips in the pot, plus the ante, making 11 in all. A, B, and D now receive their third cards (see diagram 7) and there is another betting interval. B, who has drawn a 2 to the ace, pairing with the 2 in the hole, is still the highest hand and is again the first to bet. B decides to test the mettle of the other two players, and bets four chips. D, having drawn ♣7, has three to a flush and, having correctly judged that B cannot have better than a pair of 2s, decides to call.

At this stage A, who should be dropping out with only K, Q, 6, decides on a bit of bravado, possibly thinking that it might persuade the other players that the card in the hole is a king, queen, or jack. A, therefore, sees B's four and raises eight. B is not impressed and calls, secretly hoping that D will drop out. D disappoints him and calls. There are now 47 chips in the pot.

In the next round of dealing, A is rewarded with ♠A, B with ♦10, and D with ♣8.

This time, A has the bet. A is showing three to a straight, as well as having the highest hand on the table. A decides that a strong bet would be best in the circumstances – it might force the other two players out of the hand. A bets eight chips. B's hand has not improved: if either D or

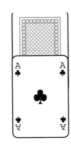

Diagram 6 First round of a sample game of Stud Poker

Diagram 7 The second round

 process. A will probably be taking up Patience in the near future. D wins the pot of 107 chips.

VARIATIONS

As with Draw Poker, there are many variations of Stud Poker. Some merely involve the designation of one or more cards as wild cards; other variations allow one or more changes of cards, with additional rounds of betting, after the first five cards have been dealt. A few of the commoner variations are described here.

Mexican Flip

This is exactly the same as Stud Poker, except that you can receive each card up or down. Two cards are dealt face-down to start with, and at an agreed signal all players turn up one of the two. They are then asked by the dealer

A is dealt a pair in the last round, it will certainly beat a pair of 2s, and D looks increasingly like holding four to a flush. B folds. D doesn't believe that A has got anything more than is showing on the table, and, with 55 chips in the pot, decides that it is worth taking a chance on drawing the fifth card to the club flush. D calls, making a total pot of 63.

A and D now receive their final cards. A fails to improve with ♦3, but D draws ♣5 to complete the flush.

D can be sure of holding the winning hand – A cannot win – but A nevertheless still wins on the table and has the first bet. A is now deeper into the game than is sensible, and suspects that D has not got a flush but more likely a pair of 7s or 8s. If that is the case, a large and confident bet might just persuade D to fold. Checking at this stage would be an invitation to D to put in a large bet, whether D has the flush or not. So A unwisely bets 16 chips. D is very happy with this and raises a further 16. A is beginning to regret the earlier failure to fold, but feels a need to see the game through to the bitter end. A sees D, losing handsomely in the

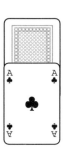

Diagram 8 The third round

whether they want subsequent cards up or down: if they choose down, they must turn up the hole card; if they choose up, they leave the hole card face-down.

Seven Card High-low

More or less any Poker game can be played "high-low" – that is, the pot is split between the player with the highest hand and the player with the lowest. Effectively, they are combinations of Low-ball games (see above) and straight Poker. The most popular of the high-low games is Seven Card High-low Stud, although Seven Card Stud can also be played as a straightforward high-only game.

Each player receives two cards facedown followed by four faceup cards. There is a round of betting between each of the faceup cards. After the betting on the fourth faceup card, a further card is dealt facedown and there is a final round

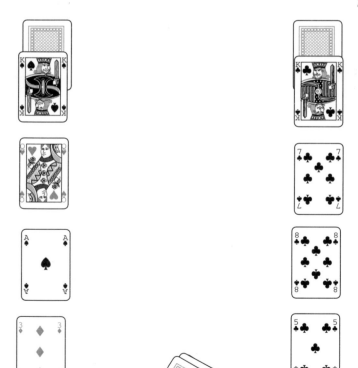

Diagram 9 *The fourth round*

of betting before the showdown. Players make the best five-card hand possible from the seven cards they hold. The hand may be either high – in which case the highest hand is determined in the usual way – or low, when precedence follows the rules of Low-ball (see above), and the lowest hand is A, 2, 3, 4, 6, not of the same suit. Players may try for both the high and the low hand, and may use as many of the same cards in each hand as they like. For example, a player holding ♥A, 2, 3, 4, 5, 6 and ♠6 can make an almost unbeatable high hand of a straight flush – ♥6, 5, 4, 3, 2 – and a winning low hand of ♥A, 2, 3, 4 and ♠6.

At the end of the final round of betting, players must declare whether they are aiming for the high hand or the low hand, or both. This is usually done by selecting different colored chips to represent the three options. Each player conceals a chip in their hand, and reveals it on top of the table at an agreed signal from the dealer. Alternatively, many players simply use their thumbs: thumbs up for high, thumbs down for low, and thumb horizontal for high-low, again all declaring simultaneously at an agreed signal from the dealer.

High-low games can be hazardous for the inexperienced – and even for the experienced – Poker player. This is because of what is known as the "squeeze." If, for example, you hold 7, 5, 3, 2, 1 of different suits, with 7, 5, 2, and another card showing, you stand a very good chance of winning the low hand. But there are two other players in the game. One is showing three of a

Diagram 10
D's winning hand

kind and is fairly certainly aiming to win the high hand. However, the other has 7, 4, 3, 2 showing and also looks set to be going low. The player with the high hand is sitting pretty (although even in situations like this, players can come unstuck), and will continue to raise for as long as possible. Your rival for the low hand is probably going to take advantage of the situation, and indulge in continuous raising of the high hand until you are forced out by the sheer expense of staying in. It is for this reason that many Poker games limit the number of raises possible during a betting round. But if you ever find yourself in a Poker game where no limit has been set, be very careful before getting into a "squeeze" situation in a high-low game. If you are not determined to play the hand to the end, whatever the cost, you should fold immediately.

TEXAS HOLD 'EM

One of a family of related Poker games, Texas Hold 'em is a favorite game of professional Poker players, particularly in Las Vegas, and a popular dealer's choice variation everywhere.

Players: up to 10, but no more than seven is best
Equipment: one pack of playing cards; gambling chips or tokens
Difficulty: requires strategic skill
Duration: an hour to a whole evening

Playing the game

Hold 'em is one of a number of Poker games in which cards are dealt into a common pool in the center of the table – known as community cards or the "flop" – and each player may use them, together with cards in the hand, to produce the best possible combination of five.

In Texas Hold 'em, each player is dealt two cards facedown, and five cards are dealt facedown to the center of the table. There is a betting interval – as in Stud Poker, players must either bet or fold in the first round – and then three of the five facedown cards in the flop are turned up. There is another betting interval, after which the remaining two cards are turned up, one at a time, with a betting round between them. There is a final betting interval and then the showdown.

VARIATIONS
Cincinnati

In this variation, each player receives five cards facedown, and a further five are dealt facedown in the middle of the table. The flop cards are then turned up one at a time, with a round of betting between each.

Omaha

In Omaha, players receive four cards in their hands rather than five, with the usual five in the center of the table. Betting takes place as in Texas hold 'em, with betting rounds after the deal, after the first three cards of the flop, and after the fourth and fifth cards. The distinctive feature of Omaha is that players must select two cards from their hand and three from the flop to make their final hand. When played high-low, a low hand must "qualify" to be eligible by going no higher than 8, and A, 2, 3, 4, 5 is the best hand.

Spit in the Ocean

This popular variation is something of a hybrid between Texas Hold 'em and Draw Poker. Each player receives four cards, as in Draw Poker, but the fifth card is taken from the top of the pack and placed faceup in the center of the table. This card is wild, as are all others of the same rank. All players have to use the center card in making their final hand. There is a single betting interval, followed by the showdown.

An interesting variant of Spit in the Ocean involves several more rounds of betting. After the initial betting interval, each player turns up one card faceup. There is a further betting interval, and then a second card is turned up. Play continues in this way until all cards have been turned up and there is a showdown.

NON-TRICK GAMES

In non-trick games, points are scored by forming certain combinations of cards, as in Rummy or Cribbage, or by "capturing" them, as in Casino and Scopa.

Along with Bridge and Poker, Rummy is one of the most popular card games. The name comes directly from "rum" – as well as drinking it, the early players used rum as their betting currency rather than money. It is a simple game that has lent itself to many variations that can be played by between two and eight players.

Gin Rummy is the most popular of the two-handed versions: from its origins in Spain, the game reached its peak of popularity during World War II, when it was taken up with much publicity by a number of Hollywood film stars, who used it to fill in time between takes. It then became an essential part of sophisticated adult social life.

Canasta, one of the most complex Rummy games, is the most popular form for four players. Taking its name from the Spanish word for "basket," it was introduced to the USA from South America in the 1940s. After becoming the most popular card game in the USA, it spread to Europe and became very popular there too. The object of a game of Rummy is to make, or "meld," sets of three or more cards of the same rank or sequences of three or more cards of the same suit, and declare them to the other players by exposing them on the table.

Casino, and the simpler version that is called Scopa, is an unusual game that can be traced back to the fifteenth-century gambling games in France. In the USA, its era of greatest popularity was eclipsed by the Gin Rummy boom of the 1930s. In both Casino and Scopa, the object of the game is to "capture" cards from the table by matching them in specified ways with cards from the hand.

Cribbage is a very old English game that has hardly changed at all in the last 350 years, since it was first played in clubs and taverns. It is still played using a wooden "noddy" board and pegs for scoring. The best boards are made of fine wood and use ivory pegs to keep score, but bone, wood, or plastic pegs are just as good and used matches are also commonly used to keep score in many households. If nothing else is available, a scoresheet drawn up on paper will also serve the purpose just as well. Originally Cribbage was a two-handed game, but variations for three and four players are now played. Cribbage is particularly popular as a partnership game, still played in pubs and clubs of its birth.

Although simple in essence, Cribbage is a game of skill and to play it well, you must be able to choose the best cards to put in the crib and be able to score points in the play. Points are scored according to a system that is unique to the game of Cribbage.

CRIBBAGE

A popular but quite complicated game, Cribbage is thought to have been devised by the English poet Sir John Suckling in the early seventeenth century. He may have used elements of a now almost entirely forgotten game called "Noddy."

Players: *best played by two, or by four in two partnerships; variations allow satisfactory games for three*
Equipment: *one pack of cards, with the jokers removed; a Cribbage board for scoring (or paper and pencil).*
Difficulty: *quite complicated*
Duration: *about half an hour*

Beginning to play

Where there are two players, the game begins with a cut to determine the dealer: the player with the lowest card takes the deal. The dealer shuffles the cards and offers them to the second player to cut. Six cards are then dealt facedown, one at a time, to each player (there are five-, six-, and seven-card variations of the game, but only the six-card version is described here). The players then consider their hands and each throws two cards into the middle of the table: these four cards form the "crib" or "box" and will be turned up at the end of the hand, with their score, if any, accruing to the dealer.

Once each player has contributed to the crib, the non-dealer cuts the pack again, and the dealer turns up the topmost card of the lower part of the pack. If the card is a jack, the dealer immediately scores two points – known as "two for his heels." The card is placed faceup on top of the pack, and later plays a significant part in the game.

Playing the game

Each player in turn, starting with the non-dealer, places one card faceup on the table, and announces the cumulative numerical total of the cards. Kings, queens and jacks score 10; aces are low and score one. For example, the non-dealer plays a king and announces "10;" the dealer plays a 7 and announces "17." The non-dealer then plays a 9 and announces "26." The maximum total allowed is 31. If a player cannot lay down a card without exceeding the total of 31, they call "go." The opposing player must then play any cards in their hand that will not bring the total to more than 31. Making a total of exactly 31 scores two. Otherwise, the player of the last card scores one point for "last." The cards that have been played are turned over, and the player who called "go" begins a new round. Play continues in this way until all cards have been turned up. The player of the last card of all scores one for last, or two if the total is 31.

There is more to the play of the cards than this, however. While laying down their cards, players may also score points, according to a scoring system that is unique to the game of cribbage.

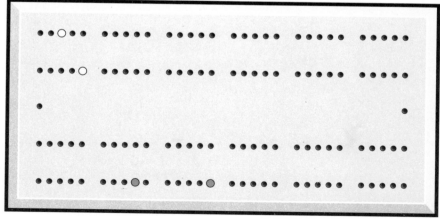

Diagram 1 A Cribbage board

Scoring during play

When played with a board, the aim is to be the first to get round the board either once (61 points) or, more often, twice (121 points). There are various combinations that can score during play. These are:

Fifteens

If the cumulative total of cards played is 15, the player of the last card scores two. For example, if the first card played is a 7, the second player can lay down an 8 and score two.

Pairs

In pairs, it is only the rank of the card that counts, not its pip, or numerical, value. A jack and a jack form a pair, but a jack and a queen do not. To form a pair, the second card must be played immediately after the first – 8, Q, 8 does not constitute a pair, but Q, 8, 8 does and scores two points.

Pairs royal and double pairs royal

If a third card is played in succession that is of equal rank to the previous two cards, for example an 8 following a pair of 8s, the player scores a "pair royal," worth six points (because a pair is worth two points and three possible pairs can be made from three of a kind). If a fourth card of the same rank follows, the player scores a "double pairs royal" worth 12 points.

Runs

Any three cards laid down that are in sequence of rank, for example 6, 7, 8, or J, Q, K, form a run of three and the player of the final card scores three points. The order in which the cards are laid down is irrelevant – 7, 8, 6, or 6, 8, 7, or 8, 6, 7, are all equally valid. Runs of four, five, and six are also possible, each scoring the same number of points as there are cards in the sequence. The same rules apply as for a run of three: it does not matter what order the cards are played in, it only matters that the last four, five, or six cards can be ordered into a ranking sequence. For example, if the first player plays a 4, the second a 7, the first a 3, and the

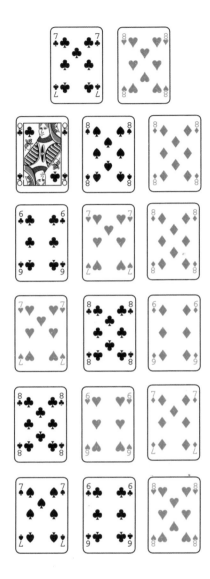

Diagram 2 Scoring combinations

second a 6, the first player can then make a run of five, scoring five points, by playing a 5.

At the end of the play, the players pick up their hands, and the "show" begins. Each player in turn lays down their hand, and announces any scoring combinations, counting out the score at the same time. Finally, the dealer turns up the cards in the crib, and calls out the scoring on this as well.

Scoring in the show

Scoring in the show is similar to scoring during play, but with a number of additional features. It is during the show that the turned up card or "start" comes into play, since it is treated as a fifth card in each player's hand and in the crib. It can therefore be combined with any card or cards in the hand to score points (2 points for a pair).

Fifteens

As in play, any combination of cards that adds up to 15 scores two points. In the show, there is the opportunity for multiple combinations adding up to 15, because each card may be used more than once, provided that each combination it makes is different. For example, say the "start" card is a 7, and a player is holding 8, 8, 7, 7. Each of the two 7s can be combined with each of the two 8s, giving six combinations of 15 – scoring 12 points (in addition to two for the pair and six for the pair royal).

Pairs and pair royals

As during play, two cards of the same rank (not value) make a pair and score two. Three of the same rank form a pair royal and score six; four of the same rank form a double pair royal, scoring 12.

Runs

The rules for forming runs are the same as during play. Again, it is the rank and not the value of the cards that matters. The same cards can be used in runs, pairs and fifteens. A hand of 9, 8, 7, 6, for example, with a 6 as the "start" can make "fifteen six" by combining each of the 6s with the 9 and the 8 with the 7. The two 6s score a further two points as a pair, and each 6 forms part of a run of four, scoring another eight. The hand is thus worth 16 points.

Flushes

Unlike during play, flushes score in the show. Four cards of the same suit in a hand score four points, or five if the start is also of the same suit. This does not apply to the crib, however, where a flush only scores if all four cards and the start are of the same suit.

One for his nob

If a player has the jack in the same suit as the start card, he or she scores one point, referred to as "one for his nob." If the start is ♥5, then ♦J scores one for his nob.

Muggins

In some games it is a rule that, if any player fails to claim a score to which they are entitled – for example, by failing to notice a run during play, or counting short during the show – then the opposing player is allowed to call "muggins" and thus claim the points. It is, however, considered particularly poor etiquette to operate this rule when playing against inexperienced opponents.

Once both hands, and the crib, have been shown, the hand comes to an end. The deal passes to the other player. New hands are dealt, and play continues as before.

The game comes to an end when one player reaches the agreed target score of, say, 121. Once this has been achieved, no further scoring is allowed, even though the loser might have been able to overtake the winner during the show.

VARIATIONS
Three- and Four-handed Cribbage

In both the three- and four-handed versions of Cribbage, the scoring and general rules of play are the same as in the two-handed version, with the following exceptions:

In the four-handed version of Cribbage, the players are divided into two partnerships, with partners combining their scores. Only five cards are dealt to each player, and each discards only a single card into the crib. In the show, the non-dealing partnership shows first.

In the three-handed version, the three players score separately (triangular Cribbage boards are available for this). Five cards are dealt to each player, with each discarding one card into the crib. The show proceeds clockwise, starting with the hand to the dealer's left.

GIN RUMMY

Originally a Spanish game, the ancestor of Rummy reached the USA in the nineteenth century and developed many variations. One of these, Gin Rummy, became enormously popular in the mid-twentieth century, by which time the modern game had taken shape.

Players: two
Equipment: one pack of cards with the jokers removed; paper and pencil for scoring
Difficulty: requires some skill
Duration: 5 to 10 minutes per hand

The aim of the game

To acquire a hand composed as nearly as possible of threes or fours of the same kind – three kings, or four 8s, say – and "sequences" containing three or more cards of the same suit in ranking sequence – ♣8, ♣9, ♣10 for example (note that ♣K, ♣A, ♣2 does not make a sequence).

Beginning to play

Players cut for deal, and the person with the highest card has the option of dealing or not. Thereafter, the winner of each hand or game deals the next round. The dealer shuffles the cards, and the non-dealer cuts. Ten cards are dealt to each player, facedown and one at a time, starting with the non-dealer. Card number 21 is turned over to become the "upcard" and laid beside the remainder of the pack, or the "stock." The non-dealer may take the upcard, in which case they replace it with another card from their hand. If the non-dealer refuses the upcard, the dealer has the option of picking it up and

Diagram 3 *A sample hand for Gin Rummy*

replacing it in the same way. If both players refuse the upcard, the non-dealer must take a card from the top of the stock, and place a card from hand on top of the upcard (so that the original upcard is concealed). The dealer may now either pick up the new upcard, or take a card from the top of the stock, laying down a card from hand (which may be the card just drawn from the stock) on top of the discard pile.

Playing the game

Play continues in this way until one or other player feels that the time has come to "go down," or "knock." It is not necessary for every card in a player's hand to form part of a set (a "gin hand") for a player to go down. Cards that are not in matching sets or sequences are called "deadwood," and a player may go down whenever the value of "deadwood" cards is 10 or less. In practice, most players would not want to go down with a deadwood score of more than five.

Players are allowed to go down after they have drawn a card during their turn – they indicate their intention by knocking on the table, or by throwing their discard on the table facedown rather than faceup. There is then a showdown. The knocker spreads out their hand on the table in the appropriate sets and sequences – no card may belong to more than one set or sequence – with deadwood cards to one side. The opponent does the same, with the difference that they are allowed to "lay off" cards from hand on the knocker's sets, provided that they match. A sequence of ♠5, ♠6, ♠7, in knocker's hand can be added to by ♠4 or ♠8 from the opposing hand, and a jack can be added to a set of three jacks. The exception to this is when the knocker has a gin hand (one with no deadwood), in which case the opposing player is not allowed to lay off at all.

If neither player goes down and the hand continues until there are only two cards left in the stock, the hand is a "washout" and declared a draw. The cards are reshuffled and a new deal begins.

Diagram 4 A set and a sequence

Scoring the game

The court cards (king, queen and jack) score 10; aces are low and score one. First, the values of the deadwood cards are counted. The player with the lower value of deadwood wins the hand and scores the difference between the two totals. If the points are equal, the opponent wins the hand. The points are written down in the form of a table (see diagram 5), with the points for each hand recorded in a separate "line" or "box." The points for each hand are added to the previous score so that a cumulative total is always shown. Various bonus points are also scored.

A	B
15	12
27	61
31	68
58	
88	
115	
75	
100	
290	
-68	
222	

Diagram 5 A score table for a game of Gin Rummy

If the opponent wins, 25 points are scored, referred to as the "undercut." If the knocker goes out with a gin hand, this too scores a bonus of 25, plus all the opposing player's deadwood points. Gin cannot be undercut, even if the opponent also has a gin hand. In addition, the winner of each hand will have a "line bonus" of 25 points per win added into their final total, at the end of the game.

The first player to reach 100 points (not including line bonuses) receives a "game bonus" of 100 points. If the loser has won no hands at all, the result is termed a "skunk," a "schneider," a "blitz" or a "washout" and the winner's score, including the game bonus but not (unless by prior agreement) the line bonuses, is doubled.

Hand 1: A knocks with 6; B has 21; A scores 15.

Hand 2: A knocks with 2; B has 14; A scores 12 and now has 27.

Hand 3: B knocks with 5; A has 17; B scores 12.

Hand 4: B goes gin; A has 24; B scores 24 plus 25 bonus for gin, making 49, and now has 61.

Hand 5: A knocks with 3; B has 7; A scores 4 and now has 31.

Hand 6: B knocks with 6; A has 4; A scores 2 plus 25 for the undercut and now has 58.

Hand 7: A goes gin; B has 5; A scores 5 plus 25 bonus for gin, making 88 in all.

Hand 8: B knocks with 1; A has 11; B scores 10, making the total 68.

Hand 9: B knocks with 5; A has 3; A scores 2 plus 25 bonus for the undercut. This brings A's score to 115, which is over 100, and the game comes to a halt.

A now adds three line bonuses of 25 each for winning three more hands than B, as well as the 100-point game bonus. This brings a total of 290. B has scored 68, which is deducted from A's total to leave A with a final winning score of 222.

VARIATIONS
Partnership Gin Rummy

Four-handed rummy involves playing two separate games simultaneously. Two packs of cards, with different patterns on their backs, are used. Players cut for partners, the two higher cards playing against the two lower cards.

The game is played in exactly the same way as Gin Rummy. At the end of each hand, the scores are reckoned in the usual way, and then each partnership combines its scores to give a final partnership total. For example, if one partner loses by five points and the other wins by nine, the combined score is plus four, which is entered on the scoresheet as a line or box.

Players change places between hands so that each partner plays each of the opposing partners in turn. In the most commonly played form of Partnership Rummy, the target score for game is set at 150 points.

Hollywood Gin

Hollywood adopted Rummy in the late 1930s and early 1940s and the well-heeled residents of Beverley Hills and Malibu turned it into a fad that swept the USA. This high-scoring game has the added thrill for the gambler of winning or losing large sums.

Essentially, Hollywood Gin involves scoring three (sometimes more) games of Gin Rummy simultaneously. The scoresheet is ruled into three sets of columns rather than one. A player enters their first winning score into the first column only. The second winning score is entered into both the first and second columns, and the third into all three. When a player reaches a score of 100 in any of the three columns, the column is closed and no further scores are added to it. In Hollywood Gin, a "whitewash" or "blitz" doubles the total score, including the line bonuses.

Play continues until one or other player has reached 100 in each of the three columns. The total score for each column is then calculated in the usual way. The winner of the game is the player with the higher total for all three columns, and the winning margin is the higher score minus the lower score.

CANASTA

A member of the Rummy family, Canasta was imported into America from Argentina and Uruguay in 1949, and became for a while the most popular game in the history of cards; the fad has passed, but it retains its popularity to this day.

Players: *four, in two partnerships*
Equipment: *two packs of cards with jokers*
Difficulty: *some skill required*
Duration: *about half an hour*

The aim of the game
Canasta is entirely a point-count game: the aim is to be the first side to reach a score of 5000 –

unlike Rummy, there is no great virtue in being the first to "go out." In scoring, cards are allocated the following values:

jokers	*50 points each*
2s	*20 points each*
aces	*20 points each*
K, Q, J, 10, 9, 8	*10 points each*
7, 6, 5, 4	*5 points each*
black 3	*5 points each*

Red 3s are given special treatment: they score 100 points each, or 800 if a side has all four of them, but these are bonus points rather than points earned during play. All jokers and 2s are wild cards: that is, they can stand for cards of any rank.

Points are scored by forming "melds." These are combinations of three or more cards of the same rank – for example, 8, 8, 8, or K, K, K, K. Wild cards may be used, so that 8, 8, 2, or K, K, joker, 2, are also valid melds. A meld, however, must contain at least two natural cards and must

Diagram 6 Melds and canastas

not contain more than three wild cards. Combinations held in the hand are not melds and have no scoring value. They must first be laid down or "melded," with the cards faceup on the table.

A meld containing seven cards is known as a canasta, and players should aim to make as many canastas as possible because they have the highest scoring value. Natural canastas – with no wild cards – score higher than mixed ones. Wild cards and red 3s may not be melded, but black 3s may be melded when a player is going out.

Beginning the game

Players cut for partners, with the two higher cards playing the two lower cards. Any player cutting the joker cuts again, as do players showing identical cards. The highest card deals first.

Cards are dealt in a clockwise fashion, facedown and one at a time, starting with the player to the dealer's left. After each player has received 11 cards, the remaining cards are placed in the middle of the table and the top card is turned faceup beside them (the "upcard") to form the basis of the discard pile. The remaining cards are the "stock."

Playing the game

The player to the dealer's left begins play by laying down, faceup, any red 3s in the hand, and drawing a replacement from the stock. They then pick up the upcard or a card from the top of the stock. At this stage, the player is entitled to meld if able to do so (see below). The turn ends with the discarding of a card from hand onto the discard pile. Play then passes to the player on the left.

Any player dealt a red 3 must immediately lay it down and take a replacement from stock. The same applies to red 3s taken from stock during play. Only red 3s acquired by capturing the discard pile (see below) are not replaced, although these too must be laid down. If a red 3 is the first card to be turned up, another card is turned up to cover it. The same applies if the first upcard is a black 3 or a wild card.

Play continues in this way, with each player drawing, melding and laying off as desired, and discarding, until either one side "goes out" (see below) or until there are no more cards left in the stock. When the stock is exhausted, play continues using the discard pile. If the upcard can be placed on an existing meld, the player must take it. There is, however, no obligation to take the upcard to make a new meld – that is for the player concerned to decide. Once there are no players willing or able to take the upcard, the deal is at an end.

If the last card is a red 3, the card is turned up and the player who drew it is then entitled to make as many melds as he wishes. However, in this situation no discard is made, and the deal ends immediately.

One rule of play is that no player may draw from a discard pile containing only one card. By convention, a player with only one card left in hand is required to announce "Last card" while discarding.

Melding

Melding is laying down a set of three or more cards of the same rank. Any player can meld in turn, after drawing a card and before discarding. However, this does not apply to the initial meld. In this case, the total point value of the meld must come to at least a certain minimum, depending on cumulative scores from previous deals. The initial meld requirements for different cumulative scores are:

Cumulative score	Requirement
minus	15
0 to 1495	50
1500 to 2995	90
over 3000	120

If a player uses a card from the top of the discard pile to make an initial meld, the value of this card can be added to the value of the meld to make up the initial requirement.

In the first deal, the initial requirement is

obviously 50, since both sides have a cumulative score of zero. If a player is found to have insufficient points in an initial meld, and provided the next player has not drawn a card, the player is obliged to rectify the situation, either by increasing the value of the meld, or by withdrawing it. The initial meld requirement for that side is increased by 10 points, and there is a 100-point penalty for each exposed card that is taken back into the hand. The same penalty applies for any incorrect meld.

Once one player in a side has melded, the other partner can meld without meeting the initial requirement. A side can only meld one set of cards of a particular rank. A meld of 5, 5, 5, cannot be laid down separately if 5s have already been melded: the cards must be "laid off" on the existing meld. Players can lay off cards on their own and their partner's melds whenever their turn comes, but they cannot lay off on their opponents' melds. Partner's melds are laid side by side on the same part of the table, and not

kept separately on opposite sides of the table.

When a meld contains seven cards, it becomes a canasta. The cards are collected into a single pile, with a red card on top if the canasta is natural, and a black card if it is mixed. Cards may be laid off on a canasta, including wild cards, but the limit of three wild cards in any meld must be observed, and the addition of wild cards to a natural canasta converts it to a mixed one of lower value. Canastas are not only desirable because of their very high values (300 for a mixed and 500 for a natural canasta), but also because no side can go out without at least one canasta – and many canasta players insist on two.

Capturing the discard pile

Winning at Canasta is a matter of adding as many cards to your hand as you can, and the way to do this is to capture the discard pile. This means taking the top card of the discard pile and combining it with two or more cards in your hand to form a meld. Once you have done this,

Diagram 7 *Capturing the discard pile*

you are entitled to pick up the remainder of the discard pile and add it to your hand.

In the official version of the game (Canasta is one of the few card games to have official rules), the discard pile has two alternative states – "frozen" and "unfrozen." The pile is frozen to any side that has not made an initial meld, and it is frozen to both sides if it contains a red 3 (as the initial upcard) or a wild card (as the initial upcard or as a discard).

The difference between these two states depends on whether you follow the official rules or adopt generally accepted practice. Officially, when the pack is unfrozen, a player may take the upcard (and capture the discard pile) if it can be laid off on an existing meld, or if it can be melded by matching it with a pair in hand, one of which can be a wild card. If the pack is frozen, then it can only be unfrozen and captured if a player matches the upcard with a natural pair in hand. In the more widely played unofficial version, the upcard can only be taken by a matching natural pair, whether the discard pile is frozen or not. In this case, the only advantage of the initial meld is that further melds (and discard captures) can be made without meeting the initial meld requirement.

Whichever version you play (and it is as well to sort this out before the game begins), the pack can be "stopped" for any individual player if the previous player discards a black 3. The "stopped" player can only draw from stock. As soon as the black 3 is covered, the pack is no longer stopped. Black 3s, for this reason, are referred to as "stop cards."

Going out

When a player lays down all his or her cards in the form of melds, that player goes out and there is no further play. Players going out do not have to discard: they can add the final card to a meld if they are able to do so.

A player going out who has not previously melded is said to be going out "concealed" and earns additional points. Going out concealed still requires that the player has enough points to meet the initial meld requirement, and must meld at least one canasta if his or her partner has not already done so.

It is legal, but not necessary, to ask your partner "May I go out partner?" before going out. Your partner must then reply "Yes" or "No" and you are bound by the reply. This routine is often used as a device to warn your partner to meld as many cards as possible because you intend to go out in the next round, and the reply is automatically "No." Only cards that have been melded contribute towards the final score: cards remaining in the hand have negative value.

Going out is usually a defensive measure, designed to stop your opponents from making too many points. The side with the bulk of the cards has the best chance of scoring canastas, and will delay going out until most of the stock has gone.

Scoring

After a player has gone out, the scores are tallied and written down. The "basic count" is calculated first according to the following scores.

For each natural canasta	*500 points*
For each mixed canasta	*300 points*
For going out concealed	*200 points*
For going out unconcealed	*100 points*
For each red 3	*100 points*
For all four red 3s	*800 points*

If a side has no melds, its red 3s count minus 100 (or minus 800 if they have all four). If a side is found to have failed to lay down a red 3, it is penalized 500 points. It is therefore possible for a side to end up with a minus score at the end of a deal.

After the basic count has been concluded, each side counts the points in its melded cards and adds them to the basic count. Finally, the value of all unmelded cards in both partner's hands is totalled and subtracted from the score. The result is the final score. This is written on the scoresheet and added to the cumulative total from previous deals. The first side to reach 5000 wins the game.

CASINO

This unusual game has its origins in medieval France and is still popular in Italy and eastern Mediterranean countries. It has more in common with traditional Chinese "fishing" games than with most other Western card games.

Players: *two, but can be adapted for three or four*
Equipment: *one pack of playing cards with the jokers removed*
Difficulty: *requires skill; suitable for adults and older children*
Duration: *about half an hour*

The aim of the game

The aim of the game is to capture cards from the table by "matching" them in specified ways with cards from the hand. Certain cards have scoring value: aces score one, and 2 to 10 score their face or "pip" value. Court cards (king, queen, and jack) have no value. The player with the highest score at the end of the game is the winner.

Playing the game

The cards are cut, and the player with the lower card becomes the first dealer. Cards are dealt two at a time, first facedown to the non-dealer, then faceup to the table, and finally facedown to the dealer. A second round of two cards is dealt in the same way, so that each player has four facedown cards, with four faceup on the table.

Play begins with the non-dealer placing a card faceup on the table. This card can be used to capture matching cards from the table. For a card to match, it must either form a pair with a table

Diagram 8 *Capturing and a sweep*

card of the same rank, or its value must be equal to the combined values of two or more table cards. A card can match several cards or combinations of cards simultaneously. If the table cards are, for example, A, 2, 5, 8, and you have an 8 in your hand, you can capture the 8 by pairing, and the A, 2, 5, by matching their combined value. You will also have captured all the cards on the table at once, making a "sweep."

Captured cards are placed in a pile, facedown, in front of the player. Sweeps are indicated by turning the hand card face-up on top of the captured cards. Court cards can only be captured by pairing since they have no value. A player can capture a single court card to make a pair, or three court cards to make a four, but it is not permissible to capture two court cards to make a three.

Building

If you cannot capture cards from the table, there is another option known as "building." The pur-
pose of a build is to position cards for capture the next time around, and you must have a card in your hand capable of making the capture. If, for example, you have a 9 and a 3 in hand and there is a 6 on the table, you can play the 3 on the 6, announce "building 9," and capture both cards the next time round with the 9. There is, of course, always the danger that your opponent will also have a 9 and will therefore capture the build before you do.

It is important that you announce clearly the value of the build in order to distinguish between "single" and "multiple" builds. If, for example, you make a build of A, 3 from the table with a 4 from your hand, you can announce either "building 4s" – a multiple build – or "building 8" – a single build. A build can only be captured by a card equal to the announced value, so if you intend to capture the build with a 4, you should "build 4s" rather than "8" and vice versa. A single build can be duplicated, becoming a

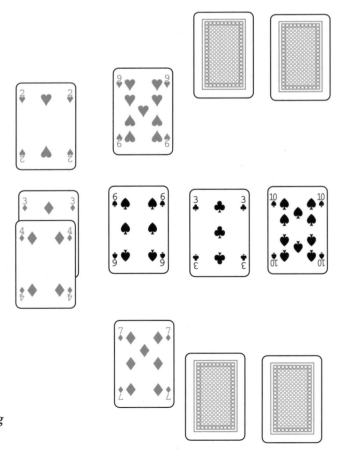

Diagram 9 *Building*

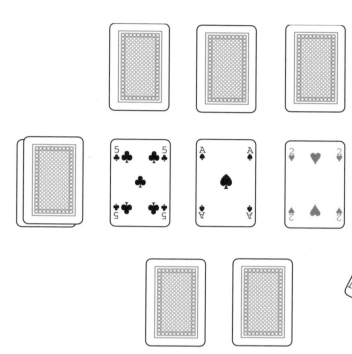

Diagram 10 *Capturing a card*

multiple build. For example, you can play a 3 from your hand onto a 6 from the table, and then add a 9 from the table, saying "building 9s." Alternatively, you can add to an existing build of nines by laying a 5 from hand on a 4 from table and then add these to the build. Obviously, multiple builds may have a total value well in excess of 10. However, their announced value – the value of the basic building block – can never exceed 10.

There is another important difference between single and multiple builds. A single build can be increased in value, provided its value does not exceed 10, and provided the player making the increase has a hand card of equal value to the new total value of the build. If one player places a 4 on a 3 from the table to make a build of 7, the opposing player can add a 2 and announce "building 9." If the first player does not have a 9, there is little that can be done, unless they have A, 10 in hand and can therefore add the ace to the build, announcing "building 10." A build can only be increased with a card from hand, and not with a card from table. The value of a multiple build cannot be increased.

Once you have made or increased a build, you cannot trail a card on your next or subsequent turns (unless, of course, the build has been captured by your opponent). You must either capture it, start a new build or add to an existing build. When both players have played all four cards in their hands, a new round or four cards each is dealt, two at a time as before. The table receives no more cards in the second or subsequent deals. The game ends when neither player has any more cards in hand and there are none left in the stock. Any cards remaining on the table are taken by the player who made the last capture. This does not count as a sweep, unless the final cards are taken by a sweep in the course of normal play.

Scoring

Players do not continue to play until an agreed score is reached: each deal is regarded as a separate game. Points are scored as follows:

For capturing most cards	*3*
For capturing most spades	*1*
For capturing ♦10 (Big Casino)	*2*
For capturing ♠2 (Little Casino)	*1*
For each ace captured	*1*
For each sweep	*1*

If there is a tie for most cards or most spades, neither player scores a point.

SCOPA

A simpler game than its close relative, Casino, Scopa is particularly suitable for children. The name comes from the Italian for "scoop" or "sweep," referring to a characteristic aspect of play.

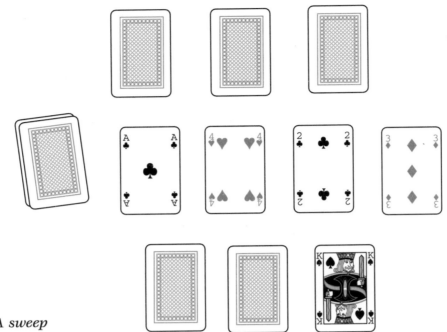

Diagram 11 A sweep

Players: two
Equipment: one pack of cards, with the 8s, 9s and 10s removed, leaving 40 cards in all
Difficulty: suitable for children
Duration: about half an hour

The aim of the game

To capture cards from the table by "matching" them with a card from hand. Each card is given a value: aces count as one; 2 to 7 are given their face, or "pip" value; jacks count as eight; queens count as nine; kings count as 10. Points are scored by capturing the majority of cards and also by capturing certain specific cards. Capturing all the cards on the table at once – a "sweep" – also scores. The winner is the first to reach an agreed score, usually 11.

Beginning the game

Players cut for deal and the player with the lower card deals first. Three cards are dealt, face-down and one at a time, to each player, starting with the non-dealer, followed by four cards face-up on the table. The remainder of the pack is placed facedown beside the table cards: this is

the "stock." Play begins with the non-dealer.

Playing the game

Each player has two options – to capture, or to "trail." To capture a card, or cards, from the table, a player must play a matching card faceup on the table. There are two ways in which a card can match: it can form a pair with another card of the same rank; and it can match any combination of two or more table cards that have the same total face value. For example, a jack in your hand can match another jack on the table, or it can match 5, 3, or A, 5, 2, on the table. But it cannot match both at once. If the table cards are A, 5, 2, J (see diagram 10), and you play a jack from your hand, you are obliged to capture the jack rather than the combination – the pair always takes precedence. You do not have to play the jack at all if you do not want to: you can play any other card in your hand instead.

If you lay down a card that does not make a capture, you "trail" the card. It simply stays face-up on the table, where it is available for capture by either player. It is generally accepted that a card cannot be trailed if it can make a capture. If it is able to capture any of the table cards, then once it has been played it must do so.

Players place captured cards facedown in a pile. The exception is in the case of a "sweep." A sweep means capturing all the cards on the table at once. When this happens, the hand card used to make the capture is turned faceup on top of the pile, making it easy to count the number of sweeps at the end of the deal. Since the number of table cards varies during play, it can sometimes be quite easy to make a sweep.

Once you have made a sweep, your opponent can only "trail" a card, because there is nothing there to capture. If you can do this by pairing, then you have made another valid sweep.

When both players have exhausted their cards, three further cards are dealt to each of them, face-down as before. In all, there are five deals of three cards each in a game. The game ends when neither player has any cards in hand and there are none left in stock. Any cards remaining on the table are deemed to have been captured by the player of the last card and are added to the other captures. This does not, however, constitute a sweep, even if the player could have made a valid sweep in normal play.

Scoring

At the end of the game, players add up the points they have scored using the system in the table below.

For capturing 21 or more cards	1
For capturing 6 or more diamonds	1
For capturing ♦7 (the "sette bello")	1
For "primiera" (see below)	1
For each sweep	1

The primiera is arrived at in rather a peculiar fashion. From the pile of captures, each player extracts the highest card in each suit. However, the cards have different values in the primiera: 7 = 21; 6 = 18; A = 16; 5 = 15; 4 = 14; 3 = 13; 2 = 12; and K, Q, J = 10. The values of the four cards are totaled, and the player with the highest total wins the point for primiera. If a player has no cards in one or more suits, he or she cannot win the point. If the scores are equal, neither player wins a point. Once both players have totaled their scores, they add them to their scores from previous games. The first to reach 11 points is the winner, and the game comes to an end.

TRICK GAMES

Historically played in many locales, from gaming clubs to Victorian drawing rooms and lowly taverns, trick games have attracted players of every level through their combination of skill and luck.

A trick is a round of play at cards, with the cards being won by the person playing the highest card or trump. With all trick games, more than in most other card games, the secret of success lies not necessarily in the quality of the cards you are dealt, but in how you play them. Piquet is one of the oldest trick games, having survived virtually unchanged since it was first played amongst the fine ladies and gentleman of the royal courts of sixteenth-century Europe. It is generally considered to be the best card game for two players ever to be devised. Pinochle also originated in Europe. It has never attracted English card players, but is popular in the USA. Originally a game for two, American card players have developed a large number of variations for three or four players.

Euchre and Whist are almost certainly derived from the French game Triomphe. Euchre reached the USA from Europe and really began to take hold in the 1860s. It is a game for two to six players depending on the version played: of the several versions available, four-handed Euchre is the most popular. Whist was the most popular four-handed card game of mid-to-late Victorian England. The rules of this game are comparatively simple, but skill is needed to play really well. Both Euchre and Whist waned in popularity in the early twentieth century, when a new and much more complex game – Bridge – took center stage. Modern Contract Bridge is the most fascinating and highly developed of card games, and is played in houses, clubs and tournaments throughout the world. It is a complicated game that uses many devices, gimmicks, conventions and systems. These bear the names of the illustrious players who invented them – Baron, Barton, Culbertson, Goren, Blackwood, Gerber. These names may not be familiar to all, but to the Bridge enthusiast, they represent figures of heroic proportions. The most popular system today is called Acol, named after a road in Hampstead, London, where a group of enthusiastic experts met and tried out various forms of bidding, before finally settling on this particular one.

Bridge can be played by two pairs playing against each other for the best of three games , known as a rubber, as described here. Rubber Bridge has an element of luck in the dealing of the cards. Duplicate Contract Bridge is very popular amongst advanced Bridge players. It is the only form played in international tournaments. All groups of players are presented in turn with the same deal of cards. A duplicate board is used at each table: this has four pockets, an arrow or label indicating North's side, and markers indicating the dealer and vulnerability of partnerships. In this way the game relies more on skill than on the luck of the deal. Duplicate Bridge relies entirely on skill rather than on the luck of the deal.

WHIST

Once played in drawing rooms, clubs, and drinking establishments throughout the Western world, whist was superseded in popularity by bridge in the early twentieth century. Nevertheless, it remains a very good game, requiring great skill to play well, despite its apparent simplicity.

Players: four, in two partnerships
Equipment: one pack of cards
Difficulty: requires skill to play well
Duration: about one hour for a rubber

Starting to play

Players cut for partners and for deal, with the two highest forming one partnership and the two lowest forming the other. Partners sit opposite each other and, as in bridge, are usually referred to as North, South, East, and West. The player drawing the highest card is the first dealer. Cards are ranked as in bridge, with aces high (except during the cut for deal when an ace counts low). Suits are not ranked, but any card from the suit drawn as trumps beats any card from any other suit.

Aim of the game

To take as many tricks as possible, and by doing so to score points toward game. The first side to win two games wins the rubber. A trick consists of four cards, one from each player, and is taken  by the highest card of whatever suit was led, or by the highest trump if any have been played.

Playing the game

The dealer deals 13 cards, facedown and one at a time, to each player, starting with the player to the left. The last card is turned faceup in front of the dealer, and whatever suit the faceup card belongs to becomes trumps for this particular hand (see diagram 1). The card is added to the dealer's hand.

The player to the dealer's left has the first lead. Play proceeds clockwise around the table, ending with the dealer. Players must follow suit if they can – that is they must play a card of the same suit as the initial lead. Failure to follow suit when able to do so is known as revoking, and carries penalties (see below). If you have no cards of the suit led, you may play a card of any other suit, including trumps. The trick is won by the player of the highest trump, if any have been played, or by the highest card of the suit originally led. The winner of the trick then leads to the next trick. Once all 13 tricks have been played and won, the result is scored and the deal passes to the player to the left of the previous dealer.

Scoring the game

Various systems of scoring are used. However, all share the basic feature that the side taking most tricks scores one point for each trick taken over six. For example, if North–South take eight tricks and East–West take five, North–South score two points while East–West score none.

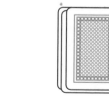

After this, however, differences emerge, particularly between the standard American and English forms of the game. In the American system, the first side to reach seven points wins the game, whereas in the English system only five points are required. Also, in the English

Diagram 1 *For this round hearts will be trumps*

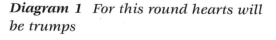

game, points are scored for honors. If a side has all four trump honors (A, K, Q, J) between them, they add four points to their score. If they have three of the honors, they score two points. Honors are not scored, however, if the side concerned is one point short of a game. In the American system, no attention is paid to honors at all. Many modern players prefer the American system on both counts – a target of seven makes it more difficult to win a game in a single hand, and the elimination of honor points removes an entirely arbitrary, non-skilled element from the scoring.

4 points

2 points

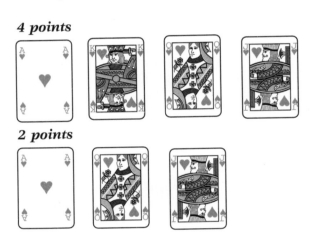

***Diagram 2** The English system of scoring for honors*

When one side or the other has won two games, they score two points for the rubber. The winning margin is the difference between the winners' and the losers' overall scores.

The penalties for revoking are also different in American and English systems. In the English system, three points are deducted from the offending side's score; or, if this gives them a negative score, three points are added to their opponents' score. In the American game, two points are transferred from the revoking side to their opponents. In both systems, there is no penalty for revoking if the player remedies the mistake before the cards are gath-

ered up and placed face-down on the table. However, the card mistakenly played must be left face-up on the table, and the opposing side may demand that it is played whenever a lead of the appropriate suit is made.

Hints and tips

On the face of it, whist might seem like a simple form of bridge. But, while the two games share many subtleties of play, the absence of bidding in Whist and the fact that there is no "dummy" hand as in Bridge, make them very different games (although there is no doubt that Whist provides excellent training for any would-be Bridge player).

Unlike bridge, the only way to exchange information about your hand with your partner is through the cards you play, particularly when you have the lead. Essentially, you should try to indicate any good "long" suits — with at least four, and preferably more cards, and with one or more honors — and the way to do this is to lead a card of that suit. There are complicated con-

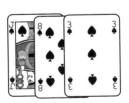

***Diagram 3** Establishing a suit*

ventions dealing with exactly which card you should lead in order to indicate the strength as well as the length of your best suit, but to describe these would take more space than is available here. However, unless you have very strong honors, a good general rule is to lead the fourth highest of your longest and strongest suit.

Once your partner has won a trick, they should then lead either a card from their best suit, or a card of the suit that you originally led. By doing this, you are trying to "establish" a suit. Say, for example, that you hold ♠A, 10, 9, 7, 4, 2 and your partner has ♠J, 8, 3. You lead ♠7 (see diagram 3). Your opponents have four spades between them. With any luck, these will be distributed two and two; so two rounds of spades – of which you will lose one to the ♠K or ♠Q – will leave you with four winning spades, provided that they are not trumped. Also, look for the opportunity of establishing voids. If both you and your partner can establish voids in the other's long suit, you can cross ruff (trump) for as long as your opponents have cards left in those suits. In this way, a weak trump can beat what would otherwise have been a certain winner.

CONTRACT BRIDGE

Preeminent among the Whist family, Contract Bridge is the most sophisticated and highly developed of all intellectual card games. It can take months for beginners to reach a reasonable level of skill, and years to reach the standard required for club and tournament play.

Players: *four, in two partnerships*
Equipment: *two packs of cards*
Difficulty: *requires considerable skill*
Duration: *about an hour for a rubber*

Brief history

The modern form of Contract Bridge has its roots in the various different forms of Whist, which can trace their origins back to at least the seventeenth century, if not earlier. One of these was a game called "Triumph" which gave us the term "Trump." Whist was the most popular card game of mid-to-late Victorian England, and was played very seriously indeed – so seriously, in fact, that the rules became ever more elaborate, and increasingly difficult to master. Bridge arrived in England toward the end of the nineteenth century, possibly from Russia or even India, and initially took the form of "Bridge-whist." This, for the first time, incorporated the notion of choosing trumps by nomination, rather than by the turn of a card. The dealer nominated the trump suit, and the dealer's partner's hand was immediately turned up to become the "dummy" (a practice derived from a French form of Whist).

Bridge-whist was superseded early in the twentieth century by Auction Bridge. This introduced the concept of competitive bidding for the right to nominate trumps. Effectively, players were guaranteeing to make a certain minimum number of tricks provided a particular suit was declared trumps – failure to do so carried penalties "above the line" so that Auction Bridge became a competition for points rather than tricks.

By 1930, Auction Bridge had, in its turn, given way almost entirely to Contract Bridge (partly due to an energetic publicity campaign waged by an American eccentric, Ely Culbertson). Contract Bridge introduced (or formalized) three important new concepts. The first was that only tricks that had been contracted scored toward the game ("below the line"), so placing a heavy premium on bidding for the optimum contract. The second was to introduce bonus points for taking all 13 tricks (a "grand slam") or 12 tricks (a "small slam"). The third was to make a team that had already won a game "vulnerable" and subject to heavy penalties for failure to make a contract. These innovations remain enshrined in the game to this day.

Outline of the game

Bridge is a game for four players in two partnerships, normally represented as North–South and East–West. Partners sit opposite each other at a square table. A single pack of 52 cards is used, although by convention two packs, with differently patterned backs, are made available so that one can be shuffled by the dealer's partner while the other pack is being dealt.

Cards rank in normal sequence, with ace as the highest, followed by K, Q, J, and so on down to 2. Suits also rank. Spades are highest, followed by hearts, then diamonds, and finally clubs.

Players cut for dealer and partners (if not already agreed), with the two highest cards forming one partnership and the two lowest cards the other. The player with the highest

card is the dealer. Cards are dealt one at a time, facedown, starting with the player to the dealer's left, until each player has 13 cards. Players arrange their hands into suits, and the auction, or bidding, begins.

The auction

The purpose of bidding is to find the best possible contract to be in or, if your opponents win the contract, to learn as much as possible about both your partner's and your opponents' hands. Bids are announced not in terms of the total number of tricks to be won, but the number in excess of six. A bid of 4♥ is an undertaking to make 10 tricks altogether if hearts are declared trumps. Each bid must be higher than the preceding bid, and both the number of tricks and the suit are taken into account. The lowest possible bid is 1♣, which is beaten by 1♦,

Diagram 4 The rank of suits

with 1♥, 1♠, and 1NT (no-trump) following in ascending order. A bid of 2♣ or higher is required after a bid of 1NT. The highest bid of all is 7NT.

At the end of the auction, when there have been three consecutive passes, the team that has bid the highest wins the contract. The player who first bid the suit that now becomes trumps (or no-trumps if the winning contract is in no-trumps) is the declarer and actually plays the hand. Declarer's partner becomes dummy: after the player to declarer's left has led the first card, dummy lays all their cards down faceup on the table and plays no further part in the hand.

The cards are then played out, each side trying to take as many tricks as possible. Declarer must make at least as many tricks as stipulated by the contract, while the opposing team must try to ensure that they "go down" (fail to make the contract) by one or more tricks.

When all 13 tricks have been played, the hand comes to an end and the result is scored. Each team keeps a single combined score, and the first team to reach 100 points "below the line" wins the game. It is possible to win the game in a single hand: if no points have yet been scored toward game, a team must bid, and make, at least three no-trumps, or four of a major suit (hearts or spades), or five of a minor suit (diamonds or clubs) to make game. More often, it will take several hands before one side or the other reaches the 100-point target.

Once a side has won a game, it becomes vulnerable, which makes it considerably more expensive to fail to make a contract, as well as, in certain circumstances, more profitable to succeed. A "rubber" consists of the best of three games, so the rubber comes to an end as soon as either team has won two games. The scores from the individual games in the rubber are combined to give the final total for the rubber.

Evaluating your hand

Many words and much ingenuity have been deployed on the topic of bidding at Bridge. The subject is considerably complicated by the fact that many bidding "conventions" have been developed over the years, in which a bid may mean something entirely different from what it appears to be saying. For example, in certain circumstances, a player may bid four clubs without the slightest desire to end up with clubs as trumps – which might even be catastrophic. If you understood the relevant convention, however, you would realize that the bid is in fact a request for information about the number of aces in your partner's hand. Nevertheless, there are some fairly simple basic principles in bidding that all aspiring Bridge players need to learn.

The essence of bidding is to convey to your partner the overall strength of your hand in terms of the number of potential winning cards it holds, and also to give some indication of the distribution of the cards. The generally accepted way of assessing the strength of a hand is to assign a point value to each of the honor cards: A = 4, K = 3, Q = 2, and J = 1.

Diagram 5: Honor cards

Hands can also be assessed according to the number of honor tricks, or quick tricks (qt) they can be expected to make in the first two rounds of play in any particular suit: A, K = 2 qt, A, Q = 1,1/2 qt, A = 1 qt, K, Q = 1 qt, and K, x (any other card) = 1/2 qt.

Points may also be added for distributional oddities. However, care should be exercised when using these, since their value varies according to the circumstances. Having no cards in a particular suit (a void) is not much help if your partner needs support for a no-trump bid. However, the following points are usually added when you are considering making an opening bid.

For a void	*3 points*
For a singleton	*2 points*
For a doubleton	*1 point*
For all four aces	*1 point*
Distributional points are also deducted.	
For no aces	*1 point*
For each unguarded honor	*1 point*

Unguarded honors are those that cannot be protected against higher cards of the same suit. For example, a singleton K will fall to A, and a Q, x will fall to the A, K. But a Q, x, x stands a reasonable chance of making a trick because the two low cards can be discarded on the A, K, leaving the Q as the highest card in the suit. This can be particularly valuable in no-trump hands, since it can prevent your opponents from establishing a long suit and winning tricks with low-ranking cards.

The value of distributional points is different if you are responding to your partner's opening bid. If you are raising your partner in the same suit, you can count five for a void and three for a singleton in another suit, and honors in the bid suit can be increased by one point (unless they already total four). A point should be deducted if you have only three in the bid suit.

An opening bid is generally considered to require a hand with at least 12 points. However, depending on circumstances, the opener's partner may respond with as little as six points. To make game in no-trumps or a major suit (3NT, or 4♠ for example), a combined partnership score of 26 points is usually required. Game in a minor suit (5♦ or 5♣) usually needs at least 28 points. A small slam normally requires about 33 points, and a grand slam 37.

Opening the bidding

The first player entitled to bid is the dealer. There are two options: to pass or to open the bidding. If the dealer passes, the next player to the left must pass or bid, and so on around the table until either someone has opened the bidding or all players have passed. If all players pass, the hands are thrown into the center of the table, reshuffled, and redealt by the player to the previous dealer's left.

If you have enough points to open the bidding you should do so, whether there is an obvious biddable suit in your hand or not. How you open the bidding is determined by a combination of the total point count and the distribution of cards in your hand. If you have a balanced hand, with a split of 4, 3, 3, 3 or 4, 4, 3, 2 between the suits, and 12–14 points, it is best to bid no-trumps. (Note, however, that some players prefer a "strong" no-trump opening bid, indicating 16–18 points – you should agree on a "strong" or a "weak" no-trump with your partner before the game begins.) You might also consider a no-trump bid if the distribution is 5, 3, 3, 2, and the long suit is weak and in a minor suit.

4 points

3 points

2 points

1 point

1 point

Where the hand has 13–21 points and a strong five-card suit with a controlling honor, for example ♥A, Q, x, x, x, the bid should be one of the relevant suit, in this case 1♥. If there are two five-card suits, you should generally bid the higher suit first, so that you or your partner can test the water with a response or rebid in 2 of the lower suit, which allows you to revert to 2 of the original suit without having to

Diagram 6: Counting points for quick tricks

step up to the 3 level. The same applies if you have two four-card suits with, say, 4, 4, 3, 2 distribution.

Strong bids

A strong hand with 23 points or more (or less if you have a strong six- or seven-card suit) gives you a very good chance of achieving game, and demands a strong opening bid. There are two possibilities. The first is a bid of 2♣. This is a convention, and is entirely artificial. It is, however, "forcing" to game: that is, it obliges your partner to keep responding to your bids until a game contract is reached. For this bid, you need at least 23 points, and five quick tricks in your hand. The other possibility is to open 2 of a suit, or (if you have good "stoppers" in the other suits) 2NT. This is a genuine bid, indicating your longest and strongest suit. Your partner must reply, but a response of 2NT is allowed as a way of indicating "I have an unbiddable hand and can't help you"—after which your partner is not obliged to bid again.

Preemptive bids

However strong your hand, there is usually no point in opening the bidding at anything higher than the 2 level. This is because bids at the 3 and 4 level are reserved for preemptive bids. If you have a weak hand (less than 10 points), but one very long suit with seven cards or more and reasonable honors, it is worth making a preemptive bid. The distribution of cards is likely to be uneven in all the hands, and your opponents are likely to have the majority of points. The idea of the preemptive bid is to make it risky and potentially expensive for them to enter the bidding since they will have to open at the 3 level or higher. The best position in which to use a preemptive bid is when you are third in the bidding. There is no point in preempting if you are fourth, because there is no one left to pre-empt. The best time to preempt is when your opponents need only a contract of one or two to reach game, and it is worth the sacrifice of going one or two tricks down to prevent them from doing so.

Partner's response to the opening bid

If your partner has opened the bidding, the situation is very different. For one thing, by opening, your partner has assured you that they hold at least 12 points and may have more. As few as six points may therefore be sufficient for a game contract and you should respond. With fewer than six points, you should pass, unless your partner has made a forcing opening bid. The negative response to an opening 2♣ is 2♦. Any other opening 2 bid should be responded to with a higher 2 bid or, if that is not possible, 2NT.

With anything between six and 10 points, the response should be the lowest possible realistic bid. If you have a biddable suit of your own – for example five cards with an honor – you should bid that unless you have to bid at the 2 level. You can bid 1♠ after an opening bid of 1♥. However, if your biddable suit is diamonds or clubs, it is better to bid 1NT than either 2♦ or 2♣ – this would indicate a hand with more than ten points. You should also bid 1NT if you have no obvious biddable suit. You should raise your partner's opening bid to the 2 level if you have at least four cards of the bid suit, or three with an honor. With more than 13 points, and at least four of the bid suit, you should raise to the 3 level, indicating that, between you, there are enough points for game.

What should you do if you have a really strong hand of 19 points or more? Barring a very bizarre distribution of the cards, you will certainly make game and should be exploring the possibility of a slam. You need, therefore, to make a strong response. This is usually done by bidding one level higher than necessary: bid 2♠ or 3♦ or 3♣ after an opening bid of 1♥, and 2NT or 3NT on a balanced hand with stoppers in the unbid suits. A jump bid in a new suit is forcing to game – your partner must continue the bidding until a game contract is reached.

Preemptive bids require a response only if you have support in the bid suit – three cards or two with an honor will generally do – and stoppers (which may include a void) in the unbid suits.

If you were the opening bidder, your decision whether to continue the auction or not depends on the strength of your hand as well as your partner's response. If responder has raised your opening bid in the same suit, or bid 1NT, you should pass, unless you have 16 points or more. In this case, you can offer your partner an alternative suit if you have one strong enough and provided that the bid does not rule out a return to the original suit at the 2 level. If you have bid 1♠, for example, but you also have a good heart suit, you should rebid 2♥. Your partner then has the choice of leaving you in hearts, or of rebidding spades if they can offer stronger support in spades than in hearts.

If responder has jump bid, indicating a good hand, you should always rebid. You certainly have enough points for game and a slam is a possibility. It is usually sensible at this stage to indicate where your other strengths lie – do you have a good, unbid, four-card suit to offer? It may be that there will be a better "fit" between you and your partner in your second best suit. Or, if between you, you have good cards in all suits, you may be better off in a no-trump contract. If you suspect that a slam is on, however, do not jump to game. Your partner will take this as meaning that you do not have the strength for a slam, and that you should stop at game. Instead, you should bid according to one of the conventions that govern slam bidding.

Defensive bidding

There are, of course, two sides in Bridge, and often it will be your opponents who open the bidding. In this case, you will find yourself in the position of making defensive, or "intervening," bids. The requirements for these are different from those of either the opening bidder or the responder. Fewer points are required for an intervening bid (about 10) and provided you have a biddable suit, you can "overcall" the opening bid. The reason is that there is very little risk of being stuck in an unsuitable contract. If your partner has a weak hand, your opponents will have strong ones, and the bidding will continue in any case. In the meantime, you have imparted some potentially valuable information about what your partner should lead during the course of play. And if your partner has a good hand, you should be bidding for the contract anyway.

There are two other bids available to the first intervening bidder. One is to overcall in the opening bidder's suit – for example to call 2♥ in response to an opening bid of 1♥. This is known as a cue bid and is the strongest of all intervening bids. It is the equivalent of an opening forcing bid, and indicates that you have a stopper in the bid suit and strong cards in all other suits. The other bid is the "double." This also indicates a good hand, but usually without an obvious strong suit. It demands that your partner bids their strongest suit: it is not intended as a genuine point-scoring maneuver. Doubles in these circumstances are referred to as "take-out" doubles. If your partner has 10 points or more, they should jump bid. The double can also be used if you are worried that an overcall might be passed by the other three players, meaning that a potential game contract could be missed. Doubling after the first round of bidding is generally best avoided unless you really think that you can defeat the contract.

If you are the responder, and your partner's opening bid has been doubled, you have the option of redoubling. As a first round tactic, this bid is used to show that you have a good hand, although it does not necessarily imply support in your partner's suit. As with doubling, redoubling should usually only be used at game level if you are confident of making the contract.

Slam bidding

If you and your partner have established that you have enough points for a slam, the only remaining thing is to check that the points are distributed correctly. A missing ace and a guarded king could be sufficient to bring down a small slam contract. You need to check, therefore, that you are covered in all four suits. Two well-known conventions are used for this purpose. The first is Blackwood. This begins with a bid of 4NT, and your partner's response tells you how many aces they hold – 5♣ = no aces, 5♦ = one, 5♥ = three, 4♠ = four. The 4NT bid is followed by 5NT, asking in exactly the same way for the number of kings. The responses allow you to determine whether a grand slam is possible, so that you can make your final bid with confidence.

Blackwood has its dangers, because it commits you to a high bid whatever information it yields. Some players therefore prefer Gerber, which allows for a lower final bid. Gerber takes the form of a 4♣ bid in circumstances where the bid could not possibly have its usual meaning. A response of 4♦ = one ace, 4♥ = two aces, and so on. To ascertain the number of kings, the asking partner would bid the next highest bid to the response: if the response was 4♥, showing two aces, then a bid of 4♠ would be asking for the number of kings. The responses follow the same pattern as before – 1NT = no kings, 4♣ = one, 4♦ = two, and so on.

Cue bidding

Cue bidding can be used to provide information about aces or voids, both of which provide first round control. If you and your partner have clearly agreed a trump suit, for example by bidding 1♥ followed by a response of 3♥, then a switch to another suit such as 4♣ would be interpreted as saying "We know we have a fit in hearts, but I also have first round control in clubs. What do you have?" First round control in all side suits and a sufficiently high point count are enough for at least a small slam.

Playing the cards

The basic rules of play are simple, but making the maximum number of tricks requires great skill.

The initial lead is played by the player to declarer's left. The dummy hand is then laid out, and declarer plays a card from dummy. The leader's partner then plays a card, and finally declarer. The winning card is the highest in the suit led, or the highest trump if any have been played. The winner of the trick then leads to the next trick, followed by the other players in clockwise rotation. Declarer must lead from dummy when dummy has won the previous trick. Players must always follow suit if they can: failure to do so, as demonstrated by subsequent play of a card of the relevant suit, is known as "revoking" and carries a penalty. If the revoke trick is won by the offending side, their opponents are entitled to take two of the offenders' tricks at the end of play, and treat them as though they had been won in the normal course of play. If the revoke trick is won by the non-offending side, the penalty is a single trick.

Once dummy has been laid down, declarer will normally take a short time to consider the hand and plan out the sequence of play. This is important, even if it is obvious that there are enough winning cards in the combined hands to make the contract. One mistake easily made by inexperienced players is to end up with the lead in the wrong hand. It is no good having winning cards in dummy if you cannot lead to them from your own hand. The order in which you play the cards can, therefore, be crucial.

In most circumstances, declarer will "draw" trumps at an early stage of the play. Assuming that, between you, you have the majority of the trump suit, you should be able to clear trumps from defenders' hands and so prevent them from "ruffing" (trumping) your winners in other suits. Another good principle is to lose tricks early in suits where you have no first (or second) round control. If, for example, you have ♣K, Q, x, you should try to draw out the ♣A in order to be sure that you can regain the lead with the ♣K or ♣Q if your opponents play another club (see diagram 7).

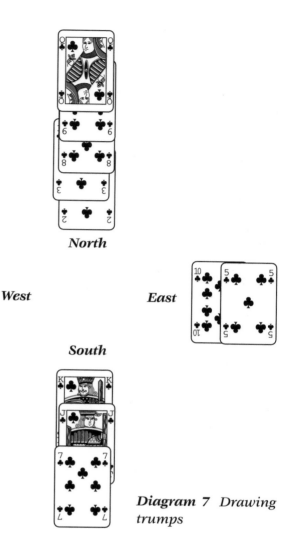

Diagram 7 Drawing trumps

Establishing a suit

Often it will be far from clear, when you first examine the hands, where all the tricks are going to come from. In these cases, look to see if there is a long suit that can be established. If, for example, you have ♣K, J, x, and dummy has Q, x, x, x, x, you know that your opponents have five clubs between them. With luck, these will be distributed three to two, so by playing three rounds of clubs, and assuming that you have drawn trumps, you will be left with two clubs in dummy's hand that are winners – even if they are only the ♣3 and ♣2. If both you and dummy have long trump suits – say five each – you will probably clear your opponents trumps in two rounds, and will then be left with three trumps in each hand. If you can establish voids in different suits in each hand, you will be able to cross-ruff, making as many as six more tricks.

Finessing

Sometimes these tactics do not work because of unequal distribution of the cards. This is where the "finesse" may be needed. Say you have ♦A, x, x, and dummy has ♦Q, J, 10 (see diagram 8). Normally, you would expect to lose a trick to the ♦K – it is extremely unlikely that the ♦K is a singleton and will fall on the ♦A. However, if the player to your right has the ♦K, you can make all three diamond tricks. Lead the ♦Q from dummy: if the ♦K drops, play ♦A, if not play a low diamond, then return to dummy and do the same again. Whatever happens, three diamond tricks are made. There is of course a chance of the finesse failing. The only clues you have to the position of the ♦K are your opponents' bids dur-

ing the auction, and the leads the defenders have made to each other. But these can be misleading, and the maneuver fails if the ♦K is to your left.

Defender's lead

If you are a defender you cannot see your partner's hand, and must guess at what cards they hold. The first problem is what to lead before dummy is laid down. It is generally best to avoid leading a suit that your opponents have bid. If your partner bid a suit during the auction, it is normal to lead a card of that suit – the ace if you have it, or the high card of a doubleton or a sequence headed by an honor. However, circumstances may alter this. In a trump contract, lead a singleton to create a void in a non-trump suit. If you have a long suit (other than trumps) headed by an ace, you should lead the ace to avoid it being ruffed later: in a no-trump contract, you should lead a lower card. A good general rule, if no other obvious lead suggests itself, is the fourth highest of your longest and strongest suit. This tells your partner that you have three cards higher than the card you led, which can provide valuable information about what the declarer may hold.

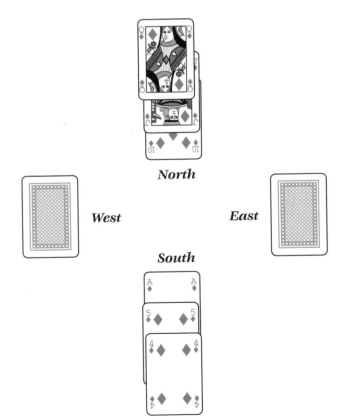

North

West   *East*

South

Diagram 8 *Finessing*

Scoring

One member of each partnership records the scores on paper in the form of a table (see diagram 9). Scores are of two types: "below the line," which is reserved for tricks contracted and made; and "above the line," where overtricks, undertrick penalties, bonuses and honors are scored.

Trick scores

These can only be scored by the declarer's side and are only awarded if the contract is made. Only those tricks that were bid for score "under the line;" overtricks are scored "above the line." If the contract fails, declarer's side scores nothing for the tricks they have made.

Trick values vary according to whether the contract is in no-trumps, or in a major or minor suit.

	NT	♥♠	♣♦
For the first trick above six	40	30	20
For subsequent tricks	30	30	20

If the contract is doubled, all scores are doubled. If the contract is redoubled, all scores are doubled again

Overtricks

When declarer has made the contract, any overtricks are scored above the line. Values are higher if declarer is doubled or redoubled or vulnerable.

	Trick value
Each overtrick, undoubled	?
Each overtrick, doubled	100
Each overtrick, redoubled	200

	If vulnerable
Each overtrick, undoubled	?
Each overtrick, doubled	200
Each overtrick, redoubled	400

Slam bonus

Points are scored above the line for a small slam (12 tricks in total) or a grand slam (all 13 tricks).

	Trick value
For a small slam	500
For a grand slam	1000

	If vulnerable
For a small slam	750
For a grand slam	1500

Undertricks

If declarer fails to make the contract, the opposing side is awarded penalty points above the line.

	Trick value
Each trick, undoubled	50

First trick, doubled	100
Subsequent tricks, doubled	200
First trick, redoubled	200
Subsequent tricks, redoubled	400

	If vulnerable
Each trick, undoubled	100
First trick, doubled	200
Subsequent tricks, doubled	300
First trick, redoubled	400
Subsequent tricks, redoubled	600

Other premium scores

The following points are awarded above the line, regardless of whether the declarer is doubled or vulnerable.

Winning rubber if opponents have won one game	500
Winning rubber if opponents have not won a game	750
Winning one game in an unfinished rubber	300
Having the only part score in an unfinished rubber	50
Making a doubled contract ("for the insult")	50

Honors

These are scored by either side, above the line.

Five-trump honors (A, K, Q, J, 10) in one hand	150
Four-trump honors in one hand	100
Four aces in one hand in a no-trump contract	150

At the end of the rubber, all scores, both below and above the line, are totaled and the highest scorers are the winners – even if they only won a single game and did not get the rubber bonus.

A sample game

Here is an example of how the bidding and play

of a hand of Bridge might proceed in an average game. Assume that this is the first hand of the game, and that neither side is vulnerable.

Bidding. North is the dealer, so East is first to bid. The bidding proceeds as follows:

East:	*1♣*
South:	*Pass*
West:	*1♠*
North:	*Pass*
East:	*1NT*
South:	*Pass*
West:	*2NT*
North:	*Pass*
East:	*3NT*
South:	*Pass*
West:	*Pass*
North:	*Pass*

The contract is 3NT, scoring 100 points and game if made, and the declarer is East. West is dummy and South makes the first lead.

At first sight, it might look as though E–W should be in a diamond contract. But this is not the case. For one thing, they would have had to bid 5♦ to reach game; for another, the bidding indicates that neither partner has an obvious suit with both strength and length, but that both have balanced hands with reasonable cover in all suits. 3NT is undoubtedly the right contract.

Play. South leads ♣Q and dummy is laid down. East can see immediately that there are only six certain tricks – four diamond tricks and two heart tricks. He or she will have to make the remaining three by winning with both ♠Q J and with the ♣K. The chief weakness is in clubs. If South has the ace, the contract is doomed. There is also a danger in spades: if North has ♠A and the K or the 10, it could be very difficult to make two spade tricks. A great deal will depend on the defenders' play.

North takes the first trick with the ♣A, and returns the ♠10, indicating control of spades. South takes this with the ♠K, and leads ♦9, presumably reasoning that diamonds were not bid and that partner might have at least one of the

outstanding honors. East safely takes this with the ♦10. East then cashes in the three remaining diamond tricks, and embarks on the attempt to clear the ♠A. North duly obliges, overplaying West's ♠9, and leads ♥5. East wins this in dummy with ♠A, and takes the two remaining spade tricks. At this stage, declarer knows that only clubs and hearts are left. He or she has masters in both suits, with one losing club. Declarer therefore leads ♣7 from dummy, losing to South's ♣J. South can only lead a club, which falls to East's ♣K. The ♥K then takes the final trick and the contract is made.

The scoresheet

First game: we bid 1NT and take eight tricks, scoring 40 below the line for 1NT and 30 above the line for one overtrick. On the next hand we bid 3♥ and make the contract, scoring 90 below

A	B
500	500
150	150
30	500
40	
90	
	120
120	
930	1270

Diagram 9 The scoresheet

the line, with 150 above the line for honors. The game comes to an end and a new one begins. Second game: we bid 4♠ and go down by two tricks. We are now vulnerable, so they score 500 undertrick penalties above the line. They now bid and make 6♦, a small slam, scoring 120 trick points below the line, 150 in honor points and a slam bonus of 500. Third game: we bid and make 4♥, scoring 120 below the line and 500 above the line for the rubber. The final scores are We = 930, They = 1270. They win by 340 points.

HEARTS

This is the ideal game to play when your opponents claim that they never receive any good cards, because the idea is to lose any trick that contains a heart. Doing so, however, is not nearly as easy as it sounds.

Players: *three to seven*
Equipment: *one pack of playing cards*
Difficulty: *not difficult, but some skill helps*
Duration: *about half an hour for a round*

The aim of the game and scoring
The basic game of hearts, along with its numerous variations, is played to the fundamental rules of Whist. The main difference between the two games is that in Hearts the aim is to lose any tricks in which a heart is played. (In some variations, players must attempt to lose tricks containing the queen, king, and ace of spades as well.) Aces are high, there are no trumps, and players must follow suit if they are able to do so.

A player winning a trick containing a heart scores one penalty point for each heart in that trick. Any player who fails to follow suit when able to do so is fined 13 penalty points; the hand ends and all penalty points previously incurred during it are canceled.

At the start of a game, the players agree a number of penalty points that will finish the game – either 50 or 100 is usual. When a player

reaches that score, the game is over and the winner is the player with the lowest number of penalty points.

Playing the game
The pack of cards is adjusted according to the number of players so that each person has the same number of cards: with three players, one card of value 2 is removed; with four or six players, no cards are removed; with five players, two 2s are removed; with seven players, three 2s are removed. The ♥2 is always left in the deck.

The pack is cut and the person with the low-

Diagram 10 The 2s are removed to ensure equal cards for each player

est card deals. The cards are dealt facedown and one by one, starting with the player on the dealer's left and working clockwise. The players pick up their hands and the one to the dealer's left plays the first card. Going clockwise, the other players must follow suit if possible; if not, any card can be rejected – it is a good idea to lay down the highest heart in your hand, to avoid the risk of it winning a trick if the suit is hearts. A card in the wrong suit cannot win a trick, whatever its face value.

The winner of each trick collects the cards, marks down any penalty points incurred and

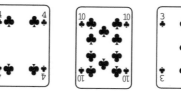

Diagram 11: Discard a high heart if you cannot follow suit

then plays the next card. Play continues until no cards are left. At this point, the players add up their scores and a new round starts, with the deal moving to the player to the left of the one who dealt the previous round.

VARIATIONS
Black Maria

This variation on basic hearts is the most popular form of the game in Europe — a "black Maria" is the British slang name for a police van. In this game, players are not only penalized for winning tricks with hearts, but also for the ace, king, and queen of spades: ♠A costs seven points; ♠K costs 10 points; and ♠Q (the Black Maria) costs 13 points.

The game starts in the same way as basic hearts, but after the deal you select three cards that you do not want and pass them facedown to the player on your right. All the players do this at the same time, so that nobody can see what cards they have received before deciding which ones to discard. Beware passing off the ♠Q; often it is better to give yourself a void and get rid of unwanted point-cards during play.

Diagram 13 Discarding two clubs leaves a void in clubs. ♠A is discarded instead of ♠Q because it may win a spade trick, and the ♠Q can be discarded on a club trick

in the exchange of cards after the deal – some players have rather predictable strategies – cards are passed off in successive hands: left, right, across, and hold (no pass). Players generally add up point-cards in their piles after play, rather than keep a running score.

American Hearts or Black Lady

In this widely played variation ♠Q carries a penalty of 13 points, but capturing all the hearts plus the ♠Q – "shooting the moon" – reverses the usual scoring. All 26 points are lodged against each of the opponents. (Falling short – even by one point – is of course a disaster.) In order to avoid any advantage

7 points

10 points

13 points

Diagram 12 Penalty cards

 1 point

 2 points

 11 points

 12 points

 13 points

Diagram 14 Penalty points for Spot Hearts

Spot Hearts

This variation gives penalty points for each heart card according to its face value.

EUCHRE

Derived from the ancient French game of Triomphe, Euchre became the national game of the USA in the 1800s. Jokers were first introduced to card games in the USA in the 1860s specifically for use in Euchre, where the joker is known as the "benny." The game's popularity there waned with the introduction of Whist and Bridge, but it is still a favorite in Australia and England's West Country.

Players: four in two partnerships
Equipment: one pack of cards with 2s to 8s removed and a joker included (25 cards)
Difficulty: some skill required
Duration: about 45 minutes for a round

The aim of the game and scoring

Euchre has elements of both Whist and Bridge. Play follows the same rules as whist, but it also has a bidding system. It also has a somewhat arcane system of nomenclature.

Players bid for the right to try to win three tricks, and are awarded one point if they do so. No extra point is awarded for winning four tricks, but two points are awarded if five tricks are won (this figure is increased to four points if one member of the partnership plays alone). If only two tricks or less are won, two points are awarded to the opponents.

A game is won by the first side to win five points. However, matches are divided into legs and a leg is won by the first side to win 21 points. The match itself is won by the first side to win two legs out of three.

Trumps

The order of trumps is different from that of other games. The joker, or benny, is the highest

Diagram 16 The trump sequence with diamonds as trumps

trump card, followed by the jack of the trump suit — this card is known as the "right bower." The jack of the same color is the third highest trump, and is known as the "left bower."

In descending order, the other trumps are the ace, king, queen, 10 and 9 – the ace, therefore, is the fourth highest trump card. The other non-trump suits are valued from ace down to 9, though the suit of the same color as trumps will not have a jack.

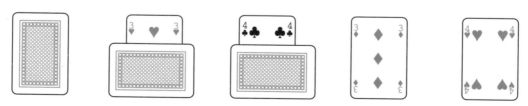

Diagram 15 Two 3s and two 4s from the pack are reserved by each partnership for use in scoring

77

Starting to play

The 25 cards are shuffled by the dealer and then cut by the player to the dealer's right. Five cards are dealt facedown to each player in two rounds, with three cards in the first round and two in the second. The remaining five cards are placed facedown in a pile in the center of the table and the top card is turned faceup. This card shows the suit that might be trumps. If the card turns out to be the joker, the dealer nominates trumps, but does so before looking at his hand.

Diagram 17 A deal

Bidding

The player sitting to the left of the dealer has the first opportunity to bid. After viewing your hand, you must decide whether it is possible to win three or more tricks if the turned-up card were to be trumps. This decision will be affected by the fact that on the first round only, the dealer has the option of picking up the trump card after the bidding is complete and discarding a card, placing it facedown at the bottom of the pile in the center of the table.

If you decide that three tricks cannot be won with that hand and the suit that is trumps, you say "pass." If you decide that three tricks can be won, you say "I order it up." You are then known as "the maker" and must immediately indicate whether you will play the hand alone or with the help of your partner. If you decide to play alone, you say "up, down;" if in partnership, you say just "up." Bidding stops as soon as one player "orders it up" and declares their intentions, and then play starts.

If all the players pass, another round of bidding starts, but this time each player is allowed to say which would be their trump suit of choice – and this time the dealer is not allowed to pick the upturned card up from the center pile. If you wish to play the hand alone with spades as trumps, for example, the bid is "alone spades" or "spades, down." If you wish to play in partnership, the bid would be "spades, up." Again, bidding stops as soon as a player bids for a game and plays starts. However, if no player has bid for a game at the end of this round the cards are reshuffled and dealt again, by the player to the left of the previous dealer.

Playing the game

The partner of a maker who has declared "down" or "alone" places their cards facedown on the table. The opponents then have the option of playing alone or together, though if one of the two players is the dealer and the upturned card has been picked up, that player must take part.

The opening lead is played by the player on the left of a lone player if there is one, or by the player on the dealer's left if there is not. Play obeys normal trick rules: the players must follow suit wherever possible; and the highest card or highest trump wins the trick. When all five tricks have been decided, the hand is over and the scores are noted. The deal then moves one player to the left and another hand is started. The process continues until a game, leg, or match has been won.

Hints and tips

As each hand has so few tricks there is little chance of planning a strategy once play has started, so it is in the bidding that a hand of euchre is won or lost. Considerable thought is needed at this stage. For example, if you are the dealer and you deal yourself a hand consisting of ♠K, ♠9, ♣Q, ♥A, and ♥J, and the turned-up card is a diamond (see diagram 19) it would be very unwise to bid. This is also true if the turned-up card is a spade or a club, because even then your ♠K will only rank as

Diagram 18 A sample deal

the fifth highest trump. But if ♥K is turned up, you hold the second, fourth, and fifth highest trumps and could win the hand by picking up the ♥K and discarding ♣Q, because you will then have two void suits that can be trumped.

Your position at the table is also significant when playing euchre. If the first two players pass, this indicates that they have weak hands. This means that the third and fourth players have to be sure that they can win without much assistance from their partners. If all the players pass on the first hand it is likely that the dealer is weak in the suit that was turned up and does

Diagram 19 The dealer's hand

not feel sufficiently strong to win three tricks even if the turned-up card – the ♥A, say – is added to the hand. In diagram 19, the dealer's opponents should examine their hands to see if they could make a game in diamonds, while dealer and partner should look more to the two black suits.

PINOCHLE

This is the extremely popular American version of two-handed bezique, the difference being that the 8s are taken out of the double pack as well as the 2s to 7s. Both games are derived from the German game Binokel.

Players: two
Equipment: two packs of playing cards with identical backs; pencil and paper
Difficulty: complex and skillful
Duration: 45 minutes to several hours

The object and scoring

To win tricks and combine, or "meld," cards and so score points over two phases of play. Points are obtained from winning tricks according to whether the trick contains high-value cards. The total number of points available from tricks is 250 points.

In addition, 10 points are awarded to the player who wins the last trick in the second phase of play. The points scored by melds (combinations of cards that can be placed on the table after winning a trick) are as follows:

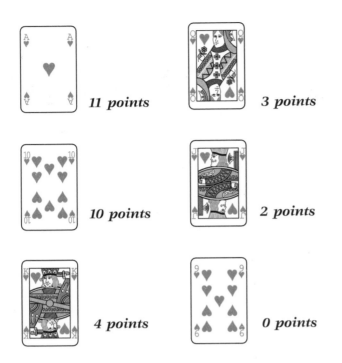

11 points   *3 points*

10 points   *2 points*

4 points   *0 points*

Diagram 20 *Scoring*

a flush (all the trump cards minus the 9) =
150 points
four aces of different suits ("a hundred
aces") = 100 points
four kings of different suits ("eighty kings")
= 80 points
four queens of different suits ("sixty queens")
= 60 points
four jacks of different suits ("forty jacks")
= 40 points
the king and queen of trumps (a "royal
marriage") = 40 points
♠Q and ♦J - ("pinochle") = 40 points
a king and queen of any other suit
(a "marriage") = 20 points
a 9 of trumps on its own (a "dix")
= 10 points.

Points won for melds are counted as the melds are placed on the table. The points for tricks are worked out at the end of each hand, but the number is rounded up or down to the nearest 10. The player who reaches 1000 points first wins the game, but if both players exceed 1000 points after the same hand the winner becomes the first player to reach 1250 points, and so on.

Starting to play
All cards with a face value of from 2 to 8 inclusive are removed from both packs, leaving 48 cards for play. The cards rank as follows, from high to low: ace, 10, king, queen, jack, 9. The players cut the cards to decide who is to deal first, the winner being the player whose card is highest — the ranking of cards for the cut is the same as that for the game. After the first hand the deal alternates between the two players.

The dealer shuffles the deck, hands it to the other player to be cut, and then deals four cards at a time facedown in three rounds, so that each player has 12 cards. The next card in the deck is turned faceup in the center of the table and determines trumps for the hand. Traditionally, the remaining cards in the deck, known as the "stockpile," are placed crosswise on top of the trump card. If the card that has been turned up proves to be a 9, it is now a dix, because it has become the 9 of trumps. When this happens the dealer is immediately awarded 10 points.

Playing the game: the first phase
The player who did not deal leads. As in whist, a trick is won by the highest card in the suit that was led, or by the highest trump. However, in the first phase of a hand of pinochle the player to whom the lead is made does not have to follow suit. For example, a player does not have to respond to a ♥J lead, say, with a ♥K if it is the only heart in the hand: the player might want to reserve the ♥K for a meld later and can play a card from any other suit instead.

When a trick has been decided, the winning player picks a card up from the stockpile and places it to one side, and the loser does the same. The winner then leads the next trick, and so on. However, the winner also has the option of placing a meld on the table before picking up from the stockpile and so scoring points; the loser

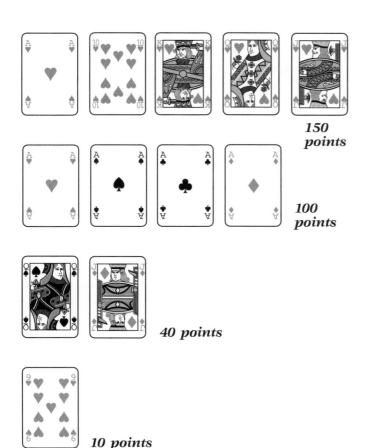

150 points

100 points

40 points

10 points

Diagram 21 Meld scoring

does not have this option. Melding is governed by some fairly complex rules, which are described below, but it is important to note here that any melds that have been put down on the table are still considered to be part of the hand of the player who put them there. As a result, a player can pick up a card from any of their own melds and play it during a trick. To put it another way, each player's hand contains 12 cards at all times.

First-phase play continues until only one card is left facedown in the stockpile. At this point no more melds are allowed and the player who won the last trick can choose to pick up either the faceup card that designated trumps or the remaining facedown card, but in either case the opponent must be shown the card. The hand now moves to the second phase of play.

Playing the game: the second phase

At the start of the second phase of the hand, the players pick up the melds that they have laid down during phase one, so that they are again holding 12 cards. The player who won the last trick in the first phase leads and play continues as before — but this time the players must follow suit if they are able to do so, and in the event that they cannot they must play a trump if they have one. If the lead is a trump, the receiving player must play a higher trump if possible. There is no stockpile in this phase of the hand and points are calculated from the winning tricks when all cards have been played. A new hand then begins as before.

Melding rules

The following rules govern melds and melding:

1. A meld can only be put down when a player wins a trick.

2. Only one meld can be placed on the table at once; another trick must be won before a player puts a second meld on the table.

3. Melds that are not put down on the table do not score points.

4. A player has the option of adding to melds that are already put down on the table. For example, if the ♠K and ♠Q of spades (a marriage) has been put down, another meld can be scored by adding cards to it: another three kings would make eighty kings, while another three queens would make sixty queens; if a ♦J was added, a pinochle would be scored. However, a player cannot add another card to form the same type of meld as the one already on the table: for

Diagram 22 Melding rules: (a) marriage was the first meld; (b) three queens added to the marriage give sixty queens as a second meld

example, if a pinochle is on the table, a player is not allowed to add another ♦J to make another pinochle.

5. A player may move cards around between melds after they have been put down on the table, but only when at least one card has been put down from the hand.

6. A card cannot be picked up from a meld, played in a trick and then put back on the original meld at a later stage; nor can the original meld be reformed by adding the second card of the same value or suit, as appropriate, from the deck. If a player does this, they lose the points that were scored for the original meld. It is therefore important to remember what melds have already been played.

7. One — and only one — meld has two scoring possibilities: if a player puts down a flush, the score awarded is 150 points, but if the king and queen of trumps are placed down first, 40 points are scored for the royal marriage; when the ace, ten and jack are added on the next occasion that the player wins a trick, 150 points are scored, making a total of 190 points.

8. The first dix to be melded is put in place of the upturned trump card, which is taken into the player's hand and can be used if wanted to form a meld immediately. When the second dix appears it can be placed down on the table alone, winning 10 points, and the player can then put down another meld straightaway.

PIQUET

Pronounced "peekay," this is one of the great card games and has remained virtually unchanged since it was first played in sixteenth-century Europe. It even retains an arcane, and sometimes bewildering, language of its own.

Players: *two*
Equipment: *one pack of cards; pencil and paper for recording scores*

Difficulty: *hard; requires considerable concentration and great skill to play well*
Duration: *half an hour for one game of six deals*

The aim of the game

Piquet is a very complex and subtle game whose elements do not necessarily follow from one to another in a logical order, so it is sensible to read to the end of this description before trying to start a game.

One game, called a "partie," consists of six hands that are dealt alternately by each player. The object is to accumulate more points than your opponent during these six hands. (As piquet is often played as a betting game, with a monetary value given to each point, it is worth noting that if the loser has failed to reach 100 points they are said to be "rubiconed" and the winner is awarded a bonus.) There are two ways of scoring points: through declarations made after the discards but before play, and during play by leading or winning a trick.

Starting the game

Remove the 2s to 6s from the pack, leaving a 32-card deck in which aces rank high. Cut the deck to decide who will deal first: the winner is the one with the highest card, and can choose to deal or to receive. (Usually the choice is to deal first, because there is a slight advantage to be gained from receiving on the sixth hand.) In each deal the dealer is known as "the younger" and the receiver is called "the elder." So each player is the elder or the younger in alternate games. Having shuffled the cards, the younger deals 12 cards to each player, starting with the elder and alternating between the two. The eight cards that remain after this, known as the "talon," are placed facedown in the center of the table.

Playing the game

In the first stage of the game the two players pick up their hands and examine them. On rare occasions a player will have a "carte blanche" — that is, no court cards (a king, queen, or jack). If

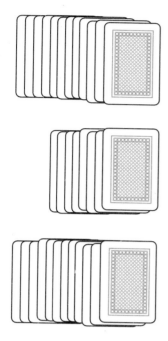

Diagram 23 *The deal for a game of Piquet*

this is the case, the player must declare the fact. If the younger has a carte blanche, the cards are placed one after another face-up on the table as soon as the elder has discarded. If the elder has a carte blanche, how many cards will be discarded is announced so that the younger can decide which and how many cards to discard and put them on the table, before seeing the elder's hand. A player with a carte blanche wins 10 points.

Whether or not one or other player has a carte blanche, the elder has the option to first discard up to five cards; the discards are placed facedown in a pile alongside the player who discards them. When played under English rules, at least one card must be discarded; under American rules this is not a requirement. Any cards that are discarded are replaced from the talon. If the total of five cards are not exchanged, the elder is allowed to look at the remaining cards in the talon up to the fifth card — so if three cards are discarded and replaced from the talon the elder can examine two more cards from the talon before replacing them. The younger can then discard the same number of cards as are left in the talon - according to English rules (but not to American), at least one card must be discarded. The younger can examine the remaining cards in the talon later, after the elder has led the first card. In practice, it is to the elder's advantage to discard five cards – generally those of a lower value, unless a void in one suit is desired – because this stops the younger

from discarding more than three unwanted cards. The discards are not used again in the hand, but each player can look at their own discards during play for reference purposes if so desired.

Declarations and scoring

Before play starts, declarations must be made by means of a question and answer routine. Scores can be made in three ways: through points, sequences, and sets. It is important to note that both players must tell the exact truth at all times.

Points

The elder adds up the number of cards in the longest suit and declares it. If, for example, there

Diagram 24 *Counting points*

11 points

10 points

10 points

Diagram 25 *Counting points*

9 points

8 points

7 points

Diagram 26 Counting points

are five cards in one suit, the declaration is "point of five." If the younger cannot match this, the elder scores five points — a point for each card. But if the younger has more than five cards in a suit, the reply will be "not good," and the younger will score one point for each card. If the younger has an equal number of cards in one suit, the reply is "equal, counting." The elder then declares the number of points according to the value of the cards, with an ace counting 11 points, court cards 10 points each and the other cards their face value. Again, the younger replies "good," "not good" or "equal" as appropriate. The player who has the highest number of points is the winner and scores one point per card, as before. If the count is equal, neither player scores.

Sequences

The next declaration is in respect of the number of cards in sequence in any one suit, with three cards in a run being the minimum number that can be declared. Again, the elder declares first and has to use the correct terminology, saying "I have a quint," for example. The names for the

different sequences and the scores that are awarded to them if a successful declaration is made are:

A "tierce" for three cards, scoring three points.
A "quart" for four cards, scoring four points.
A "quint" for five cards, scoring 15 points.
A "sixieme" for six cards, scoring 16 points.
A "septieme" for seven cards, scoring 17 points.
A "huitieme" for eight cards, scoring 18 points.

As before, the younger replies to the declaration. However, in this case the response to the same sequence is "to?" and the elder has to name the highest card of the run — for example, the reply might be "quint to queen." If the highest card is an ace, the reply is "quint major," and "quint minor" if the highest card is a king. The highest card wins, and the points are awarded; if both highest cards are equal, no points are scored.

It is not necessary for the elder to declare all sequences at this point or even the highest one, as long as at least one sequence is declared. The elder can note down and receive the appropriate number of points for any further sequences that have not been declared. It might be advantageous to disguise a long sequence if a shorter one is available for declaration in order to have a better chance of scoring points by winning tricks (see Hints and tips).

Diagram 27 Sequences

Sets

Finally, the elder declares any sets of cards of the same face value, but of different suits — only "trios" (threes) or quatorze (fours) can be declared, and only if their value is between ace (high) and ten. A quatorze beats a trio, but otherwise the set of cards that has the highest rank wins: three points in the case of a trio and 14 points for a quatorze. It is not possible for elder and younger to be equal during this declaration, unless neither has anything to declare. As in the case of sequences, the winner need only declare for one set, but can score for any others in the hand.

3 points

14 points

Diagram 28 Sets

Pique and repique

At the end of the declarations, the elder leads the first card and scores one point for doing so, saying "one for leading." However, before the younger responds, the points that have been won up to this point are added up and noted, by sections in the order in which they were scored: carte blanche, points, sequences and sets. If either player has accumulated 30 points without the opponent having scored at all in the sections so far counted, they have a "repique" and win a bonus of 60 points (the elder is not allowed to use the one point for leading in this calculation).

A "pique" can only be scored by the elder, because achieving one, as opposed to repique,

depends on the use of points awarded during trick play. If the point awarded for leading tips the scales, so that the elder now has 30 points and the younger has none, the elder is awarded a bonus of 30 points. Even if the elder does not have as many as 30 points, they can still achieve pique and be awarded a 30-point bonus if they accumulate up to 30 points through play during tricks without the younger having won a point.

Trick play

Once points have been totaled and it has been established whether there is pique or repique, the younger can reply to the elder's lead and trick play begins. This follows simple rules: there are no trumps; the players must follow suit if they can; the players may discard a card if they cannot follow suit; the highest value card wins the trick; and the winner of the trick leads the next one, with both players calculating their running total of points before the new trick and stating it. One point is awarded for each winning trick that has been led, and two points for any winning trick that has been led by the opposing player; an additional point is awarded to the player who wins the last trick. The player who wins the most tricks — seven or more — wins an extra 10 points, and a player who wins all 12 tricks is said to have made a "cabot" and scores 40 points.

After the six deals comprising the partie, the player with the highest score is awarded a bonus of 100 points, plus the number of points they have scored, minus the number of points scored by the opponent. However, if the opponent has not managed to accumulate 100 points, the winner scores 100 points, plus their own score, plus the opponent's score: the loser is said to be "rubiconed."

Hints and tips

The elder can discard more cards, so has a much better opportunity to improve a hand than the younger does. As a result, the elder can usually afford to play more offensively, while the younger has to take a more defensive approach.

During declarations, neither player has to declare a winning combination if they do not want to do so. A player might wish to confuse the opponent and increase the chance of winning more points during trick play. For example, the elder could declare a sixieme, even though it is a huitieme (this is not, of course, an untrue declaration). The reasoning for this is that as the elder leads the first trick, they could cabot the younger by winning all twelve tricks. Nevertheless, any declaration must be the exact truth: you cannot declare a trio of jacks unless you hold three jacks, but you can do so if you hold a quatorze of jacks.

FIVE HUNDRED

In 1904 The US Playing Card Company invented Three-handed Five Hundred as an alternative to Auction Bridge. A variant of Euchre with similarities to Whist, it is very popular in the USA; the four-handed version is regarded as the national card game of Australia.

Players: two to six
Equipment: one pack of cards including the joker
Difficulty: a fair degree of skill is required
Duration: half an hour

The aim of the game
To be the first player to score 500 points, by winning tricks to fulfil a contract that has been bid. If two players pass 500 points during the same hand, the player who has bid beats an opponent; if two opponents pass 500 points during the same hand the first opponent to reach 500 during the hand wins.

Starting the game
Depending on the number of players, low-value cards are removed to leave 10 cards per player and two spare or "widow" cards. In three-handed games, the 2s to 6s are taken out to leave 32 cards; in four-handed and two-handed games, the 2s, 3s and black 4s are discarded to leave 42 cards; in five-handed games the whole pack is used. A special pack of 62 cards can be bought from specialist shops for use when six people are playing, or cards can be added from another pack. As in Euchre, a joker called a "benny" is added to the pack in each case as an extra card.

The cards are shuffled, and the player who cuts the highest card becomes dealer for the first hand; the next hand is dealt by the player to the left of the first dealer, and so on. The cards are dealt facedown in batches: three cards, then four cards, followed by another three. After the first deal of three cards to each player, three cards are placed facedown in the center of the table to form the kitty or "widow."

Trumps
The joker is always the highest trump card. The jack of the trump suit, called the "right bower," is the second highest trump and the jack of the same color, the "left bower," is the third highest trump. The other trump cards descend in normal order, with the ace being the next highest, followed by the king, queen, 10, 9, and so on. (The fact that the ace is only the fourth highest trump card is the main thing that distinguishes Five hundred from Bridge and Whist.) In a no-trump game the jacks revert to their normal ranking and the joker is the only "trump."

The bidding
The players examine their 10 cards and the player to the left of the dealer opens the bidding. The lowest possible bid is six tricks and the highest is ten, or the player can pass. The suits rank from no-trumps (the highest), through hearts, diamonds, and clubs to spades (the lowest), so a bid of ♦6, for example, beats a bid of ♠6. Once a player has passed they cannot come back into the bidding during the hand (though some play-

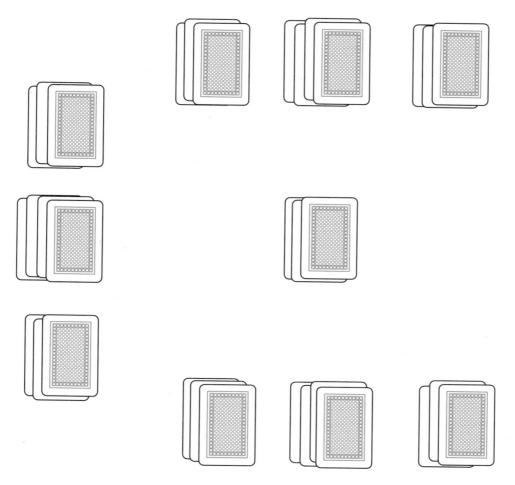

Diagram 29 *A deal for three-handed Five Hundred*

ers do allow further bids), and the bidding stops when there have been two passes in succession. It is possible to raise bids in successive rounds of bidding, but in practice this rarely happens. Each bid carries a points value that is awarded to the player whose bid is successful or is deducted from their score if the bid is unsuccessful.

Two other types of bid are possible. The first is "nullo," or "misère," and it means that the player thinks they will win no tricks in a no-trump game. Its value ranks between a bid of ♠8 and ♣8 and is worth 250 points. If the bid fails, the opponents win 10 points each for every trick the bidder won. An "open misere" outranks all other bids and is worth 520 points. This is the same bid as a misere, but it means that the bidder must lay their hand faceup on the table before play starts so that the other players can see the hand as it is being played. The prize is substantial but of course you lose the element of secrecy in playing your hand.

Bidding points for trumps

Tricks	6	7	8	9	10
Spades	40	140	240	340	440
Clubs	60	160	260	360	460
Diamonds	80	180	280	380	480
Hearts	100	200	300	400	500
No trumps	120	220	320	420	520

Misère	250
Open Misère	520

Playing the game

The player who made the highest bid must now try to make the contract by winning the specified number of tricks with the suit that was bid as trumps, or with no-trumps, as the case may be. The other two players unite in a temporary – though unspoken – alliance to defeat the contract.

Before play starts, the highest bidder has the option of picking the widow up from the center of the table and discarding three cards facedown on the table. Then they play the opening lead. The player to the bidder's left responds, and play continues clockwise. Players must follow suit where possible, otherwise they can play any card. A trick is won by the highest trump or highest card in the suit that was led, and the winner of one trick leads the next one. The benny can be played at any time, with the following exceptions and restrictions: if no-trumps was bid, the joker can only be played as the sole trump if the player is void in the suit that was led; and if a player leads the benny, they must declare which suit it represents, but this cannot be a suit in which they had a void at the start of the hand.

Each player keeps the tricks that they win, and at the end of the hand they are counted up and 10 points are awarded for each trick won. If the bidder makes the contract, points are awarded as shown in the table on the previous page. If the bidder wins all 10 tricks the score is either 250 points or the score shown in the table, whichever is the greater. If the bidder fails to make the contract (in this situation the bidder is said to be "set"), the number of points shown is deducted from their score. As a result, it is possible for the bidder to end up with a minus score — or in the "hole" —and the score is marked on the scoresheet inside a circle.

Hints and tips

On the face of it, it seems difficult to make any successful bid when the lowest possible bid is six of a suit. However, remember that 10 cards — a third of those in play — are trumps. Bear in mind, too, that as you usually have only one chance to make a bid, it is vital to bid as high as

possible to gain the maximum number of points. It is unwise to rely on the widow to produce a specific card. Instead, use the widow either to lengthen a suit, or to produce a void by discarding to it. On discard though, retain all trumps, all long suits, and high cards in consecutive order.

The order of play is significant in five hundred. If it is inevitable that you will loose a trick, it is best that the player on your left wins it. This will mean that you are the third player on the next trick, so you may force two high cards out. Try to make the bidder the second player to play a card.

The situation of the game is important, too, in that it is not always wise to join forces with another player against the bidder. If the bidder cannot make 500 points even by winning the contract, but your temporary "partner" will exceed 500 points if the bidder loses, it is wise to play with the bidder to ensure that your partner cannot win the game.

VARIATIONS
Four-handed or "Australian" Five Hundred

This is the most popular trick-playing game in Australia and has now become the version of the game that is most often played in the USA. Four players play in two partnerships using a deck that has been reduced to 42 cards by taking out the 2s, 3s and the black 4s. The joker (also known as the "bird" in Australia because the card depicts a kookaburra) is added to make a pack of 43 cards in all.

The dealer is chosen at random, but the deal passes clockwise after each hand. As before, the cards are dealt in batches of three, four, and three, but a single card is put facedown in the center of the table after each batch to form the widow.

If misère or open misère is bid, the bidder's partner drops out, their cards are laid out facedown on the table and the bidder plays alone. Misère can only be bid if someone else has bid 7 of a suit; it cannot follow a bid of 6. However, a bid of open misère can follow any other bid. A player who has passed once cannot reenter the bidding, which continues until three players have passed. The highest bid becomes the contract and the player who bid it is said to be the "contractor."

The contractor starts the play by picking up the three cards in the widow without showing them to any other player and making three discards to it. In a misère or open misère contract the joker must be played if the player has a void in the suit that has been led. The joker can be led and nominated as being in a suit so long as that suit has not been led previously.

The difference in scoring in the four-handed game is that partners keep their scores together, so that it is the first partnership to reach more than 500 points that wins the game. The game is lost by a partnership that reaches a score of more than 500 minus points — losing in this way is commonly known as "going out the backdoor."

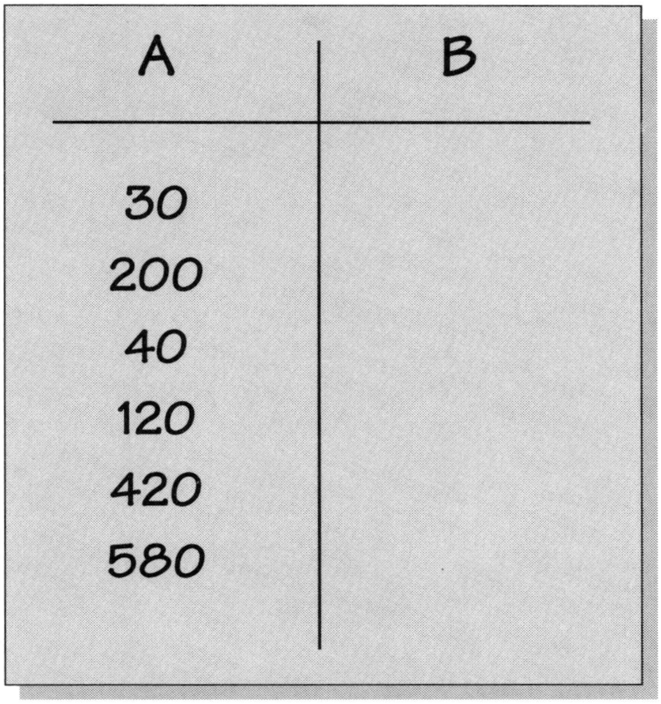

Five-handed Five Hundred

This version of the game is played in the same way as four-handed five hundred, but in each hand the contractor can choose to play either with a partner or alone. If the contractor chooses a partner, the contract score is divided between the two temporary partners. The points are kept individually.

There are several variations to this form of the game. In one of them the contractor nominates a particular card and the holder of that card becomes the contractor's partner. In another, the person holding the nominated card need not tell the other players that they are teamed with the contractor, and only the play of the round will make it evident who the partner is — this rule also allows the contractor to nominate a card in their own hand so that the opponents will not realize the contractor is playing alone until the nominated card is actually played.

Misère is often banned in five-handed games. Open misère is only worth 230 points, but "super open misère" (in which the bidder's cards are

A	B
30	
200	
40	
120	
420	
580	

Diagram 30 *A score card for a four-handed game. A circled score shows minus points*

placed faceup on the table and played by the opponents) is worth 430 points.

Six-handed Five Hundred

This version is played as above, but each partnership has three players, with the partners taking part in rotation. A special pack of cards with 62 cards is used, which has 11s, 12s and red 13s added to the normal pack and ranking above the 10s but below the court cards. These packs can be bought from specialist shops, but if you do not have one you can add the 2s, 3s, and red 4s from one normal pack to another one.

CHILDREN'S GAMES

These games are easy for children to play amongst themselves, or

with adults, and give a great deal of enjoyment while developing their

concentration and coordination.

For many adults, memories of childhood vacations are bound together with learning to play simple card games. Rainy days, especially on vacations, can be made to fly by with just a set of ordinary playing cards. As soon as a child can spot that two cards have the same rank or face value, they are old enough to start playing cards. Snap is one of the simplest and most well-known card games for children. Special Snap cards can be bought, but the game is just as much fun with standard playing cards, and this is a good way of familiarizing young children with them. Slapjack can also be enjoyed by the very young – the only requirement is that players can recognize a jack. Beggar my Neighbor is another easy game, requiring virtually no special skills, only an ability to recognize the honor cards and count to four. The way the cards move backwards and forwards is the cause of much amusement, and the game is most fun when played fast and furiously.

Much of the fun in children's games is that they are fast-moving and involve making a lot of noise. Go Boom falls into this category – young children delight in shouting out exuberantly when they have won. Cheat is always very popular, too, especially when it is understood that to play it well you have to lie without being found out. Spit is more suitable for older children because it requires considerable concentration and speed, but still involves a great deal of shouting, thus being the cause for much hilarity.

Pelmanism and other card-matching games are an excellent way of improving concentration. For older children it is fine to play with a standard pack, but for young ones you can buy special cards printed with colored pictures, patterns, or symbols. To make play simpler for very young children, the cards may be laid out at the start of the game in rows, and fewer pairs may be used. In games of this sort, a child who is concentrating can often remember more cards than a grown-up player, a fact that some adults find most embarrassing – and most children find very satisfying.

A Victorian card game, called Authors, used to be played with special cards showing different writers with quotations from their works. It was thought of as being very "educational" – which no doubt spoilt the fun for a lot of Victorian children.

Since then there have been a variety of special packs of cards, some of which are now valuable collectors' items. The game can be played equally well with standard playing cards. The object of all versions of the game is to collect sets of four cards of the same value, but in Go Fish, described here, the element of luck in winning is greater.

SNAP

Most families with children have played this classic card game. It is always amusing and invariably annoying – and it can be very irritating when the children win.

Players: *two or more*
Equipment: *one pack of cards for two or three players; two packs for four or more players*
Difficulty: *easy if you concentrate*
Duration: *five minutes*

Starting to play

The dealer shuffles the cards thoroughly, and then deals them facedown to each player in turn until all the cards have been dealt out – it does not matter if this means that some players have more cards than others.

Playing the game

The player on the dealer's left turns the top card of their pile faceup and places it next to the pile. The player to that person's left does the same, and so on, around the table. If any two cards on a faceup pile have the same value (suits are irrelevant) the first person to say – or yell – "Snap" takes both piles and adds them to the bottom of their facedown pile. Play then continues, with the player to the left of the one who cried "Snap" turning another card faceup.

If a player runs out of facedown cards they can still call "Snap" when appropriate, in an attempt to get back into the game. However, any player who has neither a facedown pile nor a faceup one is out of the game. Any player who makes a mistake by yelling "Snap" when there are not two cards of the same value on display, has to pay a forfeit of one card from their facedown pile to every other player. The game is won by the player who captures every card on the table.

Hints and tips

The faster the game is played the more amusing

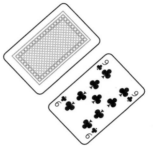
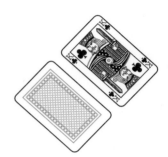

Diagram 1 Playing Snap

and entertaining it is. However, it is a good idea to have an adult standing by to adjudicate on which child shouted "Snap" first.

SLAPJACK

A member of the same family of card games as Snap, this is a game in which success depends on speed of hand and quickness of eye. But Slapjack is so easy that even very young children can master it.

Players: *two or more*
Equipment: *one pack of cards, or two packs when there are four or more players*
Difficulty: *the only skill required is the ability to recognize a jack*
Duration: *10 minutes*

Starting the game

The dealer shuffles the cards thoroughly and deals them facedown, one by one, to each player until the supply is exhausted. It does not matter if some players have more cards than others. Each player picks up their pile of cards, but is not allowed to look at them.

Playing the game

The player on the left of the dealer places one card faceup in the center of the playing area, which can either be a table or the floor. Going clockwise, each player in turn adds another card as quickly as possible to the pile until a jack is put down. At the sight of a jack, each player has to try to be the first to slap their hand down on the pile and cover the jack. The player who succeeds takes the pile and adds it to the bottom of the pile that they are holding. It does not matter if a player runs out of cards as it is possible to get back into the game by being the first to slap a hand on a jack. The game ends when one player has won all the cards that were dealt.

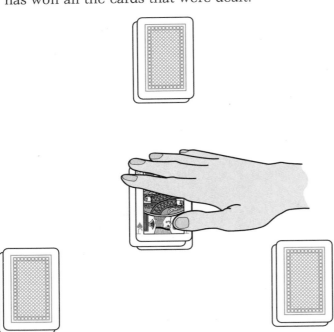

Diagram 2 A game of Slapjack

SPIT

Spit is a race between two people that depends on speed, luck, timing, and considerable powers of concentration. It is quite normal for a game of Spit to degenerate into complete chaos.

Players: *two*
Equipment: *one pack of cards*
Difficulty: *requires alertness and speed; for older children*
Duration: *10 minutes*

Starting to play

The deck is cut by all the players and the one with the highest card (aces rank low throughout the game, so the highest card is a king and the lowest is an ace) acts as the dealer, though there is no advantage to being the dealer. The cards are shuffled thoroughly and dealt alternately to each player until the whole pack is finished.

Both players then place the first five cards in their pile facedown in a row in front of them. Another row is placed on top of the first, starting with the second card of the first row, so four cards are laid down by each player in all. A further row is then laid down, starting with the third card of the first row, and so on, until one card is placed on the last pile in the row. This procedure uses up 15 cards from each player's hand.

The remainder are placed in two stockpiles, one for each player, in the center of the table. The top card in each player's row of piles (the first card of row one, the second card of row two, and so on) is then turned faceup. The top card of each stockpile is turned faceup and placed alongside it — this forms two discard piles.

Playing the game

To start the game, the two players say "One, two, three, Spit" in unison. On "Spit," the two players start to build on either of the two discard piles, working as quickly as possible. They do this by placing any faceup card from the rows in front of them, regardless of suit, but in either ascending or descending order, on the top card of either discard pile. When a card is taken from the rows, the card beneath is turned faceup. For example, if the top card on a discard pile is ♥7, either a 6 or 8 of any suit can be added to that pile. However, an ace or a king must be covered by either a 2 or a queen because aces are low.

An ace cannot be covered by a king, or a king by an ace. The players also have the option of building in either ascending or descending order on faceup cards in the rows in front of them.

If neither player can put a card down, either on the discard piles or their own row, play stops. Another card from each stockpile is then placed on its discard pile. Play resumes after another shout of "One, two, three, Spit."

The first round ends when both stockpiles are empty, at which point each player tries to slap their hand on the smallest of the two discard piles, shouting "Spit" at the same time. The discard piles are now turned over and form the new stockpile and play resumes with another round.

Finishing the game

There are now two ways to proceed. Which one you choose depends on whether you want to have a short game or a longer one. In one version of the game, the player who finishes their stockpile first is allowed to choose the smallest stockpile for the next round. The problem is that it is likely that the player who wins this round, and so obtains the smallest stockpile, is likely to finish their stockpile first in the next round, too (though it is not inevitable). It is therefore preferable to continue as for the first round, with play continuing until both stockpiles are exhausted and each player then having to slap a hand on the smallest pile — this at least gives the losing player the chance to get back into the game. The game is won when one player eventually gets rid of all their cards, both from the stockpile and their hand.

Diagram 3 A game of Spit

BEGGAR MY NEIGHBOR

*A fast and furious game for children
that requires no skill, but is great fun.*

Players: two or more
*Equipment: one pack of cards, or two with
more than four players*
Difficulty: depends wholly on luck
Duration: 10 minutes

Playing the game

The cards are shuffled thoroughly and dealt face-down to all players, starting from the dealer's left. The players can pick their cards up to put them in a neat pile, but they must not look at them.

Diagram 4 *A game of Beggar my Neighbor*

The player to the dealer's left turns the top card in their pile card faceup and places it in the center of the table. If the face value of the card is between 2 and 10, the next player, going clockwise, puts the top card from their pile on top of it, and so on around the table. If the card turned up and put down is an honor card (king, queen, or jack) or an ace, the player whose turn it is must place four cards on top in the case of an ace, three cards if the card is a king, two for a queen, and one for a jack. As long as no honor card or ace is put down while this is happening, the player who put down the ace or honor card picks up the pack and places it at the bottom of their own pile. The same player then puts the top card of their pile down to continue the game. If, for example, an ace is put down by player A, player B must play four cards; but if any card up to and including the fourth card is an honor card or ace, then no more cards are played and player A must put down the number of cards applicable to that card. (A jack is therefore the most useful card, because there is less chance of the opponent playing an honor card or ace with only one card to be played.)

As soon as any player runs out of cards they are out of the game. The winner is the last player left to have cards.

DONKEY

*This extremely simple game can be enjoyed
by very young children, who find the idea that
the loser becomes "The Donkey" very
amusing indeed.*

Players: three to six
*Equipment: four cards of equal face value for
each player (for example, four aces, kings,
queens, and jacks if there are four players)*
Difficulty: can be enjoyed by very young children
Duration: five to 10 minutes

Playing the game

The dealer deals four cards to each player. The players pick up their hands and examine them, and then each player has to discard one card – if, for example, a player has two jacks, a king, and a queen, either the king or the queen can be discarded, because it is sensible for that player to try to collect four jacks if two are already held. When all the players have made their choice, each player discards one card, placing it facedown in front of the player to the left, who picks it up. The player making the discard will receive a card from the player on the right.

Play continues in this way, with each player attempting to collect four of a kind. The first one to do so places the four cards on the table, without making any fuss about it. As the other players realize what has happened they also place their cards – whatever they are – on the table. The last player to react loses the game and becomes "Donkey."

The cards are then scooped up and shuffled, and the game is repeated – ideally until all the children playing have had a turn at being "Donkey."

Diagram 5 Cards for a game of Donkey

VARIATION
Pig

This a more subtle variation of Donkey. In Pig, a player does not put a set of four cards down on the table, but signifies that four of a kind have been collected by touching the side of their nose. The last child to realize what has happened is called "Pig" for the next round.

GO FISH

Like several other children's games, Go Fish is simple enough but its arcane phrases and element of strategy make it entertaining nonetheless.

Players: *two to five*
Equipment: *a pack of shuffled cards*
Difficulty: *luck plays a major part*
Duration: *five to 10 minutes*

Starting the game

If there are two or three players, each player is dealt seven cards; if four or five are playing each player is dealt five cards. The rest of the deck is placed facedown in a pile in the center of the table and forms the "fish pond." All the players examine their cards and decide which fours they are going to collect. The player to the left of the dealer starts.

Playing the game

The first player asks the player on their right for a card — for example a jack, because they already have two jacks. If that player has a jack, it must be handed over and another request can be made. If there is no jack, the reply is "Go fish," and the player making the request must take a card from the "fishpond" and add it to their hand. If it happens that this card is the same as the one originally requested, the player must say "I fished upon my wish," and can then request another card from the player on their right. If the card is not the same, that player's turn is over. Play then moves clockwise, and the next player can make a request of the player to their right (the one who has just finished playing).

As players collect fours of a kind, they place the cards on the table in front of them and are allowed to request another card from the player on their right.

The winner is the player who first succeeds in putting all their cards down on the table in sets of four. It is unusual for anybody to achieve this, however, so the winner is normally the player with the most sets of four on the table when the fishpond is exhausted.

Diagram 6 *A game of Go Fish*

GO BOOM

Young children love this game, probably because of the amount of noise that can be made as the winner announces his or her success.

Players: *two to 12, though the game works better with three to four*
Equipment: *one pack of shuffled cards, or two if six or more people are playing*
Difficulty: *straightforward, even for very young children*
Duration: *15 minutes*

Playing the game

Seven cards are dealt facedown to each player. The remainder of the pack is placed facedown in a pile in the center of the table and the players pick up their cards and can examine them. The player to the left of the dealer starts the game, leading with any card of their choice and placing it faceup on the table. The next player, going clockwise, follows by playing a card either of equal value (aces are high, so the lowest card is a two) or of the same suit. For example, if the first card played is a ♥5, the next player must play either a heart or a 5 of another suit.

Play continues around the table until a round has been completed – that is, everybody has played a card – or until a player cannot match the previous card. If this happens, the player has to pick cards up from the central deck one at a time until a card that can be played is turned up; cards that cannot be played are added to their hand. (If the central pile has been exhausted, a player who cannot play must pass.) After each player has played a card, the cards put down during the round are examined, and the winner is the player who has put down the highest card during the round. If two players have played the same highest card, the winner is the one who played

Diagram 7 *A game of Go Boom*

the highest card first. The cards that had been played during the round are then discarded, and the winner of the trick leads off the next round with a card of their choice.

The winner of the game is the first player to get rid of their cards, or – if all the players have to pass during a round – the player with the fewest cards held. Traditionally, the winner announces success with a loud and exuberant yell of "Boom!"

VARIATION

The game can be continued when the central pile has been exhausted by picking up the cards discarded at the end of each round, shuffling them, and placing them facedown to form a new pile.

Diagram 8 *Go Boom trick*

CHEAT

Also called I Doubt It, Cheat can be viewed by cynics as a way of training children to play Poker.

Players: three or more
Equipment: one pack of cards
Difficulty: easy, but requires the ability to keep a straight face
Duration: five to 10 minutes

Starting to play

The cards are shuffled and dealt one at a time, facedown, to all of the players – it does not matter if some players have more cards than others. The players pick up their hands and sort them out by value from high to low, irrespective of suit. It is important that all the players make sure that nobody else can see their cards.

Playing the game

The whole point of Cheat is to get rid of all your cards through minor bluffing or outrageously lying, when necessary or appropriate, about their value. The player to the left of the dealer starts the game by placing a card facedown in the center of the table while naming its value – the player has the option of telling the truth or lying. The next player, going clockwise, puts another card facedown on top of the first card and also says what its value is — the claim may be true or false, but it must be higher than the value of the previous card. Each player around the table takes it in turn to put down a card and either lie or tell the truth.

If one player suspects another of cheating, and as the game progresses this becomes more and more likely, that player yells "Cheat" and the card that has just been played is turned faceup. If the person who played the card did cheat, they have to pick up the pile on the table and add it to the bottom of their hand. If it turns out that the claim as to its value was accurate, the player who made the false accusation has to add the pile to their hand. If more than one player shouts "Cheat" at the same time, the player nearest to the left of the person accused is deemed to be the accuser. It is therefore perhaps wise to err on the side of caution and wait for braver or more foolhardy players to take the risk. The first player to be left without any cards is the winner.

VARIATION

Instead of putting one card at a time, the rules can be varied to allow two or even three cards of the same value to be put down in one go if a player wishes to do so. For example, a player might claim to have put down three queens: this sounds outlandish, but it could just be a clever double-bluff.

Hints and tips

Success in Cheat depends on the ability to look either innocent or guilty, as appropriate, in order to fool the other players. As a result, children who excel at the game often grow up to be extremely good Poker players.

PELMANISM

Also known as Pairs and Concentration, Pelmanism tests both memory and concentration. A child who is concentrating hard can often remember more cards than an adult.

Players: two or more
Equipment: one pack of cards
Difficulty: easy, but requires concentration and good observation
Duration: five minutes

Starting the game

The cards are shuffled and spread out facedown on a table or the floor. They can either be placed in neat rows or at random in any position – the latter method makes the game more difficult.

Playing the game

The first player turns over any two cards of their choice, keeping them in exactly the same position as they were when facedown. If the two cards make a pair of the same face value – two jacks or two 7s, for example – the player wins them. The same player can then turn up another two cards at random, continuing until the cards turned up are of a different face value. Having given all the players time to see which cards have been turned faceup, the player then turns the odd cards facedown again, in exactly the same position as they were before. The next player to the left then has a turn.

At the start of the game it is more luck than a good memory that allows pairs to be collected. However, as the game progresses and more cards have been revealed, concentration and memory start to play the major role. But the game becomes progressively easier as the number of cards on the table diminishes. The player who has the most pairs when all the cards have been picked up wins the game, and is the dealer for the next game.

Diagram 9 *A game of Pelmanism*

Chapter 2
BOARD GAMES

The first games played on a board were primarily games of chance. Players competed to complete a circuit of the board by throwing dice to determine the number of moves that could be taken at any one time. The only element of choice was which piece to move, or how many pieces to move from one position to the next.

Increasingly, chance was combined with strategy. Games of strategy seem to have emerged when societies increased in complexity to such an extent that there was a need for diplomacy and strategic warfare. In the ancient Chinese game of Weichi, from which Go is derived, players attempt to surround each other's pieces using a blockading kind of warfare. Chess has been likened to a battle between different social orders, with the status of each member – from pawn to king – being carefully stated. The aim of the game of Chess is not to surround the enemy, but to capture and exterminate them. The modern game of Risk® is the ultimate conquest game, with players competing to take over the whole world.

Some board games are symbols of personal success and achievement. Mancala, the strategic game of the African continent, first played in ancient Egypt, involves each player having a number of pieces distributed about the playing board. With each move, a player must make estimates involving numerical skill and good judgement in order to capture the opponent's pieces. In Mancala, and in games such as Ludo that are derived from it, the accumulation of property is at issue. The contemporary game of Monopoly® is similar in this respect.

Many board games were intended to be educational. This was particularly the case during the eighteenth and nineteenth centuries, when scores of games were designed to impart useful information. Scenes from the past, famous people and battles were all popular subjects, and were accompanied by dates and descriptive information. Some games were based on maps of different parts of the globe, illustrated with landscapes and animals. The boards were beautifully colored by hand or stencil, and are now popular collector's items. Today, of course, many board games can be played on a computer screen and are more popular than ever.

FAMILY BOARD GAMES

The twentieth century has seen an explosion of commercial board games.

Games such as Monopoly®, Trivial Pursuit®, and Scrabble® have sold in

their millions and achieved worldwide popularity.

Most families are familiar with the fun and excitement provided by a board game. Many contemporary games are simple enough to be played by both adults and children – the outcome often depends solely on the throw of the dice. Other games are more sophisticated and require strategy, though they can usually be played to accommodate all levels of skill.

Monopoly® is perhaps the best-known and most popular family board game. It is a game of make-believe property deals and financial bargaining, in which real estate is bought and then rented or sold profitably, so that you become the wealthiest player and bankrupt the other players. Monopoly® started in the USA, but is now played in many different countries using different currencies and on boards showing different cities. It is a game, too, in which the more fiercely competitive members of the family can sometimes get a little heated. Be warned!

Risk® was invented by a Frenchman but, like Monopoly® and the other board games in this section, is played in many different countries, sometimes with slightly different rules. In this world conquest game, the winner is the one who manages to eliminate all the opponent's forces.

Clue® is a mystery game in which each player attempts to solve a murder that takes place in a large house. Players move their pieces around the board from room to room. By a process of questioning and deduction, they seek to discover the murderer, the weapon and the scene of the crime. Clue® is one of the few board games that has enjoyed the rare honour of being adapted for the big screen.

Scrabble® is a word game in which two, three or four players, using up to seven lettered tiles at a time, try to build words on a grid pattern board. It can be played by anyone from young children to expert players at tournament level. The game quickly became popular when it appeared in the late 1940s, and is now played in 31 languages as well as in Braille.

Just as Scrabble® is the ultimate word game, Trivial Pursuit® is the ultimate quiz game. Players answer questions in six different categories, represented by different colors. The game is particularly good for team play, with those deemed strong in various categories dispersed among the teams.

As in earlier times, many modern games combine pleasure with learning. There are historical and geographical board games that differ little from the type of game played a couple of hundred years ago. Other games deal with current topics such as property deals, finance, space travel, or political maneuvering. Games that are specifically designed for young children are a useful way of teaching the rudiments of counting and reading, and of encouraging a child to plan and think ahead.

MONOPOLY®

Monopoly® is perhaps the definitive family board game. Since it was acquired by Parker Brothers in the mid-1930s, over 125 million Monopoly® sets have been sold in more than 40 countries and upward of 20 languages.

Players: *two to six*
Equipment: *board, two dice, cards and pieces*
Difficulty: *ideal for families; requires a combination of strategy and luck*
Duration: *tournament games are usually restricted to one and a half hours, at which point each player's assets are added up and recorded. After three games have been completed, the five players with the highest totals go into a "to the death" final game.*

Brief history

The history of Monopoly® is inextricably linked with an unemployed heating engineer named Charles Darrow from Germantown, Pennsylvania, who secured a patent for it in 1933 and went on to become a multi-millionaire from the proceeds of his "invention". However, its origins date back to the late 1800s, when property games started to become popular. In fact Monopoly® has striking similarities to "The Landlord's Game," which was patented by Elizabeth Magie 30 years before Darrow's patent. Although Magie never marketed her game properly, it gradually grew in popularity in the form of hand-made sets that were copied by friends and acquaintances.

By the time Darrow played The Landlord's Game in the early 1930s, it had developed from a simple property game where rents were charged for landing on a rival's properties to include many of the elements that were to make it a success: names for the individual properties; the concept of collecting groups of properties and erecting houses and hotels in order to increase rents; and the introduction of Community Chest and Chance cards. However, the fundamental change that was to make Monopoly® such a success had nothing to do with the rules of the game and everything to do with the spirit in which it was played – Monopoly® became a game of acquisition and competition at a time (the Great Depression) when people needed a means to escape from the harsh realities of life.

Magie had developed her original game as a means of anti-capitalistic propaganda. She had intended to show how unscrupulous landlords could charge unfair rents. It is somewhat ironic, therefore, that Monopoly® evolved to become one of the greatest symbols of capitalism, with players battling to acquire property and wealth and to bankrupt their rivals. Indeed, one of Fidel Castro's first acts after seizing power in Cuba was to ban Monopoly® and confiscate all existing sets

Diagram 1 Monopoly® – the game for all budding property tycoons

on the island, denouncing it as "symbolic of an imperialistic system." It is still banned in Cuba, as well as in China and North Korea.

Although Darrow cannot be given credit for inventing the game, he contributed two vital ingredients: the draughtsmanship skills that enabled him to produce a much more attractive game board, and business acumen. Having copyrighted "his" version, he immediately set about selling hand-made sets to friends and local shops but soon realized that a more commercial approach was required. It was then that he approached the games manufacturers Parker Brothers, who initially rejected the game, claiming that there were "52 fundamental errors." However, Darrow was not discouraged and began to manufacture and sell the game himself. Having sold more than 5000 sets to department stores in Philadelphia and New York by Christmas 1934, Darrow was reapproached by Parker Brothers and offered an attractive royalty, which he "gladly accepted and never regretted." At the age of 46 he was able to retire to become a gentleman farmer in Bucks County, Pennsylvania. When he died in 1967, he was able to leave his heirs a fortune in royalties.

Monopoly® also came along just at the right time for Parker Brothers, who had been badly hit by the Depression themselves. By the end of 1935 they were forced to increase their workforce to cope with demand for over 20,000 copies a week. However, they also had to deal with a nasty surprise when they discovered the existence of Elizabeth Magie's very similar patent and of another extremely closely related game called Finance (which itself owed much to Magie's prototype). In a deft piece of damage limitation they purchased all the rights to both Finance and The Landlord's Game (the latter for only $500), thereby saving themselves a potential scandal (it was not until the 1980s that the true story came out) and perhaps millions of dollars of royalties.

Such was the success of Monopoly® that Parker Brothers were rapidly able to secure licensing arrangements for foreign editions. In the UK Waddingtons enthusiastically took up the new game, with the small modification of pounds for dollars and the substitution of London street names for the original Atlantic City names, Boardwalk and Park Place becoming Mayfair and Park Lane.

During the Second World War, Waddingtons were commissioned by the War Office to send special sets to prisoner-of-war camps. However, these special editions were not for recreational purposes: they contained an escape map hidden in one side of the board and Monopoly® money was replaced by real German, Italian or Austrian money. These POW sets brought whole new meaning to the expression "Get Out of Jail." It is also said that the perpetrators of the Great Train Robbery in England in 1963 passed the time playing Monopoly® with real money – the two million pounds from the heist.

Beginning to play

The board consists of an outside track of squares, including properties, railway stations, jail and parking squares. Each player chooses one token to represent them while travelling around the board. Players move their pieces around the board, throwing the dice to determine the number of squares they may move. According to where a player lands, they may be entitled to buy real estate or other properties – or be obliged to pay rent, pay taxes, draw a Chance or Community Chest card, "Go to Jail," etc. Each player buys, sells and rents properties to become the wealthiest person on the board – and drives his competitors to bankruptcy in the process.

One player is nominated as Banker and must keep their personal funds separate from those of the Bank. The Bank pays salaries and bonuses and holds the Title Deed cards and houses and hotels prior to purchase and use by the players. It also sells and auctions properties and hands out the appropriate Title Deed cards; it sells houses and hotels to the players and loans money when required on mortgages. The Bank

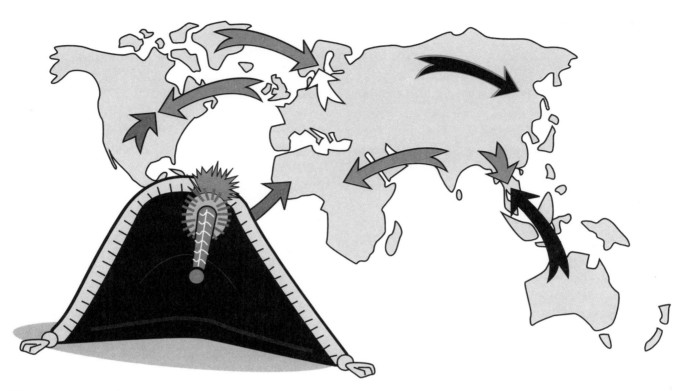

Diagram 2 *Dominate the world with Risk®*

collects all taxes, fines, loans and interest, and the price of all properties that it sells and auctions.

Strategy

American computer expert Tom Friddell has shown, using probability theory, that some properties are much more advantageous than others. All of the red and orange properties are good value. The red properties, clockwise, are Kentucky Avenue, Indiana Avenue, and Illinois Avenue. The railroads, also valuable, are Reading Railroad, Pennsylvania Railroad, B&O Railroad, and the Short Line.

Winning the game

The object of Monopoly® is to amass enough wealth to bankrupt one's opponents and force them out of the game. The last player left in the game wins. In the "short" version, the game ends with the second bankruptcy, regardless of the number of players, at which point the players' assets are totted up and the richest player is declared the winner.

RISK®

The world conquest game of Risk® is one of the most popular games to have been published in the post-war period. Players attack and counter attack one another in 42 countries on six continents, with the aim of taking over the world.

Players: *two to six*
Equipment: *board, five dice, cards and pieces*
Difficulty: *very strategic; some luck*
Duration: *usually more than one and a half hours*

Brief history

Although the principles are basically the same, the precise rules of Risk® vary quite markedly from country to country – and sometimes even from edition to edition! Risk® was invented by a Frenchman named Albert Lamorisse, but publishers in different countries adopted slightly different rules. The version discussed here follows the current English rules and is sometimes known as Secret Mission Risk.

Beginning to play

At the start of the game the board is laid out and each player selects a color with which to play. One player should be nominated as General, and they will be in charge of handing out and collecting cards and reinforcements. Each player is given one card which describes a secret mission that they must fulfil, such as destroying a particular army, conquering a certain combination of continents or occupying a certain number of territories.

The Risk® Cards are then dealt out, each card representing a territory which that player will occupy at the start of the game. This stage is a vital juncture of the game – players must decide from which territories they may wish to launch an attack, and which strategically important territories they need to fortify for defense.

Strategy

Overall strategy will generally depend on the mission that needs to be accomplished. However, it is generally not a good idea to focus on your strategy immediately, as your mission will become harder to achieve once other players know what it is. In principle, it is considered to be a good strategy to conquer Australia first, gaining additional Battalions on each turn for occupying a continent, and then amass forces in Siam, delaying an attack on Asia until sufficient forces are in place. South America is also a very useful starting point, although it will require a great deal of fortification. It is hard to hold Europe and Asia in the early stages of a game, as they are so large and can be attacked from so many different directions.

Winning the game

In a three- to six-player game, the winner is the first player to achieve the strategic objective stated on their Mission Card, so a player who seems to have an overwhelming advantage may in fact be nowhere near completing their mission in some cases. In a two-player game (which is played without Mission Cards), the winner is the player who manages to eliminate all the opponent's forces. Even with more than two players it is still possible to play the world domination game, although it will take much longer to complete.

CLUE®

The classic "Whodunnit" game of Clue® remains one of the most popular family games. (It was invented by an English clerk, Anthony Pratt, in the 1940s, under the name of Cluedo®.) Each player has to use his powers of deduction to work out which suspect is guilty, where the murder was committed and how.

Players: *three to six*
Equipment: *board, two dice, cards and pieces*
Difficulty: *easy to grasp strategy; some luck*
Duration: *usually less than half an hour, depending on the number of players*

Beginning to play

The object of Clue® is to discover which of the six suspects (Colonel Mustard, Professor Plum, Reverend Green, Mrs Peacock, Miss Scarlett and Mrs White), using which of the six weapons (dagger, lead piping, candlestick, rope, wrench and revolver), committed the murder of Dr Black, and in which of the nine rooms (kitchen, lounge, ballroom, billiard room, hall, dining room, study, library or conservatory) it took place.

At the start of the game the board is laid out with each of the playing pieces on their starting spaces and each of the weapons in a different room. Each player chooses a character and takes a sheet from the Detective Notebook, on which they will write down their deductions. The character cards (one for each of the six characters), weapon cards (one for each of the six weapons) and room cards (one for each of the nine rooms) are shuffled in turn. One card from each pack is placed secretly in the Murder Envelope and the remaining cards shuffled together and dealt out. The players eliminate the cards that they have received on their Notebook sheets, taking care not to allow their cards or notes to be seen by the other players.

The players then roll both dice and move their tokens around the board. If that player reaches one of the rooms they can make a "suggestion;" this involves calling any character and weapon into the room the player has entered in order to establish whether that character, weapon or room was involved in the murder. On entering the kitchen, for example, one could say "Mrs Peacock in the kitchen with the spanner."

Moving

Each player moves around the board from room to room, eliminating characters, weapons and rooms from their inquiries until someone is ready to make an "accusation." To make an accusation the player must write down the character, weapon and room that they suspect and look at the cards in the Murder Envelope. If they are correct on all three counts, they may then show their accusation and the cards to their opponents. However, if they are incorrect, they must replace the cards into the envelope and stay in the game to answer suggestions by the other players.

Strategy

Early in the game you may wish to try and obtain as much general information as possible by basing your suggestions around cards other than those you hold in your hand. However, as your suspicions solidify, you may wish to combine, say, a character that you strongly suspect with a weapon and room that you yourself have. If none of the other players have that character, then you have found the murderer and you can then focus your efforts on finding where the murder was committed and how. It is also sometimes worth making suggestions that are deliber-

Diagram 3 Clue® – the ideal armchair detective game

ately designed to confuse your opponents and put them off the scent.

Winning the game

The winner is the first person to make a successful accusation.

SCRABBLE®

The world's premier word game, Scrabble®, has been sold in 120 countries and is now produced in 31 languages. Its universal appeal owes much to the use of a unique combination of vocabulary and strategy to score points.

Players: *two to four*
Equipment: *board, four letter-racks, letter-bag and 100 letter-tiles. A dictionary is also highly desirable for verification purposes.*
Difficulty: *suitable for ages 10 and above; requires vocabulary skills*
Duration: *usually around one hour per game (25 minutes each for a competitive two-player game)*

Brief history

The founding father of Scrabble® was a New York architect by the name of Alfred Butts. Like Charles Darrow, the mastermind behind Monopoly®, Butts found himself unemployed as a result of the Great Depression. As a fan of anagrams, crossword puzzles and other word games, he decided to devise his own game. At the time there were no commercial word games and, recognizing a gap in the market, Butt developed a prototype game known as Lexiko in 1931. Although Lexiko utilized the same 100 letter tiles that came to be used in Scrabble®, there was no board. The object was simply to form a seven-letter word on one's rack. On every turn tiles could be exchanged for new ones from the pool of unused ones and the game finished when one player was able to win by constructing a seven-letter word. Subsequently a further dimension was added when point values were given to the letters, thereby enabling scores to be collated for each player after every round.

Butts tried to sell Lexiko to various manufacturers but he was turned down. He then hit upon the idea of using a board with premium squares, and tried again to find a manufacturer but was again rejected. It was only at the end of the Second World War, by which time Butts had teamed up with Jim Brunot, a social worker, that any real progress was made. Brunot and his wife refined the game, protected it with a unique brand name, Scrabble®, and in 1949 began to manufacture sets by hand. In the first year, 2400 sets were sold, but the company made a loss. Production doubled in the following year, but still no return was made. It was only when Jack Strauss, the chairman of Macey's, the New York department store, became hooked on Scrabble® in 1952 that the Brunots achieved their long-awaited breakthrough. Strauss made a large order for sets for his store, backed up by a large in-store promotion. Suddenly demand snowballed: four and a half million sets were sold in the next two and a half years as Scrabble® fever gripped America.

Such was the demand that the Brunots decided to license Selchow and Righter, one of the leading American games companies, to market Scrabble® in North America. Soon afterwards UK distribution rights were granted to J.W. Spear & Sons plc. In the first year alone they sold four and a half million sets. It was not long before Scrabble® became a worldwide phenomenon as other countries took up and became obsessed with the game. Nowadays Scrabble® is not only available in standard form, but also in a variety of other board editions, in Braille and on computer.

Beginning to play

At the start of a game of Scrabble® the board is laid out, all the tiles are placed in the bag, and each player is given a rack. To decide who will play first, each player draws a tile from the bag; the player who draws the letter nearest to the beginning of the alphabet starts the game. The tiles that have been drawn are then returned to the bag and the players decide who will be scorer. The players then take seven letters each from the bag and place them on their racks.

The first player must then form a word using two or more letters and arrange it either horizontally (from left to right) or vertically (from top to bottom) on the board in such a way that one letter is placed on the square with the eight-pointed star in the middle. That player then declares a score based on the total value of the tiles they have placed, which the scorer notes down. The player replenishes their stock of tiles from the bag so that they again have seven on their rack. The second player must then place one or more letters from their rack in a straight line to form at least one new word. If more than one word is created a player gains full credit for all the words that have been created. If one of the other players wishes to challenge a word, the dictionary is consulted for verification.

Strategy

There are several interesting strategic factors that add to the appeal of Scrabble®. First, there

Diagram 4 *Vocabulary is the Scrabble® player's main tool*

are two blank tiles which may be used as any letters. Another important component is the 'premium squares' concept: specially colored squares give double or triple scores for the letters or words placed on that turn. If a player manages to place all seven tiles on their rack on the board in one turn a 50-point bonus (or bingo) is scored in addition to the points scored on that turn. Finally, at any point in the game a player may elect to use a turn to discard some or all of the letters on their rack, returning them to the pool in exchange for an equal number of new letters.

The most important ingredient in a Scrabble® player's armory is vocabulary. Champion Scrabble® players spend hours learning rare words that may make the difference between winning and losing a key match. However, novice players can improve their play simply by memorizing all 100-odd words and as many three-letter words as possible. It is also worth knowing the allocation of tiles for each letter of the alphabet.

The most useful tile in Scrabble® is the blank. Top players recommend that you should hold back a blank tile for later use unless it improves any other move by a least 25 points. It is also desirable to keep a balanced rack with a roughly similar number of vowels and consonants (optimally four consonants and three vowels) in order to retain flexibility. Furthermore, if you have two or three identical letters (say three Ts), it is a good idea to play two or more of these in order to remain balanced. Remember that a

seven-letter word scores a 50-point bonus. The most useful tiles to help achieve this are the letters that make up the word RETAINS, and of course the blank tile. One should therefore hold on to these letters if possible, in order to achieve potential high scores later in the game.

However, Scrabble® is not just about tiles and vocabulary – you also need to be aware of the board situation in order to take advantage of premium squares. Try to place the highest scoring letter in your rack on a double or triple letter square if possible, and avoid placing vowels next to premium squares, as these may present your opponent with an invitation to amass a big score. It is usually worth sacrificing a few points if this restricts your opponent's possibilities. The high scoring J, Q, X and Z will enable you to score well in the early part of the game, but could become a problem later on when there are fewer possibilities, particularly if you are left with two or more of these on your rack. You should also always be careful where these tiles are placed in order to avoid opening up double and triple word opportunities for the opponent.

It is important to decide whether you are aiming for an open board, on which there are plenty of scoring opportunities for all the players, or a blocked board, on which it is difficult to make any high scoring words. Generally, you should keep the board open if you think your word power is superior to that of your opponent or need to make a big score to catch up, and block the position if you are ahead by a fair way (say 40-60 points) or are wary of your opponent's word power. A very useful device for blocking the board is the "hook," such as the B added to the front of EAT to form BEAT, or the S added to the end of it to form EATS. Also, in a blocked low-scoring situation, it is worth considering changing tiles if you have a poor allocation of letters. Although this involves the loss of turn, you may be able to obtain some good tiles in order to break the game open with some high scores.

Finally, at the end of a two-player game, nearly all the tiles will be on the board, so you may be able to take a reasonable guess as to which tiles your opponent has left, and then make a play based on that. It is important to be the first to play out, as then extra points are gained for the letters left on your opponent's rack. If you leave one last tile in the pool for your opponent to take, at least you have the assurance that you will have the advantage of being the first to try and play out.

Winning the game

The game ends when all the letters have been drawn from the pool and either one player has used up all the letters on their rack or no further plays are possible by any player. The players' scores are then added up and the value of any unplayed tiles deducted from each player's score. If one player has used up all their tiles, their score is increased by the sum of the other players' remaining tiles.

VARIATIONS

There are numerous variant forms of Scrabble®. Here is a small selection of the most popular.

Solitaire Scrabble®

Although Scrabble® was devised as a game for two, three or four players, it is also possible to play it on your own. The solo player draws seven tiles from the pool and makes a word in the usual way. Having noted the score, they then draw from the pool and make another word, and so on. At the end, the score is added up and compared to scores from earlier games.

Duplicate Scrabble®

Duplicate Scrabble® was invented by a Belgian, Hippolite Wouters, and is more popular than the standard game in French-speaking countries. Any number of players can play, each with their own board. At the start of the game a referee selects seven letters from the pool. The players then have a set time limit to write down the highest scoring play they can find, at which point all the moves are handed in and the high-

est score identified. The referee then announces that this move is to be played on the board and selects some more letters from the pool, which are used for the next move. Play continues until all the tiles have been used. The winner is the player who has achieved the highest score, with bonuses usually awarded if a player is the only one to find the highest scoring play on any turn. Duplicate Scrabble® relies very heavily on word power, and lacks the strategic elements of board and rack management that make the standard game so enthralling.

Blank Option Scrabble®

In order to reduce the luck element associated with the two blank tiles, the American player David Gibson has invented his own variant of the two-player game. Instead of placing the blank tiles in the pool, one is given to each player at the start. At any point they can then add this to their rack instead of a seventh tile from the pool. Once on the rack, the blank tile can then be played in the same way as for a normal game.

TRIVIAL PURSUIT®

Trivial Pursuit® was the games phenomenon of the 1980s. Nowadays this quintessential family game is distributed in 19 different languages and 30 countries across the world.

Players: two to six
Equipment: board, one die, question cards, playing tokens and scoring wedges
Difficulty: straightforward strategy; requires good general knowledge
Duration: around one to one and a half hours

Brief history

In 1979 photo editor Chris Hanley and sports-writer Scott Abbott purchased a brand new game of Scrabble® – their eighth in total, because the pieces never seemed to stay in the box for long.

They began to wonder how many other people had bought multiple copies of the game, and this realization of a potential market opportunity galvanized them to develop their own game – Trivial Pursuit®. Since their background was reporting news, it was natural that they would be interested in current affairs – and Trivial Pursuit® reflects this with its focus on "who, what, when, where, and why."

Having developed a new game, the next step for Hanley and Abbott was marketing it. First they persuaded Hanley's brother John and his friend Ed Werner to join them, and then they formed a new company and set about raising capital from everyone they knew. In the end 34 original investors put in a total of $40,000. However, their initial experiences were less than encouraging – in 1982 sets costing $75 each to manufacture were being sold at $15.

The big breakthrough came when they managed to interest the American games company Selchow and Righter in the idea. The company undertook a major public relations campaign at the 1983 New York Toy Fair and mailed copies to dozens of Hollywood stars. Word of mouth did the rest, and by the end of that year three and a half million games had been sold. In the following year 20 million games were sold – Trivial Pursuit® had arrived!

Beginning to play

At the start of the game, the board is laid out and each player chooses a color and rolls the die. The player with the highest number starts the game by rolling the die again and moving his token the requisite number of squares. He then has to answer a question, read out from the next card in the pack by one of the other players, corresponding to the color on which he has landed. The answers to the questions are on the back of the cards.

Table 1 *Trivial Pursuit® color categories*

Blue	*Geography*
Pink	*Entertainment*
Yellow	*History*
Brown	*Art and Literature*
Green	*Science and Nature*
Orange	*Sports and Leisure*

If the question is correctly answered, the player rolls the die again, moves his token and answers a question from the next card in the pack. However, his turn ends with the first incorrect answer.

Each player travels around the board, answering questions and attempting to land on the designated category headquarters. If a correct answer is given while the player is at a category headquarters, he collects a wedge of that color. If an incorrect answer is given he must move away from that space before attempting another question. If a player lands on the central hexagonal hub before he has collected all six wedges, he may choose which category he wishes to answer a question on.

Winning the game

The object of the game is to collect wedges of all six colors by providing correct answers at each category headquarters. Having achieved this, the player must then make his way to the central hub. When he lands on the hub, the other players may then choose which category that player must answer a question on. If the player answers correctly, he wins the game. If not, he must leave the hub on his next turn and then attempt to reenter it and provide a correct answer.

Diagram 5 *Trivial Pursuit® for a slice of knowledge*

RACE GAMES

The common denominator of all race games is that you must be first past the post and there is nothing to kill or capture. In most games the outcome is entirely dependent on chance, but in Backgammon, for instance, strategic play can add excitement to the race.

The concept of a race is to be found in the games with the greatest antiquity. When people first started living together in groups, they had minimal contact with the outside world. The concepts of territory and fighting would most likely have been alien to them, so it is likely that the earliest attempts at constructing games would have been based on racing, running and capturing, reflecting those activities necessary for survival. When they came to create what we would now recognize as board games, it is probable that the mechanisms behind them would be analogies for these activities.

Many contemporary race games have developed from ancient games. Ludo is a modified version of Pachisi, which originated in India several thousand years ago and of which various forms are still played in Asia and South America.

Fox and Geese games originated in Scandinavia in the Middle Ages, and similar games are played in many other parts of the world. In all of them, two unevenly matched forces race against each other. The smaller force usually comprises one or two pieces and has considerable freedom of movement, while the larger force has more pieces but less maneuverability.

Snakes and Ladders is a development of a sixteenth-century Italian game called Goose, which was a favorite in Europe until the end of the nineteenth century. Goose was the forerunner of many race games in which the player's progress may be either hindered or advanced by landing on certain specially marked squares. A similar game, Moksha-Patamu (Heaven and Hell), which consisted of 100 squares, existed in India and was used by the Hindus for the religious instruction of their children. More recently, the American game of Chinese Checkers was derived from Halma, which itself was invented in England toward the end of the nineteenth century.

Backgammon is thought to have originated in India or China and spread quickly to Europe via the Middle East and the Mediterranean. One school of thought, however, credits Ardashir, a third-century Sassanian ruler of Persia, with its invention.In Backgammon, the pieces are moved round a board according to the throw of dice. Games with this principle have been known for at least 5000 years – the earliest recorded example was discovered in a Royal cemetery of the Sumerian civilization in Mesopotamia. In its modern form, Backgammon has been played since the fifteenth century, and there are several Backgammon boards that date back to the sixteenth century. However, one very important feature of modern Backgammon – doubling – was invented as recently as the 1920s.

FOX & GEESE

The hunt game of Fox and Geese is believed to have originated in Scandinavia. It is played in many different forms, in much of Europe, and Asia.

Players: *two*
Equipment: *board and 14 or 18 pieces*
Difficulty: *mainly strategy*
Duration: *usually less than half an hour per game*

Beginning to play

Fox and Geese boards may be either cross-shaped or round. The pieces may be either counters or pegs that fit into small holes. In the original version of the game 14 pieces are used, one fox (marked in black) and 13 geese (marked in red).

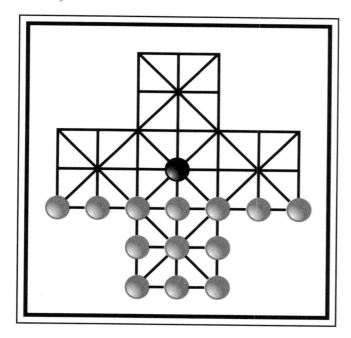

Diagram 1 Starting position for a game of Fox and Geese (14 pieces)

Sometimes 18 pieces are used instead of 14, in which case the game starts with the position in diagram 2. The fox is in the center of the board, but the fox player can in fact choose any vacant square at the start of the game in this particular variation.

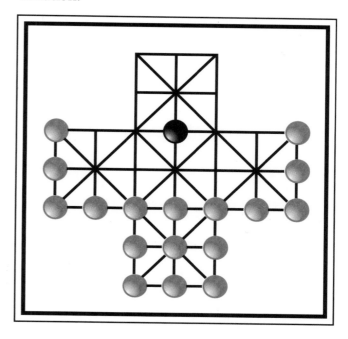

Diagram 2 Starting position for a game of Fox and Geese (18 pieces)

The players draw lots to determine who will be the fox and who will be the geese. The fox makes the first move and the players then move in alternation.

Moving

In the standard game both fox and geese move in identical fashion, one square forward, backward or sideways on each turn. However, only the fox is allowed to capture, which it does by leaping over an adjacent goose and landing on a vacant square beyond it in similar fashion to draughts. Also, just as in Draughts, it is possible for a fox to make several captures in one turn by a series of short leaps. The geese are not allowed to leap, but will try to crowd the fox into a corner. In the 18-piece game the rules are identical, except that the geese are not allowed to move backwards or diagonally. In some variations of the 18-piece game the fox is not allowed to move diagonally, which has led to the removal of the diagonal lines. However, this makes his task too difficult.

Winning the game

The fox wins if it manages to capture so many geese that there are not enough left to trap it, or if it reaches the geese's end of the board. The geese win if they can immobilize the fox by surrounding it.

FOX & GEESE SOLITAIRE

The game of Solitaire was invented - purportedly - by a prisoner in the Bastille during the French Revolution. The French version takes place on a board with 37 holes, but the American form uses a simple adaptation of the Fox and Geese board.

Players: one
Equipment: board and 32 pieces
Difficulty: easy to grasp strategy
Duration: usually less than 15 minutes per game

Beginning to play

Fox and Geese solitaire takes place on a standard Fox and Geese board on which there are no diagonal lines. The pieces are arranged as in diagram 3, with every point occupied by a piece except one (usually the center point).

Moving

There is only one type of move in this game: a short jump over an adjacent piece, removing that piece from the board. These jumps can be horizontal or vertical, but not diagonal.

Winning the game

The object of the game is to remove all the pieces from the board except one, which should

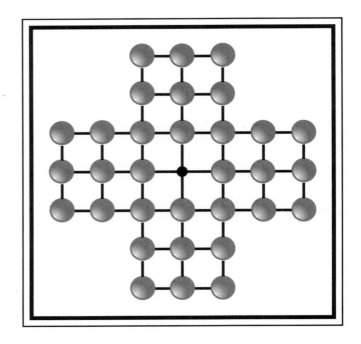

Diagram 3 Starting position for a game of Fox and Geese solitaire

end up in the central hole (or some other designated point).

COWS & LEOPARDS

Cows and Leopards originated in Sri Lanka (then Ceylon) and has many similarities to Fox and Geese. Indeed, there is even an English version that is played on a standard Checkers board.

Players: two
Equipment: board and five or seven pieces
Difficulty: mainly strategy
Duration: usually less than half an hour per game

Beginning to play

The game takes place on a 12x12 Chess or Checkers board. In the initial position the cows

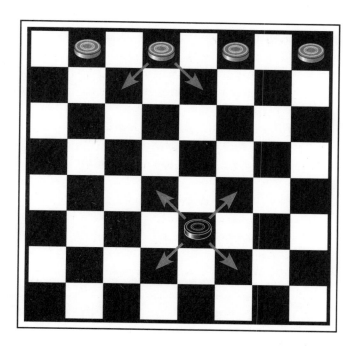

Diagram 4 *Starting position for a game of Cows and Leopards*

are arranged on the back rank, while the leopards can be placed on any black square on the board.

In England a similar game is often played on an 8x8 board, but it is still known as Fox and Geese.

Moving

In Cows and Leopards, the cows can move one square forwards along a diagonal on any turn, in a similar fashion to an uncrowned piece in Checkers. The leopard, on the other hand, can move two squares both diagonally forwards and backwards. Neither piece can jump or capture. In the English version the fox can only move one square at a time, in similar fashion to a king in Checkers.

Winning the game

The cows win the game if they are able to hem in the leopard, leaving it without a legal move. The leopard wins if it manages to break through the line of cows to reach the cows' end of the board.

WOLF & GOATS

Wolf and Goats is another form of Fox and Geese that is played on a Checkers board.

Players: *two*
Equipment: *board and 13 pieces*
Difficulty: *mainly strategy*
Duration: *usually less than half an hour per game*

Beginning to play

In Wolf and Goats the goats are placed in exactly the same formation as one would see at the start of a game of Draughts, while the wolf may be placed on any of the black squares on its back rank.

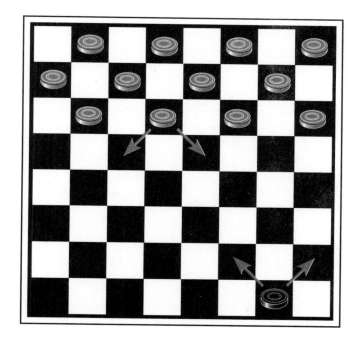

Diagram 5 *Starting position for a game of Wolf and Goats*

Moving

In Wolf and Goats the goats can move one square forwards along a diagonal on any turn, just as in Cows and Leopards. Although the wolf can only move one square either diagonally forwards or backwards, in this game it can capture goats by jumping over them and landing on the square immediately beyond.

Winning the game

The outcome of a game is determined in exactly the same way as Cows and Leopards: the goats win if they are able to hem in the wolf, leaving it without a legal move. The wolf wins if it manages to break through the line of goats to reach the goats' end of the board.

HALMA

Halma was invented in the 1880s. It can be played by two, three or four players.

Players: *two to four*
Equipment: *board and 64 pieces*
Difficulty: *very strategic*
Duration: *usually less than one hour per game*

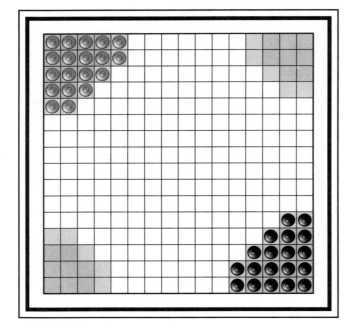

Diagram 6 *Starting position for a game of Halma (two players)*

Beginning to play

Halma requires a 16x16 Checkerboard, marked out with camps in each corner. In the two-player version, each player has 19 pieces, arranged as in diagram 6.

The thicker or double line marks the boundaries of each camp. In a three- or four-handed game each player has 13 pieces, as shown in diagrams 7 and 8.

The players draw lots to decide who will move first and then take alternate turns. In a three- or four-handed game the players act alone, taking turns in a clockwise direction. In a three-player

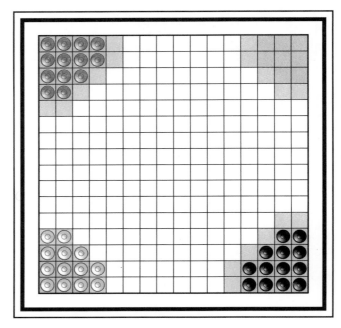

Diagram 7 *Starting position for a game of Halma (three players)*

game it is a slight disadvantage to be the one heading for the empty camp, so players should take turns to be the odd man out.

Moving

In any turn of play only one piece may be moved. There are two ways in which a piece can move: the "step" and the "jump." With a step a piece can move to an adjacent square in any direction – vertical, horizontal, or diagonal; back-

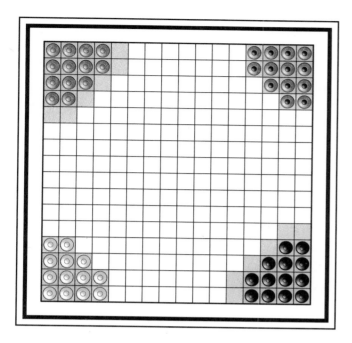

Diagram 8 *Starting position for a game of Halma (four players)*

wards or forwards. Alternatively, if there is a piece in an adjacent square – whether it be a fellow or enemy piece – it may jump over that piece to an empty square immediately beyond it in similar fashion to a capture in Checkers. Having made such a leap, that piece can jump again until all its jumps have been exhausted. However, pieces are not captured in Halma – they remain on the board even if they have been jumped over. Furthermore, unlike in Checkers it is not compulsory to jump when one is able.

Strategy

The ideal strategy in halma is to construct "ladders" across the board to enable your rearguard pieces to traverse rapidly from one side to the other through a series of hops. The ladder technique is illustrated in diagram 9, where the white piece is able to move down the board with a series of jumps. Of course, one should also try to block one's opponent from building ladders and take care to remember that one's own ladders can be used by the opponent too! It is often fatal to advance your scouts and neglect your rear men, as the stragglers may become cut off from the rest of the army.

Winning the game

The first player to occupy the opposite camp is the winner.

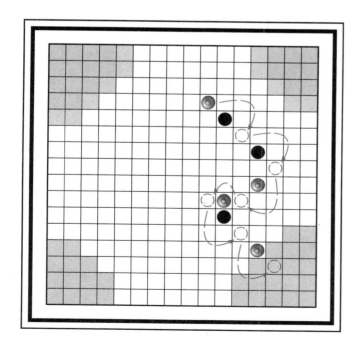

Diagram 9 *The ladder technique*

CHINESE CHECKERS

The American game of Chinese Checkers is neither Chinese nor Checkers! – but a modified form of Halma played on a six-pointed star. It was patented in the USA around 1880 by J. Pressman & Co., New York as Hop Ching Checkers.

Players: two to six
Equipment: board and 90 pieces
Difficulty: very strategic
Duration: varies, but usually less than one hour per game

Beginning to play

The Chinese Checkerboard takes the form of a six-pointed star, as illustrated in diagram 10 (below).

Diagram 10 Starting position for a game of Chinese Checkers (two players)

In the two-player game, each side has 15 pieces. If there are more than two players, only 10 pieces are used for each player. With three players the camps are arranged so that each player is heading towards an empty camp, but with four or more camps the players can choose whichever camp they like. Each player plays alone; there is no teamwork.

Moving

Moves in Chinese Checkers are identical to those in Halma: "steps" and "jumps." The strategy of the game is also similar, with the players trying to construct and block ladders.

Winning the game

Just as in Halma, the winner is the first player who manages to occupy the opposite part of the star.

BACKGAMMON

Backgammon is the ultimate race game and has been enjoyed around the world for over five thousand years. Although the play is highly skillful, the fact that the moves rely on the fall of the dice introduces a large element of luck. In the long run the better player will always win, but the beauty of the game is that even a novice can win the odd game against a world champion.

Players: two
Equipment: Backgammon board, 30 pieces (15 black and 15 white), four dice and a doubling cube
Difficulty: the basic moves are simple but the strategy can become very complex. The balance between luck and skill is finely tuned and gives the game an enduring fascination
Duration: games can be over very quickly or can develop into long wars of attrition. A typical social game takes about 10 minutes

Brief history

Backgammon is a game of great antiquity, having been played almost everywhere in the world for thousands of years. It originated in the Middle East and has survived long periods in the doldrums due to banishment by the Church. The game is strongly associated with gambling and even today this creates legal problems for those wishing to hold Backgammon tournaments. In the UK, for example, it is not possible to offer prizes in Backgammon tournaments, because it is classified as a game of chance.

The board and pieces

The Backgammon board consists of a board of 24 points, 12 on White's side of the table and 12 on Black's. The points are alternately coloured light and dark. The pieces have a set starting position as shown in diagram 11. White is playing on the side of the board marked by points 1-12, while Black has the side marked 13-24. The points

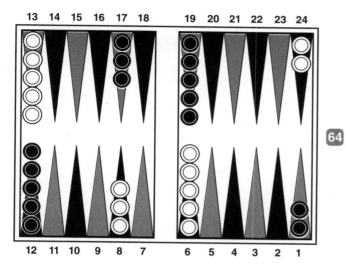

Diagram 11 *Starting position for a game of Backgammon*

indicated by 1-6 are known as White's inner table, while 19-24 represent Black's inner table. Similarly, points 7-12 are the outer table for White, as are points 13-18 for Black. White plays in an counterclockwise direction around the board, moving pieces from higher- to lower-numbered points. Black's play mirrors this movement, with pieces moving in a clockwise direction from the lower- to higher-numbered points.

There can be any number of similarly colored pieces on any point. Although White already has five pieces on the 6 point, it is possible to place more pieces there. However, pieces from opposite sides cannot share a point, so Black cannot (temporarily at least) bring any pieces to the 6 point.

The aim of the game

Backgammon is a simple race game. The object is to move the pieces around the board toward your inner table. Once all 15 of your pieces have arrived in the inner table, they can be "borne off," i.e. removed from the board. The first player to remove all his pieces from the board is the winner.

Beginning to play

Players move alternately, the throw being determined by the roll of a pair of dice. To start the

game, both players throw one die and the player rolling the higher number moves first, with the two dice counting for the initial play. For example, if White rolls a 6 and Black rolls a 2, then White (having rolled the higher number) starts the game with 6-2. If the players roll the same number, then the dice are rolled again. It is not permissible to start the game with a double.

Throwing and moving

The values on the two dice indicate how far around the board a player can move a piece. The numbers on the dice can be added together to move just one piece, or they can be used separately to move two pieces. In White's opening position given above (6-2), two possible moves with this throw are:

1. Moving a piece from 24 to 16 (using the entire roll to move one piece).
2. Moving one piece from 24 to 18 and one from 13 to 11 (using the dice separately).

Let us assume that White chooses the latter option, resulting in the position in diagram 12.

Now Black rolls 2-2 (indicated in diagram 12 by the two dice adjacent to Black's inner table). When a doublet is rolled (the same number

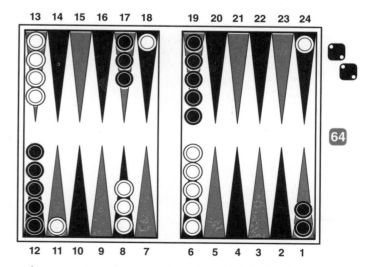

Diagram 12 *The position after White's first move*

being shown on both dice), the total for the roll is doubled, as if four dice had been thrown and all had yielded the same value. Therefore it becomes possible to move up to four pieces. Thus with the 2-2 roll Black now has numerous options, including the following:

1. Moving a piece from 1 to 9 (using the entire roll to move one piece).

2. Moving a piece from 17 to 23 and one from 1 to 3 (breaking up the roll into a 6 and a 2).

3. Moving a piece from 1 to 5, one from 12 to 14 and one from 19 to 21. The number of points moved still totals eight, but this has now been broken down into 4, 2, and 2.

4. Moving two pieces from 1 to 3 and two pieces from 12 to 14. Now four pieces have moved, each advancing two points.

Closed points

Let us assume that, from the previous diagram, Black chooses to play 2-2 by taking the last option, moving twice from 1 to 3 and also twice from 12 to 14. This results in the position in diagram 13, where White has just rolled 4-3 in reply.

Any point that has two enemy pieces on it is "closed." This means that, for the moment at least, it is inaccessible to White's pieces. In the above position, Black's last move has closed the 3 and 14 points. Therefore, White cannot move the piece on 18 to 14, nor is it possible to move a piece from 6 to 3. However, White could consider moving the piece on 18 to close the point on 11. Although moving 4-3 would not be possible – this would necessitate landing on the 14 point – White can take the move as 3-4, moving to the 15 point and then onwards to 11.

Building up a series of closed points is one of the fundamental aims in Backgammon. If one player's back pieces are stuck behind a succession of enemy-held points it can be difficult, or even impossible, to free these pieces. Sometimes a player is fortunate (or skillful!) enough to build up a succession of six closed points. As long as these points can be maintained, any enemy pieces stuck behind them cannot escape.

Hitting and reentering

Any piece that sits alone on a point is called a "blot," and a blot is always in danger of being hit by an enemy piece. When a piece is hit, it moves to the bar (the central partition between the inner and outer tables). This piece must then re-enter the game via the opponent's inner table. The player with the piece on the bar cannot make any other moves elsewhere on the board

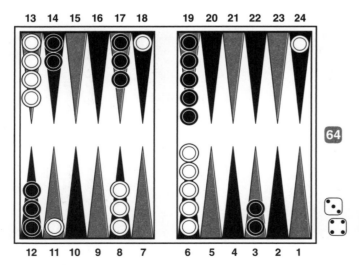

Diagram 13 *The position after Black's first move*

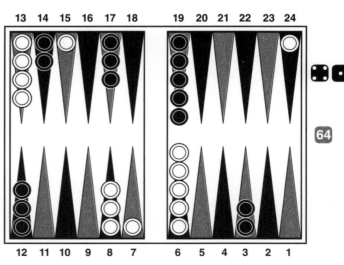

Diagram 14 *The position after White's second move*

until this has been achieved. Let us assume that from diagram 13, White used the roll of 4-3 to move from the 11 to the 7 point and also from the 18 to the 15 point. The position is now as in diagram 14, with Black having rolled 4-1 in reply.

White has blots on the 7, 15 and 24 points and with a roll of 4-1 Black can hit two of these. This Black does, moving from 3 to 7 and from 14 to 15, both moves hitting White blots. These two pieces are now placed on the bar and White rolls 6-2.

White must now immediately reenter these pieces into the game via Black's inner table (ie

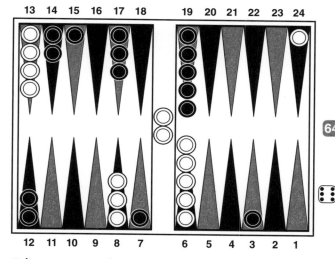

Diagram 15 The position after Black's second move

points 19-24). Rolling a 1 will enable White to place a piece on the 24 point (the 24 point being the 1 point from Black's point of view). Similarly, the roll of a 2 permits White to place a piece on the 23 point; a 3 would grant access to the 22 point, and so on.

White in fact rolls 6-2. With the 2, White places a piece on the 23 point. However, to White's dismay, the 6 is not playable, as the 19 point is closed. White's other piece, therefore, has to remain on the bar for the time being. White is not permitted to use the 6 elsewhere on the board while a piece is out of play on the bar.

Black now rolls 4-4. This is an excellent roll which allows Black a very powerful play. Black can move two pieces from 17 to 21 and two

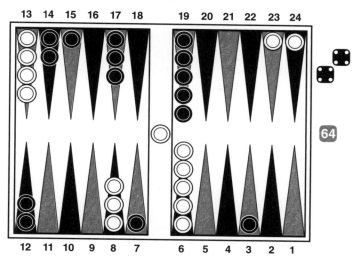

Diagram 16 The position after White's third move

pieces from 19 to 23, hitting White's blot, which has just reentered the game, and sending it scuttling back onto the bar. The position is now beginning to look very promising for Black.

White again has two pieces on the bar, while Black has created three closed points in the

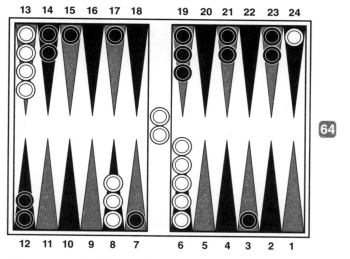

Diagram 17 The position after Black's third move

inner table. With a roll of 2-2, 4-4, 6-6, 2-4, 2-6, or 4-6, White will have to miss a turn completely as the pieces on the bar will be unable to reenter play. Black is now well ahead in the race to get around the board and the pieces in Black's outer table (on the 14, 15, and 17 points) indicate good chances to close out further points in the inner table.

Bearing off

The ultimate aim in Backgammon is to "bear off" all your pieces before your opponent. However, you cannot begin to bear off until all your pieces have negotiated their way around to your inner table. During bearing off, the pieces move in the normal way except that the pieces can move beyond the player's 1 point to an imaginary 0 point. When this occurs the piece is removed from the board.

It is only possible to bear off when all of your pieces are in your inner table. What sometimes happens is that White, for example, begins to bear off while Black still has pieces stationed in White's inner table. It is then possible that White will leave a blot that will get hit. When this piece reenters the game, White must maneuver it round to White's inner table before continuing to bear off.

It is possible to use a larger number than necessary to bear off a piece, provided that one cannot make a move with this number which does not bear off. For example, suppose that White only has pieces on the 4, 3, 2, and 1 points and rolls 6-2. The 2 can be used in the normal way to bear off a piece from the 2 point, but the 6 can be used to bear off a piece from the 4 point – the highest available point. However, if White has pieces on the 6, 2, and 1 points and rolls 4-3, he cannot bear off and is obliged to make moves from the 6 point.

The play in diagram 18 should help to clarify these points.

Both players are in the process of bearing off and White rolls 4-4. This enables White to bear off two pieces from the 4 point but then the

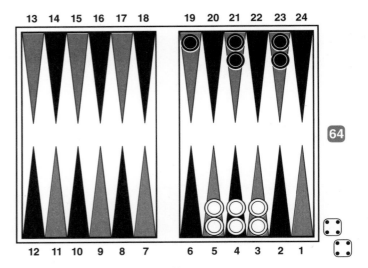

Diagram 18 *Bearing off*

remaining play must be to move the two pieces from the 5 point to the 1 point. Black now rolls 6-3 in reply. There are two ways to play this move:

1. Black can use the 6 to bear off a piece from the 19 point and then use the 3 to move from the 21 point to the 24 point.
2. An alternative line of play is to use the 3 to move from the 19 point to the 22 point. Black then has no way to play a 6 from the 19 point and is thus allowed to bear off a piece from the 21 point.

If we assume that Black chooses the former play, the situation is now as in diagram 19.

With a big double, White could win the game immediately, bearing off all four pieces. However, White rolls the more modest 4-2, using the 4 to bear off from the 3 point and the 2 to move from the 3 point to the 1 point.

Black could now also win the game with a 6-6, 5-5, or a 4-4. A roll of 3-3 would leave Black tantalizingly short of immediate victory. The first play would be to move from the 21 point to the 24 point, bearing off two pieces from the 23 point and one from 24. This would leave Black with a solitary piece on the 24 point. However, let us assume that Black also rolls a more mod-

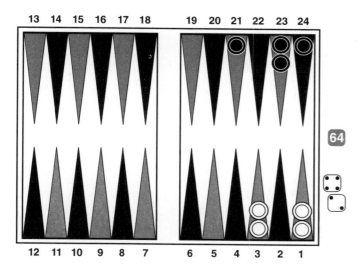

Diagram 19 Position after Black's play

est number, in this case 5-2. This roll enables Black to clear the 21 and one of the pieces from the 23 point, resulting in the following position.

Now it is inevitable that Black will be able to complete bearing off with the next roll. Even the smallest possible roll of 2-1 will enable Black to

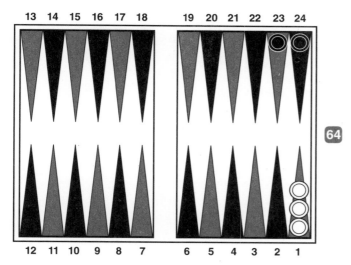

Diagram 20 The final position, with Black firm favorite

clear the inner table. Therefore, White must finish off with the next roll and to do this needs a doublet, as this is the only way to bear off more than two pieces at once. Black is now the firm favorite to win the game because the probability

of White rolling a doublet is only 1 in 6. White's chances of winning are therefore approximately 17 per cent, while Black has an 83 per cent chance of success. Black should win the game, but the dice can be very cruel!

Scoring

Normally, the winner of a game of Backgammon scores one point if a match is being played, or wins one unit if the games are being played for money. However, there are two exceptions when the winner can claim more. If a player wins by bearing off all their pieces while the opponent has not yet borne off any, they win a "gammon," which scores double. An even better result is to bear off all the pieces while the opponent, as well as not having begun to bear off, still has one or more pieces in the winner's inner table. This results in a "Backgammon," and scores triple points.

Gammon is a reasonably common occurrence and the possibility of it happening plays a large part in a player's strategy. Backgammon is very unusual and can be seen as a lucky bonus when a mere gammon was looking inevitable.

The doubling cube

Every Backgammon set has a peculiar die bearing the numbers 2, 4, 8, 16, 32, and 64. The doubling cube is an ingenious method of increasing the tension during a Backgammon game by allowing one player to insist upon an increase in the stakes if they feel that the position is favorable to them. At the start of the game, the doubling cube is put in the middle and is available to both players. Conventionally this is shown, as in the previous diagrams, by having the cube on 64 and placed in the middle of the board. At this stage the game is being contested for one unit. Play continues normally until one player decides that he has a good chance of winning the game, and maybe even achieving a gammon. When this happens, the player can then offer the cube to his opponent.

Let us assume that White holds the advantage and wishes to do this. White takes the cube from the middle, turns it so that the 2 is faceup, and places it on Black's side of the board. If Black feels that White will win, the game can be conceded and Black loses one unit. There is no further play and a new game begins. Alternatively, Black may want to continue the game. In this case, Black accepts White's double and the game continues. Now, however, the stake is two units and Black may suffer a loss of two units (or even four if White achieves a gammon) instead of escaping with the loss of a mere one unit.

However, by accepting the double, Black now gains possession of the cube. If at a later stage the play should turn in Black's favor, Black can then offer the cube back to White, insisting on an increase in the stakes from twofold to fourfold. White now has the choice of conceding the game and losing two units or continuing with the stake now at four units. This process can proceed indefinitely, with the stakes increasing exponentially from 2 to 4 to 8 to 16, etc. Games where the cube reaches 2 or 4 are quite common, 8 is rare, and 16 exceptional.

Game strategies

We have already seen how closing out points with two or more pieces can restrict the opponent, so making points is a fundamental aim in backgammon. It also means that your own pieces are secure from being hit. The best points to try to make are the high numbered ones (3, 4, 5, and 6) in your inner table, as these also impede your opponent from reentering pieces should you manage to hit their blots. Other good points are (from White's point of view) 7, 8, and 9, as these can act as landing points to bring pieces around to the inner table. It is also very useful if you can make an advanced point on the opponent's board.

Consider the position in diagram 21, where White has just rolled 4-4. This enables White to

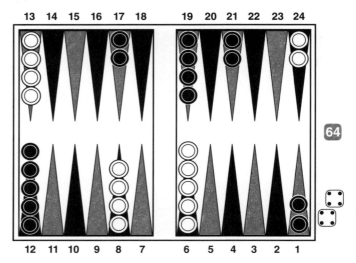

***Diagram 21** A wonderful roll for White*

advance two pieces from 24 to 20 and two from 8 to 4, achieving good points on both boards. The benefit of having the 20 point is that it is a good anchor for White. If White has to leave blots elsewhere on the board at a later stage, and these are hit, there will always be a secure point to re-enter these pieces. The pieces on 20 also put pressure on Black's outer table (the 14 to 18 points) and make it difficult for Black to create points there.

The running game

A running game occurs when both sides have successfully freed their back pieces. Contact between the two armies is then either no longer possible, or extremely unlikely. The contest turns into a straight race and whoever rolls the better dice will win. The position in diagram 22 is a typical case in point. Neither side has any pieces remaining in the opponent's half of the board, with the exception of the 12 and 13 points. However, this contact is basically irrelevant as these pieces will inevitably bypass each other. The game is a straight race. If all Backgammon games ended up as such straight races then the game would not be very interesting. Fortunately, this does not happen very often and complex interaction between the forces is far more common.

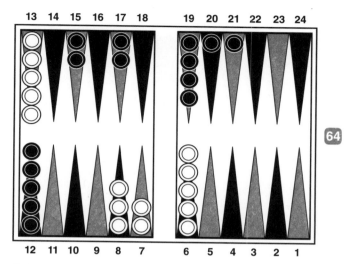

Diagram 22 *A straight race*

The holding game

If your opponent manages to free their back pieces while you do not, they will, all other things being equal, have a useful advantage. They can hope to close points in their inner and outer table and your back pieces may become suffocated. However, you can fight back. If you are unable to free the back pieces, the next best course of action is to try to establish an advanced point in your opponent's half of the board. The ideal spots to aim for are the 5 and 7 points.

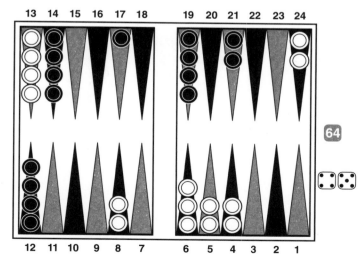

Diagram 23 *White's pieces remain stuck on the 24 point*

Consider the position in diagram 23. The Black back pieces have escaped, while White's remain stuck on the 24 point. If White now plays passively, Black will be able to bring up pieces from the outer board and close off useful points. Therefore, a good way for White to play the 5-4 roll is to move 13 to 8 and from 24 to 20. This entails a certain risk as Black now has a few very powerful rolls, such as 6-1, 6-3, and 3-1, all of which would close out the 20 point, while simultaneously hitting White's blot. However, it is better for White to put up a fight than to simply leave the back pieces where they are and watch them become entombed. Additionally, it is more likely that Black will roll a combination which

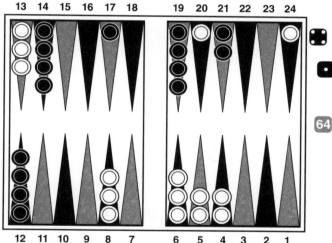

Diagram 24 *White's inner table begins to look powerful*

does not allow such a powerful play.

Black actually rolls 4-1 (see diagram 24) and cannot now hit the white blot on 20 without leaving a blot that White would have an immediate chance to hit. White's own inner table is beginning to look powerful and Black does not relish the thought of having to extricate a piece from this area. Black therefore decides to play solidly by using pieces from 14 and 17 to build the 18 point.

White now rolls 3-1 and uses this to build the 20 point. Having achieved this aim, White now

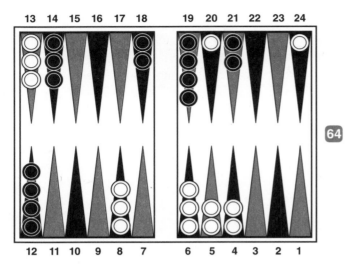

Diagram 25 Black is unable to exploit White's blot on the 20 point

has an excellent "holding" position (see diagram 25) and is well in the game. White's pieces on 20 pressure Black's outer table and make it awkward for Black to bring pieces round. Furthermore, White may soon roll a big double, such as 6-6 or 5-5, and escape with the back pieces completely to compete in a straightforward running game.

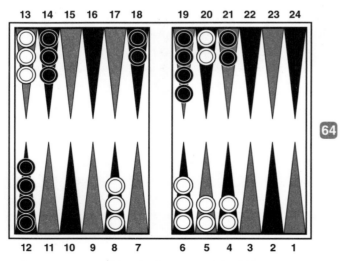

Diagram 26 White is in a good holding position

The attacking game

Let us consider again the position from the previous section where Black had to consider how

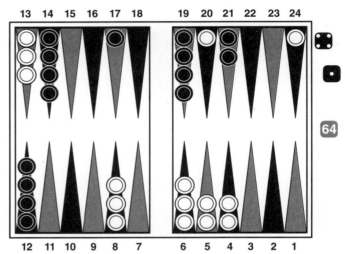

Diagram 27 Black rolls 4-1 and attacks

to play the roll 4-1 (see diagram 27).

In the previous example, Black played safely by making the 18 point. However, an alternative line of play was to launch an attack by hitting both White blots with a piece on the 19 point, reaching the position in diagram 28.

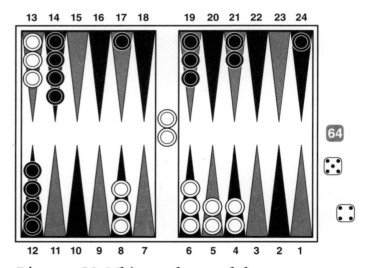

Diagram 28 White needs a good throw

White now has two pieces on the bar and only four of the six entry points are available. With a roll of 5-4, White's move is forced: one piece can be brought back into the game on the 20 point, while the other must remain on the bar because the 21 point (the place of entry for a 4) is blocked.

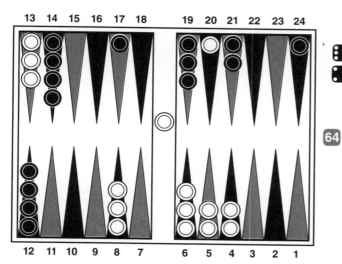

Diagram 29 Black puts White under great pressure

Black now rolls 6-4, a strong throw that can be used to move a piece from 14, hitting White's blot on 20 and then moving on to close out the 24 point.

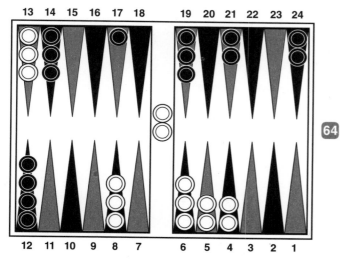

Diagram 30 White is in big trouble

White is now in big trouble: two pieces are still on the bar and Black has closed out three points in the inner table. Furthermore, the Black forces are poised to move around and close out further points. If White does not get a good roll immediately, there is a danger of being shut out of the game completely. This is the sort of position where a gammon result becomes a very real possibility.

Cube strategy

A good understanding of probability and statistics is very important in backgammon, especially in endgame positions where the cube comes into play. Consider the position in diagram 31. It is Black's turn to play.

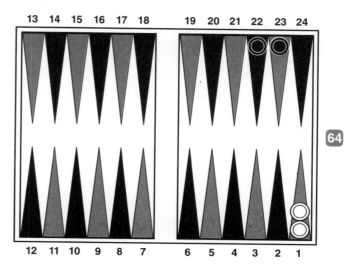

Diagram 31 An endgame position

Black will be able to bear off both pieces provided the roll does not include a 1. However, if the roll does include a 1, Black will not be able to bear off and White will win. Out of the 36 possible rolls of the dice, 25 will win for Black and only 11 will lose (1-1, 1-2, 1-3, 1-4, 1-5, 1-6, 2-1, 3-1, 4-1, 5-1, and 6-1 are the unfortunate rolls). Black therefore wants to raise the stakes and offers White the cube. Should White accept?

One way to work this out is to assume that this position is played 36 times with Black receiving each of the possible 36 rolls. We can then see what happens with White's different courses of action:

1. White concedes the game. On all 36 occasions White loses one unit and thus ends up losing 36 units.

2. White accepts the cube. On 25 occasions White will lose and the cost will now be two units, yielding a total loss of 50. However, on the other 11 occasions White will win, and these will yield a profit of 22. White's net loss will therefore be 28 units (50 - 22).

It is therefore clear that, in the long run, White will be better off accepting Black's offer, even though the chances of losing are still greater.

LUDO

Ludo is a modified form of the Indian game of Pachisi, which was enormously popular with the sixteenth-century Moguls. Ludo was patented in England around 1896. It remains popular with children across the globe. It has also been sold commercially as Parcheesi, Patchesi and Homeward Bound.

Players: two to four
Equipment: board, 16 counters (four each of four different colors) and a die
Difficulty: ideal for children; mainly luck
Duration: usually less than half an hour per game

Beginning to play

Players choose which color they wish to play with. Each player starts with four counters of the same color in their yard, as in diagram 32.

The first player to throw a six starts the game by advancing one of their counters to point "A."

Moving

Once a counter has entered the game it can be advanced in a clockwise direction according to the throw of the die. The object is to race each counter around the board to point B and then run up the middle cells of the arm to be borne off in the center. New counters can only be introduced when a six is thrown, but a six results in another throw. Enemy counters can be captured and returned to their own yard by landing on the cell that they occupy. Counters on the same side

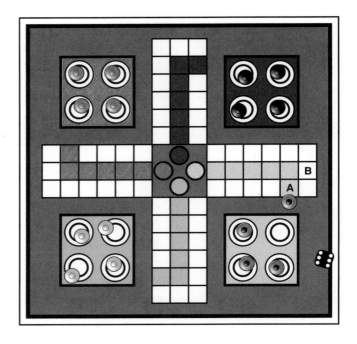

Diagram 32 The starting position for a game of Ludo

can be piled and advanced as if they were a single counter, but in that case they can also be captured as a single counter.

Winning the game

The first player to advance all their counters around the board and bear them off in the center is the winner.

SNAKES & LADDERS

Like Ludo, Snakes and Ladders has always been a favorite game for children. It is a game that relies entirely on luck and therefore enables young players to compete on equal terms with their elders.

Players: two or more
Equipment: board, four counters and a die
Difficulty: ideal for children; all luck
Duration: usually less than 20 minutes per game

Brief history

Snakes and Ladders is based on the Indian game Moksha Patamu, which was used a means of religious instruction. The board stands for the symbolic moral journey through life to heaven, with the ladders representing virtuous acts that shorten the soul's road to nirvana (the state of ultimate perfection) and the snakes representing sins that lead to reincarnation in a lower animal form, thereby delaying nirvana.

Beginning to play

Each player selects a different colored counter. Play takes place on a 10x10 board with approximately 10 snakes and 10 ladders scattered around it, such as in diagram 33. The first player to throw a six starts the game. Other players

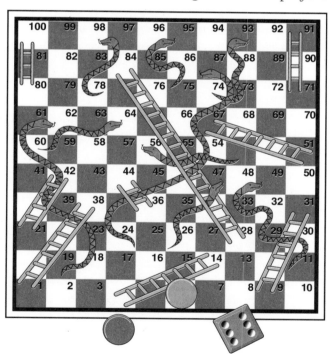

Diagram 33 *The board used for a game of Snakes and Ladders*

do not enter the game until they have thrown a six themselves.

Moving

Counters are moved according to the throw of the dice. If you land on a square with a ladder you can advance up the ladder (say from 28 to 84), but if you land on a snake, you have to slide down to the bottom of the snake (say from 49 to 11). If you land on an opponent's counter, that counter is sent back to the first square.

Winning the game

The object of the game is to reach the 100 square with an exact throw. (If you overthrow 100, you have to travel back down again from that point; thus a throw of six from square 96 means the counter advances to 100 and then back to 98.) The first player to land exactly on the 100 square is the winner.

WAR GAMES

Common to all war games is a fight between opposing armies. As with all such engagements, however, victory is not achieved through luck or sheer aggression, but through the successful deployment of a cunning strategy.

There is a feeling, often expressed in the opinion columns of newspapers and magazines, that society is becoming an increasingly violent place. Whether this is true or not – and even the most cursory glance at the history books would suggest that it is not – it is certainly the case that games involving conflict are very popular. Today, this usually means video or console games, but more traditional games such as Chess and Shogi are also based on a violent heritage.

The invention of Chess is generally attributed to the Hindus, around 600 AD. It spread to Persia, and with the conquest of Persia by the Arabs, Chess, known at this time as Shatranj, spread throughout the Islamic world and eventually reached Europe. It later came to England with the Norman Conquest. The objective of each player is to capture, or "checkmate," the opponent's king. Originally, the game was played with a die, which decided which piece a player should move. In the course of time this was dropped, and it was agreed that the player must decide which piece it was best to move. A number of other changes have also taken place over the centuries.

Shogi is the Japanese version of Chess, and there have been many different forms since the game was first introduced in the eighth century. A feature peculiar to Shogi since the sixteenth century is that captured pieces become members of the capturing side, and can be returned to any position on the board.

Checkers was played in southern Europe in medieval times and appears to have been derived from much older games in the Middle East. Each player attempts to capture and remove the opponent's pieces or to confine them so that they cannot be moved. Uniquely, in the USA and in Canada the game is called Checkers after the actual board, and the pieces are usually red and white instead of black and white. Many countries have their own version of the game. In most European countries the game is named after the matriarchal playing piece: *Dama* in Italy, *Damenspiel* in Germany, and *Jeu de Dames* in France. In the UK it is known as Draughts.

While it is true that Chess, Shogi, and Checkers do indeed involve a fight between opposing armies, a keen player does not become more prone to violent outbursts – but does become more adept at concepts of strategy. Chess in fact was devised as a test of courage and mental fortitude. For this reason, some players even play blindfold as a demonstration of their highly developed intellectual prowess. Astute employers on the lookout for recruits in areas such as financial management will always look favorably on a resumé that demonstrates an interest in strategic games.

CHESS

Chess is the classic war game, combining elements of art and science. It is a game of pure skill, requiring both strategy and tactics.

Players: *two*
Equipment: *board and 32 pieces. Tournament games also use a Chess clock*
Difficulty: *although Chess is a difficult game to master, it can be enjoyed by all ages*
Duration: *tournament games will typically last between four and five hours. However, with a chess clock, games can be played much more quickly and tournaments where games are completed in one hour, or even 10 minutes, are frequently held. A leisurely social game will probably take between 30 minutes and one hour*

Brief history

Chess is one of the world's oldest board games. Since its invention in India around AD 600, it has experienced many changes in the rules and the movements of the pieces to arrive at the version we know today. The original Indian version of Chess featured pieces directly based on warfare, such as infantry, cavalry, elephants, and chariots. These have metamorphosed into the modern pieces: kings, queens, rooks, bishops, knights, and pawns. The queen was once a male minister or adviser to the king, but when the game reached Europe this piece became a queen and much greater powers were conferred on her. Until the twentieth century, Chess was regarded mainly as a pursuit for the leisured classes; now it is played by many millions of people.

Before the breakup of the Soviet Union, Chess was the national sport in Russia and, until recently, Russian players have dominated world chess. Russia remains the strongest nation, but many other countries, including the UK and the USA, are fast gaining ground.

Every now and again, the classic confrontational nature of a major Chess match can capture the public imagination and thrust Chess onto the front pages of the world's press. Battles for the World Championship title, often played over several weeks, can become very big news. The various encounters between Bobby Fischer and Boris Spassky in Reykjavik in 1972, Anatoly Karpov and Viktor Korchnoi in the late 1970s, and Garry Kasparov and Anatoly Karpov in the 1980s generated tremendous public interest thanks, in part, to the political subtext of all three clashes. When Garry Kasparov famously lost a six-game match to IBM's Deep Blue computer in May 1997, the moves of the games were relayed in real time on IBM's Chess website. The final and decisive game generated a world record 22 million hits on this site. In comparison, the 1996 Atlanta Olympics attracted a mere 10 million over a three-week period. The IBM record was surpassed only by NASA's reporting of the Mars landing.

World champions

There has been a recognized World Chess Champion since 1886, and the roll of honor reads as follows.

WORLD CHAMPIONSHIP ROLL OF HONOUR

1886–1894	Wilhelm Steinitz	Austria
1894–1921	Emanuel Lasker	Germany
1921–1927	José Raoul Capablanca	Cuba
1927–1935	Alexander Alekhine	USSR and France
1935–1937	Max Euwe	Holland
1937–1946	Alexander Alekhine	USSR and France
1948–1957	Mikhail Botvinnik	USSR
1957–1958	Vassily Smyslov	USSR
1958–1960	Mikhail Botvinnik	USSR
1960–1961	Mikhail Tal	USSR
1961–1963	Mikhail Botvinnik	USSR
1963–1969	Tigran Petrosian	USSR
1969–1972	Boris Spassky	USSR
1972–1975	Bobby Fischer	USA
1975–1985	Anatoly Karpov	USSR
1985–	Garry Kasparov	USSR/ Russia

In the years up until the end of 1946, the world champion was expected to play matches to defend the title against the leading challengers of the day. However, there was no formal structure to enable players to qualify for matches against the incumbent champion and this enabled some of the champions to avoid their more dangerous contemporaries or postpone the matches. After Alexander Alekhine's death (while World Champion) in 1946, the World Chess Federation (FIDE) stepped in and organized a five-player tournament, which was won by Mikhail Botvinnik, to determine the new champion. They also established a structure of tournaments and matches to decide a challenger to the champion. In general, this resulted in a match for the World Championship being played every three years.

In 1993, the World Championship cycle was won by Nigel Short of England, who thereby acquired the right to challenge Garry Kasparov for the world title. However, the two players had a dispute with FIDE and therefore broke away to form their own rival organization, the Professional Chess Association. Their 1993 match, which resulted in a comfortable win for Kasparov, was played under the auspices of this new organization. FIDE, meanwhile, organized its own match, contested between the runners-up in the qualifying cycle. This match was between Anatoly Karpov of Russia and Jan Timman of the Netherlands, and was won easily by Karpov.

Kasparov subsequently defended his PCA title against Viswanathan Anand of India in New York in 1995. Kasparov's tournament record demonstrates that he is unquestionably the strongest player in the world, but he is not the world champion of the official governing body. As of early 1998, the PCA has more or less ceased to function but there has been no rapprochement between Kasparov and FIDE. In late 1997 and early 1998 FIDE organized a World Championship knockout event that resulted in a final between Viswanathan Anand and Anatoly Karpov. The match resulted in a 3-3 tie; Karpov subsequently went on to win the speed play-off 2-0.

The board

Chess is played on a board of 64 squares, alternately colored light and dark. The board is always set up with a light square in the lower right-hand corner. In contemporary Chess notation, the squares are referred to using letter and number coordinates. In diagram 1, the square

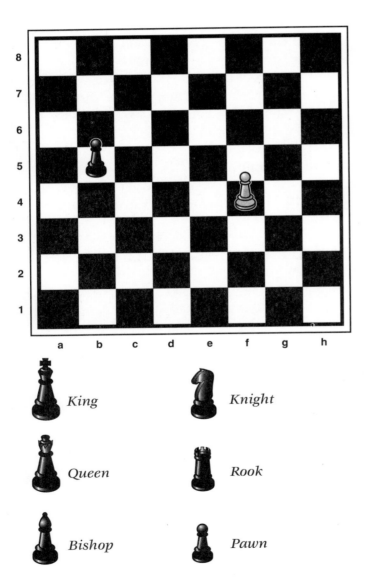

Diagram 1 The Chessboard and pieces

King

Knight

Queen

Rook

Bishop

Pawn

with a black pawn is b5, while the square with a white pawn is f4.

There are various other terms used to describe areas of the Chessboard, and it is useful to be aware of these. The lines across the board are known as ranks. For example, the third rank stretches across the board from a3 to h3. The lines running vertically up the board are known as files. For example, the d-file consists of the squares running from d1 up to d8. Additionally, the four left-hand files (ie the a-, b-, c-, and d-files) are collectively known as the queenside, while the four right-hand files (ie the e-, f-, g- and h-files) are collectively known as the kingside. Therefore, in diagram 1, the square with a black pawn (b5) is on the b-file, the fifth rank, and is also on the queenside.

The pieces

Each player starts the game with one king, one queen, two rooks, two bishops, two knights and eight pawns. The symbols representing the pieces are shown on the previous page.

Diagram 2 *Starting position for a game of Chess*

At the start of the game the pieces are arranged as in diagram 2.

In Chess diagrams it is conventional to display the board from White's point of view. Thus the white pieces start the game along the first and second ranks, while the black pieces start on the seventh and eighth ranks. However, when discussing positions, it is sometimes convenient to refer to, for example, "Black's second rank." This actually means the seventh rank, but from Black's point of view, sitting at the top of the board, it is the second rank.

Beginning to play

White always moves first and from then on the players move alternately.

The moves of the pieces

The Chess pieces move around the board in very distinct ways. Some have more mobility than others and this makes them more valuable. A fundamental aim in Chess is to win material by exchanging your lower-ranking pieces for the opponent's more valuable ones. When an opposing piece is captured it is removed from the board.

The rook

The rook operates along the ranks and files and can move any number of squares, as long as there are no intervening pieces. In diagram 3, the black rook has complete freedom of action to operate along the a-file or the eighth rank. The white rook is more restricted, only being able to move as far as g5 along the g-file and c3 along the third rank, where it would capture the black knight. The rook cannot "jump" over intervening pieces, so a3, b3, g7, and g8 are not available. The white rook could capture the black knight on c3 (the white rook would move to the c3 square and the black knight would be removed from the board), but the g6 square is currently occupied by the white queen and is thus also unavailable. You cannot capture your own pieces.

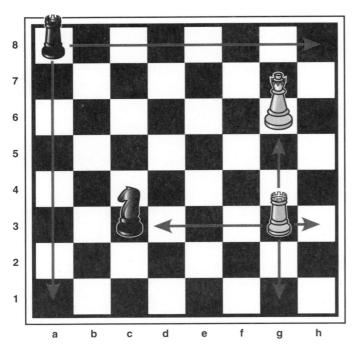

Diagram 3 The rook in action

The bishop

The bishop operates along the diagonals and, like the rook, can move freely as long as there are no other pieces in the way. In diagram 4 the

Diagram 4 The bishop in action

black bishop can move to any of the squares d8, c7, a5, a7, c5, d4, e3, f2, and g1. The white bishop has less mobility, only being able to move to g4 or g6, or to capture the black queen on f7. The bishops are permanently restricted to the color of the square on which they start the game. So in this example, Black has a "dark-squared bishop," while White has a "light-squared bishop." Each player starts the game with one dark-squared and one light-squared bishop.

The queen

The queen is the most powerful piece on the board, and combines the activities of both the rook and the bishop. The white queen in diagram 5 can

Diagram 5 The queen in action

move as indicated by the arrows and capture the black knight on g5. As with the rook and bishop, the queen cannot jump over pieces and so the squares a5, h5, g2, and h1 are not available.

The knight

Of all the chess pieces, the move of the knight is probably the most difficult to grasp. It moves in an L-shape, two squares along any rank or file and then one square at right angles. Another way to perceive this is to visualize a 3x2 "box" of squares; the knight can move from one corner to an opposite corner. This movement is much easier to understand from a graphical representation rather than a textual one.

In the diagram 6 the black knight is able to move to any of the five squares b8, b6, c5, e5, or

Diagram 6 The knight in action

f6. The f8 square would be available, but it is currently occupied by the black queen. The white knight can move to f3 and h3, or capture the black rook on e2. Note that the knight, unlike other pieces, is not restricted by intervening units of either colour. Thus the presence of the two white pawns on f2 and, g2 and the black bishop on h2 do not prevent the white knight from being able to move to f3 and h3.

The pawn

The pawns are the foot soldiers, or infantry, of Chess. They begin the game on the second row (for White this is the second rank, while for

Black it is the seventh rank) and move forward along their respective files. From their initial position pawns can move either one or two squares, but are then restricted to a move of just one square. So in diagram 7, the white pawn on a2, being on its initial square, can move to either a3 or a4, while the pawn on b3, which has already moved, can only go to b4. Similarly the black pawn on e3 can advance only to e2, while the pawn on f7 has the option of moving to f6 or f5. The black pawn on h5 is blocked by the white knight and thus has no moves available at all.

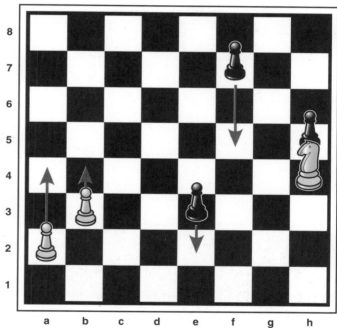

Diagram 7 The pawns in action

The pawns are unique among the Chess forces in that their method of capture differs from the method by which they move. In diagram 7, one might expect that the black pawn on h5 would have been able to capture the white knight on h4, but this is not the case. Pawns capture by moving one square forwards diagonally rather than along a file. So in the diagram 8, the white pawn on b4 can capture either the black queen on a5 or the black knight on c5. The black pawn on h7 can capture the white bishop on g6.

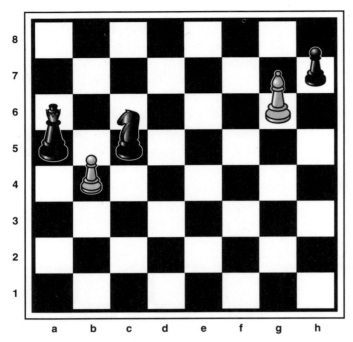

Diagram 8 Pawn captures

The king

The king is able to move one square in any direction: horizontally, vertically, or diagonally. In diagram 9, the black king can move to g7, g8, and

h7. The white king has seven possible moves: six are indicated by the arrows, while it is also possible for the white king to capture the black pawn on f3. If White chose to play this move, the king would come to the f3 square and the black pawn would be removed from the board. The e5 square is not available as this is occupied by one of White's own pieces.

Check and checkmate

As we shall see later, the fundamental aim in Chess is to capture the opponent's king. Thus whenever the king is threatened by an opposing piece (the king is then said to be "in check") immediate action must be taken to defend against this threat. There are three possible ways to do this:

1. The king can move away from the check.

2. The opposing piece can be captured.

3. A piece can intervene to block the check. (Note that if a check is delivered by a knight, then this option is not available, as it is not possible to block a knight move.)

Diagram 9 The king in action

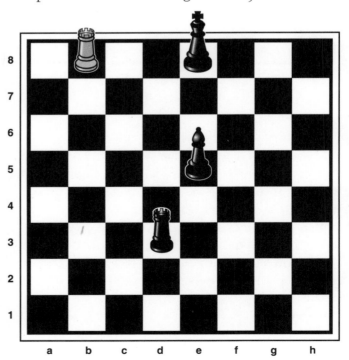

Diagram 10 Black is in check

If no such action is possible, and it is inevitable that the king will be captured on the next move, then "checkmate" has occurred and the game is over. In diagram 10, the black king is in check from the white rook on b8.

In this situation all three of the responses indicated above are possible:

1. The king can move to d7, e7 or f7, escaping from the check. Moving to d8 or f8 is not possible, as the king would then remain in check from the white rook.
2. The black bishop on e5 can capture the white rook.
3. The black rook on d3 can move to d8, blocking the check.

***Diagram 11** Black is in checkmate*

Let us now change the situation by adding further pieces. In diagram 11, Black is still in check but the options for escape have been removed.

1. The black king cannot move to d7, as this square is threatened by the white pawn on c6 (pawns capture one square diagonally). It can-

not go to e7 as this square is threatened by the white knight and the f7 square is now blocked by Black's own rook.
2. The black bishop can no longer capture the white rook as the pawn on c7 is in the way.
3. The black rook on d3 cannot move to d8 to block the check as the white knight on d5 prevents this.

The black king is in check and cannot escape. Black has been checkmated and the game is over.

Stalemate

It sometimes happens – often between expert players – that checkmate is not possible: not enough pieces remain to either player to confine a king in checkmate, or a position has been achieved in which a king is driven in check back and forth onto the same squares in an unending repitition ("perpetual check"). The players have reached a draw, or "stalemate." This may arise, as well, when either player offers a draw, and the other accepts. There is a special rule, too, that allows either player to call, at any time, for

***Diagram 12** Castling*

"fifty moves"; the game is drawn if checkmate has not occurred within that interval.

Unusual moves

The main moves of the pieces are described above, but there are three other possible moves which do not conform to the above conditions.

Castling

During the course of the game it is possible to make a move known as "castling," which can occur either on the queenside or kingside. When castling occurs, the king and rook move simultaneously along the back rank. The king always moves two squares and the rook hops over the king to land on the square beyond. Thus, in diagram 13, Black can castle on the queenside by moving the king from e8 to c8 and the rook from a8 to d8. White can castle kingside by moving the king from e1 to g1 and the rook from h1 to f1.

Castling is only permitted if the following conditions apply:

1. The king and rook must not have moved earlier on in the game.
2. The king must not be in check nor must the king pass through check.

In diagram 13, Black cannot castle queenside and white cannot castle kingside. Black is in check from the white queen, while the white king would have to pass through the f1 square, which is controlled by the black bishop. However, White would be able to cas-

Diagram 14 Pawn promotion

tle queenside, by moving the king to c1 and the rook to d1. There is no impediment to this move.

Pawn promotion

As we have seen, the pawn is the weakest of all the pieces, being very restricted in its movements. However, if a pawn manages to break through to the opponent's back rank it "promotes" to a new piece that takes the place of this pawn. The player who promotes a pawn can choose which piece to replace it with. Any piece is possible, with the exception of the king. In

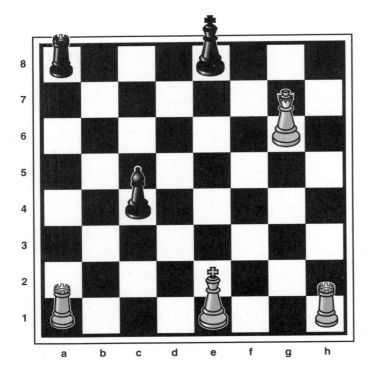

Diagram 13 Exceptions to castling

almost all cases the player will choose the queen, as this is the most valuable piece.

In diagram 14 the white pawn can advance from d7 to d8, when this pawn will be removed from the board and replaced with a white queen,

Diagram 15 The en passant *rule*

rook, bishop, or knight, according to the choice of the White player. Similarly, the black pawn can promote on e1, but could alternatively capture the white bishop on f1, when it would also promote.

En passant

The *en passant* (French for "in passing") rule is the one that confuses most beginners. It occurs when a pawn advances two squares on its initial move and finds itself adjacent to an opposing pawn. The opposing pawn then has the option to capture this pawn as if it had only moved one square.

In diagram 15, if Black advances the pawn from b7 to b5, White can respond by capturing this pawn as if it had only moved one square, ie from b7 to b6. Similarly, if the white pawn advances from h2 to h4, Black could take as if the pawn had only moved to h3. The *en passant* capture

is only possible if the pawn moves from its initial square. Thus, if the white pawn on f3 moves to f4, the capture is not possible. *En passant* only applies to pawns and can only be made in immediate response to the advance of the pawn. Thus if Black did advance the pawn on b7 to b5 but White chose to make a move elsewhere on the board, the chance to make the *en passant* capture is lost forever. White cannot come back later to make this capture.

Chess notation

There is a huge literature on Chess and to understand it successfully it is necessary to understand Chess notation. Fortunately the modern style – algebraic notation – is very straightforward and is now in more or less universal use.

Algebraic notation

If you have looked through the previous material you will by now be familiar with the idea of the squares on the Chessboard being referred to by coordinates. The method by which a move is recorded is to give the symbol of the piece

Diagram 16 Starting position for a game

followed by the square to which the piece moves. When a pawn is moved, only the square on which the pawn lands is given. The symbols for the pieces are as follows:

King	*K*
Queen	*Q*
Rook	*R*
Bishop	*B*
Knight	*N*

Diagram 17 An endgame position

Thus, starting from the initial position (see diagram 16), if White opens the game by playing the knight from g1 to f3 and Black responds by playing the pawn from d7 to d5, the "score" of the moves would be written thus: 1 Nf3 d5. The "1" designates the first move of the game and, conventionally, White moves first. When a capture is made, an "x" is introduced, and when a move results in check a "+" is added to the move.

Consider the position in diagram 17. Here White captures the pawn on e4 with the bishop and Black replies by taking the knight on a5, giving check.

This sequence would be recorded as 1 Bxe4 bxa5 + .

Note that with a pawn capture, the file from which the pawn has moved is given.

Occasionally, a position arises where a little extra information is required to avoid any ambiguity. For example, if White has rooks on a1 and f1 and moves the a1 rook to d1, writing 1 Rd1 will not yield sufficient information to recreate the move, as the other rook could also have moved to d1. In this case, the file from which the piece moves is added, ie 1 Rad1.

Two other moves need a mention. Castling on the kingside (for either color) is denoted by 0–0, while castling on the queenside is given by 0–0–0. When a pawn promotes, the piece for which it is exchanged is given at the end of the move, eg 1 e8Q or 1 b8N.

Chess symbols

Many theoretical works on Chess are sold around the world and these often use a completely languageless notation to describe the game. To the untutored eye, such texts can look like hieroglyphics with strange symbols denoting factors such as "small advantage to White," "Black is winning," or even "space advantage and the two bishops." However, the following special symbols, attached to individual moves, are much more common and would be used in Chess columns in the general press:

...	Black move follows
!	Good move
!!	Excellent move
?	Bad move
??	Blunder
!?	Interesting move
?!	Dubious move

The values of the pieces

Before one can make any attempt to play a game of Chess with any degree of competence, it is important to be aware of the value of the different pieces. Opportunities constantly crop up to exchange pieces, and a knowledge of their relative values is essential to gain an insight into whether a particular trade is a particularly good idea.

As the pawn is the basic unit in Chess it is convenient to assess all other pieces relative to the pawn. The following is a good rule of thumb. Remember that the king can never be exchanged, as checkmating the king ends the game, so assigning it a value has no meaning.

Piece	Value in Pawns
Knight	3
Bishop	3
Rook	5
Queen	9
King	Not applicable

From this table we can conclude that, all other things being equal, knights and bishops have approximately equal value. A rook is worth a knight or a bishop plus two pawns, and a queen is worth a rook, a bishop (or a knight) plus one pawn. Knights and bishops are known in chess as minor pieces, while the rooks and queens are referred to as major pieces. Another typical chess term is the "exchange." A player who has won a rook for a bishop is said to be "the exchange up."

Although the ultimate aim of the game is to checkmate the opponent's king, a more typical method of winning a game is to gain material. Even the advantage of a single pawn is often enough to decide a game. Remember that when a pawn reaches the opponent's back row it can promote to queen, thus creating a huge material balance in favor of the player who has just achieved this.

Chess tactics

There are various fundamental tactics that enable a player to win material, and the following are typical examples.

The fork

A fork occurs when one player attacks two pieces simultaneously, of which only one can be

***Diagram 18** The fork*

saved. Consider the positions in diagram 18.

On the queenside, White is attacking the black bishop and knight with the pawn on b3. Black can only move one of these and so the other will

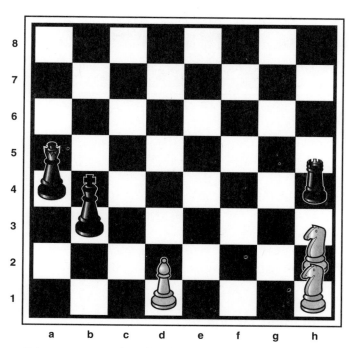

***Diagram 19** The skewer*

141

be lost. 1 ... Bxb3 will not help as White could recapture 2 axb3 and still win a piece. On the kingside, Black has forked the white queen and rook with the knight. Both of White's pieces are more valuable than Black's and so the impending trade will favor Black.

The skewer

A skewer is a device whereby two pieces along the same line are threatened and one cannot move without exposing the other. On the queenside, White has checked the black king, which will be

gram 21, White can continue with 1 Rg7+, skewering the black king and queen. At first this appears to be a mistake, as Black can simply cap-

Diagram 21 A tactical combination

Diagram 20 The pin

obliged to vacate the diagonal, allowing the white bishop to capture the black queen. On the kingside the two white knights have been skewered by the black rook.

In diagram 20 very favorable exchanges result from pinning a piece against the king – a "theme" used quite often in Chess.

Combining tactics

The real beauty of tactical play occurs when the above ideas are combined. In the position in dia-

Diagram 22 Another tactical combination

ture the rook with 1 ... Kxg7 but now comes 2 Ne 6 + and the black king and queen are forked. In diagram 22 Black can advance with 1 ... e2+. White has two ways to capture this pawn, but both allow a knight fork, eg 2 Qxe2 Ng3+ or 2 Kxe2 Nc3+.

Winning the game

The ultimate aim in Chess is to checkmate the opponent's king. As with tactics, there are various checkmating situations that arise again and again. The following is a typical, but by no

Diagram 23 Four possible checkmating positions

means comprehensive, selection.

(a) The white queen single-handedly covers all the black king's escape squares. The black king cannot capture the queen as it is protected by the pawn.

(b) The white rook and bishop combine to take away all the flight squares from the black king.

(c) The white king has been smothered by its own pieces and cannot escape the check from the black knight.

(d) Having three pawns in front of the king (a

typical situation when one has castled) is good for protecting the king from frontal attacks. However, it does leave a weakness on the back row which an enemy major piece can sometimes exploit. Here White needs to move the king to the second rank to escape from the black rook, but all these squares are taken by White's own pawns.

Chess clocks

Social Chess games are most often played with just a board and the 32 pieces, but all tournament games are nowadays played with the aid of a chess clock. Even social players would do well to consider using a clock, as this limits the amount of time that can be spent on a game.

The Chess clock is a clever device which actually consists of two clocks, one for each player. They are linked in such a way that the starting of one clock automatically stops the other and vice versa. Thus only one player's clock is running at any one time. Each player has a set period of time to complete either a certain number of moves or the entire game. Failure to comply to the time control, as it is known, results in automatic loss of the game, regardless of the position on the board. The most common version of the Chess clock has a flag which is pushed up by the minute hand as it approaches the hour mark. When the hand passes the hour mark, the flag falls and time is deemed to be up. This mechanical, and perhaps slightly unreliable, version of the clock is gradually being replaced by digital models.

In international events, the time control is typically two hours for the first 40 moves of the game, one hour for the next 20 moves and then a further half an hour to complete the game. If this time allowance were used in full, each player would have three and a half hours thinking time for the game. However, as the clocks do not run simultaneously, this would mean that the game lasted seven hours. Events which are played at faster time limits are becoming more and more popular. Typical time controls in such events are 30 minutes, 15 minutes or even just five minutes per player for the entire game. The Chess clock is a very efficient method of timing a two-player game and these clocks are used in many other competitive games such as Scrabble, Checkers, and Go.

PROGRESSIVE CHESS

This game is probably the most widely played variant of the parent game. It provides an interesting challenge that rewards creativity and imagination.

Players: *two*
Equipment: *board and Chess pieces*
Difficulty: *anyone who can play Chess can easily master progressive Chess*
Duration: *between 10 and 20 minutes*

Beginning to play
The pieces are set up as for normal Chess.

Moving
White moves first and plays as in normal Chess. Black then replies by having two moves. White then plays three, Black four, and so on, the number being incremented by one on each turn. A player may only give check on the last move of his sequence and if a player is in check, the first move of his sequence must be to escape from the check. If a player gives check before his move is complete, then the check ends his sequence. Pawn promotion is perfectly valid.

Winning the game
A game will typically last around seven or eight moves and is won, as in normal Chess, by delivering checkmate. If you are unable to deliver checkmate, often the best plan is to take as many of your opponent's pieces as you can and to give your king as much air as possible. This will make

it harder for your opponent to deliver checkmate on their next turn. A useful trick is to keep the king on the back row, as this makes it more difficult for your opponent to promote a pawn (promoting to a queen or rook will give check – only permissible on the final move of the sequence).

Diagram 24 shows a typical progressive Chess game. The pieces start as in normal Chess and the notation is the same: 1 d4 2 d5, Nh6 3 Nc3,

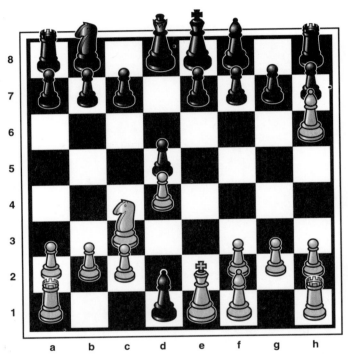

Diagram 24 *A typical Progressive Chess game*

Nf3, Bxh6 4 Bg4, Bxf3, Bxe2, Bxd1.

Black's last move was a mistake. White's reply shows the drawback of not creating flight squares for the king: 5 Nb5, Bc4, Bb3, Ba4, Nxc7 checkmate.

RANDOM CHESS

Random Chess attempts to side-step a great deal of the opening theory that has built up over the years. The middle-game and endgame remain the same but, in the opening, the players are on their own.

Players: two
Equipment: board and Chess pieces
Difficulty: the play in random Chess does not differ from normal Chess
Duration: approximately half an hour

Beginning to play

The pawns are set up as for normal Chess and the pieces occupy the eight squares on the back row. However, the order of these pieces is randomized, with the only proviso being that the two bishops cannot start the game on similarly colored squares. The initial layout of the pieces applies to both White and Black. There are many different methods of selecting the starting line-up. A typical one is that one player conceals a piece in his hand and the other player indicates to which square this piece must be placed. Diagram 25 shows a possible starting lineup.

Diagram 25 *A starting lineup for Random Chess*

Moving

The pieces and pawns move exactly as for normal Chess. However, castling is not permitted, even in the unlikely event of the king and rook(s) starting the game on their normal squares.

Winning the game

Again, after the initial configuration is determined, play follows exactly that of normal Chess – the aim being to deliver checkmate.

Bobby Fischer

The American Bobby Fischer famously defeated Boris Spassky in a World Championship match (for normal Chess) in Reykjavik in 1972. Since then he has only competed once – playing a controversial rematch against Spassky in Sveti Stefan in 1992. Fischer has attempted to popularize his own version of Random Chess and has been quoted as saying that this is the only form of Chess he will ever consider playing again.

KRIEGSPIEL

Kriegspiel is a variant of Chess that rewards detective work, reasoning, and – unusually – intuition.

Players: two and one umpire
Equipment: three boards and three sets of pieces
Difficulty: at first sight Kriegspiel is apparently little more than a game of chance. However, it is a highly skillful game
Duration: about half an hour

Beginning to play

The two players each have a board and the pieces are set up in the normal way with one player taking White and the other Black. The players must be prevented from seeing the opponent's board – this is usually accomplished by use of a screen. As the game unfolds, the players will only know for certain where their own pieces are. The complete situation, however, will be known to the umpire, who has the positions on the third board and will use this knowledge to relay information to the players.

Moving

The moves are exactly as for normal Chess and White plays first. When White has made his move, the umpire announces that he has played and it is then Black's turn. Black does not know what move White has played and now makes a move himself. White, not knowing Black's reply, then moves again. If a player attempts to make a move that is not legal the umpire will indicate this by saying "no." However, any attempt at a move which is legal must stand.

At any stage during the game a player can ask if there are any pawn captures available and the umpire will respond either "yes" or "no." A player may then try to make a capture. If this capture is not legal, the umpire will say "no." If the capture is valid the umpire says 'yes' and the move stands.

Captures are indicated by the umpire saying which player has moved and where the capture has been made. However, the identity of the capturing piece and the piece it has taken remain undisclosed. For example, after a move the umpire might announce "Black has played and captured on f3.".

When a check is given the umpire announces whether the check has been made along a file, a rank, a diagonal, or comes from a knight. For example, if White plays his queen to e7, giving check to the black king on a7, the umpire announces "White has given check along a rank."

Winning the Game

The aim of the game is to deliver checkmate.

SHOGI (JAPANESE CHESS)

The Japanese game of Shogi has many similarities to "western" Chess, and some very interesting differences. It is played on a 9x9 board with more pieces, only some of which have direct parallels in Chess.

Players: two
Equipment: board and 40 pieces
Difficulty: very strategic
Duration: several hours for tournament play; shorter time limits for friendly games

Beginning to play

Each player starts the game with 20 pieces: one king, two gold generals, two silver generals, two knights, two lances, one rook, one bishop and nine pawns. The pieces lie flat on the board with their Japanese names written on them. In Shogi notation, these pieces are represented by the symbols in diagram 26.

Shogi is played on an uncheckered 9x9 board, which is usually represented as in diagram 27.

Moves are written with the pieces first followed by the square (number first), for example G6h or P5f. If more than one piece can move to the same square, the starting square is also noted, for example G6i-5h. Captures are represented by an "x," for example Px6d; and drops are represented by an apostrophe, or sometimes an asterisk, for example P'5f or P*5f. Promotion is represented by a plus sign behind the move, for example P3c+; promoted pieces are represented by a plus sign before the move, for example +N7d.

 King (K)

 Lance (L)

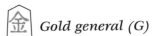 Gold general (G)

 Rook (R)

 Silver general (S)

 Bishop (B)

 Knight (N)   Pawn (P)

Diagram 26 The Shogi pieces

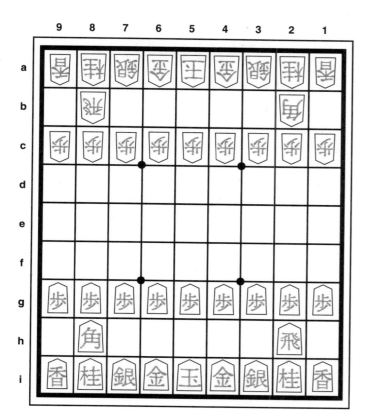

Diagram 27 The starting position for a game of Shogi (with Japanese characters)

At the start of a game, each player takes an army and positions the men facing the opposition in the formation shown in diagrams 27 and 28. The two sets of forces are distinguished solely by the way they are facing; all the pieces are the same color, although in books and magazines the player facing up the board is usually known as Black and his opponent White. Black makes the first move and from then on play is by alternation.

Moving

The pawn moves one step forward in any move, just as in a standard pawn move in Chess. The bishop moves any distance diagonally, just as a bishop does in Chess. The rook moves any distance horizontally or vertically, just as a rook moves in Chess.

The lance moves forward any distance (but not sideways or backwards). The knight moves

one step horizontally and then two steps forward — similar but not identical to a knight in Chess, (ie a choice of at most two moves). The king moves one step in any direction, just as a king moves in Chess. The gold general moves one step in any direction except diagonally backwards. The silver general moves one step forwards or diagonally (not sideways or vertically backwards).

Just as in Chess, it is possible for pawns to promote by reaching the other end of the board, but all the other pieces except the king and gold general are also allowed to promote. On promotion, pieces are flipped over to show their promoted name. Promoted silvers, knights, lances, and pawns all move like a gold general. Promoted rooks retain the rook's move but also acquire the king's move (one square in any direction). Promoted bishops retain the bishop's move but also acquire the king's move (one square in any

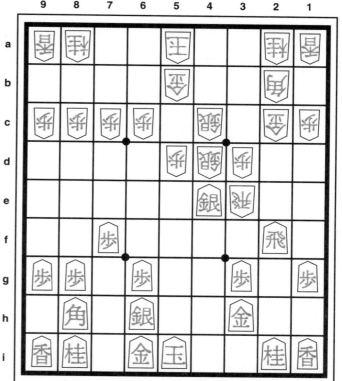

Diagram 28 A game of Shogi in progress

square in any direction). It is not necessary for a piece to reach the ninth rank to promote — the last three ranks represent the promotion zone. Nor is it compulsory to promote, except in the case of a pawn or a lance moving to the last rank or a knight reaching the final two ranks. Pieces may be promoted when moving into, inside or out of the promotion zone, but only on completion of the move.

Capturing

Capturing in Shogi is almost identical to Chess, with all pieces capturing in the same way as they move. When one piece moves to a square occupied by an opponent's piece, that piece is removed from the board. However, unlike Chess that piece becomes part of the capturing team's army. On any turn, instead of moving a piece on the board, a player can choose to "drop" one of his captured pieces on any empty square on the board. However, if that piece is a pawn, knight, or lance it must be dropped on a square from which it will have a legal move. Furthermore, it is not permitted to drop a pawn in front of the opponent's king if the king will inevitably be captured on the next move, ie checkmating with a pawn drop is not allowed. Nor is it permitted to drop a pawn on a file on which that player already has an unpromoted pawn. If a promoted piece is captured, that piece can only be dropped as an unpromoted piece. Pieces dropped on the promotion zone can only be promoted on the following move.

Diagram 28 shows a game of Shogi in progress. Note that the captured pieces that have not yet been dropped are shown by the side of the board.

Winning the game

The winner is the player who checkmates his opponent, leaving the opponent's king with no means of evading check. The possibility of dropping captured pieces means that, unlike in Chess, draws are very rare.

XIANGQI (CHINESE CHESS)

The Chinese game of Xiangqi was adapted from Indian chess in around AD 700 and is popular in Chinese communities all over the world. It is primarily distinguished from "western" Chess and Shogi by the fact that it is played on the intersections of the squares rather than the squares of the board themselves, and that there is a river that splits the board in two and a palace at either end.

Players: two
Equipment: board and 32 pieces
Difficulty: very strategic
Duration: several hours for tournament play; shorter time limits for friendly games

Beginning to play

Each player, Red and Black, starts the game with 16 pieces: one king (or general), two rooks (or chariots), two knights (or horses), two ministers (or bishops or elephants), two guards (or advisers or assistants), two cannons (or gunners) and five pawns (or soldiers). Like Shogi, the pieces lie flat on the board with their (Chinese) names written on them. In Xiangqi notation, these pieces are represented by the following symbols:

 *King (K)*    *Guard (G)*

 Rook (R)   *Cannon (C)*

 Knight (N)    *Pawn (P)*

 Minister (M)

Diagram 29 Xiangqi pieces

Approximate piece value

King	*(K)*	
Rook	*(R)*	*9 points*
Knight	*(N)*	*4.5*
Minister	*(M)*	*4*
Guard	*(G)*	*2*
Cannon	*(C)*	*2*
Pawn	*(P)*	*2 (after crossing river)*
		1 (before crossing river)

Xiangqi is played on an 8x8 board with a river across the middle. Because the game takes place on the intersections, there are 10 horizontal rows and nine vertical ones. The board is usually represented as in diagram 30.

The river between the two sides is an empty space in the middle of the board and cannot be occupied by either side. Each player has a palace, in which their king and guards reside, marked out by the areas d1-d3-f3-f1 and d0-d8-f8-f0.

In western books and magazines, moves are usually written in similar fashion to Chess, using the algebraic system of notation: first the piece moves, then the file on which it stands (if necessary), and then the file and rank to which the piece is moving. A capture is represented by an "x."

At the start of a game each player arranges their army in the formation shown in diagram 30. Red makes the first move, after which play is by alternation.

Moving

The king moves one square at a time, as in Chess, although it is not permitted to move diagonally. The king is not allowed to move outside its palace. Nor are the kings allowed to oppose one another on the same file, unless there is at least one piece of either color between them.

The rook moves any number of squares horizontally or vertically, as in Chess. The knight moves two squares horizontally and one square vertically, or two squares vertically and one square horizontally, as in Chess. However, unlike in Chess, if another piece sits on an adjacent square, the knight cannot move through that square.

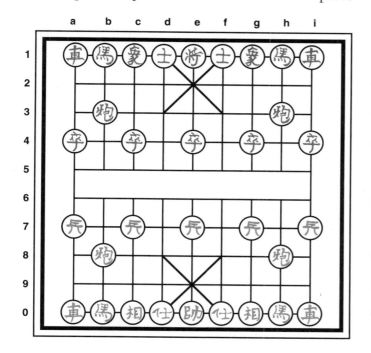

Diagram 30 *The starting position for a game of Xiangqi*

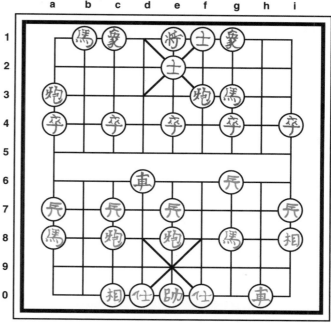

Diagram 31 *A game of Xiangqi in progress*

The minister moves two diagonal squares at a time, but is not allowed to jump or cross the river. The guard moves one square diagonally at a time. Guards are not allowed to leave the palace. The cannon moves horizontally or vertically, exactly like a rook. However, cannons can only capture by jumping over another piece to land on an opposing piece. They are not allowed to jump without a capture.

The pawn moves one square forward until it crosses the river. On their own side of the board pawns capture by moving one square ahead to occupy a square on which stands an opponent's piece. However, having crossed the river pawns can move and capture by moving one square sideways as well as one square forwards. Pawns cannot move backward and nor can they promote; on reaching the end of the board they may only move sideways.

In Xiangqi it is not permitted to undertake a perpetual check or perpetual attack on an unprotected piece, or a combination of the two; nor can two pieces attack an unprotected piece. However, pawns and kings are allowed to undertake a perpetual attack. Knights and cannons are not allowed to perpetually attack rooks, regardless of whether they are unprotected or not.

Winning the game

The object of Xiangqi is the same as Chess: to checkmate the opponent's king. The rules governing check and checkmate are the same.

CHECKERS (DRAUGHTS)

Checkers (Draughts in the UK) is perhaps the world's best-known board game. The attraction of the game is that, despite the simplicity of the rules, complex play can result.

Players: two
Equipment: board and 12 pieces. Tournament games also use a clock
Difficulty: the rules of Checkers are very simple and the game can be enjoyed by players of almost any age
Duration: tournament games will typically last between one and two hours. A social game will probably take between 10 minutes and half an hour.

Brief history

Checkers may well be a very old game, as a typical board and pieces have been discovered that date back to Egypt in the period 1600 BC. However, it is not clear that these were necessarily used to play a game that would be familiar as a precursor to Checkers as it is played today. The modern game had its beginnings in Spain in the sixteenth century and spread, via France, to the rest of Europe. In 1688, a manual on Checkers, *Jeu des Dames*, was published in France. The key publication in Great Britain followed in 1756 – *Treatise on the Game of Draughts* by William Payne. This contained much fundamental analysis on endgame positions and demonstrates that even 250 years ago, there was a great deal of knowledge about Checkers.

The modern era of Checkers features one of the most dominant champions ever of any mental sport – Dr Marion Tinsley. Tinsley was born in Ohio in 1927 and died in 1994. He was the best player in the world for 40 years, during which time he lost the incredibly small total of just seven games.

The board and pieces

Checkers is played on a standard Chessboard, using only the dark squares. Each side starts the game with 12 pieces, as indicated in diagram 32. Unlike Chess, Black is conventionally shown as starting from the lower end off the board. In a further divergence from Chess, Black always moves first.

The aim of the game

The aim in Checkers is to capture all the opponent's pieces or render them unable to move. It sometimes happens that both sides are reduced to a small number of pieces and these are unable to attack the opposition successfully. The pieces will then circle around each other endlessly with no hope of a decisive result. In such situations

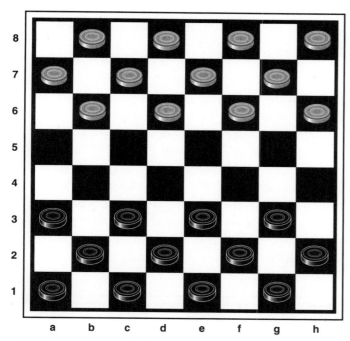

Diagram 32 *Starting position for a game of Checkers*

the players can agree to a draw (in fact the players can, by mutual consent, agree to a draw at anytime during the game). Draws are very common in Checkers, especially at a high level. For example, when Dr Tinsley played the computer program Chinook in London in 1992, the result was four wins for Tinsley, two for Chinook and 33 draws.

Moving and capturing

The pieces can move one square in a forward diagonal direction. For example, in the starting position Black can move the piece on c3 to either b4 or d4. The White piece on h6 can only move

to g5. The eight pieces that each side has on the back two rows cannot, for the moment at least, move anywhere at all.

Checkers pieces capture by jumping over an enemy piece to the square beyond. The enemy piece is then removed from the board. For example, if Black opens the game by moving the piece on g3 to f4 and White responds by moving from d6 to e5, we arrive at the position in diagram 33.

Now Black captures the White piece on e5 by jumping with his own piece on f4 to d6.

White now has a choice of recaptures, either by jumping from c7 to e5, or e7 to c5. In Checkers, unlike Chess, captures are obligatory. If you can capture an enemy piece, you must do so. If you have a choice of captures (as, for example, in the diagram 33 below) you are free

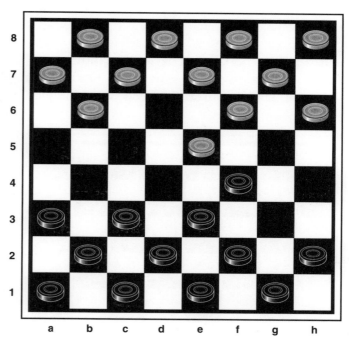

Diagram 33 *The position after Black's opening move and White's response*

to choose which one you want to make. It is also possible to capture more than one piece as in diagram 35.

If it is Black's turn to move, the piece on g1 can make a triple capture, jumping from g1-e3-

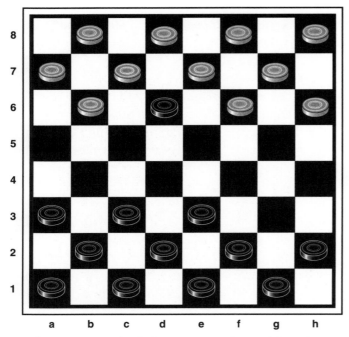

***Diagram 34** Black has captured a White piece*

g5-e7, taking all three White pieces in the process.

If you have a choice between captures and one move involves capturing more pieces than the other, you are still free to choose which play to make – you are not obliged to make the capture that removes most of the opponent's pieces.

Promotion

When a piece fights its way through to the opponent's back rank, it promotes to become a king. A king is the same as a normal piece, except that it can move and capture both forwards and backwards. A king is represented by two pieces on a square.

In diagram 36, Black can move the piece on c7 to either b8 or d8 and promote this piece to a king. If it were White's turn he could jump from g3 to e1, capturing the Black piece on f2 and simultaneously promoting to a king. Diagram 37 illustrates the power of the king.

The White king on f2 can move, like a normal piece, to e3 or g3. However, the added option of moving backwards means that the squares e1 and g1 are also available. The Black king on f6 demonstrates the capturing power of a king. The added direction of movement means that this piece is able to jump from f6 to d8 to b6 to d4, capturing the three White pieces in the process.

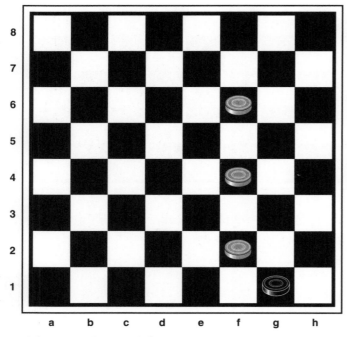

***Diagram 35** A triple capture*

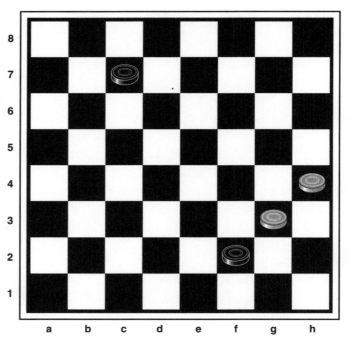

***Diagram 36** Promoting a king*

The endgame

The endgame in Checkers can be very subtle and is often finely balanced between a win and a draw. Consider the position in diagrams 38 and 39.

In the upper half of the board, White can move safely by playing a7-b8. If Black responds with c7-

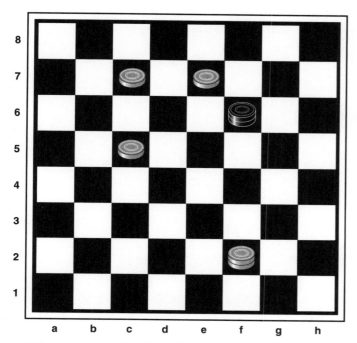

Diagram 37 *The king in action*

b6, White can simply go back with b8-a7 and the position is a draw. In the lower half, the White king is stymied and any move is met by immediate capture. However, if it were Black's turn to play, then Black would not be able to maintain the blockade and the game would be a draw.

Here Black has a king and White only a piece. If it is White to play, for example, d4-e3 h4-g3 e3-d2 g3-f2 d2-c1/K f2-e1 c1-b2 e1-d2 b2-a3 d2-c3, the White king is trapped as in the previous example. However, if it is Black to play, then the timing is wrong and the game will be a draw. Try it and see!

Tactics

The fact that captures are obligatory in Checkers creates many opportunities for tactical play. Pieces are often sacrificed in order to create

Diagram 38 *A typical endgame position*

opportunities to make multiple jumps and recapture many pieces at once. Diagram 41 shows a typical example. Black wins the game with a neat combination by playing the king

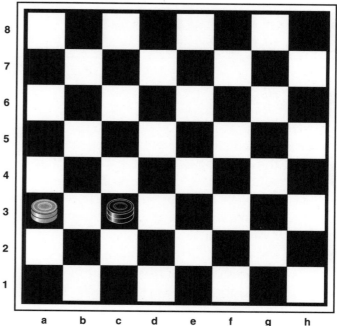

Diagram 39 *Another endgame position*

from d4 to c3. White is now obligated to capture this piece with b4 x d2 (the 'x' signifying a capture). Now Black plays the killer blow, f2-e1.

White now has only one move. He is forced to play his king from c1 to b2, when Black wins the game with the double jump, e1 x c3 x a1.

Different methods of play

As Checkers has been studied to a deeper and deeper level, the theory of the opening moves

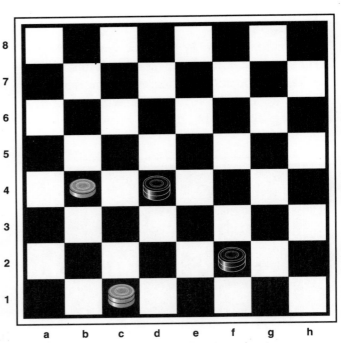

Diagram 41 *An example of sacrifice play*

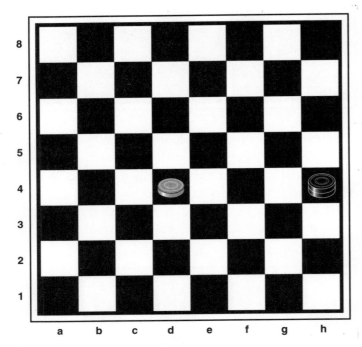

Diagram 40 *Another endgame position*

has become increasingly well understood. This presents a problem for expert players, because many of the openings are now known to fizzle out to drawn positions. This is unsatisfactory for tournament play, because weak players would have the chance to make easy draws with their stronger opponents simply by playing out a drawing sequence. Three main styles of play have been developed to combat this problem.

Go as you please (GAYP)

This is not a solution to the problem; in fact, it completely ignores it. Both players can make

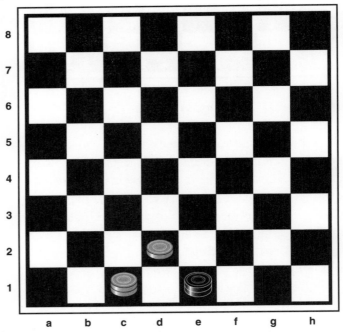

Diagram 42 *Black wins with a double jump*

any move they wish. Playing like this is perfectly satisfactory for social players or club players who are less well versed in the subtle nuances of the game.

Eleven-man-ballot

In this version, each players starts with 11 pieces rather than the standard 12. The missing piece is selected by ballot and is the same for each player.

Three-move-ballot

This is by far the most popular solution to the problem. A number of three-move sequences (Black's opening move, White's reply and Black's second move) are written on cards, one of which is drawn at random. The players then play two games, each taking one Black and one White, using this opening sequence. If the sequence is favourable for one side, then this becomes like serving at tennis and then having to receive the serve. This is by far the most popular form of the game and is used in almost all major tournaments and championship matches.

LOSING CHECKERS (DRAUGHTS)

In Losing (or Giveaway) Checkers the winner is the first player to get rid of all their pieces. It is an amusing variation that particularly appeals to young players.

Players: two
Equipment: board and 24 pieces
Difficulty: easy to grasp strategy
Duration: usually less than 20 minutes

Beginning to play

The board and pieces are arranged in the same way as for Checkers, and the rules are the same.

Moving

Just as in the parent game, players are obliged to capture if they can. If a player fails to capture an opponent's piece when it is possible to do so, the opponent can insist on the move being replayed and the capture made. After the opening stages, it is desirable for players to move their men out from the back rank, leaving spaces between those pieces and the ones in front, since of course it is almost always fatal to make a king.

Winning the game

The player who is first to get rid of all their pieces or be placed in a position in which they cannot move is the winner.

ITALIAN CHECKERS (DRAUGHTS)

Italian Checkers is almost identical to the British and US version, with slightly differing rules on captures. It dates from at least the sixteenth century.

Players: two
Equipment: board and 24 pieces
Difficulty: strategic
Duration: usually about one hour

Beginning to play

The board and starting position are identical to British and American Checkers, except that the board is placed with a white square in the bottom left-hand corner. Play still takes place on the black squares.

Moving

The moves in Italian Checkers are exactly the same as in the conventional version, except that there are slightly different rules for captures. In Italian Checkers kings cannot be captured by uncrowned pieces. In addition, a player who has a choice between two or more captures must make the move that captures the greater number of pieces. If the number of pieces is equal,

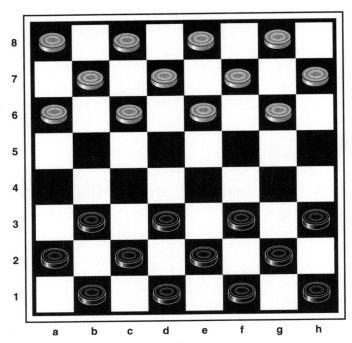

Diagram 43 Starting position for a game of Italian Checkers

but a player faces a choice between capturing a king and an uncrowned piece, they must capture the king.

Winning the game

Just as in conventional Checkers, the winner is the player who captures all the opponent's pieces or immobilizes those that remain.

SPANISH CHECKERS (DRAUGHTS)

Spanish Checkers is identical to Italian Checkers, except for the power of the king, who can move any distance along a diagonal and can land beyond the captured piece any distance. Spanish Checkers can also be traced back to the sixteenth century.

Players: two
Equipment: board and 24 pieces
Difficulty: strategic
Duration: usually about one hour

Beginning to play

The board and pieces are arranged in exactly the same way as for a game of Italian Checkers.

Moving

The rules are the same as for Italian Checkers, except in relation to the king. In Spanish Checkers a king can move any number of squares along a diagonal, as long as it is unobstructed by its own pieces. If there is an opposing piece on that diagonal, it can be captured provided that there are no pieces in front of it and that there are one or more squares immediately beyond it for the king to land on. The king may land on any of the vacant squares beyond the captured piece, but having made that capture, the king must capture another piece on a different diagonal if it is possible to do so. The move is only

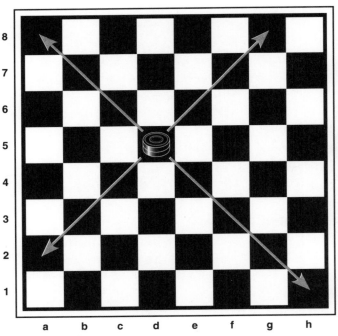

Diagram 44 King captures in Spanish Checkers

156

completed once the king has made all the captures it can. The captured pieces are removed from the board once the move is completed, but the king can jump over each of them only once – dead pieces form an impassable barrier.

Winning the game

Just as in conventional Checkers, the winner is the player who captures all the opponent's pieces or immobilizes those that remain.

GERMAN CHECKERS (DRAUGHTS)

German Checkers is identical to Spanish Checkers except in relation to the capturing powers of uncrowned pieces. The pieces are arranged in the standard way on a 64-square board. Instead of being made kings, pieces that land on the opponent's back row are made queens or dames.

Players: two
Equipment: board and 24 pieces
Difficulty: strategic
Duration: usually about one hour

Beginning to play

The board and pieces are arranged in exactly the same way as for a game of Spanish Checkers.

Moving

The rules of German Checkers are identical to those of Spanish Checkers, apart from one very important aspect: in German Checkers uncrowned pieces can capture in both a forward and backward direction. Furthermore, an uncrowned piece's move is not necessarily completed if it reaches the coronation square. If it can then capture other pieces by moving back-

wards it must do so. In that case it does not promote to a king on that move.

Winning the game

Just as in conventional checkers, the winner is the player who captures all the opponent's pieces or immobilizes those that remain.

RUSSIAN CHECKERS (DRAUGHTS)

Russian Checkers is very similar to German Checkers, but with slight variations in the rules on capturing and promotion. Capturing is not compulsory, and the moment a piece hits the king's row, it is crowned.

Players: two
Equipment: board and 24 pieces
Difficulty: strategic
Duration: usually about one hour

Beginning to play

The board and pieces are arranged in exactly the same way as for a game of German Checkers.

Moving

There are two rules that distinguish Russian and German Checkers. First, when a piece reaches the coronation square it cannot again capture backwards, but in Russian Checkers it does become a king. Second, when there is a choice between two capturing moves, there is no obligation to choose the move that captures the highest number of pieces.

Winning the game

Just as in conventional Checkers, the winner is the player who captures all the opponent's pieces or immobilizes those that remain.

POLISH CHECKERS (DRAUGHTS)

Polish or Continental Checkers, which was deveoped around 1725, is identical to German Checkers, but is played with a larger board and more pieces. Nowadays, it is the form of Checkers played in France, Belgium, Holland, and the French-speaking cantons of Switzerland.

Players: *two*
Equipment: *board and 40 pieces*
Difficulty: *strategic*
Duration: *usually about one hour*

Beginning to play

In Polish Checkers the board and pieces are arranged in exactly the same way as for a game of German Checkers, but on a 10x10 board with a white square in the bottom right-hand corner. Each player starts with 20 pieces, five on each of the first four rows.

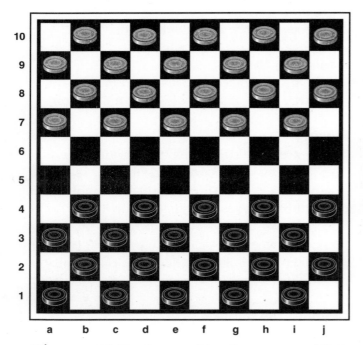

Diagram 45 *Starting position for a game of Polish Checkers*

Moving

The rules for Polish Checkers are identical to those of German Checkers. Interestingly, crowned pieces are known as queens rather than kings in Polish Checkers.

Winning the game

Just as in conventional Checkers, the winner is the player who captures all the opponent's pieces or immobilizes those that remain.

CANADIAN CHECKERS (DRAUGHTS)

Canadian Checkers is identical to German and Polish Checkers, but with an even larger board and more pieces. It was devised by the French settlers of Quebec, who called it the Grand Jeu de Dames.

Players: *two*
Equipment: *board and 60 pieces*
Difficulty: *strategic*
Duration: *usually about one hour*

Beginning to play

The board and pieces are arranged in exactly the same way as for a game of German Checkers, but on a 12x12 board. Each player starts with 30 pieces, six on each of the first five rows.

Moving

The rules for Canadian Checkers are identical to those of German Checkers.

Winning the game

Just as in conventional Checkers, the winner is the player who captures all the opponent's pieces or succeeds in immobilizing all those that remain.

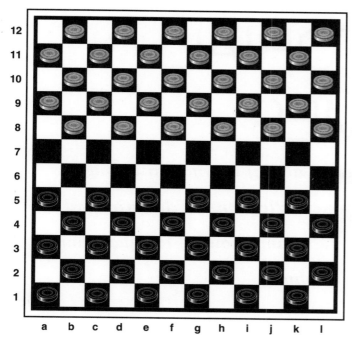

Diagram 46 Starting position for a game of Canadian Checkers

TURKISH CHECKERS (DRAUGHTS)

In the Turkish form of Checkers play takes place on both the white and black squares, and pieces can move forwards or sideways but not diagonally.

Players: two
Equipment: board and 32 pieces
Difficulty: strategic
Duration: usually about one hour

Beginning to play

The pieces are lined up side by side on the second and third ranks of a standard Chessboard.

Moving

Unlike other forms of Checkers, a move in Turkish

Checkers can be forwards, lateral or backwards (for the kings) but not diagonal. Uncrowned pieces can move one square in a forward or lateral direction. They capture by jumping over the opponent's pieces, again either forwards or laterally. On reaching the other side of the board, a piece becomes a king, after which it can move any number of squares forwards, backwards or sideways (but not diagonally) and capture by moving forwards, backwards or sideways in similar fashion to a king in Spanish Checkers. Captured pieces are removed from the board immediately, and cannot impede further captures. Just as in Spanish Checkers, it is compulsory to capture a piece if it is possible to do so and, given a choice of captures, the move that involves the greatest number of captures must be made.

Winning the game

As in conventional Checkers, the winner is the player who captures all the opponent's pieces or immobilizes those that remain. However, it is also possible to win by reducing one's opponent to a single uncrowned piece.

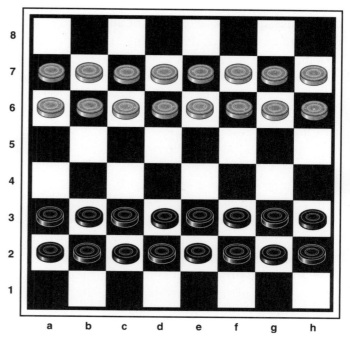

Diagram 47 Starting position for a game of Turkish Checkers

TERRITORIAL GAMES

If war games reflect the human race's ability to triumph through cunning strategy, then territorial games reflect one of the principal reasons why war occurs in the first place: ambitions of conquest and the defense of land.

Observations of nature show that many species will fight hard to establish their own personal territory and go to great lengths to defend it. The human species is no exception: on a global scale countless wars have been fought to settle disputes based on ownership of territory. Even on a personal level, an invasion of one's space can cause psychological distress. In general, we all like to have our own space, and the development of territorial games is perhaps a reflection of this.

The objective of territorial games is to capture a playing area or an opponent's pieces. Go, which originated in China, is thought to be one of the oldest games in existence. The first books on the game were published during the Tang Dynasty (618–907 AD), though there are earlier references to it dating as far back as 625 BC. It was later adopted by Japan and other oriental countries. Two players compete to secure as much of the playing area as possible. Go is considered to be one of the greatest games of strategic skill.

Mancala is the generic name for a group of ancient African games. Names, boards and rules differ from region to region, but the basic principles of play are the same – seeds are moved from cup to cup around a board in an attempt to capture opposing seeds. Owari, which is played in West Africa, is a typical Mancala game.

Nine Men's Morris is one of the oldest European games, and was particularly popular during the Middle Ages. Remains of Morris games have been found in places as far apart as the first city of Troy and in a Bronze Age burial site in Ireland and cut into the deck of a tenth-century Viking ship and the steps of a shrine in Ceylon.

More recent territorial games include Reversi, which was invented in England in the late nineteenth century. Since 1971 a modified form, known as Othello®, has more usually been played. The aim of both Reversi and Othello® is to have a majority of your pieces on the board at the end of the game.

Hex was invented by a Danish mathematician in the 1940s. This game has similarities with Go in the way that moves are made and in that play takes place on the point of intersections, but the aim is to form an unbroken line of pieces.

An important lesson to be learned by playing and studying territorial games is that having a large territory is all well and good, but it is also necessary to have a large army to defend it. A small army defending a large territory is vulnerable to pincer movements from the opposition.

GO

Go is the ultimate territory game. Players take it in turns to place stones on the board, attempting to surround territory. The apparent simplicity of the game is deceptive and even the very strongest computers only play at the level of a competent beginner. Go has been compared to playing five games of Chess simultaneously – one in the center and one in each corner.

Players: two

Equipment: Go board and Go stones. Tournament games also use a clock

Difficulty: the rules of Go are very simple and the game can quickly be enjoyed by anybody. However, the intricacies of the game take decades to master

Duration: tournament games can last a day or more. However, a leisurely social game will probably take between 30 minutes and one hour

Brief history

The origin of Go is steeped in mystery and legend, but the game almost certainly developed several thousand years ago in China. The most popular story is that Go was invented by the Chinese Emperor Shun to "strengthen his son's weak mind." From China, Go spread to Japan and Korea and eventually throughout the rest of the world. It is revered in Eastern tradition in much the same way as the physical sport of Sumo. In fact, even though Go is not a physical sport, it is categorized as a martial art because study of the game is regarded as a process of self-development.

Although there has been a recent upsurge in interest in the UK and USA, the game remains most popular in the East, where the top Go players are huge stars. For example, Lee Chang-Ho, a brilliant young player from Korea, was ranked as the eighth most recognized person in the world in a survey in Korea.

The Go board and stones

The classic game of Go is played on a 19x19 board as in diagram 1.

There are 19 horizontal and 19 vertical lines on a standard board, yielding 361 intersections, called "points." The nine darker points are reference markers and are used to locate your position. As a game on the full-size board can take a great deal of time, the game is also often played on a smaller 13x13 board. Beginners can also play on a further reduced 9x9 board. The game obviously simplifies as the size of the board decreases, but all the rules and the basic principles remain the same.

The game is played by the two players ("White" and "Black") taking it in turns to place stones on the board. The stronger player takes White, as Black plays first and thus holds a small advantage.

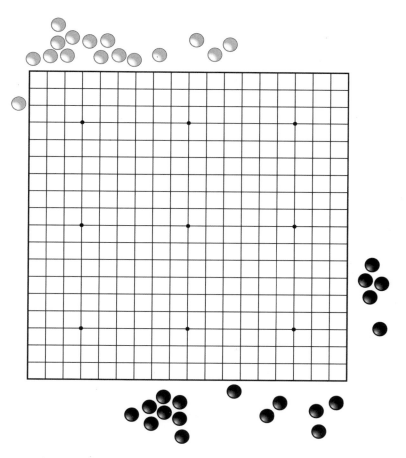

Diagram 1 A Go board and stones

The stones are placed on the intersections and not the squares themselves. The traditional nature of the game of Go can be discerned from the fact that players are expected to place the stones by using the index and middle fingers. At the start of the game the board is empty, unless one player is far superior to the other, in which case a handicap system may be used. The weaker player takes Black and can receive a head start of up to nine stones. These stones are placed on the star points, White plays first and the game continues as for an even game. Once the stones have been placed on the board, they cannot be moved. The play consists only of adding further stones to the board on unoccupied points.

The aim of the game

The aim of Go is extremely simple – it is to capture territory. At the end of the game, the size of the Black and White territories are compared. Whoever has captured more is the winner. Territory is defined as points surrounded by stones of the same color. For example, in diagram 2, White has succeeded in capturing four points, while Black has done better with nine. If the game were now concluded, then Black, having captured more territory, would win.

Rules of play

In the battle to capture territory, it is possible that your stones may be captured, or you may capture those of the opponent. A key concept in the fight to capture stones is that of "liberties." A stone's liberties are adjacent points horizontally and vertically.

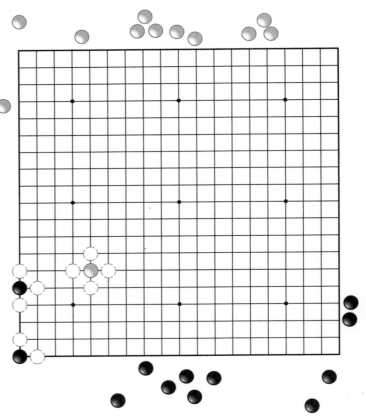

Diagram 3 Liberties

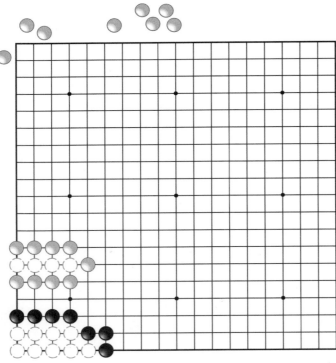

Diagram 2 Capturing territory

A stone in the center of the board has four liberties (see the White stone in diagram 3), while ones on the edge or in the corner have three and two respectively (see the Black stones). When enemy stones block all the liberties of a stone, the stone is surrounded, deemed to be captured, and then removed from the board.

In diagram 4, the White stone in mid-board has been captured,

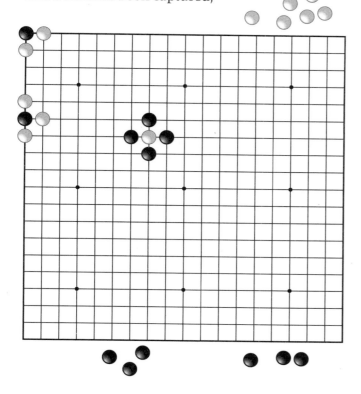

Diagram 4 *Captured stones*

and will be removed from the board. The same applies to the Black stones on the edge. A captured stone is a prisoner-of-war. It has value at the end of the game because it can be used to "fill in" points that the opponent has gained, thus reducing his territory.

Atari

Stones that are threatened with imminent capture are said to be in "atari." In diagram 5, three of the White stone's liberties are already blocked. If Black were now to play a stone on the point marked with an "x," the White stone would be captured. The White stone is therefore in atari. However, it is White's turn to play and save the situation, temporarily at least, by playing a stone to the "x." Black cannot now capture both stones.

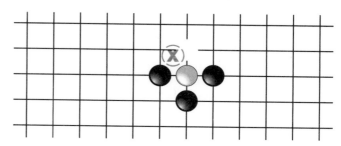

Diagram 5 *White is threatened with capture*

Regardless of how many stones there are in a group (see diagram 6), if all their liberties are taken away, the stones are captured.

If Black now plays a stone as indicated, the four White stones will have been deprived of all their

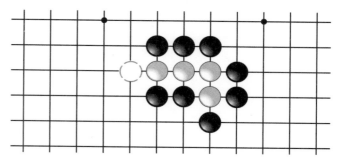

Diagram 6 *Capturing a number of stones*

liberties and the result is shown in diagram 7. Black has captured four White stones and gained four points of territory.

As play in the game progresses and the stones become intertwined the possibilities for captur-

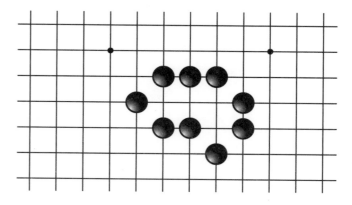

Diagram 7 *The White stones have been captured*

163

ing, both stones and territory, can become complex. In diagram 8, the group of four white stones in the lower half of the board are in atari and seem to be in trouble. White could try to keep these alive by playing on "x" but then Black

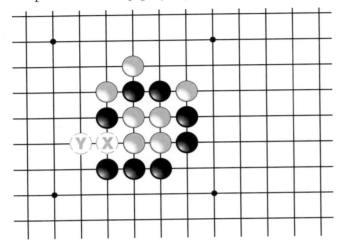

Diagram 8 Attack and counterattack

would play on "y" and the stones would still be captured.

However, White has a much better move. In diagram 9, the two highest black stones are captured and removed from the board. The lower group of four white stones is thus no longer in atari.

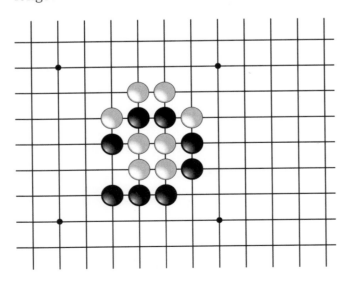

Diagram 9 White captures the Black stones

Legal and illegal moves

You may only place a stone on the board if that stone will have liberties. In diagram 10, White cannot place a stone on the point marked with an "x" because this stone will have no liberties and will simply be removed from the board by Black. However, the white stone marked with a triangle is not the same. It is connected to other white stones and thus shares liberties with them. White would not place a stone here – this would make no sense as the stone would simply reduce White's territory – but if this configuration arose during play, there would be no problem.

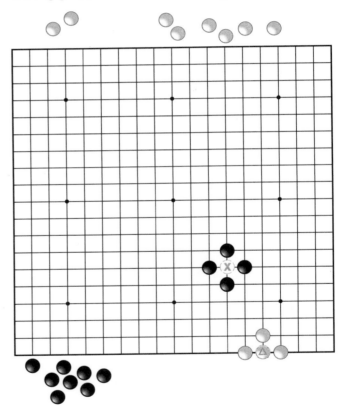

Diagram 10 Legal and illegal moves

However, you are allowed to place a stone on a point where it has no liberties if, by doing so, you capture enemy stones and thus create liberties. In the upper group of diagram 11, Black cannot place a stone at "x" as this stone would be part of a group that has no liberties. However, in diagram 12, Black can play at "y" as, by so doing, the he would capture the white stone marked with a triangle. His group of stones would then have liberties.

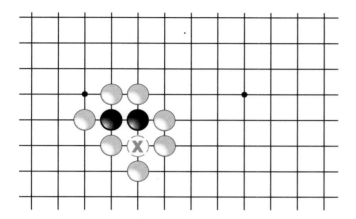

Diagram 11 *An illegal move*

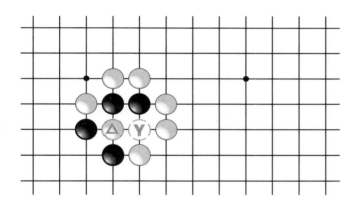

Diagram 12 *A legal move: Black captures a White stone*

Life and death

A key element in the strategy of Go is whether a group of stones are alive or dead. If a group of stones is dead, they will be picked off and any territory they have gained will be transferred to the opponent. If a group is alive this will not happen. Ensuring that your groups are alive is crucial. In diagram 13, the group of Black stones has been completely surrounded, but White will never be able to capture these stones. It is not possible to play a stone to either of the points marked "x," as they have no liberties. The Black group is "alive."

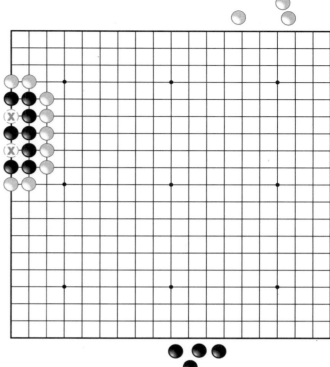

Diagram 13 *The Black stones are alive*

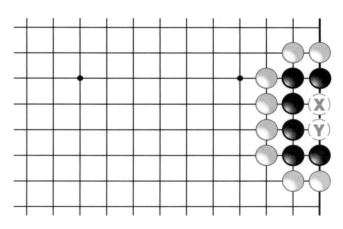

Diagram 14 *The Black stones are dead*

The situation in diagram 14 is different. Here, although the Black group has two points of territory, the stones can nevertheless be captured. White is able to play a stone to either "x" or "y" as these points have liberties. Let us assume that White plays to "x." White now threatens to play to "y" and capture the group. Black could capture the white stone by playing to "y," but now the position in diagram 15 arises.

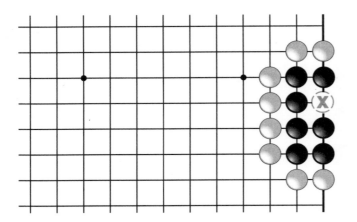

Diagram 15 *White captures the Black stones*

Now White hits back by playing to "x" and killing off the Black group. In fact, in the original position, White is in no hurry to attack this group, as it is defenseless. This group of stones is "dead."

The Rule of Ko

The rule of Ko is important in Go because it prevents a situation where the game could have no resolution. Consider the position in diagram 16.

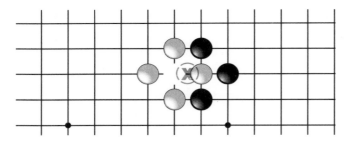

Diagram 16 *A White stone is in atari*

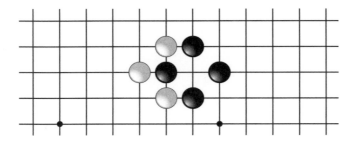

Diagram 17 *Black captures the White stone*

The White stone to the right of the group is in atari, so Black can play to "x" and capture this stone. The position in diagram 17 results.

Now, however, the Black stone that has just made the capture is itself in atari, so White can perform the same manoeuver and capture in return. This leads to the position illustrated in diagram 18.

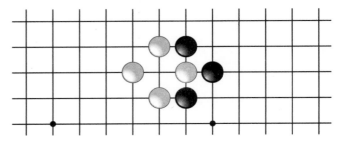

Diagram 18 *White recaptures*

We are now back where we started. Between two particularly stubborn players, it is possible that this little exchange of captures could continue indefinitely. However, the rule of Ko (Ko is, in fact, the Japanese word for eternity) prevents this. When a stone captures in Ko, it may not be captured immediately. In our previous example Black played to "x," capturing

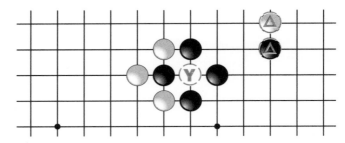

Diagram 19 *The rule of Ko*

the White stone and leaving the position in diagram 19.

White is not now allowed to play to "y" but must play elsewhere on the board. If White plays as marked by the triangle and Black does the same, White can now return to the point "y" and make the capture. White has captured in Ko, and now it is Black's turn to find something else to do.

Strategy

A basic element of Go strategy is to form strong chains of stones. Such stones are said to be connected. If stones are prevented from connect-

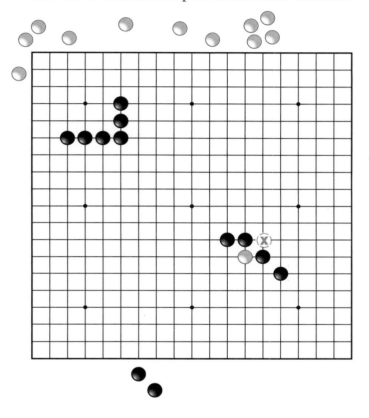

Diagram 20 Connecting and cutting

ing, they are weak and can become vulnerable to capture. Stones are strongest when they are connected in a straight line.

The upper group of stones in diagram 20 is very secure. It is very difficult for White to mount an attack against them and they can form the basis of plans to gain territory. Any group of stones which is connected horizontally or vertically constitutes a powerful unit. Groups which contain a diagonal connection, as in the lower group in diagram 20, are less secure.

The key point here is "x." If Black can play to "x," this will make a strong connected group of stones. However, if White plays to "x," the black stones are "cut," and more vulnerable to attack.

HORSESHOE

The simple game of Horseshoe is played in many parts of the world, including China.

Players: *two*
Equipment: *board and four counters (two black and two white)*
Difficulty: *easy-to-grasp strategy*
Duration: *less than 10 minutes per game*

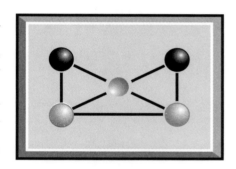

Diagram 21 Starting position for a game of Horseshoe

Beginning to play

The Horseshoe board can easily be drawn on a sheet of paper. Diagram 21 shows the starting position.

Moving

The game starts with one player moving their counter to the center point. The opponent must now move one of their counters to the point vacated by the first player. Play then continues alternately, with each player in turn moving one of their counters to the vacant point.

Winning the game

The player who manages to block the opponent so that they cannot move either of their counters

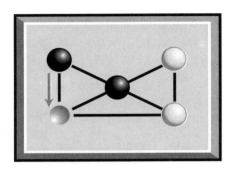

Diagram 22 Achieving a winning position in Horseshoe

achieves victory. In Diagram 22, Black can achieve a winning position by moving the counter in the direction of the arrow.

NINE MEN'S MORRIS

Nine Men's Morris ("Mill" in the USA) is one of the oldest board games in the world.

Players: *two*
Equipment: *board and 18 counters (nine black and nine white)*
Difficulty: *requires good strategy*
Duration: *usually less than half an hour per game*

Brief history

Nine Men's Morris reached a peak of popularity in Europe in the Middle Ages, when the grid was often marked out with a trowel on the turf. It was probably to this in fact that Shakespeare was referring in *A Midsummer Night's Dream* (II, I, 96-8):

The folds stand empty in the drowned field,
And crows are fatter with the murrion flock
The nine men's morris is filled up with mud.

Today the board is usually made of wood or

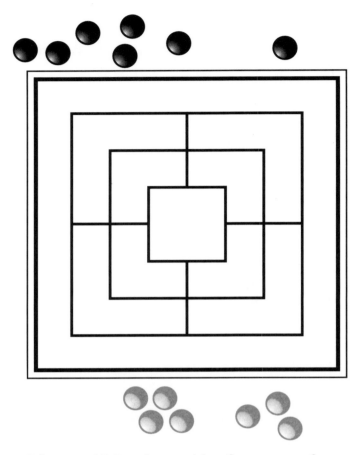

Diagram 23 Starting position for a game of Nine Men's Morris

pasteboard. It comprises three squares, one inside the other, linked by four lines, two horizontal and two vertical (see diagram 23).

Beginning to play

Each player starts with nine men, which they take turns to place on any vacant point of intersection on the board. If one of the players manages to achieve a row of three counters, known as a "mill," they can remove one of the opponent's counters from the board, but not one that itself stands in a mill – unless there are no other men available. Once counters have been removed from the board they are then deemed to be "dead."

Diagram 24 shows the position after one counter has been introduced by each side, Black moving first. After two moves each (diagram 25) both sides are close to forming a mill. However,

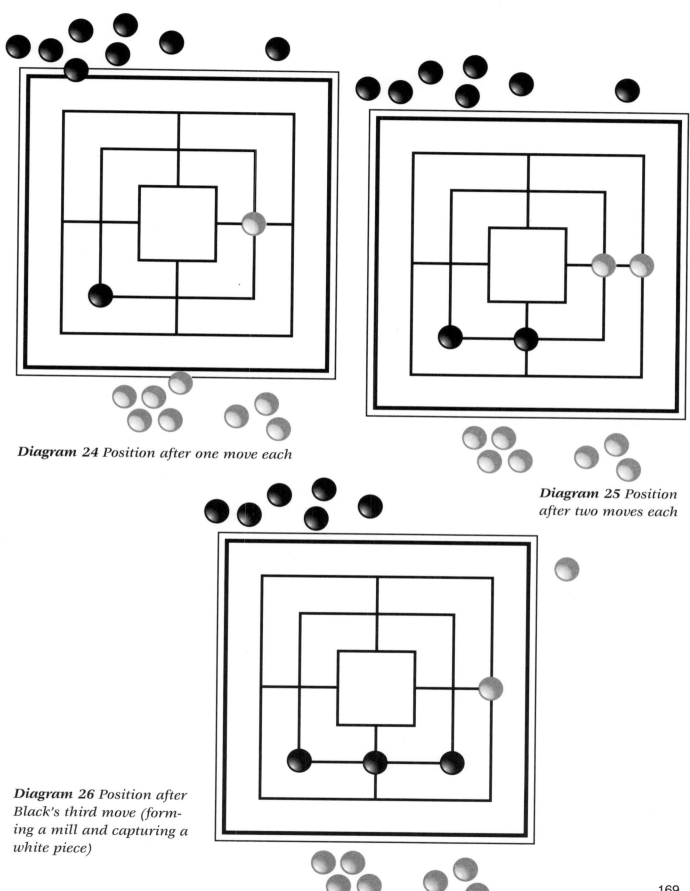

Diagram 24 *Position after one move each*

Diagram 25 *Position after two moves each*

Diagram 26 *Position after Black's third move (forming a mill and capturing a white piece)*

Black moves first and is able to form a mill, thereby removing one of White's counters from the board (diagram 26).

Moving

Once all the counters have been placed on the board, the players continue in alternate turns by moving a piece to an adjacent vacant point along a line, attempting to create a mill. A mill can be made and broken any number of times, an enemy counter being removed each time a mill is formed. It is particularly desirable to set up a double mill, whereby a counter can oscillate from one mill to another and then back again, capturing an opposing counter on every turn.

The hop

This common optional variation is often used to prolong the game. If used, it enables a player with only three men left to hop one of their pieces to any point on the board, rather than being restricted to adjacent points. This is a big advantage and often enables a player to regain a great deal of lost ground. Of course, if the opponent is then reduced to three men, they are also entitled to hop. (It is interesting to note that centuries later this idea of hopping reemerged in the late 1970s in the guise of "hyperspace" in video arcade games.)

Winning the game

The winner is the player who manages to leave their opponent with only two men. If hopping is not allowed, victory can also be achieved by blocking the opponent's men so that they cannot be moved.

HEX

Hex was invented by the Danish mathematician and poet Piet Hein in the 1940s and enjoyed a brief period of fashion both there and in North America. Although relatively little known nowadays, it is simple to play and has an elegant and intriguing cut and thrust.

Players: two
Equipment: board and 122 counters
Difficulty: very strategic
Duration: usually less than one hour per game

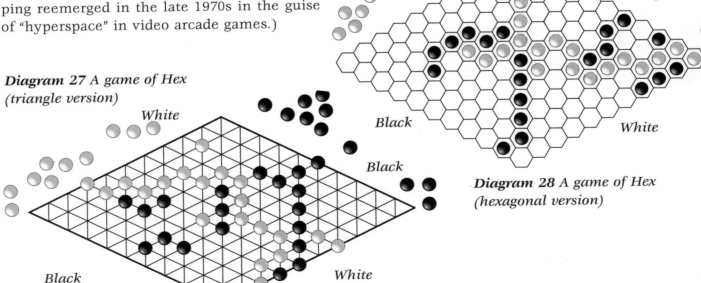

Diagram 27 A game of Hex (triangle version)

Diagram 28 A game of Hex (hexagonal version)

Beginning to play

Hex is played on a diamond-shaped board ruled into equilateral triangles. The standard size board has 10 triangles along each edge (see diagram 27). Just as in Go, play takes place on the points of intersection between the triangles, and not within the triangles themselves. Sometimes the board is shown instead as a series of adjoining hexagons (hence the name "Hex"), as in diagram 28, but this is harder to draw. In the hexagonal version, play takes place on each of the hexagons.

Moving

Like Go, the game starts with the players alternately placing counters on any vacant point, Black moving first. Once these counters have been placed, they remain in that position for the whole game. Counters cannot be moved or captured.

Winning the game

The winner is the first player to complete a continuous line of counters from one of the sides marked with their colour to the other. A winning chain can be of any length and can turn and double back on itself as many times as it likes provided that there are no gaps. Note that the four corner points belong to both players.

REVERSI (OTHELLO®)

"The game that takes a minute to learn – and a lifetime to master." Reversi (nowadays usually played in the modern form of Othello®, since its resurrection from a long period of obscurity) is a fast-moving and skillful test of wits in which the more territory you claim the better.

Players: two
Equipment: board and 64 discs with different colors on their two sides (usually black and white)

Difficulty: very strategic and complex; not suitable for young children
Duration: usually less than one hour per game

Brief history

Like Halma (see Race Games, Chapter 2), Reversi was invented in the 1880s. It is usually credited to Lewis Waterman, whose company, Jacques and Sons, published a book entitled *Handbook of Reversi* in 1888, written by Walter H. Peel. Nowadays it is usually played in a modified form known as Othello®, which was invented by Goro Hasegawa in 1971.

Champions

Japanese players have dominated the World Othello® Championships since their inauguration in 1977. The current human world champion is Makoto Suekuni, who took the title in Athens, Greece in 1997. However, there are some computer programs that can defeat the top human players. The program Logistello defeated the 1996 world champion Takeshi

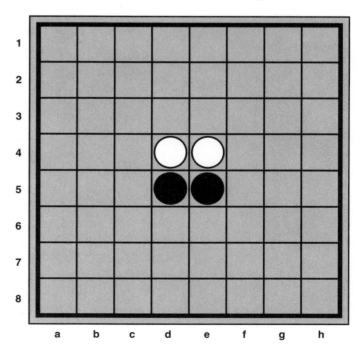

Diagram 29 Possible starting position for a game of Reversi

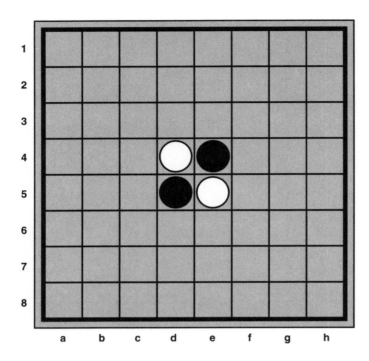

1 2 3 4 5 6 7 8

a b c d e f g h

Diagram 30 Starting position for Othello® (and possible starting position for a game of Reversi)

Murakami in every game of a six-game match in August 1997.

Beginning to play
Reversi starts with an empty board and 32 discs for each side. The two players first decide which color they will play with and then take it in turns to place discs of their color in the four center squares, with Black starting. In Othello®, however, the location of these four discs is already determined, thereby eliminating one of the two possible starting configurations of Reversi.

Notation
Reversi uses a similar system of notation to Chess. However, the top left-hand corner is labelled "a1" in Reversi, whereas it would be "a8" in Chess notation.

Moving
Once the initial discs have been placed, Black must then place a disc on a vacant square adja-

WORLD CHAMPIONSHIP ROLL OF HONOR

Year	Venue	World Champion
1977	Tokyo	Hiroshi Inoue, Japan
1978	New York	Hideshi Maruoka, Japan
1979	Rome	Hiroshi Inoue, Japan
1980	London	Jonathan Cerf, USA
1981	Brussels	Hideshi Maruoka, Japan
1982	Stockholm	Kunihiko Tanida, Japan
1983	Paris	Kenichi Ishii, Japan
1984	Melbourne	Paul Ralle, France
1985	Athens	Masaki Takizawa, Japan
1986	Tokyo	Hideshi Tamenori, Japan
1987	Milan	Kenichi Ishii, Japan
1988	Paris	Takeshi Murakami, Japan
1989	Warsaw	Hideshi Tamenori, Japan
1990	Stockholm	Hideshi Tamenori, Japan
1991	New York	Shigeru Kaneda, Japan
1992	Barcelona	Marc Tastet, France
1993	London	David Shaman, USA
1994	Paris	Masaki Takizawa, Japan
1995	Melbourne	Hideshi Tamenori, Japan
1996	Tokyo	Takeshi Murakami, Japan
1997	Athens	Makoto Suekuni, Japan

cent to an opponent's disc in such a way that one or more of the opponent's discs are trapped between that disc and another black disc – with no empty spaces in between. All enemy pieces that lie between those two discs are flipped over to show the black side. In diagram 31, Black plays a disc to f5, thus flipping over the black disc on e5. Captures may be horizontal, vertical or diagonal and it is possible to capture in several different ways with one move, as in diagram 32. Here White can play to f4, flipping over the discs on e4 and f5, or alternatively he can play to d6, flipping over the discs on e6 and d5.

Play continues by alternation and discs may change ownership several times during a game. If a player cannot move, they miss a turn. If neither player can move, or one player runs out of discs on the board, the game is over. In Reversi

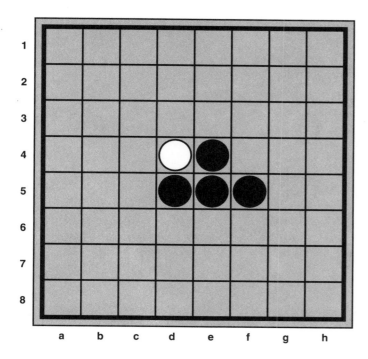

Diagram 31 Capturing at the start of a game

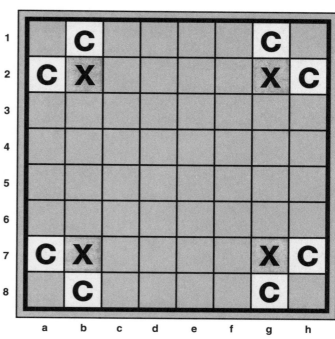

Diagram 33 Special squares

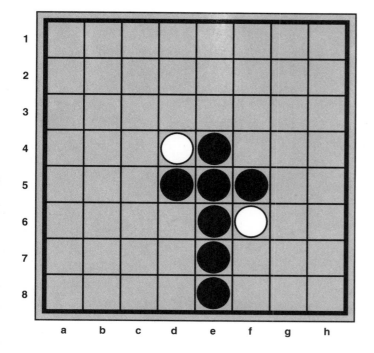

Diagram 32 Capturing at a developed stage of a game

the game also ends if one player runs out of discs with which to play. However, in Othello®, that player can draw on their opponent's stock.

As the game reaches its conclusion the situation on the board can change dramatically as each move results in numerous captures. Indeed, it is the fast-changing nature of the game that forms one of its principal attractions.

Strategy

Since the object of the game is to end up with more discs than your opponent, most novice players concentrate on playing moves that capture the most pieces on every turn. However, this strategy is invariably mistaken – it is the quality rather than the quantity of discs that usually decides the game. The strongest discs are those that are "stable," ie invulnerable to being flipped over by your opponent. In fact, adherents of the brute-force strategy of capturing a maximum number of pieces on each turn often find that in the later stages of the game they are left without good moves, since by definition the more discs you have, the fewer your options on

173

each turn to flip over your opponent's discs. Inevitably, they are thus forced to make poor moves, allowing their opponents to seize numerous discs on every turn and thereby win the game. Most experts agree that the best way to take control of the board is to maintain fewer discs on the board than your opponent in the early and middle stages of the game.

It is important to realize that certain squares are far more important than others, as possession of these key squares will usually determine who has the initiative in the crucial final few moves of the game, when large numbers of discs may be won and lost. The four corner squares, a1, h1, a8, and h8, are especially significant. Once you hold these key squares they can never be taken away from you, so they are stable and can be used as key points in the battle for possession of the outside of the board and the long (a1-h8 and h1-a8) diagonals. It is very dangerous to play your discs adjacent to the corner squares, as these may then be used as "stepping stones" by your opponent to seize the corners. In Reversi the diagonal squares next to the corner (highlighted in red) are known as "X" squares and the other squares next to the corner (highlighted in pink) as "C" squares, as shown in diagram 33.

Apart from the corner squares, the next most important squares to seize are the outside squares, b1-g1, h2-h7, b8-g8, and a2-a7. These discs act in five directions but can only be captured in two (left and right, or top and bottom, depending on the location of the disc) and are therefore often more powerful than discs in the middle of the board, which are vulnerable to capture from all directions. However, strong players are often reluctant to seize territory on the outside of the board until the later stages of a game, in order to restrict their opponent's chances of capturing the corner squares. Note, however, that of the 64 squares that make up the board, no less than 28 are on the extreme outside edges, so it is almost impossible to win without some control of these rows.

However, these strategies are only guidelines – in certain situations it may pay to ignore them altogether.

Winning the game

Once all 64 squares on the board have been occupied by discs, the game is over. The players then tot up the number of discs of each color. The player with more discs is the winner, although ties are possible.

FOUR FIELD KONO

Four Field Kono is one of a family of Korean games that includes Five Field Kono and Six Field Kono. It takes its name from the fact that it is played on a 4x4 board, which creates 16 intersections.

Players: two
Equipment: board and 16 counters (eight each of two different colors)
Difficulty: mainly strategy
Duration: usually less than half an hour per game

Beginning to play

Four Field Kono is played on a square board of 16 points. Each player has eight counters, arranged in the starting position shown in diagram 34.

Moving

The players move in alternate turns. If a counter is able to jump over another counter of the same color and land on an opponent's counter, it can capture the latter. If no capturing moves are possible, a counter may only move to an adjacent point along one of the lines.

Winning the game

The winner is the player who is able to capture

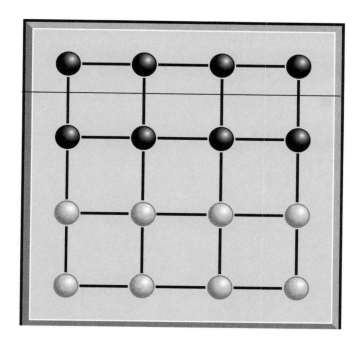

Diagram 34 *Starting position for a game of Four Field Kono*

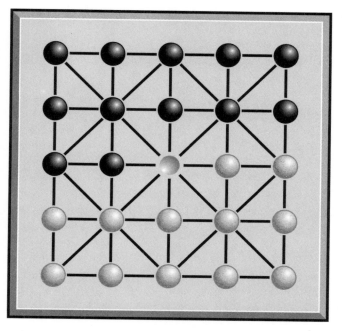

Diagram 35 *Starting position for a game of Alquerque*

all the opponent's counters or block them so that they cannot move.

ALQUERQUE

Alquerque is a board game for two players that has certain similarities to Checkers (Draughts).

Players: *two*
Equipment: *board and 24 counters*
Difficulty: *mainly strategy*
Duration: *usually less than half an hour per game*

Brief history

Alquerque is thought to have originated in Ancient Egypt, and was introduced into Europe by the Moors when they invaded Spain. Originally boards would have been made out of stone, marble, wood or some other material, and the lines would have been incised on them. The Alquerque game board is incised into the roof tiles of the ancient temple at Kurna – an honor it shares with Nine Men's Morris.

Beginning to play

The alquerque board consists of 25 points connected by diagonal, horizontal and vertical lines. Each player has 12 counters, which at the start of the game are arranged on the board as shown in diagram 35.

Moving

Play is by alternate moves. On their turn players may move one counter to any adjacent empty point. If an adjacent point is occupied by an enemy piece and the point beyond it is empty, a player may jump over that counter, capturing it in the process, and removing it from the board. If a second counter can then be taken in the same fashion, this may also be removed, even if it involves a change of direction. Further captures may be made in the same way. A turn is completed when a counter is moved to an adjacent empty point or when all captures by that counter have been exhausted. In many variations of the game it is compulsory for a piece to capture if it can do so, otherwise the offending counter is "huffed", and is removed from the board.

Winning the game

The game is won by capturing all the opponent's counters.

OWARI

The West African game of Owari is one of most popular of the Mancala family of board games.

Players: two
Equipment: board and 48 stones or beans
Difficulty: easy-to-grasp strategy, but requires great skill to play well
Duration: usually less than 20 minutes per game

Brief history

Owari, sometimes called "Oware," "Wari," or "Ware" originated in Africa several thousand years ago. The game can be played by marking boards out in the sand and using seashells as pieces. The boards available in the West are often beautifully carved, and smooth stones or beans are usually used for the pieces, thus making the game both visually appealing and wonderfully tactile.

Beginning to play

The Owari board comprises 12 cups arranged in two parallel rows, with an additional large cup at each end for each player to store captured stones. At the start of the game, four stones are placed in each of the cups on both sides of the board, leaving the large cups at each end empty (see diagram 36). Each player has control of the six cups on their side of the board and may not move any of the stones in the other player's cups, although they may add stones to them, as we shall see.

Moving

The first player starts the game by lifting all the stones from any one cup on their side of the board and, in a counter-clockwise direction, 'sowing' one stone in each successive cup, starting immediately to the right of the emptied cup and continuing into the opponent's territory, if necessary, until all the stones from that cup have been sown. The second player then does

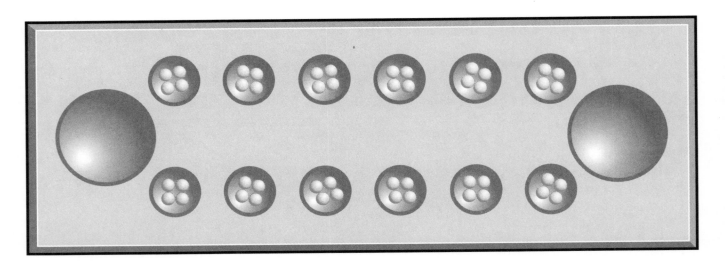

Diagram 36 Starting position for a game of Owari

the same, picking up all the stones from a cup on their side of the board and sowing the stones around the board. The players take it in turns to move until one of the players manages to place the last stone in a sowing sequence into a cup on the opponent's side of the board containing only one or two stones (ie two or three stones after the sowing has been completed). That player captures all the stones in that cup and places them in the cup to their right. If there are either two or three stones in the preceding cup, these are also captured, and so on with the cup before that. However, if there are less than two or more than three stones in a cup, these are not captured and that player's turn ends.

There are very few other rules, making Owari a very easy game to learn. First, if there are more than 11 stones in a cup, a whole circuit of the board will be carried out when these are sown. In that case the original cup from which the pieces are being sown remains empty and the player skips that cup and continues sowing around the board. Finally, it is not permissible to leave your opponent with no stones to sow on their side of the board; if it is possible to give them a stone to sow, you must do so. If this is not

possible and the opponent cannot move, all the remaining stones are captured by the first player. If both sides have stones left but no further captures are possible, the remaining stones are shared.

Strategy

The first thing that you will notice after a game or two is that it is very dangerous to leave cups with only one or two stones on your side of the board. If your opponent has a cup with the correct number of stones these will be captured. If you have a vulnerable cup you should either empty that cup to distribute the stones, empty another cup in such a way as to add a stone to it, thereby making it impregnable, or empty another cup in such a way as to cause the enemy cup to overshoot its target. By building up your right-hand cups it is sometimes possible to mount simultaneous attacks on your opponent's cups. However, if these cups become too full, they end up being sown into your own territory and are thus rendered harmless.

Winning the game

The winner is the player who has captured the most stones at the end of the game.

Chapter 3

DOMINO & DICE GAMES

Dice games were first played thousands of years ago in ancient cultures around the world, from the Aztec and Maya of South America, to South Sea Islanders and the Inuit. The origin of dominoes is less certain, but tiles dating back to AD 1120 have been found in China, and some people believe they were derived from dice. Dominoes appeared in Europe in the early years of the eighteenth century, when it became the favorite game of Italian courtiers. Of all tile games, only dominoes and China's national pastime, Mah-Jongg, are played to any great extent today. Mah-Jongg arrived in San Francisco from Shanghai early in the twentieth century, and was highly popular in the 1920s.

Dice are used mainly in gambling games. In the past they have been made from materials such as fruit stones, seeds, bone, ivory, glass, and metal. Today, dice are usually made from plastic and stamped with spots; each of the six faces is numbered with one to six spots. Most dice games use two to six dice. Their smallness makes them one of the most portable games, and they are widely used, from gambling casinos to family games around the kitchen table.

Dominoes were originally carved from exotic materials such as ivory and ebony, but today they are usually made from wood or plastic. Domino pieces may be called tiles, stones or, more commonly, bones. Each half tile is called an end; an end with no number is called a blank, and a tile with the same number at both ends is known as a doublet. The highest-ranking tile in the standard set of 28 is the six doublet, giving the set the name "double sixes." For most family games the double sixes set is suitable, but double nines (55 dominoes that go up to a nine doublet) or even double twelves (91 dominoes) can be purchased for games involving more than four players. By contrast, Mah-Jongg has no fewer than 144 tiles. As with dice, the tiles were once carved from ivory, but nowadays they are stamped with intricate designs ranging from Chinese characters and bamboo stalks to winds and dragons. By comparison with most domino and dice games, Mah-Jongg is highly complicated, and players are advised to become familiar with the design and the names of the pieces before commencing play. Many say Mah-Jongg takes an hour to learn but a lifetime to master!

DOMINO GAMES

Certain principles are common to all Domino games, which have much in common with card games. Before play commences, the bones are turned facedown and shuffled; each player also has the right to shuffle his bones separately.

Before beginning a game of Dominoes, it is advisable to give some thought as to where you are going to play. At a glance 28 bones may not look like much but they do take up a lot of space. Avoid a soft surface like a rug on the floor, and though a card table will suffice, a large kitchen or dining room table is better.

To start a game, each player draws the required number of bones at random from the pool. The bones are set out on edge so that the other players cannot see them, rather like holding a hand of cards. (Some people hold as many bones as possible in one hand, but few can manage more than five or six.)

Bones that remain facedown after the draw are known as the "boneyard." Players who cannot play from their hand must take a bone from the boneyard, much the same as drawing from the stockpile in card games.

A standard set of 28 bones is arranged in seven suits: 1s, 2s, 3s, 4s, 5s, 6s, and the blank. Each doublet belongs to one suit alone, while every other bone belongs to two suits. For example, the 5-2 belongs to both the 5 and 2 suit. When comparing the value of two bones, the one with the most spots is known as the heavier; the other is the lighter.

The basic rules of Dominoes are simple: players have to match the end of one of their bones with one end of the bones on the table. Depending on the game played, they either have to match suits (for example, playing a 1 from hand against a 1 on the table), or make matches that add up to a given number, such as 5. Play moves clockwise around the table as the chain, or layout, of bones grows. Traditionally, doubles are laid crosswise to the other bones. In most domino games a player must play any playable bone, or draw a new one from the boneyard.

There are two basic types of domino game: block games, where the sole aim is to get rid of your bones before your opponent; and point games, where you also score points at the same time. Both types of game are usually played up to a total of a specified number of points. The first to play all his bones declares 'Domino!', which means finished. If the game is blocked, which means no one can make another move, the other players add up the spots still in their hands. The winner is the one with the lowest, or lightest, total.

Initially, it might appear that Dominoes is a game of pure luck. With practice, however, it evolves into a game of strategy that demands finely honed logic.

BLOCK & DRAW DOMINOES

This is the basic game of Dominoes – the best way to learn the fundamental rules of play.

Players: two to five
Equipment: one set of double sixes (28 bones)
Difficulty: ideal for children; adults may play more strategically
Duration: half an hour upwards

Beginning to play

Turn all the bones facedown on the table and shuffle them. With two or three players, each takes seven dominoes; four or five players take five each. The player with the highest doublet begins, or "sets," laying the doublet face up on the table. Play moves to the player on the left, who adds a bone that matches it, at right angles to the doublet. The third player then plays a bone that matches one of the two open ends of the layout. Play continues clockwise round the table, each player in turn matching one of the two open ends of the layout.

In diagram 1, the highest doublet drawn, 5-5, was set vertically and 5-1 played against it. The third player had the option of either matching the 1 or the 5 on the other side of the doublet, and played a 5-3.

Diagram 1 Setting the bones

Rules of play

A player who cannot match either end of the layout must take bones from the boneyard until a match is drawn. If all the dominoes are drawn and there is still no match, the player must pass and wait for his next turn.

Winning the game

The first player to get rid of all his bones calls "Domino!" and wins the hand. Otherwise, the game continues until no player can make another move. This impasse is known as a blocked game.

Scoring

When a player calls "Domino!", the other players add up the spots on the dominoes still in their hands (blanks score zero) and this total is the winner's score. If the game is blocked and nobody can move, the players add up the spots on their dominoes and the player with the lowest total wins. The winner calculates his or her score by subtracting the total number of points in his or her hand from the number in each of the losers' hands, then adding the resulting totals together. So if one player has won a blocked game with a final total of 11, and the two other players have 13 and 15 respectively, the winner's score is 6. The first player to reach 100 wins the game (or 50 for a shorter game).

Strategic tips

Once you have mastered the basic rules, you can think about developing a strategy. In many hands there will be only one possible play, but if there is a choice of play, skill can be used. For example, if you hold four or more dominoes in one suit, try to leave both open ends in that suit because your opponents are less likely to have any. Then they will have to empty the boneyard – and when the game is closed you may gain a high score!

Dig in the boneyard early on in the game to supplement your hand, but as the game proceeds, do your best to offload your highest scoring dominoes, particularly if your hand appears weak after several plays, because otherwise they will mount up as penalty points to be added against you when someone else goes 'Domino!' If your hand seems strong, play to go out. When an opponent plays sets a doublet, aim to cover the doublet as soon as possible because the chances are that he has at least one other bone to play on it.

BLOCK DOMINOES

An easy version of Dominoes that is suitable for young children. It eliminates the draw (from the boneyard), the remaining bones being distributed after reshuffling.

The player with the highest doublet starts and the others follow in turn. Reshuffle the bones and divide them between the players. If there are two players, they take 13 each; three players take 8 and four players take 6. Any remaining dominoes are left out of play. Take turns to lay down bones until "Domino!" is called or the game is blocked. This is a game of pure luck, because chance decides whether the dominoes needed to unblock the game remain in the boneyard – or in the other players' hands.

CROSS DOMINOES

A game with more options than Block and Draw dominoes, and which has the added advantage of taking up less space.

The player with the highest doublet starts, then for the next four turns players have to match dominoes to form a cross. In diagram 2, a double 4 was set to start, then the next players laid down a 4-3, 4-6, 4-1 and 4-5 to create four open ends with 3, 6, 1 and 5 available for play. No other dominoes can be

***Diagram 2** Forming a cross to start the game*

played until the cross has been created. Play then continues as in Block and Draw Dominoes.

DOUBLE CROSS DOMINOES

This game is not – as its name might suggest – a game of double dealing and deception, but is instead a variation on Cross Dominoes.

This is played in the same way as Cross Dominoes, with the exception that a doublet must be played on one of the arms before play can continue on the four open ends. In diagram 3, a double 3 started the game, then 6-3, 1-3, 5-3, 3-2 were played. After that, a doublet has to be played on one end of the cross (players often have to draw from the boneyard for this), in this case a double 2, before play can continue as for Block and Draw Dominoes.

Diagram 3
Forming a double cross

MALTESE CROSS DOMINOES

Another variation, this time a tricky one, on Cross Dominoes.

After a doublet has been set to start, it must be matched by four dominoes, and then four doublets played at each arm of the cross before play

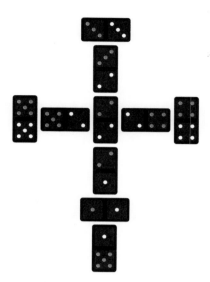

Diagram 4 *Forming a Maltese cross*

can proceed. In diagram 4, before the 1-5 could be played, doublets had to be placed at the ends of the cross. Often players have to dig deep into the boneyard to get the game going!

DOUBLE NINE CROSS DOMINOES

A family game requiring a set of double nines (55 dominoes).

With two to three players, seven dominoes are drawn; four or more players draw five each. The player with the highest doublet starts, then dominoes are matched to the two ends and two sides, as in Cross Dominoes. As play proceeds, every time a doublet is played two more ends are opened for play. In the game shown in diagram 5, the double 4 was played first, then dominoes were laid at the four sides of this doublet. After the double 9 was played, 9-1 followed it and players can lay down a domino on either side, such as 9-3 as illustrated.

CYPRUS

This game also uses a set of double nines and is a good game for four or more.

Once the dominoes have been shuffled, four players draw 13 each, five draw 11 each, six draw 9 each, seven draw 7, eight or nine draw 6, and ten draw 5 each. The player with the double 9

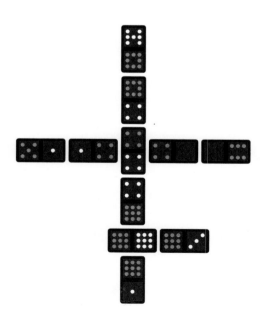

Diagram 5 *A game of Double Nine Cross Dominoes in progress*

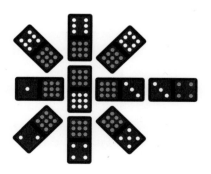

Diagram 6 *The eight-pointed star of Cyprus*

starts (if no one has drawn the double 9, the dominoes are reshuffled and drawn again). After the double 9 is played, the domino must be matched on both sides and ends to make a cross, and then diagonally to make an eight-pointed star. Play proceeds clockwise and when the star has been created then the ends of the nines already played can be matched. Play continues as for Block and Draw Dominoes.

ALL FIVES

The most popular form of Dominoes in the USA, this game is also known as the Five Game or Muggins. Players score not only by winning hands but also by scoring points during play.

Players: *two to four*
Equipment: *one set of double sixes (28 bones)*
Difficulty: *not as difficult as Five Up, but needs some arithmetical ability and keen observation*
Duration: *about half an hour*

Beginning to play

After the bones have been shuffled, each player draws five dominoes, whether it is a two-, three- or four-handed game. The player with the highest doublet begins, then play continues clockwise around the table, players drawing from the boneyard when they cannot match the ends with the same suit.

Rules of play

Whenever possible a player should try to make the open ends of the layout add up to 5, 10, 15, or 20. As is usual in Dominoes, doublets are laid crosswise and count their full value. For example, in diagram 7 Player 1 sets 5-5 and scores because the domino totals 10. Player 2 plays 5-0 and also scores because the total is still 10, the blank scoring 0 but the doublet still making 5+5. Player 1 then adds 5-3, and does not score because the total of the ends is now 3 (3+0).

Player 2 plays 0-3 and does not score because the total of spots on the ends is now 6 (3+3). Player 2 next adds a 3-3, but still does not score because this only totals 9 (3+3+3). Player 1 plays a 3-4, making 10 (3+3+4) and Player 2 adds a 3-6, also making 10 (4+6).

It is essential to keep your eyes on the game because if a player makes a multiple of 10 and does not declare it, any player can call "Muggins" as soon as the next play is made and score the points himself. Players may draw from the boneyard if they cannot play, but the last two bones in it are left unplayed.

Winning the game

The first player to go out by getting rid of all his bones calls "Domino!" otherwise the game may end when no one can make another move, in which case the player with the lightest hand wins.

Scoring

Players score the total value of each multiple of five made. For example, if one end of the layout is a 5 and a player lays another 5 on the other end, he scores 10, and so on.

After a hand is finished, players who still have bones each total up their spots and round the number to the nearest multiple of five (for example, downward for scores which end in 1 or 2, upward for scores with 3 or 4). The player who has called "Domino!" wins the opponents' adjusted points. In a blocked game, the player with the lightest hand wins and scores the difference between his spot total and that of his opponents – all scores rounded to the nearest multiple of five. The player who reaches 100 first is the winner. A cribbage board or single stroke scoring (see Five Up for description) is the best way of keeping the score.

Diagram 7 *A game of All Fives*

Strategic tips

It is difficult to score after one player has made a multiple of five because it is unlikely that the next player will have a bone that will turn the open ends into another multiple of five. Keep an eye out for the 6-1, 5-5, and 5-0, however, as they can help you score, as can the 0-0. As this is a points game, if you have a good hand do not try to finish too quickly but try to score as many points as possible to help you toward the all-decisive 100.

FIVE UP

Developed in San Francisco early in the twentieth century, this popular game demands skill and perseverance, plus the ability to add up quickly!

Players: *four, playing as partners*
Equipment: *one set of double sixes (28 bones)*
Difficulty: *easy to learn, but difficult to become proficient. Not suitable for young children, as scoring is complicated*
Duration: *about half an hour*

Beginning to play

After the tiles have been shuffled, the four players draw for partners, the two with the heaviest bones playing together. The player with the heaviest bone (the one with the highest total of spots, or, in the event of a tie, the highest number on one end) starts. Play then continues clockwise.

After the draw for partners the bones are reshuffled, each player drawing five bones. The game begins with the first player setting any bone. The next players then match ends to suits, but, as often as possible, make the open ends add up to five or multiples of five.

Rules of play

In the usual fashion of dominoes, doublets are always laid crosswise on the chain. When another bone is laid against a doublet on the other side,

the doublet becomes a spinner. This means that tiles can be played to either end, in effect, sprouting off the double to form a cross pattern – although each end can only be included in the score if a bone has been played to it. In diagram 8, the first player lays the 3-1, and the second player lays 1-1, making a total of five (see section on scoring, below) totaling the two ends $(3 + 1 + 1)$. The third player lays 1-2 and also scores five $(3 + 2)$. The fourth player lays 5-1 against the double and scores ten $(3 + 5 + 2)$. When 2-3 is laid, this totals 11 $(3 + 5 + 3)$, so the player does not score. Next, 6-2 is laid, so the total from all four ends is 17 $(6 + 3 + 5 + 3)$, and no score is recorded. From this point, as the spinner has had bones added to each crosswise end, four numbers must be included for each score, and each double added can become a spinner, opening more and more ends for scoring.

Players draw from the boneyard until a playable bone is found, although one bone is always left facedown. When this stage is reached, players who cannot play must pass. The hand is over when one player calls "Domino!" or when play is blocked.

Scoring

Each multiple of five scores 1; 10 counts as 2; 15 counts as 3; 20 counts as 4; and so on. Many players find it easiest to keep the score for this game on a cribbage board, or by recording a single stroke on a pad of paper for each 5 points.

If no one notices a score before the next player begins his turn, then no points are awarded, so all players are advised to be as observant as possible. However, if the opponents notice, they can say "Muggins" and score the other team's points.

Each team's points can be added together after each hand. The first player to declare 'Domino!' scores points for the tiles remaining in the opponents' hands. These points are scored just like the multiples of five above, but if the total ends in 1 or 2, they are rounded down to the nearest multiple of five (so 11 rounds down to 10 and two points are awarded). If the total ends in

3 or 4, it is rounded up (24 rounds up to 25 and five points are scored).

If play is blocked and no player can proceed, the team with the lowest combined number of points in hand wins and scores one point for every five spots left in the losers' hands. Play continues until one team has reached 61.

Strategic tips

Try to play bones that will force the opponents to draw from the boneyard, and try to go out first so that they will be left with a handful of bones. Hold onto tiles, known as kickers, which automatically score after an opponent scores – the double blank, and 5-5, for instance, as well as tiles that can be played off their own doubles to score (1-2, 2-4, 3-1, 4-3, 5-0, and 6-2). Try to play these to your best advantage.

Keep a close eye on the tiles being played to make sure that you are not left with an unplayable doublet after all the tiles in that suit

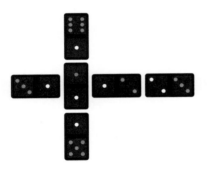

Diagram 8 A game of Five Up in progress

have been played. One way of making sure that play comes back to you is to play a doublet if you have tiles of a matching suit for the next go. As in Five Up, there are four playable faces on every doublet, so you will be able to play one of your bones.

Keep a constant check on the total of the open ends – this will let you know instantly which of your bones can score and helps you catch any scores that your opponents miss, which you can then claim for yourself.

VARIATION

In Five Up for two players, each player draws five tiles to begin. The game is usually played to 21, and two tiles must remain in the boneyard.

BERGEN

Sometimes referred to as 'the Bergen game', this is a point-scoring game that may have originated in either Norway or the Netherlands.

Players: two to four
Equipment: one set of double sixes (28 bones)
Difficulty: fairly easy
Duration: about half an hour

Starting to play

After the bones have been shuffled, if there are two players they draw six bones each; three or four players draw five each. The player with the lowest doublet sets.

Rules of play

If a player does not have a suitable bone, he can draw one (no more) from the boneyard. Two bones must always remain in the boneyard. Play is otherwise the same as in Block and Draw Dominoes, but points are given for leaving both ends open in the same suit (known as a double header), or leaving one open end in the same suit as a doublet on the other (a triple header). In diagram 9, Player 1 scores for his first play of 2-2, a doublet. Player 2 lays down 2-1 and does not score; nor does Player 1 who next lays 4-2. Player 2 then adds 1-4 and scores a double header, as there is a 4 at the other open end. Player 1 tops this by adding a doublet, a 4-4, and scores a triple header, having a doublet and an open end all of the same suit.

Scoring

Score 2 points for a doublet, 2 points for a double header, and 3 points for a triple header. A player calling "Domino!" scores 1 point. If the game is closed (no one can move) the player with no doublets wins 1 point or, alternatively, the player with the lightest doublet wins the game point. If no one has a doublet in their hand, the lightest hand wins 1 point. The first player to score 15 points wins.

Strategic tips

You should get into the habit of counting the number of occurrences of a suit in the layout. Each suit appears eight times at the ends of bones, so half of the available matching ends are used up at each doublet. Doublets are important and you should hold them as long as possible to get a valuable triple header.

Diagram 9 A two-handed game of Bergen

VARIATION

Because the total number of spots is not used for scoring, Bergen can be played by young children using picture dominoes. In the event of a blocked game, you can adjust the rules so that if, say, animal dominoes are used, the player with the doublet containing the smallest animal wins. If nobody has a doublet the player with the fewest number of dominoes wins.

MATADOR

This game of skill, which makes use of "wild" bones, is also known as Russian Dominoes or All Sevens.

Players: two to four
Equipment: one set of double sixes (28 bones)
Difficulty: strategic skill needed
Duration: about half an hour

Starting to play

First shuffle the bones. If there are two players, each draws seven dominoes; three or four players, each draws five. The player with the highest doublet sets, and play continues clockwise around the table.

Rules of the game

Matador differs in several ways from other domino games:

1. A player can draw from the boneyard even when he has a playable bone. However, if he cannot play a bone he must draw from the boneyard until he gets one, or until the boneyard is empty of all but two bones.

2. Players must match adjacent ends so that they add up to seven, rather than matching ends to suits. For example, an open end with a 6 calls for a 1; a 5 calls for a 2; a 4 calls for a 3 and so on.

3. Doublets are always laid end-to-end rather than crosswise. The bones that add up to 7 (3-4, 5-2, 6-1) and the double blank are known as

Diagram 10 Matadors

matadors (see diagram 10). They are played like wild cards or trumps – that is, a matador can be played at any time and is the only bone that can unblock an end which has been closed with a blank. In diagram 11, 3-2 has been set, and the next player must add a bone that totals 7, so a 4-4 is laid against the 3 (4 + 3), making the required 7. Several moves later, a 2-0 is played and the only way to continue playing against this bone is to add a matador, in this case 4-3.

Winning the game

As is usual in Domino games, either the first player to get rid of all his bones and call 'Domino!' wins, or the game cannot continue when it is blocked

Diagram 11 Making a Matador

Scoring

Making adjacent tiles add up to 7 does not score any points – it is the basic requirement of the game. Scoring is the same as in Block and Draw Dominoes: the player who calls 'Domino!' wins the total of all the spots left in opponents' hands. If the game is blocked, the player with the lightest hand wins and scores the difference between his spot total and each opponent's. The first to reach the agreed 50 or 100 points is the winner.

BLIND HUGHIE

This is a fast and fun game in which no one gets to see their hand before the start of play.

Players: *two to five*
Equipment: *one set of double sixes (28 bones)*
Difficulty: *great for kids because it's all luck and no strategy!*
Duration: *about half an hour*

Starting to play

The bones are shuffled facedown, then players draw to see who will play first, the heaviest bone winning. After reshuffling, all the bones are dealt equally between the players: 14 each to two players; 9 each to three players (the one left over is not played); 7 each to four players; 5 each to five players (three left over). The players do not look at their bones, but arrange them facedown in a vertical row. If there are leftover bones, one of them is played (with two or four players, the first player lays any bone), then

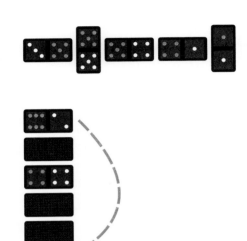

Diagram 12 Blind Hughie Dominoes

the first player turns over the top bone in his row and plays it if possible. If not, the bone is put facedown at the bottom of the row. If an unplayable doublet is turned up, this is put at the bottom of the row, but it remains faceup so that everyone can see it, as shown in diagram 12. The next player then takes his turn.

Winning the game

Play continues clockwise around the table, until either a player gets rid of all his bones and calls 'Domino!' or the game is blocked. In this case, the player with the lightest hand wins and scores the difference between his hand and each opponent's hand. The first to reach the agreed 50 or 100 wins.

MAH-JONGG

Mah-Jongg, which originated in China, is a fascinating and elaborate game. It is not, however, quite as difficult to learn as it may seem.

Players: *best with four; two or three can play but the game will not be as good*
Equipment: *144 Mah-Jongg tiles, two dice, four wind disks and counters for scoring, four racks for holding each player's tiles upright*

Difficulty: because of the exotic Chinese pieces, Mah-Jongg looks daunting, but the basic game can be learned in an hour
Duration: experienced players can play a hand in five minutes, but beginners should set aside an hour for a hand, an evening for a game

The tiles

Before you begin to play, it is a good idea to familiarize yourself with the 144 Mah-Jongg tiles. Basically, they are divided into three categories: 28 honor tiles, 108 suit tiles, and 8 optional flower tiles.

The honor tiles consist of four Green Dragons, four Red Dragons, four White Dragons, four North Winds, four East Winds, four South Winds and four West Winds.

The suit tiles consist of three different suits of 36 tiles. Each tile is numbered from 1 to 9, and there are four of each number. The three suits are Bamboos, Circles, and Characters. Bamboos are sometimes called Bams or Sticks, Circles are also called Dots or Balls, and Characters are also known as Cracks. Individual tiles are referred to as 1-Bamboo, 4-Circles, 7-Characters, and so on. The 1 and 9 of each suit (known as head tiles) are worth more than tiles 2–8 (known as middle tiles).

Some sets of Mah-Jongg come with eight optional Flower tiles (sometimes called Seasons), consisting of either four Seasons and four Flower tiles or eight of one type. These are essentially wild cards. Beginners are advised to learn the basic game before including these tiles in their play, and use of them will be discussed under Variations.

Apart from the tiles, a Mah-Jongg set includes four wind disks (marked N, S, E, W), which decide the seating arrangements of the players, two dice and counters (usually dyed bars and disks) that represent different points.

Aim of the game

There are no partners in Mah-Jongg – each player is on his own. The aim of the game is to collect 'sets' of tiles, of which there are three different kinds:

1. Chow: A sequence, or run, of three tiles in the same suit. For example, 2-3-4 Characters or 6-7-8 Circles. Only three tiles are allowed in a sequence.
2. Pung: Three of a kind, for example, three 4-Bamboos or three Green Dragons or three South Winds.
3. Kong: Four of a kind, for example, four 8-Characters or four White Dragons.

A player aims to collect four of these sets and a pair for a complete hand (also known as a 'woo'). Although any sets can help the player to go out, some carry higher points than others. For example, Chows are worth nothing in points, while Pungs consisting of middle tiles score only half as much as three of a kind with head tiles. (It is a good idea to keep the scoring system close to hand when you start to play, to help to remind you of which sets score most.)

Preparing for the game

Before you start to play there is a formal ritual that determines where each player sits around the table. However, beginners may find it easier to use this simplified method: each player throws the dice, and the highest score takes the East Wind disk. The player to the right becomes the South Wind. North Wind is on the left, while West sits opposite. The East Wind always starts.

Before play begins, each player should take counters to the value of 2000 points: two 500-point bones; nine 100-point bones; eight 10-point bones; and ten 2-point bones. In a game for beginners, remove the eight Flower tiles if they are present in the set, then turn the Mah-Jongg tiles facedown and shuffle them in the same way as for dominoes. At the same time each player should take a rack and position it in front of them.

Each of the four players picks 34 tiles, and without looking at them, stacks them facedown to make a wall that is 17 tiles long and two tiles deep. The four walls are then pushed together

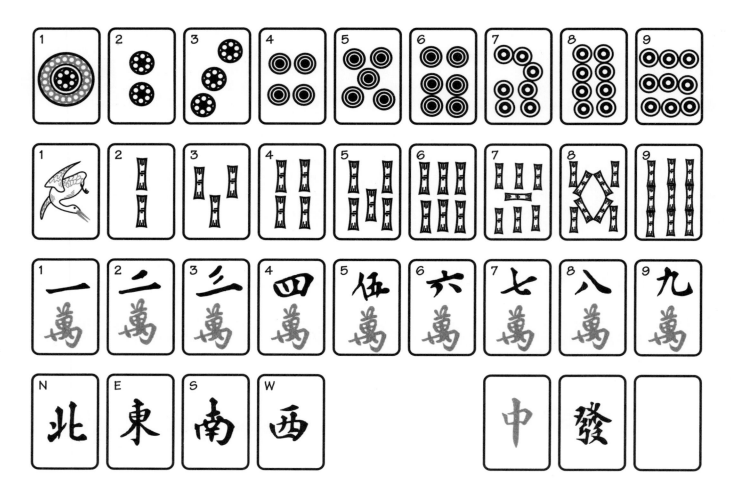

Diagram 13 Mah-Jongg tiles

with the help of the racks to form a hollow square in the middle of the table.

Beginning to play

Every Mah-Jongg game begins with the opening of the wall. East Wind throws the dice to decide which side of the wall is to be breached. This is arrived at by counting to the right and taking East Wind's wall as "one," South Wind's wall as "two," and so on, until the number shown on the dice is reached. The player designated by the end of the count throws the dice again and adds the total of this second throw to the total of the first throw. Starting at the right-hand corner of the wall, the player counts left the number of tiles indicated by this final total. For example, if East Wind's first throw was 4-1 (5) and the sec-

ond was 5-3 (8), the total is 13 (5 + 8). Starting at the right-hand corner of the chosen wall, the player counts 13 from right to left and removes the thirteenth pair of tiles from the wall and places them facedown on top of the wall to the right of the opening, as indicated in diagram 14. (These are known as loose tiles and when both have been taken, the next stack of two to the right of the break is set on the wall and become loose tiles.) If the total number from the two dice throws is more than 17, the player rounds the corner and opens the wall of the player on the left. At this point, traditionally, East Wind picks up the dice and places them in his rack, as they will not be needed until the next hand.

Now that the wall has been opened, the draw begins from the left side of the wall opening.

East Wind goes first, taking two pairs of tiles from the opening. Moving counterclockwise around the table, each player does the same, drawing four tiles at a time, until each player has drawn three times and has 12 tiles. Then players draw one more tile each, and East Wind draws one last tile. This means that by the end of the draw East Wind has 14 tiles and North, West and South have 13 tiles each. Players then arrange their tiles in suits and decide what kind of sets they will try to collect.

Rules of play

Players now try to collect a complete hand by drawing new tiles from the wall and discarding unusable ones into the hollow center. East Wind begins by discarding a tile faceup into the center, naming it while doing so: for example, "6-Circle." (All players should do this when they discard.)

Next South Wind may either take the discard or draw one from the wall, discarding a tile from hand. Play continues counterclockwise to West Wind and North Wind, each player either drawing from the wall, or picking up the last discard (none of the other discards are ever picked up), before discarding a tile.

The rules relating to the picking up of discards are as follows: a player may pick up the last discarded tile only if it can be used to make a Pung (three of a kind) or a Chow (a sequence). When the discard is picked up, it must be added to the relevant two other tiles in hand and the set immediately laid faceup on the table. The player now has an exposed hand (the set on the table) as well as a concealed hand. As the scoring system shows, sets in the concealed hand are worth more than sets in the exposed hand. After laying down a Pung or Chow, the player discards so that the number of tiles in both exposed and concealed hands still totals 13.

A player may Pung out of turn if a tile is discarded that completes three of a kind in their hand. The player simply calls : "Pung!" and takes the discarded tile. Furthermore, if a player picks

up a discard intending to Chow, and another player says "Pung!", the second player gets the tile even if the opponent has already picked up the tile. If the opponent has already revealed the tiles for the Chow, however, the tile in question can be kept.

Declaring a Kong, which is four of a kind, obeys different rules. A completed hand that

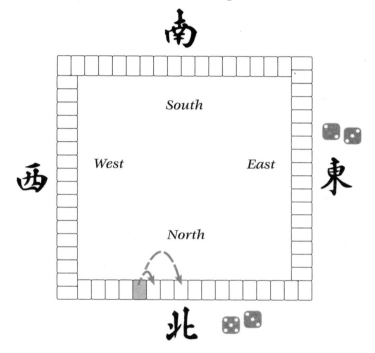

Diagram 14 *Opening the wall*

contains a Kong must contain extra tiles. (A completed hand with 1 Kong = 15 tiles; 2 Kongs = 16 tiles; 3 Kongs = 17 tiles.) To make sure that the correct number of tiles are maintained in hand a player making a Kong draws an extra tile from the loose tiles on top of the wall. For example, to convert a Pung into a Kong, a player can pick up the relevant discard and lay a Kong faceup on the table, then draw the first loose tile on the top of the wall before discarding a tile.

Another way to convert a Pung into a Kong occurs when a player draws a tile from the wall that matches an already exposed Pung. The player can simply add the single tile to the Pung, then draw a loose tile and discard another.

A player who has a Kong need not necessarily declare it. It can be saved and one of the four tiles can be used in a Chow (sequence). However, during any turn, a player must never declare a Kong after announcing a Chow or a Pung.

Winning the game

When a player has collected four sets and a pair, either by drawing the final necessary tile or by Punging or Chowing a discard from the table, they declare "Mah-Jongg!" and lay the concealed hand faceup by the exposed hand.

You can also declare "Mah-Jongg" by picking up a discarded tile. This can be done out-of-turn by any player who is one tile short of declaring "Mah-Jongg," even if the tile is to be used in a Chow or a Pung.

A player cannot discard after declaring "Mah-Jongg." Nor can a player complete a Kong and win, because a loose tile must always be drawn afterward. Furthermore, if a player declares a Kong by drawing a fourth tile to add to an exposed Pung, another player may steal the fourth tile (known as stealing the fourth, this move carries bonus points) and make Mah-Jongg.

If no one declares "Mah-Jongg," the game may be said to be a draw when the wall is reduced to the last 14 tiles. In this case, no scores count, the tiles are reshuffled and a new hand is played. The same player remains East Wind.

When each game is over, the East Wind disk and all the other Wind disks pass to the right. The tiles are turned facedown and shuffled before a new game begins. In Mah Jongg, several games, known as "rounds," are usually played until each player has had a turn as East Wind.

Scoring

The value of the winning hand is calculated first with the help of the scoring table, adding in any bonus points and doubling. Each other player pays this amount in counters to the winner. If East Wind wins, the other players always pay double. The values of the losers'

hands are then calculated and each player pays each other player who has a higher score than he does the difference between their scores.

Winning hands tend to average about 40 points, but bonuses can send scores rocketing, so a limit of 300 or 500 per hand is usually established before the game starts.

Scoring system

Exposed combinations
(completed from discards)	*points*
Three of a kind (middle tiles 2-8)	2
Three of a kind (head tiles 1 and 9)	4
Three of a kind any Winds	4
Three of a kind any Dragons	4
Four of a kind (middle tiles)	8
Four of a kind (head tiles)	16
Four of a kind any Winds	16
Four of a kind any Dragons	16
Pair of any Dragons or player's own Wind	2

Concealed combinations
(completed by drawing from the wall)	*points*
Three of a kind (middle tiles 2-8)	4
Three of a kind (head tiles 1 and 9)	8
Three of a kind any Winds	8
Three of a kind any Dragons	8
Four of a kind (middle tiles)	16
Four of a kind (head tiles)	32
Four of a kind any Winds	32
Four of a kind any Dragons	32
Pair of any Dragons or player's own Wind	2

Bonus scores
(for the winning hand only)	*points*
Mah-Jongg (for winning the hand)	20
Drawing winning tile (rather than discard)	2
Drawing winning loose tile	10*
No score other than Mah-Jongg	10
No Chow, concealed or exposed	10
Stealing fourth to win	10
Mah-Jongg on the last tile drawn	10

(* score this or the previous bonus, not both)

Double honor scores
(applies to all hands; calculated last)
Three or four of your own Wind, concealed or exposed: Double total score
Three or four Dragons, concealed or exposed: Double total score
Hand all one suit except for Dragons and Winds: Double total score
Hand all one suit: Double total score three times
Hand entirely honor tiles (Winds and Dragons, no suits): Double total score three times

Strategic tips

Make sure you maintain 13 tiles (plus one extra for each Kong) in your hand at all times, otherwise you cannot complete a Mah-Jongg and your hand will score zero. Try to assess both your chances of scoring high and your chances of making a Mah-Jongg at the beginning of the game. For example, if the original draw provides you with six or more single tiles, the chances are you won't declare Mah-Jongg. If the tiles that you draw do not improve, avoid Chows and go for high-scoring Pungs. Watch for combinations that can be completed in as many ways as possible: for example, a Chow that is open at both ends 3-4 or 6-7, rather than 8-9. Discard your least useful tiles, such as single suits and nines of a suit, because they can be difficult to combine in a run. Keep your eye on the discard pile, calculating which tiles are dead and which have yet to appear. Try to collect the pair that is necessary to complete your hand early on, because this is the most difficult part of the hand to complete.

VARIATIONS
Flowers and Seasons

The eight optional Flowers and Seasons tiles (two series of four tiles), are numbered 1 to 4, each series in a different colour. Each player has their own Flower and Season: East is 1, South is 2, West is 3, and North is 4. When a player draws a Flower or Season, it cannot be discarded and must be immediately declared and exposed, or laid face-up. The player then draws a tile from the dead portion of the wall to replace it. Each Flower or Season scores 4 points. If a player holds one of their own Flowers or Seasons, their total score is doubled; if they hold two, the total score is doubled twice. And should they be so lucky as to hold all four Flowers and Seasons of one colour, the total score is doubled three times!

Limit hands

When you gain more experience, you can incorporate the special limit hands listed on below. A player who has collected a group of them and declares 'Mah-Jongg!' gets the maximum points.

Limit hand scoring system

Hand from heaven: East picks up a complete Mah-Jongg in his or her 14 tiles at the beginning of the game and scores the limit (300).

Hand from earth: If any player other than East picks up a set hand of 13 tiles and pungs East's first discard for Mah-Jongg, this scores half the limit (150).

Lucky thirteen: If a player picks up a set hand and cannot complete it with the first discard, he or she can declare the set hand before making the first draw. Provided none of the original 13 tiles are discarded, this scores one-third of the limit (100) when the player finally draws or pungs the necessary tile.

Snake: 1 to 9 of a suit plus one of each of the Winds with any tile paired. All tiles but the last must be drawn from the wall. This scores the limit (300).

Thirteen hidden orphans: Thirteen single tiles concealed in the hand – each one of the four Winds, the three Dragons and one head tile from each suit – all drawn from the wall. Drawing one matching tile completes the hand, and it scores the limit (300). If that one tile is not drawn, the hand scores nothing.

Seven twins: Any seven pairs, making 14 tiles in all. The fourteenth can be drawn or punged, and the complete hand scores half the limit (150).

Three Great Scholars: A Pung or Kong of one of the Dragons (Red, White or Green), plus any Chow or Pung and a pair, scores the limit (300).

DICE GAMES

Dice have been used for thousands of years in gambling games. The commonest dice are cubes, but some cultures have used two-sided dice, while others have constructed five-sided and eight-sided dice for use in games of chance.

If war games and territorial games (see Chapter 2) reflect some of humanity's less appealing but ancient origins and instincts, dice games, it can fairly be said, have their origins in one of our most enduring preoccupations: is life random chance or divine will? For the roll of the dice was one of the earliest ways of divining or interpreting the will of the gods and of making major decisions. Even those who have never frequented a casino will be familiar with the phrase 'the die is cast'. The continuing appeal of dice games is simple and fundamental: with a quick roll we grapple with the future and try to outwit our fate. There is, too, of course the fact that they are cheap, and can easily be carried anywhere. Dice are also fun for children because the element of luck gives them an equal chance against adults.

The perfect dice used in casinos are as accurate to a true cube shape as possible, so that every time a die is thrown it will have an equal chance of falling on any one of its six faces. The dice for board games are not usually perfect cubes, but they are good enough to play family games. With numbered dice, the spots are always positioned so that the total of opposite sides adds up to seven: 1 is opposite 6; 2 is opposite 5; and 3 is opposite 4.

The skill in dice games lies in understanding the likelihood, or mathematical probability, of throwing a specific combination of numbers. The combinations of the six sides, as well as the number of dice in play, determine the mathematical probabilities. For example, with one six-sided die there is one chance in six that a specific side will fall uppermost; with two dice there are 36 possible combinations of numbers. To find the odds of a certain number or total appearing, work out the number of throws that will produce a desired combination and subtract it from the total possible combinations. With two dice there are six ways to throw a seven: 4-3, 3-4, 5-2, 2-5, 1-6, 6-1. So the odds against throwing a seven are 36 (total possible combinations of two dice) minus 6 (the number of ways to throw a seven with two dice) – that is, 30 to 6, or 5 to 1.

In most dice games, the dice are thrown from the hand or from a receptacle known as a dice cup. The spots that face upwards when the dice come to rest are the deciding spots that determine whether the player wins, loses, continues to throw, or has to pass the dice to the next player.

Some dice games use special dice. The six faces of poker dice are stamped with the playing card denominations of 9♠ or 9♣, 10♦, Jack, Queen, King, and Ace♠ or Ace♣.

CRAPS

Craps is the most popular dice game in the USA, thought to have been brought to New Orleans by French settlers. It is a casino gambling game that can easily be played at home, an offshoot of the British game Hazard.

Players: *from two to more than a dozen*
Equipment: *two dice, counters, and a backstop (optional)*
Difficulty: *a fast, fun game for the whole family*
Duration: *a few minutes to several hours*

Beginning to play

Players gather round the playing area: in casinos this is a table with a stenciled layout where bets can be placed; at home any level surface will do – some people like to set up a large book as a backstop for the dice to bounce against. The players then decide what the maximum bet will be. The first player (known as a shooter) announces the amount he will bet, puts the number of counters (or money) into the center, and in the language of Craps says, "I'll shoot three." This means the shooter has a bet of three counters to win. At this point other players have the option to fade, or bet against the shooter, by covering the bet and putting their money with the shooter's (in the pot or kitty).

One player can fade the whole bet or several can cover parts of it. Any part of the shooter's original stake that is not covered must be withdrawn (dragged down) before the dice are rolled and no more counters must be bet than are in the shooter's bet. No bets are written down and players need not bet each time. When the bet has been faded, the shooter shakes the dice and rolls them.

Rules of play

Although there are no official rules for Craps, it is generally accepted that no one can touch the dice after they have rolled to a standstill, until all those betting have seen them. If a die is cocked – that is, resting in such a way that it is doubtful which face is uppermost – the throw is then declared void.

If the first roll is 7 or 11 (a natural), the shooter wins; if it is 2, 3, or 12 (craps), the shooter loses. If it is 4, 5, 6, 8, 9, or 10, the shooter has a point to make. This means rolling the dice again and again until the same number is rolled. If the shooter throws a 7 before he makes a point, the bet is lost and the dice pass to the player on the left. The shooter can also voluntarily pass on the dice at any time between rolls.

Winning the game

When the shooter wins, he takes all the counters in the pot. If the shooter loses, those players who faded each take double the amount they put in the pot (their original bet plus the shooter's stake). If, for example, the shooter has bet three

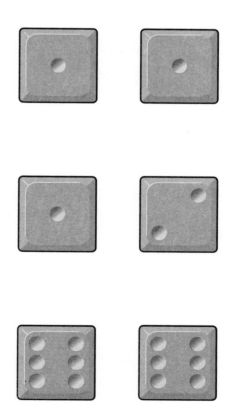

***Diagram 1** Three ways to crap out*

counters and two players have bet one counter and two counters respectively, the player who has bet one counter takes two counters, the player who bet two gets four.

In addition to the shooter's opening stake and faders' bets, players can also bet with the shooter or among themselves as to whether or not the shooter will win (come right) or lose (come wrong). For example, after rolling a point, a shooter might make a bet to come right (win) in the next series of rolls. If, for instance, the shooter rolls a point of 5, makes a come bet, then rolls an 11, this has no effect on the main bets in the pot – which can be settled only by a 5 or a 7 – but it wins the bet because 11 is a natural and the throw is functioning as a first roll.

Strategic tips

Craps is a game of chance, so there is little you can do to improve your skill, but it helps if you are aware of the odds of numbers being thrown. With two dice there are 36 possible combinations of numbers: the most common combination is 7 because there are six ways the dice can add up to that number, namely 1-6, 6-1, 2-5, 5-2, 3-4 and 4-3. This works to the shooter's advantage on the first throw, but against when shooting to make a point. Of the other combinations, the most uncommon are 2 and 12 because there is only one way to make each: 1-1 and 6-6. Similarly, there are two ways to make 3 and 11; three ways to make 4 and 10; five ways to make 6 and 8. When betting on making a point, it helps if you remember the following odds: 2 to 1 against making the point 4 or 10; 3 to 2 against making the point 5 or 9; 6 to 5 against making the point 6 or 8.

POKER DICE

Often played in restaurants or bars to see who will pay the bill, Poker Dice is Poker without the bluff!

Players: any number, but either two or five is best
Equipment: five poker dice, a dice cup, counters
Difficulty: it takes a while to become familiar with the poker hands, but thereafter it is straightforward
Duration: can range from just a few minutes to an hour or more

How to play

Players have three rolls of the dice, by the end of which each has to make the best possible poker hand (see scoring table below). The first player rolls all five dice, setting aside any that will be part of their eventual poker hand, then repeats this with the rest of the dice for a second and third roll. The first player then declares his hand – for example, 9-9-King-King-Ace is two pairs; 9-10-Jack-Queen-King is a straight. The dice and dice cup are then passed to the next player.

Hands (from low to high)

One pair	any two dice of the same number
Two pairs	
Threes	three of a kind
Straight	five in sequence
Flush	five same color
Full house	three of a kind and a pair
Fours	four of a kind
Fives	five of a kind

Table 1 Poker Dice scoring table

Winning the game

When all players have taken their turn, the highest hand wins. In the event of a tie, the players throw another round. If playing for counters, each player puts one or more counters in the pot (kitty) beforehand and the winner takes the pot.

Scoring

The best poker hand wins each round, or leg. Some games may be decided by the best of three or five legs.

Diagram 2 A full house at Poker Dice

INDIAN DICE

Poker Dice can be played with standard dice. This is known as Indian Dice, and is one of the most popular bar games in the USA.

In Indian Dice, the Ace or 1 is ranked high and play is the same as in Poker Dice, except that straights do not count. Sometimes players opt to play Deuces Wild (where the 2 counts as any number) or Aces Wild (where the 1 counts as any number). For example, if a throw is 4-4-1-2-3, the pair of 4s can be set aside and the three remaining dice thrown again. If the throw is then 1-4-5, and Aces are wild, the 4 and the Ace (which counts as a 4) can be set aside to achieve the high-ranking hand of four of a kind.

LIAR DICE

A popular gambling game in the army – but good for families if played fast and furiously.

Players: *best with two players, but more can play*
Equipment: *five dice (poker or regular dice), dice cup, counters*
Difficulty: *suitable for adults and older children*
Duration: *as long as you want*

How to play

In gambling clubs the two players are separated by a low screen so that opponents cannot see each other's dice. At home a book will be sufficient, or you can keep the dice covered under your hand or the dice cup. If standard dice are used instead of poker dice, the 1 or Ace is high; 6, 5, 4, 3 and 3 represent King, Queen, Jack, 10, and 9, respectively.

Each player starts with 10 counters. One die is rolled to determine who starts, the highest throw winning. Each player puts a counter into the pot. The first player shakes the five dice in the dice cup, then turns the dice cup upside down. Carefully peeking at the dice under the cup, the player selects the ones to keep and hides them under his hand. The player then has the option of continuing for a further two throws – by which time he must select a final hand to declare in full, saying for example "Full House – three Kings and two 9s."

However, the player is not required to tell the truth, but can understate or exaggerate the hand. The next player can either accept the hand as it is or lift the dice cup. If the first player was bluffing, he has to put a counter into the pot. If he was being truthful and the hand was as declared, or better, the other player puts a counter in the pot.

Should the next player accept the first player's call, then the dice pass to them and they have three rolls to improve on the hand – or to bluff the player to the left. Play continues in this way until only one person – the most successful liar – has a counter left and wins the game.

VARIATION

Each player takes three counters, or lives. The first player shakes the dice, upturns the dice cup and views the contents, taking care that the others do not see. The player then declares the hand, or bluffs. The next player must either accept the call or declare the first player a liar.

If the first player's hand is doubted and the hand is at least as good as declared, then the doubter puts one counter into the pot. If the shooter has lied about the value of the hand, he pays the doubter one counter and puts one in the pot. It is then the doubter's turn to play against the player to the left.

If the first player's declaration is accepted, then the next player has to better the hand, throwing all the dice or only some of them. The second player must declare a higher hand than the first. The first player then either accepts or declines this call – and so the game continues between the two until one has doubted a hand that the other has thrown or bettered. The doubter puts a counter into the pot.

A player who has lost all three counters drops out of the game. The others continue until only one player has one or more counters and, as winner, takes the pot.

YACHT

This game is similar to the Puerto Rican game General and is sold commercially as Yahtzee®.

Players: *two to ten; best for five or six. One can play solo, trying to reach a personal best.*
Equipment: *five dice, dice cup, pen and paper*
Difficulty: *suitable for adults and children over eight*
Duration: *about half an hour*

How to play

There are 12 rounds in the game. To start, all players roll a single die to determine the order of play. The first player then rolls the five dice from the cup, sets aside any dice to keep, and throws for a second and third time. Each player decides which category on the scorepad he will try for. A player may change his mind during the three throws, but at the end of a turn must assign a category. If a player throws the maximum score on the first throw, his turn ends and the dice cup is passed to the left.

The numerical categories simply mean throwing as many of the number as possible within three throws. A Little Straight is 1-2-3-4-5 and a Big Straight is 2-3-4-5-6. A Full House is three dice of one number, and two (a pair) of another: for example, 5-5-5-2-2. Four of a kind is four of one number. A Choice Hand is the highest score the player can throw in three turns. A Yacht is five of a kind.

Scoring

Before the game starts, copy the Yacht scoresheet or buy a Yahtzee® scorepad from a games store. The score in brackets after each category on the scoresheet is the maximum total score. After three throws each player adds together the numbers on the dice that have fulfilled the chosen category. For example, if trying for 4s, and after the third throw a player has 4, 4, 4, 1, 5, adding together the 4s produces a score of 12. No addition is necessary for a Little Straight or a Big Straight, which both score 30. For the Full House category, add up all the numbers – for example, 3-3-3-6-6 scores 21; the same applies to Four of a Kind – for example 5-5-5-5-2 scores 22. Add all five dice together for a Choice Hand, whatever the numbers are. Yacht always scores 50 points no matter what the numbers are.

Having scored for each of the 12 categories, players add up their scores. The highest total wins.

Hand	Maximum Points	A	B	C	D	E
Yacht	50					
Big straight	30					
Little straight	30					
Four of a kind	29					
Full House	28					
Choice	30					
Sixes	30					
Fives	25					
Fours	20					
Threes	15					
Twos	10					
Ones	5					

Table 2 The Yacht scoresheet

GENERAL

In Puerto Rico, General is played for drinks at the bar as well as for money.

In General there are only ten categories to be filled in and certain categories – General, Four of a kind and Full House – score extra points if the player fills them in one go. A Big General – five of a kind made in one go – automatically wins the game. Five of a kind made on the second or third throw scores 60 points. Four of a kind is worth 45 on the first throw and 30 on the second or third throw. A Full House is worth 35 on the first throw and 30 on the second or third throw. A straight (note that there is no Big or Little straight as in Yacht) scores 25 if made on the first throw, and 20 on the second or third throw. If General is played, players should decide the value of a point before they start playing. The person with the highest score wins the difference between his score and each of the losers.

	Points scored	
Hand	*1st throw*	*2nd or 3rd throw*
Big General	Win game	—
Small General	—	60
Four of a kind	45	30
Full House	35	30
Straight	25	20
Ones to Sixes	Scored on total spot value	

Table 3 The General scoresheet

SHUT THE BOX

This game is also known as Round Dozen because players have to close exactly "12 boxes."

Players: *two or more*
Equipment: *two dice, paper, pencil, and 12 counters for each player*

Difficulty: *a good family game*
Duration: *about an hour*

How to play

Each player draws 12 boxes on a piece of paper and places it on the table with the 12 counters

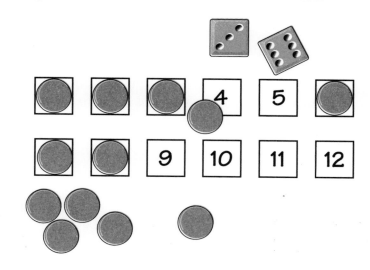

Diagram 3 A game of Shut the Box

nearby. Each player aims to cover as many of the boxes as possible. The first player throws both dice, adds the total value and then decides which boxes to close by placing a counter over them. For example, by throwing a 9, boxes 6 and 3, or 5 and 4, or 7 and 2, or 8 and 1 can be closed. The player throws again and closes more boxes, and continues throwing until there are no more combinations available. After closing boxes 7, 8, 9, 10, 11 and 12, only one die can be thrown. Play then continues clockwise round the table and the player who has either closed all the boxes or who has the lowest number of open boxes left wins. Players can play as many rounds as they choose.

PIG

This game can be played almost anywhere because it requires the minimum of equipment. The player who throws first usually has the advantage.

Players: two to any number
Equipment: one die, pencil and paper
Difficulty: all ages; a fun game for holidays
Duration: about half an hour

How to play

Each player first throws the die to decide the order of play, the lowest score going first, the next lowest second, and so on. The first player throws the die as many times as he wishes, adding up the numbers on the top face of the die. An Ace immediately cancels out the total score made for that turn, and the die passes to the next player. The die can be passed on at any time, in which case (so long as an Ace has not been thrown), the player can claim the score thrown on that turn.

Scoring

The player who first makes 100 wins. Because this game gives an advantage to the first person to throw, the rules can be adapted to allow all players to have a turn. When a player reaches 100, those players who have not yet had the chance to throw in that round are allowed to throw, and if any of them go over 100, then the highest score wins. This does not make the game any fairer, because now the last player has the advantage. The last player knows what scores have been made and with nothing to lose can continue throwing (unless an Ace is thrown) until the score betters all the others. But this method does at least give everyone a go!

ACES IN THE POT

In this game players' fortunes rise and fall quickly. Anyone can win, right up to the last throw!

Players: two to any number
Equipment: two dice, one dice cup and counters
Difficulty: no strategy, all luck
Duration: about half an hour

How to play

Each player takes two counters. Players take it in turn to throw one die. The highest number starts, then play moves clockwise round the table, each player taking it in turn to throw the dice. Any player who throws an ace puts one counter in the kitty, known as the pot, in the center of the table. If two aces are thrown, both counters go in the pot – hence the name Aces in the Pot. If a player throws a 6, he gives a counter to the player on their left. If a player throws two 6s, both counters are given to the player on the left. All other throws do not count.

Only players who have counters may continue to throw the dice; all other players are out until the next round. When the dice come to the last player to hold a counter, the dice are thrown three times. If there is no 6 in those three throws, the player wins the pot. However, if a 6 is thrown, the last counter and the dice are passed to the player on the left. The first player to throw the dice three times without throwing a 6 wins the pot.

Each player is given two counters for the next round and the person to the left of the first player in the last round starts.

HEARTS DUE

A straightforward roll 'em and count 'em game that all the family can play.

Players: two to any number
Equipment: six dice, paper, and pencil for scoring
Difficulty: no strategy, all luck
Duration: about half an hour

How to play

Originally this game was played with six special dice, each one having the letters H E A R T S inscribed on its six faces instead of spots. However, regular dice can be used: 1 = H, 2 = E, 3 = A, 4 = R, 5 = T and 6 = S. The players first roll a die to see who will start; the lowest number goes first.

Players take it in turns to roll the die once per player and score (see table 4). When doubles or triples of the same number are thrown, then only one number can count in the score. If three ones are thrown then the player loses his entire score and must start again from zeros! The first player to make 150 points wins the game.

	Points scored
H (1)	5
H-E (1-2)	10
H-E-A (1-2-3)	15
H-E-A-R (1-2-3-4)	20
H-E-A-R-T (1-2-3-4-5)	25
H-E-A-R-T-S (1-2-3-4-5-6)	30

Table 4 Scoring table for Hearts

HELP YOUR NEIGHBOR

In this fast, fun and extremely old, game you can win or lose a fortune in counters within an hour!

Players: *two to six*
Equipment: *three dice, a dice cup, 10 counters per player*
Difficulty: *no strategy, all luck*
Duration: *one hour*

How to play

Each player has 10 counters. If six are playing, each person chooses a number from 1 to 6. The first player is 1, the next 2, and so on. If there are five players, the 6 is not in play and is ignored when it comes up in a throw. With four players, both the 5 and 6 are ignored; with three players, each takes two numbers; with two players, each takes three numbers.

Each player throws the three dice in turn, play moving clockwise round the table. When a player's number comes up, they must put a counter

in the pot, one for each number. For example, if a player throws 4-2-2, the number four player puts in one counter and the number two player puts in two counters. The first player to run out of counters wins the round. The next round begins with the number two player.

DROP DEAD

Similar to Yacht but far simpler, this is a good game for families who have a few minutes to spare, rather than a whole evening.

Players: *any number*
Equipment: *five dice and a dice cup*
Difficulty: *no strategy, all luck*
Duration: *varies according to how many rounds are played*

How to play

Each player rolls one die to determine who will start, the one with the lowest number going first. Then each player in turn rolls the five dice and adds up the numbers. If there is a 2 or a 5, the score is nothing, and each die with a 2 or a 5 on it is taken out of the throw, being effectively dead. The remaining dice are rolled again and the player continues to throw until all the dice are dead. The player keeps a running total of the score gained from throws that did not contain the fatal 2 or 5. The dice then pass to the player on the left.

For example, if the first throw yields 2-3-3-4-6, there is no score because of the 2, and this die is eliminated. The other four dice are rolled again, and this second throw produces 1-3-4-6, scoring 14. All four dice go back in the dice cup. The third throw yields 1-5-5-5, no score and only one dice can be thrown. This produces a 2, so the player has to pass the dice cup to the next player. The score for the turn is 14.

The player with the highest score after one round wins, or the length of the game can be extended by playing three or five rounds.

Chapter 4

FAMILY GAMES

All over the world, and all through the ages, games have been an important feature of family life. Playing games is considered by many people to be a vital part of a child's development, and an excellent means of communication with adults, especially parents. Some of the games described here are for children to play by themselves, in the school playground or at parties. Others are best for family entertainment – recent studies have shown that adult involvement increases a child's concentration and the capacity to play imaginatively and creatively.

Many of the family games played today have a very long history, originating hundreds, or even thousands, of years ago. In ancient Greece, Pollux wrote about the children's game of Blind Man's Buff, calling it "The Brazen Fly." According to his writings, the person whose eyes were covered with a bandage shouted out "I shall chase the brazen fly." The other player replied "You may chase him, but you won't catch him," and they hit the "blindman" with whips made from papyrus husks until one of them was caught. Pollux also wrote about Hide and Seek, referring to the game as "Apodidraskinda."

Markings of a game that looks very similar to Tic-Tac-Toe have been found at ancient Roman archaeological sites. This simple mathematical game, which can be played with pencil and paper or simply scratched out on the ground, was an early version of the board game Nine Men's Morris. The three-dimensional version of Tic-Tac-Toe may well have been the inspiration for the modern Rubik's Cube.

Family games were at their most popular in the eighteenth and nineteenth centuries, before there was radio and television for entertainment. Their appeal has not been completely diminished, however, because many of today's popular television game shows are derived from traditional games. Password, for instance, was based on Twenty Questions in reverse: given a word, a teammate coached his fellow player backwards, arriving at, say, chicken, by a string of ever more delimiting clues.

PARLOR GAMES

Although few people nowadays may claim to have a room called a parlor, the term "parlor games" is still used to describe a whole range of indoor games that can entertain children and adults alike.

Nowadays parlor games are played mainly at children's parties, but in the past they were popular entertainment for the whole family. Samuel Pepys, the English diarist, records that on 26 December 1664 he went to bed leaving his wife and household "to their sport and blind man's buff, which they did not leave off until four in the morning..." Under its various names, Blind Man's Buff is probably more often mentioned in English literature than any other informal game, and in one form or another is part of the social history of many parts of the world. It is one of a family of blindfold games that also includes Squeak Piggy Squeak and Pin the Tail on the Donkey.

Hunting games have also been popular, and there is a great variety of games of this type. In some, players hunt for hidden objects, while in others, the seeker hunts for the other players and the game is often played in the dark – Sardines and Murder in the Dark are popular examples. Children find the suspense of such games highly exciting. Adults may also find them exciting, although for a different reason, as when played in adult company, the games often become a subterfuge for romantic liaisons and general misbehavior.

Luck is the major component of blindfold and hunting games, as it is with gambling and guessing games such as Scissors, Paper, and Stone, and Spoof, although the latter is also a good test of psychology and the ability to calculate probabilities. Other games require a degree of ingenuity or dexterity in order to outwit the opponents. Grandmother's footsteps falls into this category, as do games in which teams of players race to pass objects to each other in different ways. In Apple Ducking, the Matchbox Race, and Pass the Orange, the contestants need to strike a balance between speed and skill in order to be successful. Buzz and Buzz-Fizz rely on concentration.

To play acting games well, you need a lively imagination and a little acting ability. Dumb Crambo, much played in the nineteenth century, was the forerunner of games such as Charades, The Game, and In the Manner of the Word. In acting games one team, or a member of the team, mimes a word for the other team to guess. Amusement derives not only from the players' acting attempts, but also from the often bizarre guesses made by the other team.

Games like Charades remain as popular with adults as with children, and there are various 'revelation' games – such as I Have Never and Likes and Dislikes – that are suitable only for adults as after-dinner entertainment.

APPLE DUCKING

This game has been played for centuries – you can see it in many paintings of medieval life. Apple Ducking is still great fun today, for young and old alike. Play it in the kitchen, if you have enough space, or play outside.

Players: from two upward, depending on the size of the tub
Equipment: a large tub of water and some apples
Difficulty: harder than you would think, especially if the aim is to stay dry; children love it, but adults can enjoy the game too
Duration: a one-off game can last half an hour, but players often want to go back for another bout

Beginning to play

Place a tub of water – an old-fashioned zinc bath is ideal, or a rain barrel from the yard will do just as well – in the center of a large space. If your bathroom is large enough, you could always use the bathtub. (A word of warning if you play in the living room: it's as well to cover the surrounding area with something that will protect your carpet from splashes.) Drop some apples into the water – preferably as many apples as there are people taking part – and ask the players to gather around.

Playing the game

The most fun, and the maximum mayhem, comes when everyone plays at the same time. You might prefer, though, to let players take turns individually. The aim is to get as many apples out of the water as you can without using your hands or elbows: this means that you can use only your head and mouth – and teeth, of course. Getting hold of even a single apple is much easier said than done, though large mouths and sharp teeth are distinct advantages. The winner can either be the first person to get

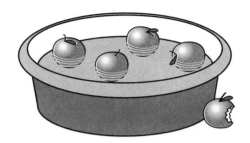

Diagram 1 A game of Apple Ducking

an apple out of the tub, the person who gets the most apples out in a set time, or – if you are taking individual turns – the person who gets an apple out faster than everyone else.

BEETLE

A good way to keep children occupied for hours on a rainy afternoon.

Players: two to eight
Equipment: one die, a sheet of paper and pencil for each player
Difficulty: all luck; children from five upward will enjoy this game
Duration: about half an hour

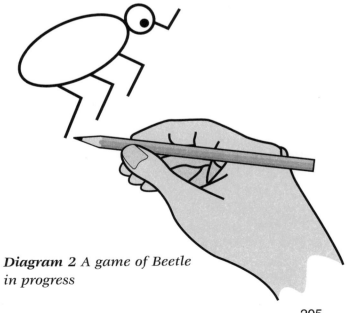

Diagram 2 A game of Beetle in progress

How to play

The parts of a beetle are numbered to correspond with the numbers on the dice. Players take turns to roll the dice until they get the right numbers to draw the insect's 13 parts. A completed beetle must have a body, a head, a tail, two eyes, two feelers, and six legs.

Each player must throw a one to start, which entitles them to draw the beetle's body, as in diagram 2. A player who doesn't throw a 1 must pass the dice and throw again on their next turn – and possibly several turns after that. After the player has thrown a one, his or her task becomes easier. The dice can now be thrown for parts that connect with the body: a 2 for the head; a 3 for a leg; a 5 for the tail. Until the head is drawn, eyes and feelers cannot be added. The first player to complete a beetle shouts "Beetle!" and wins the game.

MATCHBOX RACE

One of the simplest – and silliest – games that there is, Matchbox Race is a standby of children's parties. But it is not only children who enjoy this game, because it has been used to break the ice at many an adult party, too.

Players: six or more
Equipment: the sleeves of two matchboxes
Difficulty: much harder than it would appear, though children have an advantage because they have smaller noses
Duration: unlikely to last for more than 15 minutes

Beginning to play

Divide the players into two teams and ask each team to stand in line one behind the other, with the players clasping their hands behind their backs. (Depending on the age of the players, and whether they would giggle or be embarrassed, it is worth considering alternating men and women along each line.)

Playing the game

The first person in each line puts a matchbox cover on their nose, and, on the call of "start," passes it down to the next player along the line, using only noses – and so on, to the end of the line. If any player drops the matchbox, it is returned to the first person in the line and the process starts all over again. The first team to get the cover to the end of the line wins.

Horse or currant bun?

Some people think the entire human race can be divided into two groups according to what type of nose an individual has: according to the theory, we are all either "horse" or "currant bun." Placing your friends (and enemies) in the appropriate category is a game in its own right, but debating which player fits into which type can add considerable spice to a matchbox race – especially because a succession of "horses" plunging their noses into a matchbox can make it hard for a "currant bun" to get much of a grip.

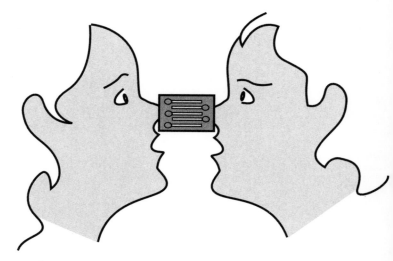

Diagram 3 A Matchbox Race

PASS THE ORANGE

Oranges are something of a tradition at Christmas, so it is not surprising that this game has always been a part of the Christmas festivities. For earlier generations, a variant of Pass the Orange was traditional at teenagers' parties.

Players: *ideally, six or more on either side*
Equipment: *two oranges*
Difficulty: *this game is far from easy, but it is the ludicrous contortions needed that make it fun, rather than success itself; it is suitable for both children and adults*
Duration: *about half an hour*

Beginning to play

Divide the players into two teams, and ask them to sit in lines, with each player side by side; the teams should face each other across the floor. The first player in each team is then given an orange.

Playing the game

At a signal, the first player on each team puts the orange between his or her feet and, using only feet, passes it on to the next player. The orange is passed down to the end of the line in the same way, and then returned back up the line to the first player. Any player that drops the orange must pick it up again – no matter where it has rolled – using feet alone. Any orange that has been dropped has to be returned to the first player in the team, and the process repeated – if this means that players have to shuffle around the room on their bottoms, so be it. The first team to get the orange from one end of the line to the other and back again wins.

VARIATION

In another version of this game, the players hold the orange not between their feet, but between

Diagram 4 Passing the orange between chin and neck

their chin and their neck, again, passing it without the use of hands. This version can be quite uncomfortable – in both senses of the word – but used to be very popular at teenage dances, many years ago.

WINKING

Winking has weird and sometimes frightening connotations in some cultures. Perhaps this is why this game – though thoroughly domesticated – can still be surprisingly tense and has deliciously scary overtones.

Players: *four or more*
Equipment: *a pack of playing cards*
Difficulty: *with practice, this game can become surprisingly complex; it might be scary for children under seven*
Duration: *about an hour, with a number of adult players*

Beginning to play

Select cards from the pack to the same number as there are players – one card must be the Ace of Spades, but the others can be random. Lay the cards down on a table, with the players sitting around it, and ask each player to pick a card, keeping its identity secret. The person who draws the Ace of Spades is "the murderer," but whoever it is must keep their identity secret.

Playing the game

"The murder" is committed by catching the eye of another player and shooting a deadly wink in his or her direction. The victim waits a few seconds so as not to give the game away before slumping over dead. Any other player who spots the wink can reveal the identity of the murderer and a new game can begin.

Strategic tips

On one hand, players try to avoid eye contact with each other because they do not want to become victims, but on the other hand they want to catch the murderer before they become a victim themselves. Staring fixedly at the table will get you nowhere – you will just become the last victim – but trying to wink at everyone at the table at the same time, if you are the murderer, rarely works. Winking is best played by friends who know each other reasonably well, because then they can try to second-guess the strategies and reactions of the others.

Diagram 5 Winking

DUMB CRAMBO

The forerunner to Charades and The Game, Dumb Crambo was an extremely popular parlor game in the nineteenth century, in the days before people had television for entertainment. It is extremely simple, but its very simplicity gives it a rumbustious charm.

Players: six or more
Equipment: none
Difficulty: fairly easy, but the charm of the game lies not in winning but in the pure pleasure of acting, which both adults and children can enjoy
Duration: an hour, on average

Beginning to play

As with The Game and Charades, the players are divided into two teams. One team leaves the room while the other team thinks of a word – usually, but not necessarily, a verb. When the players in the first team are summoned back to the room, they are not told the actual word that has been chosen, but a word that rhymes with it. For example, if the word chosen was "bite," the word given to the opposing team could be "night." This is the only point in the game when the teams actually speak to each other – hence the name Dumb Crambo.

Playing the game

The opposing team is allowed to leave the room for a few minutes to consult, and has to decide on three words that rhyme with "night." The team then returns to the room and mimes the first of their three words: for example, they might mime "fight." Since, in our example, this is incorrect, the members of the first team then boo, hiss, and stamp their feet, and generally express their complete disdain and disgust.

The opponents might then mime "light" – someone might act out lighting a cigarette, for example, or another member of the team might pretend to flick a light switch – to more boos and hisses from the other team. Then they might try "bite," with one person miming a dog that bites the others. Huge applause then comes from the the other team. You only have three guesses at the word, and then the teams swap roles, the spectators becoming the actors, and the ex-actors – trying to think of some really difficult word for the opposing team – become the rumbustious spectators. Remember that not a word must be uttered, apart from the one and only rhyming clue that is given at the start. Even so, the whole point of the game is to make as much noise as possible, and to exaggerate responses to a ridiculous extent.

THE GAME

Many games players have no doubt that this is the best game in existence. There may be room for argument about this claim, but the only way to see whether it is true is to play The Game yourself.

Players: *a minimum of four*
Equipment: *pencil and paper*
Difficulty: *can be tailored for both adults and children*
Duration: *anything from half an hour to a whole evening*

Beginning to play

First the players divide themselves into two teams. Then comes the question of which version of The Game to play: the first version is the more relaxed of the two – almost a spectator sport – with only one person in the spotlight at a time; the second version requires everyone to participate at the same time, and is usually chaotic and noisy – but all the better for that.

A single protagonist

In this version, the two teams each compile a list

of phrases in secret: they can be titles of books, films, songs, proverbs, or whatever the players can think up – the number of phrases chosen should equal the number of players in the opposing team. Team One then gives the first player from the second team one of the phrases that has been chosen, and that player has to act out the phrase to his or her teammates, without using words. The teammates have to guess the answer, while the members of Team One look on and, at least as a rule, snicker. When the phrase has been identified – or the second team has given up, as the case may be – the round is over. The teams reverse roles and the second team takes its turn at trying to outwit the players of the first team. And so the game goes on until both lists are finished. The advantage of this version is that the lists can be tailored so that they bring out the best, or the worst, in individual members of the opposing team. There is a danger that doing this can bring an element of cruelty to the game, but this need not be the case.

A joint effort

In the second version, players compete in two teams and a quizmaster is elected who belongs to neither team. The quizmaster compiles the list of phrases, and gives the first phrase to one player from each team at the same time. The players then return to their respective teammates and attempt to act it out. The first person to guess the phrase correctly dashes to the quizmaster to get the next phrase, and so on – until all the phrases have been acted out. The winning team is the one that reaches the end of the list first.

The problem with this version is that there is ample opportunity to cheat, either by watching the other team acting, or by listening to their guesses. But the likelihood is that the players will be too absorbed to do this, because as it is essentially a race, the pressure is on to perform quickly and appropriately. Nevertheless, the quizmaster should keep an eye on events to ensure fair play. This version is very exciting and things become very noisy, as members of both teams shout, cajole, abuse, and mock the actors.

Playing conventions

Whichever version of The Game you play, it is important to know the conventions that are used. These indicate whether the phrase about to be acted is a movie title, a book title, a television program, or whatever. They take the form of sign language: opening your palms, for example, signifies a book; drawing the rough shape of an arch with your fingers indicates a play; pulling sound from your open mouth means a musical or an opera; drawing quotation marks in the air says that the phrase is a proverb; drawing a square in the air signifies a television program; and winding an old-fashioned movie camera indicates a movie title.

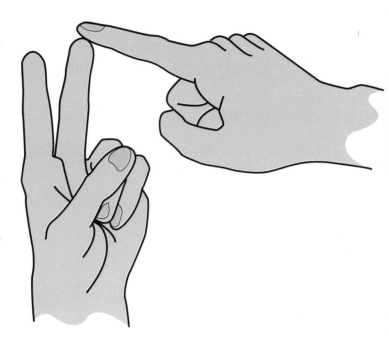

Diagram 7 *Indicating the second finger means that you are acting the second word*

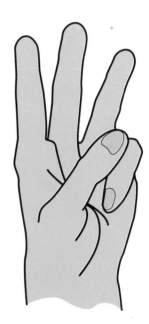

Diagram 6 *Holding three fingers in the air signifies that the phrase contains three words*

By holding the appropriate number of fingers in the air, you tell the others how many words a phrase contains. To indicate which of the words you are acting at any point, you indicate the relevant finger.

To indicate how many syllables there are in the word, you lay the corresponding number of fingers across your forearm. If the word or syllable rhymes with something easier to act – you pull your ear lobe. Small words such as "in," "of" and "but" are indicated by holding your thumb and forefinger up slightly apart. And if you are brave enough to act the whole phrase out in one go, you draw a circle in the air with both hands. Your teammates are allowed to shout out questions but you can only nod or shake your head in response.

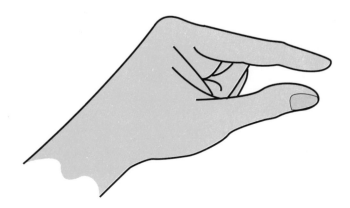

Diagram 8 *Indicating a small word*

There must be no talking, whispering, or even mouthing between the actor and the team.

An example

If you are going to act out *To Kill A Mockingbird*, the title of a book by Harper Lee, you start by opening your palms to indicate a book. Then you put up four fingers to indicate the number of words. Next, indicate your first finger to show that you are acting the first word, and hold up your thumb and forefinger slightly apart to show that it is a small word. If you could not think how to act out "kill," you could pull your ear lobe and act out "pill" or "hill." Again, with "a" you would show that it is a small word. "Mockingbird" could be split into "mocking" (rhymes with "stocking," "rocking," or even "locking") and "bird."

Hints for successful play

There is no fun in The Game if you choose a phrase that is too easy to act out. But if you are feeling unkind, it is not difficult to come up with some real horrors. In such uncharitable moments, try these: *Persuasion*, by Jane Austen; *Oscar and Lucinda*, by Peter Carey. Some easier ones are: *Gone With The Wind*; *Three Men in a Boat*; and *A Tale of Two Cities*.

SARDINES

An old favorite for people of all ages, this game was devised as a country-house frolic with amatory overtones. While it is important to have a fair amount of space, a mansion is not necessary.

Players: four or more
Equipment: a large house
Difficulty: easy, though frustrating at times, for people of all ages
Duration: half an hour with just four players, but can be several hours depending on the number of players and the amount of room

Playing the game

This game is a variant on Hide-and-Seek, so the first thing you must do is to draw lots to decide who is to go off and hide – though sometimes it is easiest to give the most tired and reluctant player the task of hiding, to save them from energetic seeking. Whoever it is leaves the room to find a suitable place in which to hide, and after a decent interval – five minutes, say, depending on the size of the house – the rest of the players separate to hunt for them. The first player to find the person who is hiding waits until any other players are out of sight and then jumps into the hiding place, wherever it may be – for example, under a bed, in a cupboard, or on top of a child's bunk bed. The two of them wait for the next player to discover them, and so on, until all but one of the players are in the same hiding place together, packed in like sardines in a tin – hence the game's name. The last player to discover the rest of the group has to be the next sardine.

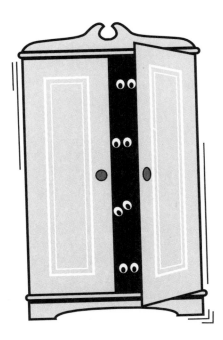

Diagram 9 A game of Sardines

Hints for successful play

Obviously, the success of this game relies largely on the resourcefulness of the first sardine, who must find a spot in which the rest of the players can hide, no matter how uncomfortably. It becomes progressively harder for each subsequent sardine to find a hiding place that is both difficult to find and also big enough to accommodate the other players.

MURDER IN THE DARK

There are many detective games, but this one has the great advantage of being played with the lights out, which can lend the game a surprisingly exciting sense of tension, suspense, and scariness.

Players: eight or more
Equipment: pencil and paper and, preferably, a large house – the darker and gloomier the better
Difficulty: suitable for adults and older children – but not for the faint hearted
Duration: an hour or more, depending on the number playing and the size of the house in which it is played

Diagram 10 Slips of paper marked for a game of Murder in the Dark

Beginning to play

Tear some sheets of paper into as many slips as there are players. Mark one with a black cross and another with a circle. Fold the slips over and place them in a hat, then ask everyone to choose one. The player who picks the piece of paper with the cross is the murderer, but must not betray the fact in any way, keeping totally quiet. The player who picks the circle is the detective, and should identify himself or herself to the other players. Then the lights are turned off and all the players except the detective disappear in all directions.

Playing the game

The murderer roams around until he comes across a victim, and whispers "You're dead," or puts his hands around the victim's neck – though this is sometimes going too far in a dark and scary house if people are of a nervous disposition. The victim lets out a bloodcurdling scream, while the murderer slinks away to some suitably innocent and distant location. When the screams are heard by the other players, they must all stay exactly where they are. The detective then hurries to the scene of the crime and switches on the lights, before noting down where everyone is. The suspects are then summoned to a main room and questioned about their movements and where they were at the time of the crime. The innocent must tell the truth, but the murderer is allowed to lie as necessary – but if there is a direct challenge that a suspect is guilty, the truth must be told. After all the evidence has been assembled, the detective is allowed just two guesses as to the murderer's identity.

CHARADES

This classic parlor game has a special appeal for children because it involves dressing up and using props, though adults enjoy it too. Charades certainly has its devotees – among whom, reputedly, are Britain's royal family.

Players: six or more
Equipment: a dressing-up box, containing old clothes, and a few props
Difficulty: as easy or as hard as you wish to make it
Duration: from an hour to a whole evening

Playing the game

Charades differs from The Game in that speech, clothes, and props can be used to help convey the syllables that make up a word or phrase. Otherwise, the two games are very similar. In

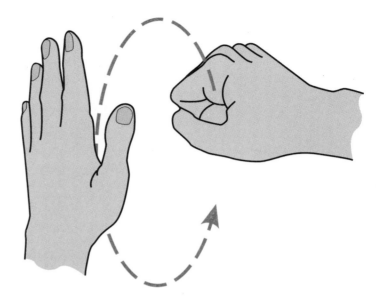

Diagram 12 It's a movie...

Charades, two teams are formed and each one chooses a two- or three-syllable word that is acted out to the opposing team, syllable by syllable. Finally, the whole word is acted out. For example, "incubate" could be split for acting purposes into "in," "queue," and "bait." The conventions used are the same as those for The Game.

The trick is to disguise each syllable as cunningly as possible and to try to fool the other players with red herrings and high drama. There are really no winners and losers in Charades, unless, perhaps, one team guesses far more

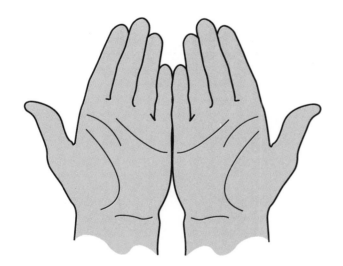

Diagram 11 It's a book...

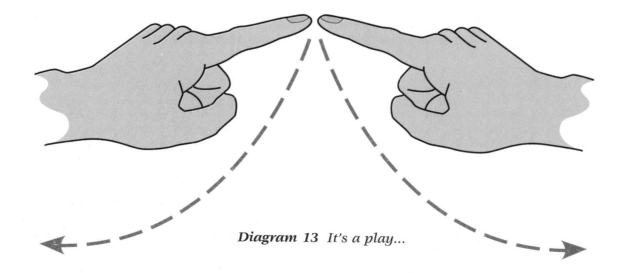

Diagram 13 It's a play...

quickly than the other or fails to solve the puzzle at all. However, winning is not really the point. Charades is boisterous and noisy, and, as a result, is normally very popular with children. It is simpler than The Game too, and has the advantage that you can dress up – the sillier the props and the wilder and more ridiculous the clothes, the better.

SCISSORS, PAPER, & STONE

An ancient game, played all over the world, which is based on the simple principle of anticipation. As with Poker, the game depends on bluff and double-bluff: a knowledge of your opponent's foibles is therefore vitally important.

Players: *two (but there is a team variant – see Elves, Gnomes, and Giants)*
Equipment: *none*
Difficulty: *adults and children from seven upward*
Duration: *anything from 15 minutes up to an hour*

Playing the game
Both players put one hand behind their backs and at the count of three bring it out, either in a representation of scissors, paper, or stone. Scissors are represented by a horizontal hand with two fingers extended; paper is indicated by a hand held out horizontally and flat; stone by a clenched fist. The point of the game is that scissors cut paper; that paper wraps stone; and that stone blunts scissors. Therefore, scissors wins over paper; paper beats stone; and stone beats scissors. If both players use the same shape, that round is a draw. One of the great advantages of the game is that it can be played anywhere at all – in the car, on a train, or sitting in the garden.

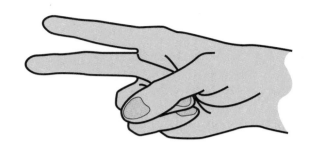

Diagram 14 Scissors,

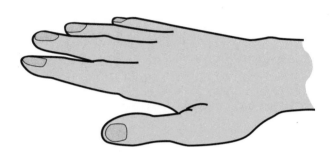

Diagram 15 Paper,

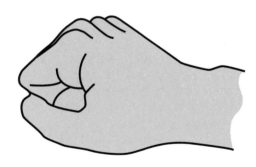

Diagram 16 And Stone

ELVES, GNOMES, & GIANTS

This game is for the exuberant and uninhibited – it involves two teams charging toward each other across a room, shouting their identities, and brandishing the gestures that match them.

Players: the more the better, but ideally at least 12
Equipment: none
Difficulty: easy, but tense for grown-ups and fun for children
Duration: half an hour for adults; an hour for children

Beginning to play

The principle is as for Scissors, Paper, and Stone, but the execution is very different. The players divide into two teams and retreat to either end of a room – ideally, it should be large and cleared of furniture. Each team forms a huddle and debates whether all its members should be elves (the same as scissors), gnomes (paper), or giants (stone) – the teams make the same gestures as in Scissors, Paper, and Stone to indicate their choice. After making their decision, the teams wait for an umpire to start the game. As with Scissors, Paper, and Stone, elves beat gnomes; giants beat elves; and gnomes beat giants. Identical selections mean that the round is tied.

Playing the game

On the umpire's call, each team rushes toward the other, shouting their identity and brandishing the appropriate gestures – though if played with sufficient enthusiasm, these gestures might not be very exact. The team that wins stays in the middle of the room, and the team that loses retreats back to its original position. Both teams then huddle around to choose what they will be in the next round. However, if both teams chose to be elves, say, in a round, and the result is consequently a draw, they both stay in the middle of the room and are forced to choose in secret, by means of nods and winks, what they will be in the next round. The first team to overrun the other, by winning two rounds in a row, wins the game – but the law of averages dictates that, for most games, there is a fair amount of rushing backward and forward before one team does actually win.

SPOOF

A guessing game with an element of bluff that gives it added interest. Raffish types have been known to play to determine who pays a bar bill.

Players: two or more
Equipment: small objects, such as coins or buttons
Difficulty: chance plays a major part, but bluffing – and the ability to spot bluffs – adds an element of skill. Enjoyable for both adults and older children.
Duration: as long or as short a time as you wish

Playing the game

Each player finds three objects that are small enough to be concealed in a clenched fist – coins, matches, or buttons are ideal. The players then put some or none of these objects in their hand and hold their fists out in front of them.

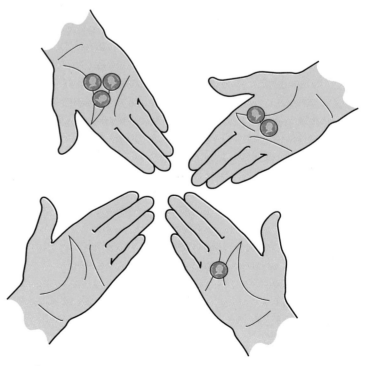

Diagram 17 *A game of Spoof*

Then each player, going around clockwise, guesses the total number of objects that have been concealed. The first player to make a guess can say whatever number he or she pleases, but each subsequent guess must be different from any that has been made previously. When the round of guesses is complete, the objects are counted and the player whose guess is closest to the correct answer is the winner.

Hints for successful play

The player who has the first guess has the advantage of being able to guess any number, from zero to three times the number of players. The rest of the players have the advantage of time to try and work out who is bluffing and who is not. But the possibilities are intriguing: does a high number mean that the person guessing holds the maximum of three objects, or is it a bluff? Does a low number mean that the player has put no objects in his or her hand, or is it a bluff?

IN THE MANNER OF THE WORD

This very popular parlor game, thought to date from the nineteenth century, has a special subtlety that derives from its dependence on adverbs – and so, of course, it teaches young people what adverbs are. It appeals to natural show-offs and tempts even the shyest people to be extrovert.

Players: four or more people
Equipment: none
Difficulty: as hard as you make it, but the game is enjoyed by both adults and older children
Duration: a whole evening, when good friends are playing

Diagram 18 Acting "In the Manner of the Word"

Playing the game

There are two versions of this very popular game, which can be played by any number of people.

A single protagonist

In this version, one person leaves the room and those remaining choose an adverb, for example "slyly," "madly," "sexily," or "naughtily." When the choice has been made, the person returns to the room and has to guess what the adverb is – they can either ask questions that the others have to answer "in the manner of the word;" or ask any number of them to act out a situation, such as cleaning windows or crashing your car, "in the manner of the word." Some combinations can be wonderfully inappropriate – such as cleaning windows "naughtily," or directing traffic "slyly."

A joint effort

In the second version, two people leave the room to think of an adverb. When they return, the others have to guess what it is by giving the pair situations to act, "in the manner of the word" – for example, milking a cow, or washing a car. Many people prefer this version of the game because it is less inhibiting: the person acting has someone with whom to share the agony. It also tends to be funnier, because you can tailor the situations to suit the participants. You could try asking your elderly uncle to conduct an orchestra "groovily," or a rock music-loving teenager to play the guitar "loftily."

BLIND MAN'S BUFF

There is no record of when this game was first played, but it has certainly been in existence for many centuries and has been played by countless generations of children – and adults, too. Try the original game, or play one of its variations for added spice.

Players: six or more players
Equipment: a blindfold
Difficulty: either easy or hard, depending on the abilities of the "blind man," but enjoyed by both adults and children
Duration: playing for an hour is generally enough

Playing the game

One player is selected to be the "blind man." He or she is blindfolded, led to the center of the room and turned around three times – the idea is to make the blind man disoriented. The other players scatter around the room. The blind man then searches for the other players, who are not allowed to move their feet, but may twist their bodies to escape. But once the blind man has found a body, its identity has to be established by touch. If the blind man guesses the person's identity correctly, that person becomes the next blind man; if unsuccessful after one go, the blind man has to try to catch someone else.

VARIATIONS

There are a number of variations to this game, all of which have their own adherents.

Blind Man's Circle

In this variation, the players walk in a circle around the blind man until he or she claps three times: the players must come to a standstill and the blind man points to the edge of the circle. The player most closely identified by the point must enter the circle and try not to be caught for two minutes. If caught, that player becomes the blind man.

Blind Man's Staff

Here the blind man carries a stick and the players walk around in a circle that is sufficiently tight for the stick to reach them. When the blind man points his stick, the players stop walking and the one closest to it takes its end. The blind man says "Who's there?" and the person, in a voice disguised as much as possible, answers: "It's me." If the blind man recognizes the voice, the one who has been identified loses, and changes places. If the blind man gets it wrong they try again.

Seated Blind Man's Buff

This is for more risqué gatherings. All the players except for the blind man sit on chairs placed in a tight circle. The blind man sits on the lap of one of the players and has to try to identify the player without touching the body any further. Usually the player who is being sat upon will giggle – but not always. If the blind man guesses correctly, he or she changes places with that person. If not, another lap must be tried.

Diagram 19 A game of Blind Man's Buff

BUZZ & BUZZ-FIZZ

Games that rely on concentration, such as this one, are easy in theory and infuriatingly hard in practice. Children can take great delight in beating their elders if they keep their mind on what's going on.

Players: *just two are sufficient, but the game is more enjoyable with additional players*
Equipment: *none*
Difficulty: *irritatingly difficult, but enjoyed by adults and children of all ages*
Duration: *about half an hour*

Playing the game

The players sit in a rough circle and try to concentrate their minds so that they can play fast and furiously – which is the key to enjoyment in this game. The game starts with the first player calling out "one;" the next "two;" the next "three" – but as soon as you reach number five, or any multiple of five, you must say "buzz" instead of the number. If the number contains five, but is not a multiple of it, only the five part of it is replaced by "buzz": for example, 51 would be "buzz-one." If just two people are playing, the game is over when one player hesitates too long or forgets to say "buzz;" played by three or more, the player who hesitates or forgets is out of that round. A typical game played by six people might go like this:

Player one: "thirty-nine"
Player two: "buzz"
Player three: "forty-one"
Player four: "forty-two"
Player five: "forty-three"
Player six: "forty-four"
Player one: "buzz"
Player two: "forty-six"
Player three: "forty-seven"

Player four: "forty-eight"
Player five: "forty-nine"
Player six: "buzz"
Player one: "fifty; oh, no!"

The important thing is that all the answers should be quick, so that nobody has time to think carefully about what they are saying.

VARIATIONS

When several people are playing, it is possible to add another dimension to the game if the player who is saying "buzz" has to get up quickly and then sit down as the word is said. Then, if you manage to get as far as 55 ("buzz-buzz"), the player must stand up and sit down twice. Players have three lives each, and lives are lost by saying "buzz" at an inappropriate time, forgetting to say it, or hesitating too long.

Fizz

Fizz is the same game, but sevens and multiples of seven are used. This is difficult enough, but Buzz-fizz is much more terrifying. In this, the sequence after you get to five is: "buzz"; "six"; "fizz;" "eight;" "nine;" "buzz;" "eleven;" "twelve;" "thirteen;" "fizz;" "buzz;" "sixteen;" "one-fizz;" and on you go. You need a clear head and superb concentration for this game, but when it works it can be great fun.

I HAVE NEVER

A deceptively simple game that reveals surprising facts about the players and tends to lead to considerable argument – all of which makes it an ideal after-dinner entertainment.

Players: *three or more*
Equipment: *none*
Difficulty: *not as easy as it first appears; for adults*
Duration: *15 minutes for each round, up to an hour at least*

Playing the game

Each player in turn has to declare something that he or she has never done, selecting on the basis that there is a probability that everyone else playing has done it. For example, a player might say: "I have never eaten a grapefruit;" "I have never possessed a pair of jeans;" "I have never swum in the sea;" or "I have never had a school meal." If your "I have never . . ." proves to be unique, you score a point; and the first person to gain three points wins the game. It is import ant that all the players are honest about their claims, because it is almost impossible to prove or disprove negatives, but there is still some scope for challenging claims that seem too extravagant. It can become surprisingly difficult to think of something that you have not done but that everyone else has – which all adds to the fun of the evening.

GOING BLANK

The questions are relatively easy in this game, at least in principle – but its point is that the Inquisitor fires them at you with intimidating speed. Thankfully, though, each player takes a turn at being the Inquisitor, so humiliation is a possibility for all.

Players: four or more
Equipment: none
Difficulty: varies according to the questions; for adults only
Duration: 30 minutes of fast rounds, with another game when everyone has recovered

Playing the game

Speed is of the essence in this game. One person is elected Inquisitor, and has to designate three categories for questions: for example, actors, flowers, and big cats. The other players stand, or sit, in a circle, with the Inquisitor in the middle, and he or she points a finger aggressively at one

of them, demanding an instant answer to the question. For example:

Inquisitor: "actor?"
Player One: "Robbie Coltrane"
Inquisitor: "flower?"
Player Two: "rose"
Inquisitor: "actor?"
Player One: "Marlon Brando"
Inquisitor: "big cat?"
Player: "er, um"
Inquisitor: "OUT!"

The Inquisitor has to be alert, too, because they can only ask the same player the same question three times. Even so, one's mind can go blank surprisingly quickly – hence the name of the game. In theory, the winner is the last one in – or, more likely, the last ones in after the Inquisitor has asked the three questions of each player. But as in so many parlor games, there are no real winners or losers, just fun or humiliation!

GOOD MORNING MADAM

A wonderfully silly game that necessitates paying close attention to the cards as they are turned up. It depends for its success on the enthusiasm and boisterousness with which the responses are made.

Players: four or more
Equipment: one or two packs of cards
Difficulty: easy, if sufficient attention is paid; enjoyed by adults and children alike
Duration: 30 minutes is generally enough

Playing the game

One or two packs of cards are dealt, depending on the number of players. Taking turns, each player puts a card down, faceup, on a central pile. If an Ace, King, Queen, or Jack appears, each player tries to be first to make the appropriate action – the first person to do this takes all the cards in the pile. The object of the game is to win all the cards that have been dealt. When an Ace appears, everyone tries to be the first to slam down the palm of their hand on top of it; if a King appears the first person to salute wins; when a Jack is seen, the race is to shout "boo;" and (which gives the game its name) when a Queen is put down everyone tries to shout "Good Morning Madam" as loudly as possible before everyone else. Inevitably, there is then uproar as everyone argues about who yelled it first. This game is best played late at night, but is usually a tremendous success.

LIKES & DISLIKES

A "revelation" game with a difference, this is fascinatingly oblique and depends on the fact that few people are likely to know about the obscure twists and turns of what you happen to like and to dislike, and yet they make up the complex picture of who you are.

Players: six or more players, preferably who know each other well
Equipment: paper and pencils
Difficulty: surprisingly hard; for adults only
Duration: 30 minutes or less

Playing the game
Each player writes a list of five things that they like and five things they dislike on a piece of paper – the likes and dislikes can be anything, from politics to landscapes. The pieces of paper are folded up and collected, and one player reads out the lists one after the other. The other players have to guess who wrote which list. No one really wins or loses in this game, but it can be a lot of fun.

A typical list might go like this:

Likes: *red wine*
          locomotives
          sleep
          marshmallows
          computers
Dislikes: *buses*
          oysters
          politicians
          hiking in the country
          sport on TV

The fun of the game depends on the degree of subtlety in your selections, because you obviously have to be more careful the better you know the other players.

RUBIK'S CUBE

Strictly speaking this is not really a parlor game, as it can – just about – be enjoyed anywhere. Ernõ Rubik invented his maddeningly addictive Cube in 1974, and between 1980 and 1983 it swept the world — more than 100 million were sold. Inevitably, it fell out of fashion for a while, but is now enjoying a resurgence in popularity.

Players: one
Equipment: the Cube
Difficulty: very hard to solve
Duration: until your patience runs out

The cube
Available from most good toy shops or stores that stock puzzles, Rubik's Cube is deceptively simple in appearance but fiendishly hard to solve. It consists of a cube that itself is constructed from 27 smaller cubes, linked in such a way that layers of the cube as a whole – each consisting of nine small cubes – can be rotated in both planes. The face of each small

cube is colored differently: it could be either red, black, blue, white, green, orange, or yellow.

The object

The sole point of Ernõ Rubik's puzzle is to manoeuver the small cubes so that each face of the large cube displays one color, and one color only. This sounds simple enough, but it is infuriatingly difficult to achieve. And when you have succeeded, the challenge remains: to complete the puzzle with the fewest possible moves.

Hints and tips

In the 1980s many books showing how to solve Rubik's Cube were published. Today, such books are harder to come by, but you will find page after page on the Internet filled with complex mathematical algorithms devoted to the conundrum that the Cube poses. However, there seems little fun or satisfaction in having someone solve the puzzle for you, so you will find no more than some general pointers here, though there are websites that will take you through the process step-by-step – it is up to you to find them if you wish. The official Rubik's Cube site gives a number of useful hints, and even lets you try to solve the puzzle on-line, using your computer's mouse. You will find this site, which is signed by Ernõ Rubik himself, at http://www.rubiks.com/.

For those who do not have access to the Internet, here are a few tips – with acknowledgements to the Official Rubik's Cube website. First, work layer by layer from the top, solving one face of your cube before moving on to the others; think in terms of using quarter-twists and half-twists.

Second, bear in mind that opposite colors never appear on the same small cube: for example, no single cube will have both blue and white in its color scheme.

Third, concentrate on "edge cubes" first – that is, small cubes that do not form the corners of the larger cube – remembering to work layer by layer. And, fourth, work on the corner cubes last. You may not wish to know that the mathematical theory demonstrates that Rubik's Cube can be solved from any position in just 22 moves. However, you may be consoled to know that nobody, as far as is known, has ever succeeded in doing this.

A warning

Possibly out of sheer frustration, some people disassemble a Cube in an attempt to find out how it works. If you do this, make sure that you reassemble it in the solved form, with every face being the same color. If you do not do this, you will find it impossible to solve the puzzle.

PAPER & PENCIL GAMES

Paper and pencil games need only the simplest equipment, so they are ideal for passing the time on long journeys. Many of them involve making up words, or listing words beginning with a certain letter of the alphabet.

Paper and pencil games need only the simplest equipment, so they are ideal for passing the time on long journeys and keeping children busy, as well as having a beneficial educational value. Many of them involve making up words, or listing words beginning with specific letters of the alphabet. In Guggenheim, players select and list on paper five categories such as occupations, flowers, rivers, or cities. One player then selects a five-letter word at random, and all players write it across the top of their sheets of paper, forming columns. The players then try to write a word for each of the letters in each category. In the game of Crossword, players attempt to make up a word square with words of equal length that read both horizontally and vertically. The game became popular in Britain in the nineteenth century and probably developed from Acrostics – puzzles or poems in which the first or last letters of each line spell a word or sentence.

Acrostics date from Roman times – examples have been found at Pompeii in Italy and at the old Roman city of Cirencester in England. Crosswords are a relatively recent invention that combine elements of the acrostic and the word square. The first "word-cross" appeared in a Sunday newspaper, the *New York World*, on 21 December 1913. The name was later changed to "cross-word," and soon the game became a craze in America and Britain. Many party games are based on anagrams. Players are given jumbled letters to turn into words, or they can be asked to make a word by adding one letter to an anagram. Anagrams as a pursuit in themselves have declined in popularity since the Victorian era, but they became an essential part of cryptic crosswords, and it is in crosswords that they are most commonly found today.

The game of Consequences was another popular Victorian game, frequently described in eighteenth and nineteenth-century literature. It must have been an appealing game in strict Victorian society because it enabled young people to flirt with one another under the guise of a harmless recreation, as well as digging deeper into the personalities of their peer group. The fun of the game today comes from the incongruous juxtaposition of sentences, and the fact that it is not a competitive game. While the origins of some of today's paper and pencil games – such as Tic-tac-toe and Crossword – date back to ancient times, others are more recent inventions. Battleships is said to have been developed by British prisoners-of-war during World War I, and since then has become one of the most popular paper and pencil games for two players. Stylish versions can also be bought in games shops.

TIC-TAC-TOE

One of the most enduring of games, Tic-tac-toe is also known as Noughts and Crosses in Britain.

Players: two
Equipment: paper and pencil, or any surface that can be marked
Difficulty: frustratingly difficult for both adults and children to actually win
Duration: a few minutes for each game, but generally repeats are required

Playing the game

The great thing about Tic-tac-toe is that it can be played practically anywhere – at home, in the car, on a train, or even on a beach by drawing a grid in the sand. First, draw two pairs of parallel lines at right-angles to each other to make a grid of nine squares. Then, taking it in turns, one player marks an O and the other an X in one of the nine spaces, the object being to get your Os or Xs in a row of three – up and down, across or diagonally. The player who starts the game has an advantage, so it is wise for the players to start alternately.

Hints for successful play

There are around 15,000 possible permutations for the first five moves of the game, but you can nearly always force a draw when playing second if, as O, you avoid the shaded squares as shown in diagram 1.

One winning strategy is shown in the diagram 2: if you place your X in a corner, and your opponent puts an O in the corner beneath it,

Diagram 1 Squares to avoid as second player

place your next X in the opposite corner to your first one. To stop the diagonal line, your opponent will have to place an O in the center. You can then place your next X in the remaining corner, ensuring that your next go will be the winning one.

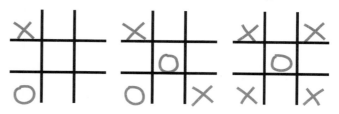

Diagram 2 A winning strategy

Even with this strategy, the majority of games are draws. And if your opponent starts, you can only win if he or she fails to spot a line developing. This should not happen, but surprisingly often it does.

HANGMAN

This word game has two advantages: first, it still has a point even when simple, straightforward words are chosen; second, its scoring system provides entertainment and even a frisson of suspense.

Players: from two to 20
Equipment: paper and pencil
Difficulty: depends on the obscurity of the word or phrase chosen; adaptable for both adults and children
Duration: depending on the number of players, from half an hour to a whole afternoon

Playing the game

When played by two people, one person thinks of a word and writes down as many dashes as there are letters in that word. For example, "cream" would be:

– – – – –

The other player then has to try and guess the letters that the five dashes represent. If the guess is "E," for example, the player who set the word fills in the third dash. If the guess is "F," say, or any other incorrect letter, the base of a gallows is drawn, and the letter "F" is written down as a reminder that it should not be guessed again. Any subsequent incorrect guess results in another line being added to the gallows, and, finally, to the person suspended from them – as shown in diagram 3. The game continues either until the word has been guessed or the loser has been hung.

A team version

If there are sufficient players, divide everyone into two teams and appoint a quizmaster to run things. The quizmaster thinks of a phrase – a well-known quotation, for example, or the title of a book, play, or movie – and writes out the necessary number of dashes, separating the individual words with a slash. So *The Full Monty*, for example, would be:

$$\_\_\_ / \_\_\_\_ / \_\_\_\_\_$$

This sequence is presented to one team as a challenge, and the members of that team try to guess the answer. If they are lucky, in our example, they might guess "E" and "L," with the result that "L" is put in wherever it appears. So:

$$\_\_e / \_\_ll / \_\_\_\_\_$$

When the phrase has been guessed – and it is often easier to guess a phrase rather than a single word – the team is awarded points according to the number of lines that would have been required to complete the hanged man before their correct guess, and the other team is challenged in its turn.

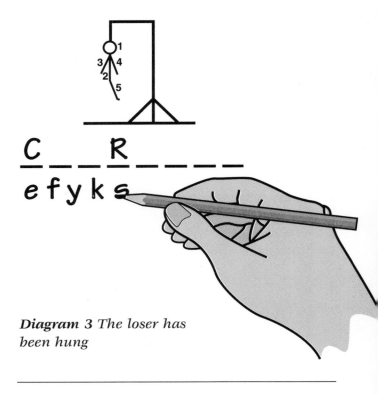

Diagram 3 The loser has been hung

BOXES

This game is deceptively simple, but in fact it demands a high level of concentration and a grasp of the strategy. The advantage constantly swings from one player to the other, and the outcome is rarely certain until the end.

Players: two players
Equipment: paper and pens of different colors
Difficulty: irritatingly difficult; for adults and children over eight
Duration: half an hour is usually long enough for a session; otherwise frustration sets in

Beginning to play

Mark out a grid of dots on a piece of paper, using the same number horizontally and vertically – 10 in a row is about right for a 10-minute game.

Playing the game

Using pens of different colors, in order to avoid arguments, the players take it in turns to draw a

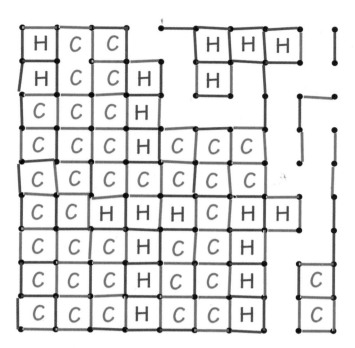

Diagram 4 A game of Boxes

line between any two dots in an attempt to form a box. When a player completes a box they mark it with their initial, and can then add another line. If this line encloses another box, they mark that one too and another line can be drawn, and so on. When all the boxes have been enclosed, each player's boxes are counted, and the one with the most is the winner.

Hints for successful play

Strategy and cunning come into play as the game progresses and it gets ever more difficult to draw a line without leaving a square that your opponent can complete. Damage limitation becomes very important – in other words, the position should be examined carefully, so that the line you draw gives your opponent the opportunity to complete the fewest squares possible. Every pair of players will have to lay down their own local rules, which add enormously to the complexity of the game.

VARIATION

If you become bored with the standard ver-

sion, make up some local rules. For example, you could decide that the player with the fewest enclosed boxes is the winner, so reversing the approach to the game.

SPROUTS

This demands the same close attention as Boxes and involves similar strategies. However, there are fewer opportunities for inventive rule-making and more for bizarre embroidery.

Players: *two*
Equipment: *paper and pencil*
Difficulty: *easy to play, but hard to win; for adults and children*
Duration: *about an hour for a session with several games*

Playing the game

Draw eight dots – the more you draw, the longer the game – well apart from each other on a piece of paper. Taking it in turns, each player draws a

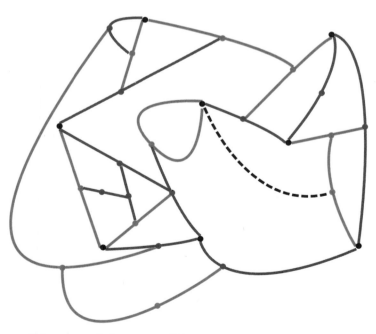

Diagram 5 A game of Sprouts

225

line joining any two dots, or joining a dot to itself, and then draws a dot somewhere along the new line. There are three rules that dictate whether a line is permissible: first, a line cannot cross either itself or any other line; second, no line can be drawn through a dot; third, no dot can have more than three lines leaving it. The winner is the player who draws the last admissable line.

ALPHABET RACE

One way of describing this game would be to say that it is Scrabble® for masochists. It is Scrabble® without the board, the tiles, or the points system. Success depends on knowledge of words and sheer imagination, but is rarely achieved completely in the straightforward version, so it is usual to agree beforehand to vary the rules.

Players: *two or more*
Equipment: *paper and pencil*
Difficulty: *adults and children*
Duration: *about half an hour in the simplest version*

Beginning to play

Each player lists the letters of the alphabet on one piece of paper, and another plain sheet of paper is used as a board.

Playing the game

The first player (toss a coin or roll dice to see who this will be) writes down a word on the piece of paper being used as the board, spacing the letters out carefully, and then crosses the letters that have been used off their own alphabet list. The next player continues by adding a word to the board and crossing those letters off their list – only the letters that have been added to the board can be crossed off, not those used by the first player. The sequence

continues until each player has had a turn, and then the first player has another go, but this player can only use the letters that remain on their alphabet list.

The rules about whether you can use a word are the same as those for Scrabble®. For example, in the example illustrated, the first player has written "MOTHER;" the second has used "TOP," using the "T" from "MOTHER," so only the "O" and "P" can be crossed off their alphabet list. The third player has taken the opportunity to cross "Z" off, by adding "ZI" to the "P;" and the first player has added an "N" to the "I" on the second go.

m o t h e r
    o
z i p
n

Diagram 6 A game of Alphabet Race

It is not too difficult to think of better words than this on the first round, but it becomes increasingly difficult to do so as the game progresses. However, a player who is stuck can say "Pass" and miss a turn. The first player to finish off their alphabet wins, but because players start with only 26 letters, it is difficult to do so. In such cases, the person with the fewest letters left is declared the winner. As you may guess, it is much more frustrating than Scrabble® because you start with only 26 letters.

VARIATIONS

There is endless scope for varying the rules of Alphabet Race, but it is important that any changes should be agreed in detail beforehand, in order to avoid arguments. One option is to double, or even triple the number of vowels (a, e, i, o, u) available to each player. Alternatively you could double the whole alphabet, with the exception of letters such as "X" and "Z." The choice is yours.

BATTLESHIPS

Said to have been invented by British prisoners of war during World War I, this game has been a favorite standby for children ever since – and it is easy to play a variation set in the future.

Players: *two*
Equipment: *pencil and paper*
Difficulty: *much luck is involved, and this is more a game for children than adults*
Duration: *15 minutes or so, but the loser normally wants revenge*

Beginning to play

Each player draws two 10x10 grids, numbering the squares from 1 to 10 down the left-hand side, and labeling them from A to J along the top. One grid is for the "home fleet" and the other is for the "enemy fleet" – this one is left blank for the moment.

Each player's fleet consists of one battleship (made up of four squares), two cruisers (three squares each), three destroyers (two squares each) and four submarines (one square each). This means each player uses up 20 of the 100 squares in the grid. Each player marks the individual ships of their home fleet on their grid, using a "b" for a battleship, a "c" for a cruiser, a "d" for a destroyer, and an "s" for a submarine. The squares that make up each ship must touch

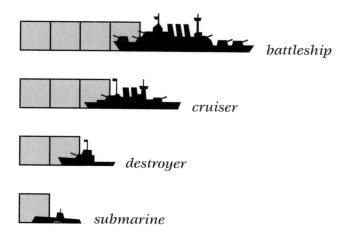

battleship

cruiser

destroyer

submarine

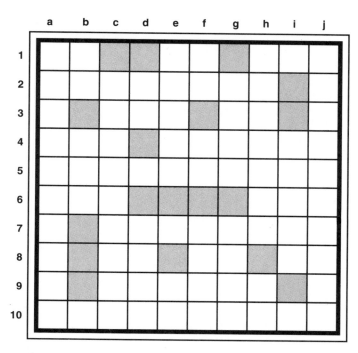

Diagram 7 The home fleet

each other, and can do so either horizontally, vertically, or diagonally. However, no two ships can touch each other by even so much as a corner – see diagram 7.

A coin is tossed to see who starts. After the first game the loser of the previous one should start any subsequent game.

Playing the game

Each player takes turns to try to hit the enemy fleet, being allowed three attempts on each turn. This is done by calling out the reference for the appropriate square. All direct hits must be declared by the enemy and the type of vessel given honestly.

In diagram 8, the player has called "D3" and missed and then "F6" and missed again. However, the third attempt reveals that part of one of the enemy's cruisers is at B8. This information, as well as which squares are empty, is marked on the first player's enemy fleet sheet. The second player then makes their challenges. The winner is the first player to destroy the enemy fleet.

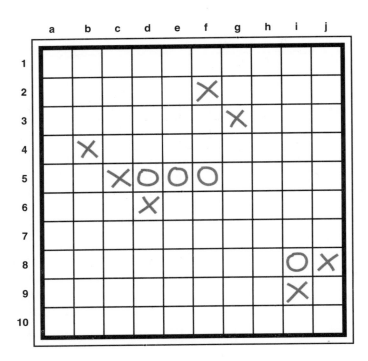

Diagram 8 Enemy fleet sheet

VARIATIONS
Starships

Great fleet actions at sea are a thing of the past, and some children may prefer playing "starships" – it is just battleships in disguise. Substitute an intergalactic battle cruiser for the battleship; asteroid smashers for the cruisers; starwarp cruisers for the destroyers; and starfighters for the submarines. Or, more sensibly, ask the children for their advice on names.

Salvo

This complex version of Battleships demands more thought and analysis by the players. The game uses the same basic grids for home and enemy fleets, but differs in the ships used and the method of play. Each player has one battleship (made up of five squares), one cruiser (three squares), and two destroyers (two squares each). Each player lays out their home fleet according to the same rules as Battleships. But unlike Battleships, in which three attempts at hitting an enemy ship are allowed each turn, in Salvo seven shots are allowed – "the salvo," of

which three shots are accounted for by the battleship, two by the cruiser and one by the destroyer. The opposing player notes where the shots have landed on the home fleet grid, but does not say whether a specific shot has been a hit. Instead, they may say: "one hit on a cruiser and one on a destroyer." If a ship has been hit more than once, this information must also be given.

The player on the receiving end of the first salvo then takes a turn, again being allowed seven shots. Meanwhile, the first player has to devise a strategy to develop the information that emerged after the first salvo, by aiming the next round of shots in such a way as to confirm which of the original shots were successful.

A ship is considered to be sunk when all of its squares have been hit, and each player must declare it when this happens. This has a critical impact on the game, because the number of shots in that player's next salvo are reduced by the number of shots that the sunken ship took. So if a player's battleship is sunk, the number of shots in that player's next salvo will be reduced by three, and only four shots will be available. As in battleships, the winner is the first player to sink all the ships in the enemy fleet.

THE POETRY GAME

A delightfully silly game that is really a rhyming and scanning version of Consequences. It is great fun to play and also has the virtue of irritating the pretentious and those who consider themselves poetry experts.

Players: *three to 10*
Equipment: *pencil and paper*
Difficulty: *moderate; adults enjoy it more than children*
Duration: *no more than 10 minutes, but the game can become addictive*

Playing the game

Do not be put off by this game's title: you do not
need to have any knowledge of poetry, nor to
excel at its composition. Each player is given a
pencil and paper. The first player writes two
lines of verse, which can either be something
remembered or made up – the two lines should
scan, but they do not have to rhyme. The paper
is then folded to hide the first line and passed to
the next player, who writes the third and fourth
line, without having looked at the first one; the
third line should rhyme with the second line,
and, preferably, have the same rhythm. The
game continues, with each player being given
the last line written and adding two more, until
a preset length is reached. Eight lines is usually
enough, though more heroic meters can be
attempted if you wish. Each poem is then read
out to (with luck) much hilarity and applause.

An example

This is a rather weak attempt, but it illustrates
the game's potential.

First player:
  I know that I shall meet my fate
  Somewhere among the clouds above;

Second player:
  Where there flew a turtle dove
  That nowhere could find a place to rest;

Third player:
  She thought she was of all least blest
  And laid her down upon a sod;

Fourth player:
  A man came by who bore a rod
  With which he set about her frame.

GUGGENHEIM

*This game is said to have been invented by a
Mrs Guggenheim, a member of the fabulously
rich American family. It is rather difficult to
play well, but making the attempt is satisfyingly
amusing.*

Players: two or more
Equipment: pencil and paper
Difficulty: can be quite hard; for adults and
older children
Duration: 10 minutes a game

	T	R	A	I	N
food	toast	radish	apple	ice cream	noodles
pleasures	talking	reading	art	ice skating	n...ng
foreign towns	Tours	Rampur	Athens	...abad	Naples
boys' names	Thomas	Ralph	Archibald		
bad habits	twitching	ranting	anticipatin...		

Diagram 9 A game of Guggenheim

Beginning to play

First, the players decide on five different categories. Any will do, such as food, drink, bad habits, countries, politicians, objects of hatred, and so on. This means, of course, that a considerable amount of heated debate normally precedes the game. Then one player opens a book and picks a five-letter word at random. Next, each player makes a grid, placing the categories running down the left and the letters of the word that has been chosen at the top – see diagram 9.

Playing the game

If the word chosen was "TRAIN," for example, the players have to think up words in each of the categories chosen that start with the appropriate letter of "TRAIN."

It is usual to set a time limit, during which each player has to write in as many words starting with the correct letter in the appropriate category as possible. The more unusual the words are, the better: two points are awarded for any word that nobody else has got, and only one point for a word if it has been used by more than one person. The player with the most points wins.

ANAGRAMS

This word game relies on a familiar device known to those who do crosswords: anagrams.

Players: two, or four or more
Equipment: pencil and paper
Difficulty: can be complex; for adults and older children
Duration: allow half an hour per game, plus half an hour to prepare for it

The two-player version

The players toss a coin to decide who will draw up a list of categories: they can be anything – movie stars, parts of the body, mammals, fish,

and so on. There can be as many categories as you like, although five is usually the maximum for a 30-minute game. Then each player devises an agreed number of anagrams (between two and five) for each of the categories. Again, there

MOVIES

Dogger Flin — Goldfinger

Hubren — Ben Hur

Primo Snappy — Mary Poppins

POP

Dan O Man — Madonna

Rum Chap Roul — Procul Harum

Teeth Bales — The Beatles

BIRDS

Pigame — Magpie

Niff Up — Puffin

But Lite — Blue Tit

FIVE-LETTER WORDS

Retbe — Beret

Bmthu — Thumb

Steap — Paste

Diagram 10 Sample anagrams

is a time limit, generally of 30 minutes, for doing this. When the lists are ready, each player spells out each anagram in a category and the opposing player writes each one down. The two players have to solve the anagrams they have been given in an agreed time, such as seven minutes per category. The player who solves the most anagrams in the time given, over all the categories, wins, and the prize is to compile the list of categories for the next round.

Playing in teams

In the team version, a question-master is appointed to devise the anagrams. Ideally, this is done several days in advance of the game, and it helps if the question-master knows who will be playing. This gives them maximum scope to tailor the anagrams to the individuals taking part, and so brings a certain spice to the game.

CROSSWORD

This is not the type of crossword that you find in your morning newspaper, but it holds the attention equally well and is something of a challenge to play well.

Players: two, or can be played in teams
Equipment: pencil and paper
Difficulty: surprisingly demanding; for adults and older children
Duration: 10 minutes for the two-player version

For two players

Each player draws a grid of squares, 5x5, on a sheet of paper. Then, taking turns, each player calls out a letter of the alphabet. Both players enter the letter into a square on their grid, in an attempt to form words that may read either across or down.

Rules for acceptable words can be agreed beforehand, but generally words must contain at least two letters and cannot be either abbreviations or proper nouns. Once in place on the grid, a letter cannot be moved. When the grids are full, the game is over and scoring begins. Each player receives one point for each word formed, reading either horizontally or vertically; however, the end of one word must be separated by one letter from the beginning of another in order for both words to count.

A bonus point is awarded if a word fills up an entire row or column. The horizontal and vertical totals are added up and the player with the most points wins.

Diagram 11 *A game of Crossword*

The team version

As many as five people can play using precisely the same rules as for the two-player version of Crossword. However, the greater the number of people who are playing, the more the game depends on good fortune rather than skill, because each player has to rely more on the letters that are chosen by the others. One way out of this dilemma is to increase the size of the grid used, perhaps to 7x7.

CONSEQUENCES

This is a group game that has been played for many generations. It has always been popular with children, but it can be fun for adults, too.

Players: *two or more*
Equipment: *pencil and paper*
Difficulty: *easy in principle, but imagination is required for success; for both adults and children*
Duration: *about 20 minutes, but one game is rarely enough.*

Playing the game

This game normally follows a set format. Variations exist, but this is probably the most common one.

1. *One or two adjectives*
2. *[Name of a male character] met*
3. *One or two adjectives*
4. *[Female character] at*
5. *Where they met*
6. *He... (what he did)*
7. *She... (what she did)*
8. *He said . . .*
9. *She said . . .*
10. *And the consequence was . . .*
11. *And the world said . . .*

The players arrange themselves in a circle. Each player takes a pencil and paper and writes down one or two adjectives to describe a male person, then folds the paper over so that the writing is hidden and passes the paper to the player on their right. This player writes the name of a male person (preferably a teasable friend or known enemy), folds the paper over to hide what was written, and passes the paper to the person on their right again. Then another one or two adjectives to describe a female person are written, followed by the name of the female character. This continues until the final

phrase "and the world said . . .". Then everyone in turn unfolds the paper they are holding and reads the story out.

The game sounds complicated, but in fact it is simplicity itself. The point is to produce wonderfully inconsequential and incongruous stories, each of which has the appearance of being sensible, that produce lots of laughter but no winners. A typical end result could be as silly as this:

"The daring but dastardly Mickey Mouse met the twitching, ululating Marilyn Monroe on a tandem. He gave her a pound of fish; she bashed him over the head with a potato; he said, "I will never forget this;" she said, "You always knew how to get round me." The consequence was a bad thunderstorm; and the world said 'We always knew it would end in tears'."

VARIATION

Children particularly enjoy a variation of this game called Picture Consequences. The idea is much the same, but in this version of the game you use drawings to create a person – or, more likely, a monster. First, each player draws a head on a sheet of paper. This is then folded over and passed to the next player on the right, who draws a neck. This is then folded over and passed to the right once more, for a torso to be drawn; then legs and, lastly, feet. As you can imagine, some pretty peculiar creatures appear as a result.

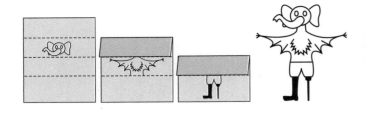

***Diagram 12** A game of Picture Consequences*

SHORT STORIES

The idea behind this game is eminently simple, and you would think that it was equally simple to play. Don't be fooled, though, because it is really annoyingly difficult.

Players: *two or more*
Equipment: *pencil and paper*
Difficulty: *surprisingly difficult; for adults and older children*
Duration: *two minutes per game*

Playing the game

Short stories can be played by as few as two people, but is more fun with three or more. All the players have to write down the longest sentence they can think of, using words of only three letters or less. The sentence must make sense. The game is as simple and as difficult as that, but the catch is that you only have two minutes. For example:

> *"I sat on a bed and I saw a cat but it did not see me, so I got off the bed and ran up to it and got a dog and an emu and we all ran off in a cab."*

If a player seems to be suspiciously good at this game, it may well be that they have played it before and memorized the best answer. If this is the case, you might want to make the game more difficult by reducing the time limit, or specifying that each word must be exactly three letters long – or do both.

LOTTO

Also known as Housey-Housey, this game is the forerunner of Bingo. No skill is required, but it demands a great deal of preparation. Children often enjoy it immensely.

Players: *from four to 200*
Equipment: *Lotto cards and numbered discs*
Difficulty: *extremely easy; for people of all ages*
Duration: *up to 20 minutes, depending on the caller*

Beginning to play

Depending on the numbers playing, there will be a great deal of preparation unless you buy the numbered discs and individual cards from a games shop. Each player is given one of the cards (see diagram 13) and the numbers on each card are unique.

If you are going to make the cards yourself, you must follow certain conventions. Each card is nine rows across and three rows deep. Each horizontal row contains four blanks and five numbers, so each card carries 15 numbers in all. The first vertical row is only allowed to contain numbers between 1 and 10; the second vertical row carries numbers between 11 and 20; the third one runs from 21 and 30; and so on, with the last row going from 81 to 90. Then you must make 90 discs, each carrying a different number between 1 and 90.

Playing the game

A card is issued to each of the players and the discs are placed in a bag, which is handed to the person who has been designated caller. The caller takes one disc at a time out of the bag, and announces it to the players. Any player who has the number can mark it off their card. The first player to mark all the numbers off their card calls out "Lotto" and wins.

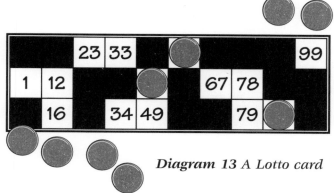

Diagram 13 A Lotto card

WORD & SPOKEN GAMES

Word games are a challenge to the imagination, and as well as being fun, they increase a player's general knowledge and vocabulary, making them a useful educational tool at whatever level they are played.

Word games are a challenge to the imagination, and as well as being fun, they increase a player's general knowledge and vocabulary and as such are useful educational tools at whichever level they are played. They can be played by one person alone, but are most fun when played with large gatherings of people at parties, or in the classroom. Some games, such as I Spy and License Plates, are simple enough for young children to enjoy. Others are extremely complex and suitable for adults only – playing a game of Ghosts demands intellectual dexterity, vocabulary skills and the ability to bluff.

There are two basic types of word game. One type consists of words of similar meanings and sounds, word association and puns, and the rearrangement and substitution of letters. The other type usually involves guessing and listing objects and words, often in a particular order. Spoken games are usually of the second type.

Question and answer games are among the most commonly played spoken games. The original game of Twenty Questions dates back to the eighteenth century, and is described in Charles Dickens's *Christmas Carol*, where it is called "Yes or No." Botticelli also falls into the question and answer category. In this game, one player selects a well-known person or fictional character and announces the initial of the last name. The other players then think of famous people whose name begins with that letter and ask indirect questions about them. Eventually one of the players guesses the correct answer by a process of elimination. In Proverbs, players have to include a word from the given proverb in the questions that are put to them. The player who is putting the questions must then guess which proverb or saying is being referred to.

The alphabet provides a natural basis for many types of word game. One of the oldest is I Love My Love, which is mentioned in Samuel Pepys's diary for 4 March 1669, and also in Charles Dickens's *Christmas Carol*. Taking it in turns, each player completes the sentence "I love my love because..." through the alphabet from A to Z. The memory game I Packed My Bag is also played by adding items in alphabetical order.

Word games and word-association techniques are sometimes used by psychologists and educationalists in intelligence and psychological testing. To be really good at word games you need to be quick-thinking as well as literate. Even the most erudite of individuals may find themselves stuck for words, which of course is part of the fun.

I LOVE MY LOVE

This game is played on the basis that you are making up silly stories about your loves. If you and your fellow players want to be really fool-hardy, you can play it for real. But be warned – this is a dangerous option!

Players: three or more
Equipment: none
Difficulty: for adults only
Duration: if you are in the mood it lasts – with interruptions – for at least an hour

Playing the game

Taking it in turns, each player completes the sentence, "I love my love because she/he is . . .," through the alphabet from A to Z. Any player who cannot come up with an adjective starting with the appropriate letter is out. For example:

"I love my love because she is Aggressive."
"I love my love because he is Balding."
"I love my love because she is Charmless."

This basic version of the game depends for its success on the players choosing the less charming and obvious attributes of their partners, rather than the more conventional soppy ones. Nevertheless, it may give your friends – and your loved one – some insight into how you view your relationship. Its essence, though, is determinedly light-hearted.

VARIATION

If you find the basic version too easy (or too revealing, or not revealing enough), you can play an entirely different version of the game. In this, instead of waxing lyrical about the qualities of your one love, who will be known to most of the other players, you list all the people you have loved in your life, or still love – or at least a selection of them. In each case, you must give the name, where he or she comes

from and his or her special quality. For example:

"I love my love with a D, because she is Daunting and her name is Dahlia and she comes from Denver."

You could put in some kind ones too:

"I love my love with an E because he is Erudite and his name is Edward and he comes from Eritrea."

If you still have an appetite for more by the end of the alphabet, try adding an adverb to the list of required elements, such as "awfully artful," "brutishly backward," "candidly cruel" and so on (it is usually more sensible to leave out X, Y, and Z).

Truth is irrelevant in this game – in fact, most people find it sensible and expedient to lie throughout.

ANALOGIES

This game was very popular around the time of World War II. As with I Love My Love, self-revelation provides the fun as well as the danger, but in Analogies there is the added frisson of indulging in vindictiveness, or even sheer slander.

Players: a minimum of four
Equipment: none
Difficulty: quite hard; for adults only
Duration: an hour to an evening (definitely not to be played in the mornings)

Playing the game

Analogies is more difficult to play correctly than it appears. It is also more dangerous, as offence can easily be taken, even if it is not intended. One player thinks of someone – it could be one of the other players, a famous person, or someone who is known to all those participating. The category that the choice falls into is given to the other players. The other players then try to guess the identity of the chosen person by making analogies.

For example, to the question, "What sort of building would the person be?," the answer could be anything from a smart town house to a badly converted barn or a public lavatory. Analogies can be made with buildings, modes of transport, drinks, smells, machines, flowers, meals, furniture, landscape – anything you can think of that can help the description.

Hints and tips

If the chosen person is one of the players, it is important not to fall into the trap of confusing what you think a person likes with their real character. For example, someone who loves champagne may really be more like fizzy lemonade in character. This is when you have to be a bit careful: stories have been told of players who spent a whole evening likening each other to dirty bathwater and overcooked spaghetti. As a result, it is often more sensible to choose absent friends or public figures. But then, of course, it isn't quite so much fun.

I PACKED MY BAG

This game relies not on intelligence but on a good memory. All too often it is humiliating for adults, because children love it and are usually very good at it.

Players: *two players or more*
Equipment: *none*
Difficulty: *ideal for mixed groups including children*
Duration: *allow 10 minutes a round*

Playing the game

The game is very simple: the first player starts the round with, "I packed my bag;" then the next player says, "I packed my bag and put in...," and adds an item. So it goes on, with each player having to remember what has gone before, in order, as the list gets longer and longer, before packing his or her contribution in the bag. After a few goes, it might run something like this:

"I packed my bag, and put in an apple, two nightshirts, 17 coins, a pair of dumb-bells, a spool of thread, my toothbrush, an imitation leopard-skin coat, a clock, two packs of cards and a tumble drier."

Whether two or 20 people are playing it is equally difficult to remember the list, but if anyone omits an item, or places it in the incorrect order, that person is out of the round.

VARIATION

If you are feeling tired – or kind – you can make a rule that items should be in alphabetical order, so:

"I packed my bag and put in four apples."

then:

"I packed my bag and put in four apples and a button."

***Diagram 1** I Packed My Bag*

and then:

"I packed my bag and put in four apples and a button and a cat."

And on you go until only one person is still packing the bag, as each of the other players has dropped out.

THE DICTIONARY GAME

This game will be familiar to all those who have seen the television programme Call My Bluff, because it is the original, home version of it. The idea is to make up your own false definitions of obscure words and the opposing team has to separate the wheat from the chaff.

Players: *four people as a minimum, but best with six*
Equipment: *a good dictionary, pencils and paper*
Difficult: *as difficult as the imagination of the players can make it*
Duration: *with preparation time, each round takes about half an hour*

Playing the game

The players form two teams, and the members of each team pick an obscure word from the dictionary – it is essential that you use a good dictionary, or you will not find words that are sufficiently obscure. One member of each team writes down the real definition of the word, while the others invent bogus, but convincing, definitions of it. The members of the first team then present their definitions to the other team, whose members have to determine which definition is the correct one; then the second team takes its turn. The game continues for as long as the players wish, with a point being awarded for each successful identification of the true definition and also for each successful bluff.

Hints and tips

The key to success lies in the degree of conviction with which both true and false definitions are presented, and in the level of detail given. Specialist knowledge of any kind comes in extremely useful: someone who knows a lot about architecture might convincingly define "stum," say, as a special type of joist used in very large rooms, such as ballrooms and conference rooms. In fact, stum is unfermented grape juice, which is added to fermented wine as a preservative. Here is how the word "placket" might be presented:

Player one: "A 'placket' was an essential tool of a printing compositor's trade in the days before lithography – when each metal-cast character was placed individually to form words, sentences, paragraphs and, eventually, pages. The assembled characters were held in place by blocks of wood known as 'furniture,' which were fixed as tightly round the blocks of type as possible by a system of screws and ratchets. But before the furniture was tightened, it was banged into place with a small mahogany mallet. So the compositors' room would ring to the sound of 'plack, plack, plack' noises as the final edition was put to bed, giving the mallet its name: a 'placket'.

***Diagram 2** Defining objects for the Dictionary Game*

And to this day, most retired compositors cannot stand watching a croquet game."

Player two: "Our great-great-grandmothers found going shopping a rather trying business. After all, in their day women didn't carry purses – or even briefcases – and, until the middle years of the twentieth century, dresses did not have pockets. If you were wealthy, your servants carried everything for you. But where could you put your tram ticket or your loose change – with delicacy, that is – if you were not? As female emancipation took hold, women decided that they would not put up with this any longer, and started instructing their dressmakers to fit their skirts with pockets. And for some reason – we know not what – these were known as 'plackets.' Perhaps a Mrs Placket started the trend. (In fact, to be technical, the hole in the skirt that gives access to the pocket is called a 'placket-hole.')."

Player three: "In the days when knights wore armor and jousted with each other to gain honor for the fair ladies whose favors they wore, accidents were not unknown. All too often, a lance – given momentum by the power of a charging destrier and about a hundredweight of metal – would pierce the breastplate of an opponent, with fatal results. Armor was expensive, though, and thrift was essential in those uncertain times. So, taking the pragmatic view, the breastplate would be cleansed of any unpleasant traces of its previous occupant and repaired, so that it could be passed on, in due course, to the poor man's son and heir. But first the hole made by the lance had to be repaired. The blacksmith-armorer would be consulted, and, having heated up the forge with much bellowing, the breastplate would be patched, hammered and burnished until it was as good as new. And the patch was called a 'placket'."

The correct definition of a "placket" is a pocket

in a woman's skirt. The slit in the skirt that gives access to the pocket is indeed known as a "placket-hole." Much of the rest of the definition, however, cannot be relied upon.

GHOSTS

This word game will test even the most literate of players. The rules are quite complicated, which makes performing a series of reasonably easy tasks a fiendishly tricky exercise.

Players: *best with six or more*
Equipment: *paper and pencil, and a dictionary to settle arguments*
Difficulty: *for adults rather than children*
Duration: *about 30 minutes a round, with experienced players*

Playing the game

The players sit in a circle and the one chosen to play first says a letter – any one that comes to mind. Then the next player, going clockwise, thinks of a word that starts with that letter, and adds another letter to the first one; this must be the next letter with which the word is spelt. (It is sensible to delegate one player to keep a record of the letters as they are added.) Then the third player thinks of a word – almost certainly it will not be the same word that the previous player had in mind – and adds a third letter, and so on, around the circle. So far so good, but the object of Ghosts – and this is where the trickery comes in – is to avoid being the player who completes an English word of more than three letters.

The scoring system

Ghosts takes its name from the rule that each player has only three lives – and lives can easily be lost. Any player whose turn it is may challenge the previous player to give the word that he or she was thinking of. If the player who is challenged fails to come up with a word that the other players accept as being valid – a dictionary can be used to check, if necessary – that player loses a life. But if he or she does provide an acceptable word, the challenger loses a life. Any player who completes a word also loses a life, but in this case a new round is started, with a different first letter.

After the loss of the first life, a player becomes a third of a ghost; a second loss makes the player two-thirds a ghost; a third and final loss turns the player into a full ghost. Once you have become a full ghost you are not allowed to join in the game, but you can have great fun haunting the living players noisily in an attempt to get one of them to talk to you. If you succeed, the tricked player joins you in the Other World immediately. Full ghosts can chatter away to each other as much – and as irritatingly – as they like. When all the other players have "passed on," the lone survivor is the winner.

Hints and tips

As with most good games, bluffing plays a large part in Ghosts. A player may have no idea of the word that the letters are building towards, but can still confidently call a letter. Remember that only the player who is next in turn can issue a challenge. Some house rules may be needed to control the full ghosts' behavior: are they allowed to pinch and throw things, for example? Are they allowed to make a lot of noise?

VARIATION

One variation on the basic version of Ghosts is Superghost, also called Fore-And-Aft. In this, letters can be added at the beginning of the words as well as at the end. For example, if the letters so far have spelt F, U, N, C, T, I, O, a player is not forced to finish the word with the letter "N," but can add an "S" to the beginning, thinking of "DYSFUNCTIONAL."

LICENSE PLATES

Car games have saved many children from perishing at the hands of their parents, so good ones are very welcome. License plates is completely mindless, but also distracting – at least for a while.

Players: *two or more*
Equipment: *pencils and paper*
Difficulty: *ideal for children*
Duration: *depends on how busy the road is, but generally 10 minutes a game*

Playing the game

One of the grown-ups specifies a number of letters and then each player writes down a word that is made up of that number of letters. Then the players have to keep an eagle eye on the road, checking the license plates of every vehicle they see. Whenever one of the letters in their word is seen, that letter is crossed off, and the first player to cross off all the letters is the winner.

Diagram 3 Playing Ghosts

Diagram 4 A game of License Plates

VARIATION

When the children grow tired of this game, you can reclaim your sanity for a while by suggesting a variation. Persuade them to write the whole alphabet down, and get them to cross off each letter as they see it. The winner is the player who crosses off the whole of the alphabet first. And when the pleasure of this variation has been exhausted, try another one: ask them to write down the numbers from 0 to 100, and cross them off as they see them. The first player to cross off all the numbers is the winner.

I Spy

The origins of this familiar game are lost in the mists of time, but it is always a firm favorite. It can be played by young children who have comparatively few words in their vocabulary, but take great delight in using them.

Players: *two or more*
Equipment: *none*
Difficulty: *only likely to appeal to children*
Duration: *can go on for ever, but patience generally limits the game to half an hour*

Playing the game

All children love this game, and most adults, playing with children, hate it after a couple of

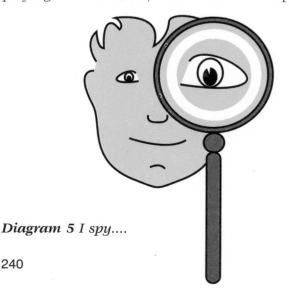

Diagram 5 I spy....

minutes. One player selects an object in the room or, more often, from the car window, and says: "I spy with my little eye something beginning with ... C." Nearly always the answer is "Car." The first person to identify the "spied" object has their turn.

VARIATION

It is possible to play a more interesting version in which the players can ask a number of "yes" or "no" questions about the object, such as: Is it gray? Is it bigger than me? Could I eat it? It may be advisable to limit this game to 10 questions each if you play in a car.

Twenty Questions

Also known as "Animal, Vegetable, Mineral," this game is an old favorite with both adults and children. It is educational as well as enjoyable, but is perhaps best played by those who have a fair amount of general knowledge.

Players: *four or more*
Equipment: *none*
Difficulty: *most suitable for groups with similar levels of general knowledge*
Duration: *five to 10 minutes a round, but a session usually lasts an hour*

Playing the game

This is the classic oral guessing game. One player thinks of an object or a concept and tells the others whether it is "animal," ""vegetable," "mineral", "abstract," or "a mixture." It is important that every player fully understands what these classifications mean. For example:

animal – includes animal products, such as butter, wool, leather and so on, as well as people and animals;

vegetable – *includes anything organic but not animal, such as paper, olive oil and pesto sauce;*

mineral – *means only something that has never been alive, such as paint or the moon;*

abstract – *indicates something non-material, such as the landscape, wickedness, or humor (this category is best not used if children are playing);*

a mixture – *means that the word includes elements of more than one of the above; in such cases it is usual to say what the primary quality is.*

The players are allowed 20 questions, including direct challenges, to find out what the word is – though an incorrect challenge means that the player who made it is out of the round. If they all fail, the person who chose the word wins. Any player who guesses correctly can choose the next word and be questioned in their turn. If an answer can be shown afterwards to have been incorrect, the player is disqualified.

An example
Player one has thought of a pair of leather shoes, and starts the round by saying: "My object is a mixture. It is mainly animal, but there might be some vegetable and mineral" (the player has glues and dyes in mind).
Then the questions start:

Question one: "Is it alive?"
Player one: "No."
Question two: "Can you eat it?"
Player one: "No."
Question three: "Would you show it to your mother?"
Player one: "Yes."
Question four: "Can you wear it?"
Player one: "Yes."

Question five: "Do you wear it on your wrist?"
Player one: "No."

And so on.

VARIATION
You can play the other way round, as a change. In this variation, one player leaves the room and those that remain choose the word. When the player returns, he or she has 20 questions in which to guess the answer. This version can be played as a knockout competition, with each player continuing in the game until they have failed to guess correctly, until the only one left is the winner.

Diagram 6 Suggestions for Twenty Questions

WHO AM I?

Best played in an informal manner, this game is simplicity itself, an yet it has hidden depths, and requires players to walk a fine line between parody and cruelty.

Players: four or more
Equipment: pencil and paper (but only to get started)
Difficulty: any age
Duration: depending on the number of players, five minutes to an hour

Beginning to play

This is a game for any number of players, but it works best when at least 10 people are involved. Ideally, it should be played informally – on a walk, or while dinner is being prepared. Each player writes their name on a piece of paper, folds it over and places it in a container. Then everyone takes one piece of paper out of the container and discreetly reads the name.

Playing the game

The game involves assuming the character and mannerisms of the person whose name is on the paper, with the other players having to identify who is being imitated. One way of playing it – the rather more organized way – is for each player to adopt an assumed character in turn, by talking, walking about, or doing anything else judged to be characteristic and identifiable. The other way of playing it – if a crowd of people are getting dinner ready, for example – is for everyone to carry on with what they were doing beforehand, but to do it in the manner of the assumed character.

Given that all the players know that someone in the room is being someone else in the room, Who Am I? is rarely very difficult. But the fun of the game lies in discovering how people perceive themselves and their friends. Be careful, though, because this game can break friendships as well as make them. And it can be quite disconcerting to discover mannerisms that you never knew you possessed.

BOTTICELLI

This game was known to games players before World War II as "The Box," perhaps because it can feel as if you are in the witness box when you play it. It is enormously versatile and great fun. Nobody knows where the name "Botticelli" came from.

Players: *three or more*
Equipment: *none*
Difficulty: *hard without good general knowledge; for adults*
Duration: *20 minutes to two hours*

Playing the game

Botticelli can be played anywhere – at home, in a train or on a long car journey. One person announces the initial of the surname of a famous

Diagram 7 Who Am I?

character, who may be fictional or real, dead or alive. The other players then think of famous people whose surname begins with the same initial letter and, taking it in turns, ask indirect questions about them. The player being questioned has to come up with the name of someone other than the person whose identity he or she has assumed who fits the criteria set by the question.

If he or she fails to do so, the player who asked the question can ask a further question, but this time it can be direct and must be answered either "yes" or "no." However, the "player in the box" can disallow a direct question by challenging the player who asked the indirect question to supply an answer if he or she has failed to do so.

Direct questions must be answered truthfully, but indirect questions need not be answered when they hit on the correct character. If, for example, you are Botticelli, you can legitimately answer the question: "Did you paint Birth of Venus?," with "I am not Botticelli." However, the same indirect question can be asked up to three times during a game.

The player who eventually guesses the answer correctly is the winner, and has the privilege of choosing the next mystery person. However, if nobody guessed correctly within 15 minutes, the player who set the puzzle announces the answer and is allowed to choose another character. Here is an example of how part of a game might go:

> *Player one: "My name begins with B."*
> *Player two: "Did you write* The Thirty-nine Steps?"
> *Player one: "I am not John Buchan."*
> *Player two: "Are you a bivalve sailor?"*
> *Player one: "Um, um . . . I don't know."*
> *Player two: "Barnacle Bill – so here is my direct question. Are you alive?"*
> *Player one: "No."*
> *Player three: "Are you a composer?"*
> *Player one: "I am not Beethoven."*

> *Player four: "Are you a king of the East who followed a star?"*
> *Player one: "Er ... sorry."*
> *Player four: "Balthazar. Are you a painter?"*
> *Player one: "Yes."*

And so on.

Hints and tips

To stand any chance of identifying a character, it is vital to get yourself in a position to ask direct questions – but it is also important that you phrase your question in such a way that the answer can either be "yes" or "no," otherwise the question need not be answered. It is surprisingly easy to make a mess of this – even people who have played the game for years sometimes make the dreadful mistake of asking: "Are you alive or dead?"

The art of indirect questioning lies in being either specific or oblique. There is little point in saying, "Are you a composer?", because there are a number of composers whose names begin with "B," and you will probably not get to a direct question (although remember that you are allowed to ask the same question three times). It is best to attach a century, nationality or other specific detail to your indirect question in order to pin a player down.

Or, even better, make your question oblique. For example, rather than ask, "Are you an actor who became an American president?" ask, "Are you the star of *Bedtime for Bonzo*?" (The answer, of course, is "I am not Ronald Reagan.") This type of question leads to lots of arguments, but that is all part of the fun. However, it is generally best to allow a consensus of the players to decide whether or not a question is unreasonably hard. There is always someone who is an expert on eighteenth-century composers or Egyptian pharaohs, but it is quite likely that anyone who falls into this category knows nothing about film stars, say, so you can always get your own back. Even so, it is sensible to tailor the game to the ages of the participants: for example, teenagers are unlikely to know much about Sir Laurence Olivier, while maiden aunts may well be unaware of Michael Jackson. And it is a major advantage, when choosing who to be, to select someone about whom you know a fair amount – it can be extremely irritating for the other players if you are unable to answer the most simple questions.

ASSOCIATION

As will become clear when you read on, this game is also known as "Chicken, Egg, and Bacon." Connections between words are made at high speed – usually these are obvious to all, but sometimes only make sense to the player who makes them, and have to be explained at laborious length.

Players: three or more
Equipment: none
Difficulty: best played in groups of roughly uniform ability
Duration: five minutes for each round, so allow an hour

Playing the game
The point of this game is to build up a long chain of associated words, so it could be extremely dull unless played fast and furiously. Unless a player is unable to make any association at all – in which case they are out immediately – success in the game depends on not using up three lives. A life is lost if a player hesitates (whether there has been hesitation can be put to a general vote) or if, after a challenge, no generally agreed association can be established between the previous word and the word that has just been played. However, if a challenge is made and the player challenged convinces the other players that an association does exist, the person who made the challenge forfeits a life. The game continues until only one player,. the winner, is left. A typical game might go like this:

Player one: "Work."
Player two: "Horse."
Player three: "Bridle."
Player four: "Cross."
Player one: "Why bridle and cross?"
Player four: "Well, you bridle when you are angry."
Player one: "OK. I lose a life. Church."
Player five: "Nave."
Player six: "Queen."

And so on.

SPELLING ROUND

This is a domestic – and original – version of the kind of game made famous by radio and television adaptations. As so often with games that have been popularized, the domestic version has a raw and pure quality generally lost with commercialization.

Players: six or more
Equipment: a dictionary
Difficulty: as hard as the players wish to make it; for groups with similar levels of knowledge
Duration: 20 minutes a round

Playing the game
In the basic version of this game, the players are divided into two teams and there is a question-master. The question-master reads out a word (making the selection with the help of a dictionary if the game is to be a hard one) and the first player in the first team has to spell it. If this is done successfully, the team is awarded a point; if they are unsuccessful, the question is offered to the first player in the second team, who has the chance to score a bonus point. The question-master then asks the second team's first player to spell a different word. When all the players in each team have had their chance, the team with the most points wins.

VARIATIONS

Another way of playing is to make it an individual game, with the players accumulating points for themselves. The question-master reads a word to the first player; if they get the answer right, another word is given – the process continuing until a mistake is made, at which point the questions move on to the next player. The player who spells the most words correctly wins.

If you are very good at spelling and find the game too simple, try backwards spelling. This is played in exactly the same way as the individual version described above, but the catch is that the players have to spell the words backwards.

Another variation is to ask two teams, with the same number of players each, to stand in a line opposite each other. The question-master then calls out a word to each player in turn, alternating between the teams. Each time a player spells out the word the opposite number on the opposing teams must shout "Right" or "Wrong." Any player who shouts "Wrong" to a word that has, in fact, been spelled correctly has to leave the game; the same thing happens if the shout is "Right" to a word that has been spelled incorrectly. The team with the last player still in the game wins.

Diagram 8 Spelling Round scoresheet

TABOO

The point of this talking game is to remember and observe silly rules that have just been made up. It seems simple, but it is irritatingly difficult to remember something that seems utterly obvious.

Players: *for three or more*
Equipment: *none*
Difficulty: *can be played by a mixture of children and grown-ups*
Duration: *children may want to go on longer, but 20 minutes is about right*

Playing the game

There are two versions of this highly entertaining game. In the simple version, a word that comes up often in conversation is chosen – for example, "and," "the" or "it" – and once all the players have agreed on the word it becomes "taboo". A question-master is chosen, and proceeds to question the other players about absolutely anything at all, in an attempt to make them use the taboo word – anyone who does so, or hesitates, is out, and the last player left in is the winner.

In the more difficult version, an individual letter is made taboo, and every word containing that letter is taboo. This is extremely difficult to play, and only for experienced games players.

PROVERBS

In this game you really have to think hard. Proverbs is not suitable for children because it assumes not only a knowledge of proverbs, but precise awareness of the way they are worded – without this, the game does not work.

Players: *three or more*
Equipment: *none*
Difficulty: *for grown-ups*
Duration: *an hour is the average length of a game with several rounds*

Playing the game

One player leaves the room while the others agree on a well-known proverb – "Too many cooks spoil the broth," for example. The player is invited back into the room and can ask the other players any question at all, and the reply must include a word of the proverb. The first player questioned must use the first word of the proverb; the second player the second word; and so on.

The questioner has to guess the proverb as quickly as possible. When all the words in the proverb have been used once, the process is repeated. In order that the game does not go on for ever, it is usual to set a time limit for each round. Here is how a typical game might go:

Q: Do you think you are a good writer?
A: No, no really I think I am too slapdash.
Q: If you had to be anyone famous on this earth, who would it be?

A: There are so many people I want to be and my ideas change every day; yesterday it was Michael Jackson.
Q: What did you have for supper last night?
A: I just had a takeaway as my wife usually cooks for me and she was out.
Q: I'm just about to paint my kitchen. Have you any ideas about what color scheme to use?
A: I would keep it very plain. Those fancy shades that are fashionable just for a few months spoil the overall effect.
Q: When was your last good holiday?
A: The last time I had a good holiday was so long ago that I can't remember it.
Q: What are you going to have for supper tonight?
A: I haven't been feeling well, so I might just have a little broth and a biscuit.

The last answer gives the game away.

Hints and tips

Here are a few suggestions for proverbs that should do very well in this game:

"A friend in need is a friend indeed."
"Still waters run deep."
"Many hands make light work."
"Let sleeping dogs lie."

VARIATION

Divide the players into two teams and give each team a prepared list of proverbs. The members of each team have to work together to translate the proverbs into the most wordy and complicated phrases that they can come up with, without losing the original meaning. For example:

"A bird in the hand is worth two in the bush."

becomes

"A feathered creature, whether plain or brightly colored as the case may be, which is kept in

your own possession by manual pressure, is of greater financial and/or symbolic value than twice that number of avian entities that are still lurking in bosky hedgerows, shrubs or undergrowth that shows a remarkable resistance to being accessible to humans."

Each team takes it in turn to read out their versions of the proverbs, while the other team tries to guess what the original proverb was. When all the proverbs have been deciphered, the team that was the fastest overall is the winner.

COFFEE POT

Sometimes called Tea Kettle, this is a word-substitution game. It requires quick thinking to work out what word has been substituted. It is just as good when played by two people in a car as it is when a group of friends plays after dinner.

Players: *four to eight*
Equipment: *none*
Difficulty: *suitable only for grown-ups*
Duration: *the enjoyment begins to pall after half an hour*

Playing the game
One player thinks of a word that has two or more meanings, such as "bolt" (a device to lock a door; a roll of cloth, or what a horse does when it gallops off out of control), or two words that sound the same but are spelt differently and have different meanings, such as "hear" and "here." This player then says a sentence using two or more senses or sounds of the word, but substitutes the phrase "coffee pot" for the chosen word or words.

For example, if the words are "hear" and "here," the player could say: "I came coffee pot yesterday but couldn't *coffee pot* anyone about." Each of the other players can then ask one question, to which the first player must reply using

one or other of the chosen words, or the chosen word in either of its meanings, but again substituting "coffee pot." The other players must try to guess the chosen word or words, and the first one to do so scores a point. If the word is not guessed, then the player who thought it up gets a point. The players take it in turns to think of "coffee pot" words, and when each person has had a turn the player with the most points is the winner.

VARIATION
In another form of this game, "coffee pot" is used as the substitute for a verb. Typical questions might be:

"Do you ever coffee pot in the office?"
"Have you coffee potted this week?"
"Does your mother coffee pot?"

There is, of course, a danger that this version may degenerate into regrettable smuttiness.

WRITTEN GAMES

Many of these games can be made as simple or as complex as you like, depending on the ages of those playing. Some written games lend themselves to long car journeys – if you have a steady writing hand!

Many written games, like spoken games, involve juggling with words and letters. You can play them alone, but it is much more fun playing in a group. Three of the games described here – Legs, Categories, and Stairway – depend on making alphabetical lists. In Legs, players have to list everything they can think of that has legs beginning with a chosen letter. Categories presents the same sort of challenge, but is simpler. Each person is given a list of categories, such as countries, towns, animals, or girls' names, to write down on their piece of paper. A letter of the alphabet is chosen and players have a set amount of time in which to write down as many words as possible in each category, starting with the chosen letter. In Stairway, each word in the list has to be one letter longer than the word before, so that you build a "stairway" of words all beginning with the chosen letter.

The two word games Transformation and Bridge the Word present the sort of exercise that you often find in intelligence and psychological tests. in Transformation, one word has to be changed into another by altering one letter at a time. Bridge the Word involves thinking of words that start and end with pre-defined letters.

The game of Pictures is a paper version of the acting game Charades. In fact, the charade started life as a written game, not an acted game, and was very popular among the leisured classes at the end of the eighteenth century. A charade plays a very important part in the plot of Jane Austen's novel *Emma*, when Mr Elton writes a charade which Emma assumes is a hidden message directed at her friend Harriet Smith, when it is really directed at Emma herself. Charades developed from a written pastime into an acting one during the nineteenth century.

Today quizzes are popular entertainment as television game shows, and are played as team games in many pubs and clubs. In the 1980s the board game Trivial Pursuit® (see chapter 2 on Board Games) took the quiz concept and remade it as a board game, becoming a phenomenal success around the world. However, it can be just as much fun compiling your own quiz at home – and the questions can be tailored to suit the ages and ability of the players.

Although most of these games take from five minutes to an hour to play, they do tend to be addictive once the players get into the flow of the game One round is rarely enough, especially for the more competitive player.

LEGS

Many people find this game compulsive, and that's possibly because the most improbable combinations of objects have legs.

Players: *three to 12*
Equipment: *pencils and paper*
Difficulty: *difficult to play well, though enjoyed by both adults and children; at its best as an after-dinner game for grown-ups*
Duration: *five minutes for a round, but many more are usually requested*

Beginning to play

Each player is given paper and a pencil, and then one person is elected to pick a letter at random. Next, note the time, because players have just two minutes to write down everything they can think of, starting with the chosen letter, that has legs (or can have them).

Playing the game

Legs might seem to be the simplest game ever invented. Play it once, though, and you will find that it is really quite difficult. In theory, the list can be considerably longer than the one shown in diagram 1. But it is surprising how quickly your mind goes blank, especially when you can see the other players scribbling away feverishly.

When the two minutes are up, everyone stops and one person starts off by reading out their list. Anyone who has the same word crosses it off their list. The next player then reads out their list, and the process is repeated. When all the lists have been read out, everyone declares how many words are left on their list, and the winner is the person with the most.

Hints and tips

The secret of success is to avoid the obvious and try to think of the more unusual things that have legs, so that you can keep your points. For example, if "C" was the letter chosen, the majority of players would immediately think of "CAT," but most likely such a commonplace word would benefit nobody. However, you might well keep your points if you came up with "COMMODE," or "CANON," or even "CARABINEER" (a soldier equipped with a carbine).

PLAYER 1

cat	chimneysweep
clergyman	chair
cupboard	cabdriver
caterpillar	camel
cheetah	canine
cheater	chinchilla
clown	cobbler
closet	cockerel
carpenter	consumer
carpetbagger	charmer
chicken	captive
cashier	chauffeur
citizen	
chiropodist	
cockroach	
chandler	

Diagram 1 A sample list of words with legs

CATEGORIES

This is a slightly simpler game than Legs, but it can be just as enjoyable. If anything, this old favorite relies more heavily on general knowledge.

Categories	D	B
five-letter nouns	dunce, duvet, diver	bidet, bench, belfry
cities	Dover, Denver, Detroit	
breeds of dog	Doberman, dachshund	
novelists	Dickens, Dostoyevsky	
composers	Debussy	
countries	Denmark	
poets	Donne	
parts of the body	duodenum, diaphragm, disc	

Diagram 2 *Scoring for Categories*

Players: *three or more*
Equipment: *pencils and paper*
Difficulty: *can be played successfully by a mixed group of adults and children, but it is perhaps more successful when played by adults only*
Duration: *15 minutes*

Playing the game

One person is elected (or take it in turns, if you intend to play more than one round) to select a list of categories. Eight is about the right number, but they should be as varied as possible and as difficult as you wish to make them. Categories might include: five-letter words, composers, novelists, breeds of dog, poets, mountain ranges, trees, dances, countries, actors, film stars, parts of the body, root vegetables and so on.

A letter of the alphabet is chosen at random (open a book and ask a player to point at a letter without looking at it) and players have 10 minutes in which to write down as many words as possible in each category, starting with the chosen letter. When the time is up, each player's list is read out and points are allotted. Scoring is simple: one point is awarded for any valid entry that is also on someone else's list; and two points are given for a valid entry that no-one else has got. Disputed words must be put to the majority vote. You can agree your own rules about eligibility beforehand, but generally only surnames count, rather than first names or titles. Foreign names – of cities, and so on – only count in their English form.

VARIATIONS

Children may find this game rather difficult, but it can be made easier by allowing any letter of the alphabet to be used when making entries in the various categories. The categories can be made more simple, too: animals, birds, and pop stars, perhaps.

A slightly more difficult version than this can be played if you write the letters of the alphabet down the left-hand side of a sheet of paper and choose a single category. Then each player must try to write down, within a set length of time, a word within the category starting with each letter of the alphabet. You can agree local rules to cope with problem letters, such as "X" and "Z." A player who achieves a "full house" of all 26 letters before the time is up wins automatically; otherwise the scoring system is the same as for the straightforward version of the game.

HEADLINES

This game imitates the outrageous newspaper headlines produced by some journalists. By the end of a game, the players may have developed some admiration for the journalists' skills.

Players: three or more
Equipment: pencils and paper, unless you have a very good memory
Difficulty: too hard for children, who rarely see the point; better for adults only
Duration: five minutes a round, but a session usually lasts for half an hour

Playing the game

The object of the game is to build amusing and attention-grabbing headlines of the type favored by the more extravagant newspapers. The first player begins a headline with a familiar word such as "millionaire." The next player adds a word before or after it. In this example, the contributions of each player are indicated by the use, or otherwise, of capitals.

CRY Baby MILLIONAIRE WON'T Pay Alimony

You can carry on for as long as you want, or until you think the headline is perfect, though the point of the game tends to be lost if the phrase becomes too long to be a genuine headline. There are no winners or losers in this game: it is played just for the fun of it.

QUIZZES

One of the best things about quizzes is that it is just as much fun compiling them as playing them. You can either play quiz games that come ready-made, or make up your own.

Players: three or more
Equipment: paper and pencil
Difficulty: as easy or as hard as you like; can be made suitable for any age group
Duration: at least an hour to prepare and an hour to play

Playing the game

There are no hard-and-fast rules about how to play quiz games, so these are just suggestions

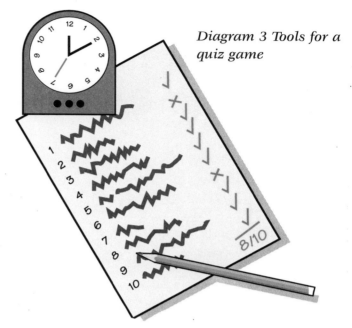

Diagram 3 Tools for a quiz game

about how to go about holding a quiz. With only a few players involved, it is best to ask the questions out loud, and allow an agreed time within which each player has to write down the answer. At the end of the quiz, the answers are checked and a point is awarded for each correct one. If four or more players are taking part, it is better to divide them into teams, and allow team members to confer (quietly) about their answers.

Obviously, though, a quizmaster is needed to set the questions, and it is best if they have a few days warning so that there is sufficient time to prepare properly. The first thing to do is to devise a theme.

The most important consideration when selecting a theme is to make sure that it is appropriate for the players, so that it is neither too easy nor too hard, and that no one person will be able to answer the majority of questions while the others are floundering. For example, it would be pointless setting a quiz on opera when one player is an opera buff and the others dislike opera. A way round the problem is to set a general knowledge quiz, taking questions from a wide range of subjects. That way everyone is sure to know at least some of the answers and it is unlikely that one person will know them all.

STAIRWAY

In this simple word game it doesn't matter if the younger players drop out as it proceeds, because they enjoy seeing what more can be done.

Players: *two or more*
Equipment: *pencils and paper*
Difficulty: *harder than you might think at the later stages, but for all ages*
Duration: *as long as you like, but an hour is usually enough*

Playing the game

Each player is given a piece of paper and a pencil, and then a letter is chosen at random. Players are given a set amount of time – five to 10 minutes is about right – to build as long a "stairway" as possible, in which each word begins with the chosen letter and each subsequent word is one letter longer than the word that precedes it. The winner is the player with the longest list when time is up; any spelling mistakes result in disqualification.

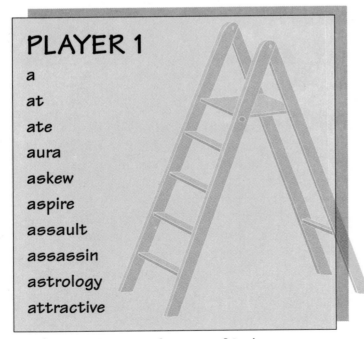

PLAYER 1

a
at
ate
aura
askew
aspire
assault
assassin
astrology
attractive

***Diagram 4** A sample game of Stairway*

PICTURES

A visual version of The Game, Pictures suits players of any age. It is particularly enjoyed by children, provided that fairly unsophisticated phrases are chosen. The game does demand at least some drawing ability.

Players: *best with four or more, though possible with only three*
Equipment: *a large blackboard and chalk, or a large drawing pad and felt-tip pens*
Difficulty: *as hard as you make it; adaptable for players of any age*
Duration: *half an hour or longer*

Playing the game

If you have ever written or received a pictorial letter, you will understand the concept of this game immediately, though in pictures you cannot use any letters of the alphabet. The players are divided into two teams, one of whom gives a member of the other team a phrase – this may be the title of a book, movie, play, or television show, a quotation, a proverb, or anything else you can think of. The player who has been given the phrase has to communicate it to the other members of the team solely by drawing. The idea is to guess what the drawing depicts as quickly as possible. Once the correct answer has been given the teams reverse roles.

Conventions

As in The Game, symbols are used to indicate the source of the phrase, but in this case they are drawn on the blackboard or pad. Generally, an arch represents a play; a camera is a movie; a book, obviously, is a book; quotation marks mean a saying, proverb, or quotation; and a face with an open mouth and musical notes represent a song – it is sensible for the teams to agree on symbols before the game starts. The number of words in the phrase is indicated by strings of dashes, one for each letter, while syllables are indicated by dots between the dashes. For "This sounds like . . .," draw an ear.

An example
If the chosen phrase was "Here We Go Round The Mulberry Bush," you would first draw quotation marks. Then you would put in the dashes and dots like this:

You might start with "bush," and draw a bush; then perhaps a berry – and hope that with "berry" and "bush" your team will have sufficient information to guess the whole phrase. If not, try drawing a circle under "round." If they still look blank, you might draw an ear, to mean "sounds like" and draw a cupped ear under "here."

This game can be quite hard, though some titles, such as *Three Men in a Boat*, lend themselves immediately to illustration. But *Persuasion* and *Casablanca*, for example, are far from easy.

TRANSFORMATION

Obvious games are often the best. Transformation involves changing one word to another by altering a single letter at a time, with the final word defined in advance.

Players: *three or more*
Equipment: *pencils and paper*
Difficulty: *depends on the length of the word chosen; for players of any age*
Duration: *from 10 minutes to half an hour, depending on difficulty*

Playing the game
This game is more difficult than it might seem at first glance. The same pairs of words are given to all the players, each of whom then tries to convert one word to the other in the fewest number of steps, changing only one letter at a time. For instance, given "dog" to "cat," you might do:

DOG, DOT, COT, CAT

This is easy enough. However, Transformation becomes harder and harder as you increase the number of letters in your words, and by the time you get up to six or seven letters success can be very hard to achieve.

BRIDGE THE WORD

In this word game you have to think of words – the longer and more complicated the better – that start and end with predefined letters. It is ideal for all levels of ability, without changing the basic idea.

Players: *three or more players*
Equipment: *pencils and paper*
Difficulty: *progressive, depending on the letters of the word chosen; for any age, but more enjoyable with older players*
Duration: *from 10 minutes to half an hour, depending on difficulty*

Playing the game
Each player draws six lines horizontally across a piece of paper. Then a six-letter word, chosen by mutual agreement, is written down the left-hand side of the paper, with each letter beginning a line. The same word is written backward down the right-hand side of the paper. with the longest words wins.

Chapter 5
SPORTING & ACTIVE GAMES

This chapter concentrates on sporting and active games, both games of skill and outdoor pursuits. In the Games of Skill section we focus on games that require ability as well as simple participation and competitiveness. These games demand not only mental agility and concentration but also the patience to practice, to become proficient and eventually, skillful.

Jacks and Fivestones are games that have developed different variations over the centuries but have an emphasis on mastering delicate moves with fingers and hands. Although having a reputation as a game for children, Tiddlywinks is also a pursuit taken seriously by many adults and considerable skill is needed to play the game at the top level. The chapter then moves on to more physical games. Carom Billiards is a cousin of Snooker and Pool while Darts is a widely played game that belies its origins in bars and taverns by requiring excellent hand-eye coordination! The chapter ends with perhaps the most active of all the games in this section, Ping-pong. Although popular around the world, no-one who has watched the game played at its peak in the Olympics could doubt the mental and physical prowess needed to compete.

The chapter then moves on to focus on outdoor games. This section deals specifically with those games that, although sometimes played inside, are best enjoyed in the environment they were designed for – the great outdoors. This is reflected in the energetic nature of these games and in the surroundings in which several are played – much of the pleasure is derived directly from the arenas and traditions that accompany them. This is especially true of Croquet and Lawn Bowls, two traditional sports that sum up the summer in all its glory and are accompanied by the chatter of good company. The chapter is not all about socializing though! It also features Horseshoe Pitching, a game that requires strength and accuracy, and Badminton, a sport whose light rackets and shuttlecocks belie the agility and speed needed to compete successfully. The chapter ends with group games that need little equipment but are lots of fun to play. These are games that many adults will remember from their schooldays: Tag, Hide and Seek, and Hopscotch. If you've any energy left after reading this chapter, a leisurely game of Marbles should renew your enthusiasm!

GAMES OF SKILL

In this section we look at games which, as well as natural ability, require a level of dexterity that demands that players make the best use of basic equipment and uncomplicated rules.

A perfect example of a game which has endured through the centuries due to its simplicity is Jacks. Played in ancient times, the game's origins lie in many different cultures and this is reflected in the different nationalities that still play the game today: the Japanese in America play Japanese Jacks, while a unique version of Jacks is still recognized in the North of England. The variations on Jacks are endless – Fivestones, Magic, Arches, Pecks, Bushels and Claws – but in essence all the different forms of this universal game rely on the skill of the competitor and the simple equipment – the knuckle-bones or jacks.

Pick-up-sticks is another old game, once known as Spillikins, which is still popular with children today. The idea behind it could not be simpler, involving as the name suggests, a set of sticks with different values. This simplicity is also mirrored in a game that so many children know and love – Tiddlywinks. It is argued that the game's origins are Chinese but it achieved worldwide popularity in the nineteenth century and was played by children in the parlor and somewhat more seriously by adults in the taverns of North America. A delightful game that relies on the individual's skill at flipping counters into a small pot, Tiddlywinks has grown into a very serious pastime with playing associations established all over the world, and uses one of the most truly bizarre sets of terms for equipment and moves that one could ever imagine.

Most will recognize the colored balls and green baize of snooker and pool from television and the local bar, but there is a much older version of these two popular sports – Carom Billiards, a game much played in the gentlemans' clubs of Georgian and Victorian England and one which still attracts large number of supporters around the world. Mary Queen of Scots is rumored to have possessed a Billiards table and been an enthusiast.

Another pastime familiar from the bar-room is Darts, a game with a fascinating martial history. Originally derived from the medieval English skill at archery, this game of high precision throwing was once the preserve of the English public house but has evolved to such an extent that its professional players compete for staggering prize money.

One of the fastest and most eyecatching tests of hand-eye coordination, Ping-pong, has risen to be one of the most popular sports in the world, played by Olympians and youth-clubbers alike. Also known as Table Tennis, this compact version of Lawn Tennis requires high levels of skill (and energy!) when played by top athletes yet is versatile enough to be enjoyed by the most leisurely of participants.

JACKS

This game was known in ancient Greece and Rome and was certainly played for centuries before that. Part of its appeal lies in the contrast between its inherent simplicity and the level of skill needed for success.

Brief history

Jacks is also known as Jackstones, Chuckstones, Dibs, Dabs, Fivestones, or Knucklebones. The last name gives a clue to its origins – the game was once played with the small bones from the knees of sheep. The game has evolved over many centuries, with local traditions developing and taking root: for example, a Japanese version of the game is now played in America, under the name of Otadama, or Japanese Jacks. The two basic games are Fivestones (the traditional version) and Jacks, which is played with a rubber ball. In both games players take turns to attempt throws that become increasingly complex — the sequence of throws being agreed between the players in advance. If a player fails to make a throw, or attempts a throw that is out of the agreed sequence, their turn is over. The winner is the player who achieves the longest and most complex series of throws correctly.

Diagram 1 A set of jacks

FIVESTONES

This is the original version of Jacks, and was known as Tali in classical times. Interestingly, it is still called Tally in some areas of the North of England.

Players: *two or more, or on your own for practice*
Equipment: *five small stones*
Difficulty: *success only comes with much practice*
Duration: *as long as the players wish*

The basic game

Place the five stones in the palm of your hand, toss them in the air and catch them on the back of your hand. Then use the back of your hand to toss the stones in the air, and catch them all in your palm. Also known as the "jockey," this is the basic throw – and it is much harder than it might seem.

One'ers

If you fail to catch any stones, your turn ends, but if you catch one or more, you can play "one'ers." In this, the stones that have been caught are transferred to your other hand and one stone is retained in your throwing hand. This is then thrown into the air, and you have the chance to retrieve one of the stones that was dropped previously before catching the stone that you threw in the same hand with which you threw it.

If you fail to do this, your turn is over; if you succeed, you can attempt to pick up any other stones that you dropped previously, one by one, in the same way.

One'ers also usually follows a successful basic throw in the sequence of agreed throws for experienced players, when all the stones have been caught. In this case, four stones are dropped to the ground deliberately, and the remaining stone thrown in the air.

Two'ers, three'ers and four'ers

Having played one'ers successfully, the next step is generally to play two'ers – though the players can agree any sequence of throws that they like before the game. In two'ers, four stones are dropped to the ground and one stone is thrown into the air. You then have to pick two stones up from the ground with your throwing hand before you catch the stone that has been thrown in the same throwing hand. As you would expect, two'ers is followed by three'ers, in which three stones have to be picked up, and then one stone. Four'ers demands that you pick up all the stones on the ground at the same time.

VARIATIONS

Experienced players move on from the basic game to challenge each other to attempt complex variations, though the basic game is normally played first, almost as a warm-up. There are endless numbers of these variations, and these are just a few examples.

Magic

This is played in the same way as one'ers, but only one stone is dropped to the ground and four stones are thrown up — all must be caught after the dropped stone has been retrieved.

Magic Flycatchers

This is the same as Magic, except that the stones that are thrown up must be snatched out of the air from above.

Pecks, Bushels and Claws

The first throw is the same as for the basic game, and if all five stones are caught on the back of the hand and then the palm the player can go straight on to Bushels. If none are caught, the player is out, as is also the case in Bushels and Claws. However, if any stones fall to the ground, one of the stones that was caught must be held between the first finger and thumb of the throwing hand, while any others are held in the same hand. Then the stone between the finger and

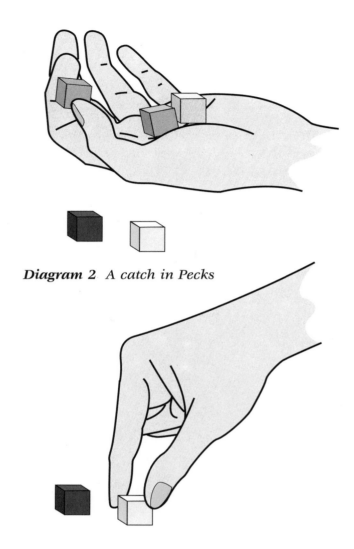

Diagram 2 A catch in Pecks

Diagram 3 Holding the stone for Pecks

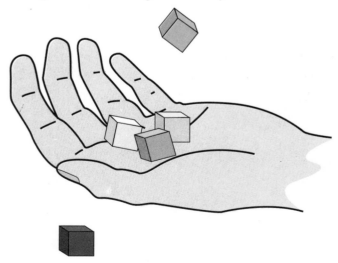

Diagram 4 Catching the stones in Pecks

thumb is thrown into the air, and one stone must be picked from the ground by the throwing hand before it is caught again. The sequence is repeated until all the stones have been picked up.

Next comes Bushels. Again, the first maneuver is the basic throw, and if all the stones are caught on first the back of the hand and then the palm, the player can go straight on to Claws. If not, all the stones that have been caught must be thrown into the air, a stone picked up from the ground and the thrown stones caught, all in the same hand. The sequence is repeated until all dropped stones have been picked up.

Then comes Claws. The basic throw starts the game, and if successful the player can go straight on to another designated throw, such as "one under the arch." If one or more stones are caught on the back of the hand, in the first part of the basic throw, the player must leave them in position and pick up the fallen stones. This time, however, the stones must be picked up individually, held between each pair of fingers on the throwing hand – without disturbing the stones on the back of the hand. Once picked up, the stones on the back of the hand must be thrown up and caught in the palm, and the stones between the fingers maneuvered into the palm.

Arches

In the basic version of Arches, four stones are placed close together on the ground and an arch is formed behind them with the thumb and little finger. One stone is thrown in the air with the other hand, and before it falls the player must flick the stones back through the arch one by one.

Not surprisingly, this variant is sometimes known as One Under the Arch. However, there are also Two, Three, and Four Under the Arch, in which, respectively, two, three, and four stones must be flicked through the arch at the same time.

Jacks

Confusingly, Fivestones is also known as Jacks, but, generally, the name "Jacks" is used to refer

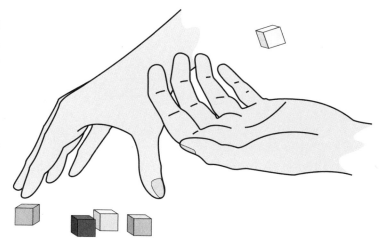

Diagram 5 *The hand position for Arches*

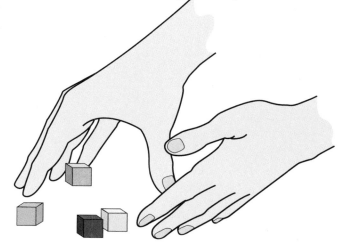

Diagram 6 *Flicking the stones through the arch*

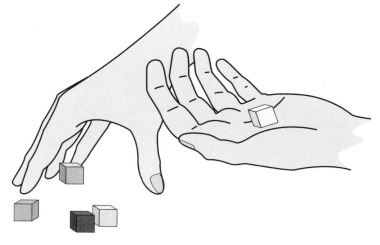

Diagram 7 *Catching the stone*

259

to a game that has evolved from it. To play the game you need a set of special jacks, which can be bought from most toy stores. The set comprises six shapes cast in metal, each with three spokes crossing and a sphere at the end of each spoke, and a rubber ball.

It is easy enough to modify any Fivestones throw for use with Jacks, with the extra difficulty that the ball must be thrown up and caught, or allowed to bounce once before being caught. However, there are also a number of games that are specifically for jacks.

The basic game

Also known as the Baby Game or Eggs in Basket, this is the first in an agreed sequence of throws. The first player lets the jacks fall to the ground from one hand, and then throws the ball in the air, allowing it to bounce only once. They must then pick up one jack, using the same hand, before catching the ball, again in the same hand. This is the equivalent of one'ers in Fivestones, and is followed by two'ers (when two jacks are picked up at a time), then three'ers, and so on. The jacks that have been picked up are transferred to the non-throwing hand, the "basket," before each pick-up.

VARIATIONS

When the basic game has been completed, the players can move on, by agreement, to more complex throws. Here are a few examples.

Crack the Eggs

This is played in the same way as the basic game, but each jack (or jacks) must be tapped once on the ground before the ball is caught and the jack is transferred to the other hand.

Pigs in the Pen

This is very similar to Arches in Fivestones. The "pen" is formed by the thumb and first finger of the non-throwing hand, and one "pig" is flicked into the pen with another finger before the ball, having bounced once, is caught. The game con-

tinues with two pigs being flicked, then three, and so on.

Pigs over the Fence

This is similar to pigs in the pen, but the non-throwing hand is laid on the ground on its side, to form the "fence." Instead of being flicked into the pen, the pigs are placed on the other side of the fence.

PICK-UP-STICKS

This test of manual dexterity and guile amuses children for hours. The modern shop-bought version is derived from the ancient game of Spillikins, in which elaborately carved strips of wood are hooked from a pile with a special tool.

The sticks

Pick-up-sticks sets can be bought at most toy stores, though they may be masquerading under another name, such as Jackstraws or Jerkstraws. Generally a set consists of about 50 sticks, each about 15cm (6in) long, made from either wood, metal or plastic. Colored rings mark the value of each stick, which is usually from one to five.

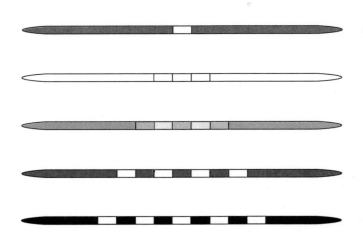

Diagram 8 Pick-up sticks

Playing the game

One player drops all the sticks on to the floor. Taking it in turns, players try to extract a stick from the pile without disturbing any other stick — if another stick moves, the turn is over. Once a particular stick has been touched, no other stick may be touched until the original stick has been taken out of the pile; if successful, a player can then attempt to move another one. At the end of the game, the points value of each player's sticks is counted, and the player with the highest score is the winner.

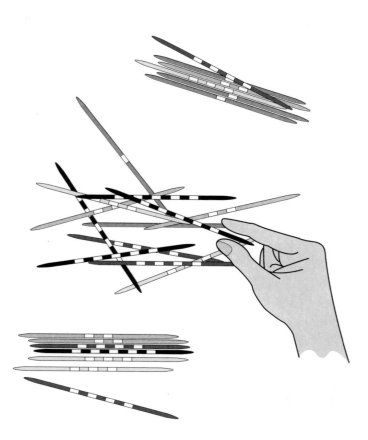

Diagram 9 *Playing pick-up sticks*

TIDDLYWINKS

Long a favorite of children, Tiddlywinks is now taken very seriously by large numbers of adults. Regular tournaments are held in both America and Britain, and there is even a World Championship.

Players: *two, with each using two sets of counters; or four, playing in pairs*
Equipment: *colored counters, a felt mat, and a cup*
Difficulty: *considerable practice is needed to compete at the top level*
Duration: *20 minutes for a singles game; 25 minutes for a pairs match*

Brief history

The first patent application of the game of Tiddlywinks – or Tiddledy-winks, as it was then called – was made in 1888, by Joseph Fincher. However, historians of the game, who take the matter extremely seriously, contend that Tiddlywinks had its origin in ancient China, and that it developed in the first half of the nineteenth century from a now forgotten game called Squails.

Originally, Tiddlywinks was played by children in the parlor and by more boisterous types in the tavern — becoming something of a fad in late nineteenth-century America. The fad soon passed, and Tiddlywinks became almost exclusively a children's pastime – until a group of students at Cambridge University, in England, took up the game in 1955. Within a few years, Tiddlywinks was being played seriously at most British universities, and in 1961 an Oxford University team embarked on a Tiddlywinks tour of America. The game quickly took hold, in particular at the Massachusetts Institute of Technology (MIT). As in Britain, it spread quickly, and today there is a North American Tiddlywinks Association (NATwA), an English one (ETwA) and a Scottish one (ScotTwA). Each holds regular competitions and tournaments to decide Singles, Pairs and Teams of Four titles. International events are supervised by the International Federation of Tiddlywinks Associations (IFTwA), which also holds a World Singles and World Pairs championship.

The conventions

The equipment and rules that follow conform to current internationally accepted practice, but it is worth remembering that pre-1960 Tiddlywink sets may come with different sets of rules. However, older sets can still provide a good deal of enjoyment.

Tiddlywinks has an extraordinary language of its own, and some words, such as "tiddlies," are now more or less obsolete. Unfortunately, there isn't sufficient space here to list all of the terms used, but if you wish to find out more, you can do so by accessing one of the many Internet sites devoted to Tiddlywinks, and consult the lexicon. Copies of the detailed rules can also be obtained from the Internet or from national associations.

The equipment

In a singles match, each player uses, separately, two sets of colored disks from a selection comprising blue, red, green, and yellow disks. In a pairs match, each player uses one set, but plays as part of a team with their partner. Blue always partners red, and green always partners yellow.

Each set of disks includes four small, round disks known as "winks." The winks are propelled by a strike from a "squidger," or by pressure from it. The winks are of a standard size: the two small ones are 16mm (⅗in) in diameter and the two larger ones are 22mm (⁹/₁₀in). The squidgers may be of any size, provided that they are round, no thicker than 5mm (⅕in), and 21–51mm (⁹/₁₀–2in) in diameter. Tournament players choose a squidger of an appropriate size and with an appropriate edge that they have personalized according to the type of shot that they are trying to make, just as a golfer chooses a club according to the nature of the shot. Any number

of squidgers can be carried, though only one for each shot.

The game is played on a felt mat 182 x 141cm (72 x 55in) in size. A straight line (a baseline) is drawn across each corner, at right angles to the diagonal of the mat and 141cm (55in) from the center of the mat – the field of play consists of all areas of the mat outside the baselines. A cup (the pot) is placed in the middle – it is 38mm (1½in) high, with a 38mm (1½in) base and a 48mm (1⁹/₁₀in) diameter top. All of the equipment can be bought as a set from most toy stores, but if you intend to play seriously check that they conform to the recognized specifications.

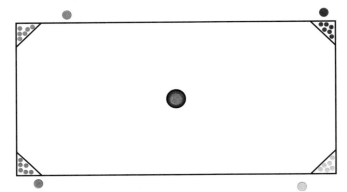

***Diagram 10** The start of a game of Tiddlywinks*

The aim of the game

At its simplest, the aim of Tiddlywinks is to shoot all of your winks into the pot (to pot out). In a pairs game the time limit is 25 minutes, followed by five extra rounds (finishing with the fifth round of the first color to play). In a singles game the time limit is 20 minutes, again with five extra rounds following.

However, the game is much more complex than this, because it involves not only skill but a thorough appreciation of both strategy and tactics. It is possible to put an opponent's wink out of play by squopping it – that is, by covering any part of the wink with one of your winks – and also possible for your opponent to free a squopped wink. As a result, it is far from common for any player to pot out. Instead, the aim is to score more points than your opponent.

Diagram 11 The potting shot

The scoring system

There are seven points to play for in each game, and there are two ways of getting them. If a player pots out, the situation is fairly simple: they are awarded four points, and all squopped winks are unsquopped, with the winks that squopped them being placed alongside the squopped ones, equidistant from the pot and, ideally, 2 mm away from it. The game then continues, but thereafter any winks that are squopped are automatically unsquopped in the same way as described above, and the time limit no longer applies. The next player to pot out gets two points, then all winks are unsquopped as before. The third player to pot out is awarded one point and the remaining player receives no points. The number of points won by the paired colors (or paired players) are then added up and one point is taken from the losing partnership and awarded to the winning one. Another game then starts – tournaments are often decided by the

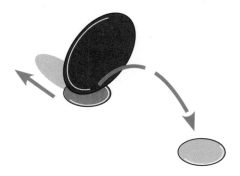

Diagram 12 A squopping shot

aggregate score over a number of games.

More often, none of the players pots out. In such cases the seven points are awarded differently. When the game finishes – the time limit having expired and five further rounds having been played – the score is calculated as follows: any wink that has been potted counts for three time-limit points (these are "sub-points" and determine the final points) and any unsquopped wink counts for one tiddly (so long as it is not still behind the baseline). The player with the largest number of tiddlies is then awarded four points; the next best player is given two points; and the third best gets one point. The number of points for each paired color are then added together to give the aggregate score. If there is a tie in the number of tiddlies, the number of points are added together and divided equally – so if the two colors are first equal, they would both receive three points.

Beginning to play

The winks are placed within the baseline at each corner, with paired colors on opposite corners (it is easy to remember the sequence if you bear in mind that the colors are arranged alphabetically – blue, green, red, yellow – clockwise). Then, taking it in turns, each player has one attempt to squidge one wink as near to the pot as possible – this procedure is known as the "squidge-off." Any wink that is potted wins, otherwise the nearest wink to the pot wins. If two players have winks equidistant from the pot, they each squidge another wink, until the victor is decided. All the winks are put back behind the appropriate baseline and then the winner of the squidge-off (who by convention plays yellow) starts the game.

Playing the game

Before the game starts a timekeeper should be elected, because the clock starts as soon as the player who won the squidge-off takes the first shot. Each color is then played in turn, going clockwise round the mat. Each shot must be played within 30 seconds of the previous one, any further time taken being taken off the time limit at an opponent's request. Only one shot is allowed per turn unless a wink is potted, in which case another shot is allowed. No player is obliged to make a shot during a turn, and can elect to pass. If any wink is squidged off the mat the next turn is forfeit and the wink is replaced in the field of play 22mm (⁹/₁₀in) from the boundary as close as possible to the point at which it left the mat. A turn is also forfeit if no winks of the color playing are available to be squidged – you are not allowed to squidge a squopped wink until it has been unsquopped by a shot from your partner or paired color. However, if neither partner in a pair has an unsquopped wink their opponents may take a "free turn" and take one shot, taking it in turns, for each wink in play that is neither squopped or squopping, before unsquopping one wink of the colors that had been unable to play by means of a "freeing shot."

There are many ways in which a shot can be made, varying from gentle pressure from the squidger to a firm strike. However, in all cases the squidger must first touch the surface of an unsquopped wink and the movement of the squidger must not start more than 5cm (2in) above the surface of the wink. If these conditions are not satisfied, or if any wink is damaged, the shot is a foul, and the opponents must either replace the winks as they were before the shot and ask the player to take another shot, or accept the result of the shot as it was played; the clock is stopped during these proceedings.

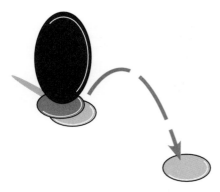

Diagram 14 A Bristol is used to move both your wink and one that you have squopped onto an opponent's wink, squopping them both

Hints and tips

When they first start to play Tiddlywinks, most people try to pot all their winks immediately. However, they soon see that this is far from easy. A player who attempts to pot out on the first turn will soon find that their winks are squopped by opponents as, inevitably, some or all of them of them miss the pot. The best strategy in Tiddlywinks is to position your winks fairly close to the pot, so that you can either pot them on your next turn or be in a position to squop an opponent's wink.

After a few rounds, a number of winks have normally been squopped – in fact, squopping winks may have been squopped themselves, as "piles" start to form. Now is the time for great caution: if, for example, you have potted two winks and your other four winks have been squopped, you will be out of the game until your

Diagram 13 A boondock is used to send a wink that you have squopped away from the pot.

Diagram 15 A blow-up shot involves shooting your wink as hard as you can at a pile to cause maximum disruption

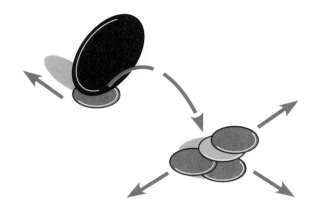

Diagram 16 A bomb shot

partner (or the other color you are playing, if it is a singles match) unsquops one of your winks. And it will be far from easy for this to be done, because your opponents will have two turns to your partner's one.

However, there are a number of squidging techniques that help to resolve difficult situations and it is as well to practise them until you are proficient.

CAROM BILLIARDS

This form of billiards – in itself a much older cue game than either snooker or pool – retains its popularity around the world, with large numbers of international tournaments held each year.

Players: two, or four in pairs
Equipment: table, 3 balls and cues (see below)
Difficulty: can be played at various levels
Duration: as long as you wish

The equipment

A carom billiards table is different from the one used to play ordinary billiards. It is smaller (304.8 x 152.4cm/120 x 60in), it has no pockets, and it has a different system of spots and markings (see diagram 17). Three standard billiards

balls are used, of which one is red and two are white (one of the white balls is spotted), and the game is played using standard snooker of billiards cues.

Aim of the game

To be the first player, or pair, to reach a previously agreed number of points. There are three versions of carom billiards, with increasing levels of difficulty, but they share the same basic rules.

Starting the game

First, the players or pairs decide who is to take the first turn by a process known as "lagging." The red ball is put on the "foot spot" (see diagram 18) and each player (or a nominated player from each pair) places their white "cue" ball – one of which will carry a spot – on the "head string" on either side of the "head spot" but within 15cm (6in) of it. In turn, the players lagging play their balls off the foot cushion, with the intention of returning them as close as possible to the head cushion. Neither cue ball must disturb the red ball or cross to the other side of the red ball and interfere with the other player's line, otherwise the stroke is a foul and does not count. The player whose ball is nearest to the head cushion starts the game.

Playing the basic game

The most simple form of Carom Billiards is called "straight rail carom." The first player to

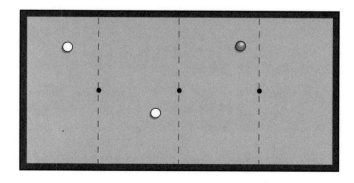

Diagram 17 A Carom Billiards table

make a stroke has to play a "break shot." The red ball is placed on the foot spot and the "object ball" is placed on the head spot – this is the opponent's ball, distinguished either by a spot or the lack of one, and each player must stick to their ball throughout the game. The "cue ball," which is to be struck with the cue, is placed as for the lagging shot — on the head string, within 15cm (6in) of the head spot.

For this "break shot," and for this shot alone, the player strikes the cue ball and has to make contact first with the red ball. The aim is to make a "carom shot" – that is, to make the cue ball hit the red ball (in this case) and then hit the other white ball (the "object ball"). In the basic game it does not matter whether or not the cue ball bounces off a cushion before doing so.

If the first player makes a successful carom shot, they are awarded a point and can continue playing. However, on any other go but the first one it does not matter whether the red ball or the other object ball is hit first. A point is awarded for any successful carom shot, in which both balls are hit in succession, but a point is deducted if such contact is not made and the player's turn ends. The next player or member of a pair, then takes to the table.

The only exception to this rule is if the player makes a successful "safety shot." To do this, a player must either strike the cue ball in such a way that it comes to rest in contact with a cushion after hitting an object ball, or that the object ball itself comes to rest in contact with a cush-

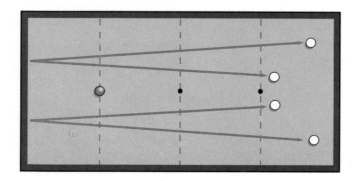

Diagram 18 *Lagging*

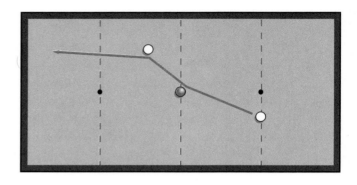

Diagram 19 *Carom shot*

ion. No point is deducted, but the player's turn ends. However, only one safety shot may be played during any one session at the table: to attempt two safety shots is a foul: one point is deducted from that player's score and their turn ends.

Fouls and exclusions

There are a number of possible fouls in Carom Billiards as well as failing to make a carom shot. For example, it is a foul to cause the cue ball to fly off the table — the penalty is the deduction of one point and the end of the turn. (The cue ball is put back on the head spot, or the foot spot if this is occupied, or the center spot if both are occupied.). If either of the object balls leaves the table the red ball is put back on the foot spot and the object ball is replaced on the head spot. In this case, however, the player can continue their turn, and still count any previous scores made during that session at the table. But if all the balls leave the table, the turn ends, a point is deducted, and the balls are repositioned as for a break shot.

If the two object balls are touching each other on a cushion, play can continue normally. However, if one of the balls is the cue ball, it must either be played away from the other object ball, or all the balls must be repositioned as for a break shot.

One of the hazards of ordinary Billiards is that it is possible to make up to 75 "cannons" – the equivalent of a carom – in succession when the object balls are stuck in a corner. This tedious problem is avoided in Carom Billiards because of the rule on "crotch" shots. The object balls are said to be "crotched" when they are both within an imaginary line drawn across each corner 12cm (4⁷⁄₁₀in) from the apex of the corner. Only three successive scoring shots may be made in this situation, and any attempt at making a fourth results in the end of the turn.

Otherwise, the normal restrictions of snooker and billiards apply. It is a foul, resulting in the end of a turn and the deduction of a point, to: make a shot while any ball is still in motion; touch the cue ball more than once in the course of a shot; push the cue ball, rather than strike it cleanly; touch an object ball with the cue; use the wrong cue ball; or have both feet of the ground when making a shot.

VARIATIONS
One-cushion Carom

In this variant of the game it is not sufficient for the cue ball to touch both object balls, whether or not it strikes one or more cushions before, after or during hitting them. A point is only awarded, and the turn allowed to continue, when either the cue ball hits one or more cushions before striking both object balls, or the cue ball hits an object ball without hitting a cushion beforehand, but then hits one or more cushions before striking the other object ball.

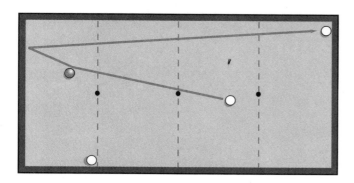

Diagram 20 Safety shot

Three-cushion Carom

This is the most complex version of Carom Billiards, since, as the name implies, three cushions must be hit – they need not, however, be different ones. A point is scored and a turn is allowed to continue only when the cue ball hits three or more cushions after striking the first object ball but before striking the second one; hits three or more cushions before striking both object balls; hits either one or two cushions before striking the first object ball and then, respectively, two cushions or one cushion before hitting the second object ball.

DARTS

Believed to have evolved from medieval archery competitions, Darts was once rarely played outside British pubs. Then, the game became popular on TV, and now it is played all around the world.

Players: *two people or teams*
Equipment: *darts and a dartboard*
Difficulty: *can be played by amateurs and professionals*
Duration: *about 10 minutes for a game*

Equipment

The standard dartboard is composed of densely-packed sisal fibers held in place by a steel band. The circle is 46cm (18in) in diameter, and is divided by steel wire into 20 wedges, each of which has a scoring value of from one to 20 points. Four more circles are superimposed on the main one, again being delineated with steel wire: the outer circle (the doubles ring) doubles the value of a wedge's points; the middle one (the triples ring) triples the value; the outer part of the circle at the center (the outer bull) scores 25; and the inner bull scores 50.

Darts come in sets of three. Each one has a steel point fused to the barrel (some players choose "dynamic" points that are screwed into the barrel — these are more expensive, but they make it less likely that a dart will hit a wire on the dartboard and bounce off it.) The barrel is made either of brass or a tungsten alloy, and often grooved to give a better grip. The shaft, made of plastic or a light metal, screws into the barrel at one end and bears the flight — the plastic or fabric "feathers," without which the dart would not fly — at the other end. A wide range of darts is available and Darts players tend to experiment with different designs and have individual favorites.

Diagram 21 A dartboard and darts

To conform with the strict rules of the game, the dartboard must be positioned precisely: it should be hung with the 20 wedge directly at the top so that the bull is exactly 172.72cm (5ft 8in) above the ground. Two throwing lines can be used, and these should be 236.85cm (7ft 9¼in) and 293.05cm (9ft 7⅜in) along a line drawn from the floor directly below the dartboard. Which line, known as the "oche," is used should be agreed before play starts and depends on the skill of the players. (To avoid damage to flooring it is sensible to place a rubber mat or spare piece of carpet underneath the playing area; the throwing lines can be marked with adhesive tape.) A blackboard or large sheet of paper on which scores are recorded should be kept behind the throwing line.

Darts can be dangerous, so it is vital that safety rules are adhered to at all times. The dartboard should be positioned where no-one (including pets) is likely to walk unexpectedly and so that darts cannot pass by the board to cause injury. No one should be allowed on the dartboard side of the throwing line during play. Darts should not be thrown recklessly, and you should not attempt to catch a dart that has bounced off a wire. Children should not be allowed to play Darts except under supervision. Shoes should always be worn to protect the feet.

General rules

Darts can be played by two people or by teams, with players from each side taking alternate turns in rotation. Each turn consists of three throws, after which the darts are retrieved during a break in play. Players are allowed to cross the throwing line during a turn to check what score has been achieved, but their turn ends if any dart is touched. A dart only counts if it sticks in the board, and no second attempt is allowed if a dart bounces out of the board or misses it. No part of a player's foot may extend over the throwing line, though leaning forward over the line is allowed.

Starting the game

The usual way to decide who throws first is for each player to throw one dart, aiming for the bull — the player closest to it starts. (On this occasion, a player is allowed another throw if the dart bounces off the board.) This procedure is known as "corking up," and traditionally the winner is allowed to decide what type of game will be played. There are two main types (though numerous other variations): 301 or 501; and Cricket (also known as Closing).

301 and 501

These two games are essentially the same: 501 takes longer and 301 is more common at professional level. Each player or team takes turns to throw the three darts. Each score is deducted from 301 or 501, with the aim of reducing the score to exactly zero. The last dart thrown to achieve a score of zero (which can be in the middle of a turn) must be a double. (A variation of the straightforward 301 and 501 is that each team player must start on a double; this is more common in games of 301.) If any dart reduces the score to less than zero, or "busts," none of the darts from that round count.

Cricket

This game bears no relationship to the game played in much of the world with a bat and ball. However, playing it does require a good sense of strategy. Darts Cricket uses only six of the scoring wedges – 20, 19, 18, 17, 16, and 15 – and the bull.

Each player, or team, attempts to score three hits (or two in the case of the bull) on these targets in any sequence, scoring points each time a dart makes a hit on the required wedge or on the bull. The winner is the player who is ahead on points when one side or the other has completed all the hits. The three hits can be made in various ways: with three individual strikes; with a double and one individual strike; or with a triple. Once a target has been hit three times it is said to be "open" — that is, it is owned by that player or team, and further hits can be made upon it. This continues until the target is "closed," which happens when the opposing player has also made three hits on it. Once a target has been closed, no further scoring hits can be made on it.

PING-PONG

Since the first Ping-pong set was marketed, in the 1880s, this game has achieved worldwide popularity. Also known as Table Tennis, it is a highly professional sport with millions of adherents — yet it is simple enough be played on a kitchen table.

Players: *two (singles) or four (doubles)*
Equipment: *table, net and paddles*
Difficulty: *can be played by amateurs and professionals*
Duration: *a professional game should take 15 minutes*

Equipment

The professional game has precise rules about the dimensions of the table: it should measure 274 x 152.5cm (9 x 5ft), and stand 76cm (2ft 6in) high. Tables can be bought from specialized stores, but one can easily be made for home use by cutting a piece of plywood to size and fixing it over an existing table. Mark the end and side lines at the edges of the table with a strip of white paint 2cm (³⁄₄in) wide. A thinner line, 3mm (¹⁄₈in) wide, runs vertically down the center of the table. The net and its supporting posts and clamps are 15cm (6in) high — these will need to be bought.

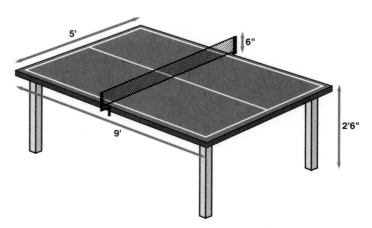

Diagram 22 A Ping-pong table

In recent years there has been considerable controversy about the composition and manufacture of paddles (or racquets, as they are called in professional circles). Now the rules forbid the use of any solvent-based adhesives and insist that only adhesives approved by the International Table Tennis Federation (ITTF) should be used to stick rubber to the paddles. Regulations also determine the thickness of the pimpled rubber that is used on the hitting sides of a paddle. It is wise to check that any paddle you purchase conforms to the international standards if you wish to play Ping-pong seriously.

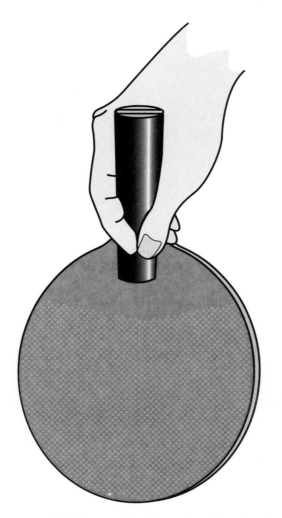

***Diagram 23** The pen-holder grip gives beginners more control*

The balls used in Ping-pong are light spheres that are made of plastic or celluloid, and these must also conform to the international regulations about exact size and ability to bounce.

Playing singles

Toss a coin to determine who is to serve first. Players must serve near court to opposite court. If you are the server, start play by placing the ball on your open palm, then raise your palm quickly so that the ball rises vertically from it. No spin must be imparted to the ball, which must be in clear sight of the service receiver at all times, and it must rise at least 15cm (6in) from its starting position and be descending before you can hit it.

The ball must first bounce on your side of the net, then cross over the net without touching it and bounce on the receiver's side before it can be played; only one bounce is allowed. If the ball touches the net, a "let" is called and the serve must be replayed. A let is also called if it is agreed that the receiver was not ready to receive the serve. If the ball does not bounce as described, or if it fails to cross over the net, the point is won by the receiver.

The receiver plays the serve by striking it over the net to the server's side. If the receiver fails to do this, the server has won the point; if the receiver returns the ball successfully but the server is unable to return the ball, the receiver wins the point. Lets only apply during a serve and not during play, when it does not matter whether the ball touches the net. Any player who touches the table with any part of their paddle or body during play forfeits the point.

At the end of each point, the game is restarted with a serve. Each server has five consecutive serves, after which the server becomes the receiver, and vice versa. The winner is the first player to reach 21 points. However, if both players reach 20 points, the winner is the player who first opens up a two-point lead, with the service alternating between players.

Competitive matches are generally decided over three or five games. Players must change ends between games.

The expedite system

Unless the two players have each reached 19 points, the expedite system comes into force when a game has lasted for 15 minutes but is still not finished. The number of successful return strokes by the receiving player are counted out loud and the receiver is awarded the point if they exceed 13. The serve then alternates between points. In professional competitions, play is halted by the umpire as soon as the 15 minutes is up, even during a rally. The serve then goes to the player who had served to start the rally.

Playing doubles

When playing doubles, the first server in a pair stands behind the right-hand court, and must serve in the same manner as in singles play to the opposite court — in other words to the opponent's right-hand court. The receiver returns the ball, which must be played by the partner of the original server; the partner of the original receiver returns this shot to the original server; and so on (if a player strikes the ball in the incorrect order, that side forfeits the point).

When the point is over, the same player as before serves to the same receiver for the next four points. When five serves are up, the service changes to the original receiver, who serves to the original server. The next player to serve is the original server's partner, serving to the original receiver's partner; then the original receiver's partner serves to the original server's partner. All serves are made from the right-hand court to the opposite right-hand court, so the players must move positions between every five serves.

If the expedite system comes into operation the serving sequence stays in force, but each player only serves once before service moves on.

Hints and tips

The secret of success in Ping-pong is an ability to play a wide range of shots (essentially the same as those used in Tennis), to impart spin to the ball and to recognize any spin that your opponent puts on the ball and take appropriate counter measures. As with most games of skill, this ability only comes with considerable practice.

When you are developing your range of strokes, here are a couple you might like to try. Forehand or backhand drives put considerable speed on your shot, making them hard to counter. Stand slightly side-on to the table, tip your paddle towards the net and hit the ball with a slicing, upward stroke, using your entire arm and finishing with the paddle above your head. If you prefer cunning rather than power, try a drop shot that barely makes it over the net, falling so short that your opponent can't reach it.

OUTDOOR GAMES

This section deals with games that are ideal for relaxed summer days when friends and family can gather to play games that combine skill and application with a little relaxed socializing.

These are games which tax the body more than the mind, although tactics and strategy are usually involved and will need to be carefully considered. Horseshoe Pitching is derived from the European pastime of Quoits, but is a game played mostly in North America. The object of the game is to throw, or "pitch" horseshoes at stake embedded in the ground, the action taking place within a rectangular court. Basically a very simple game, it does require considerable skill to get the horseshoe as near to the stake as possible and be warned – those horseshoes are not light!

Characterized by perfectly manicured lawns and gleaming clubhouses, Lawn Bowls has gained a reputation as a game for those advancing in years – but the truth is somewhat different. This apparently relaxing game requires immense concentration and a high level of skill in order to set the perfectly weighted bowls rolling as near to the smaller "jack" as possible.

Although nothing quite conjures up the image of the a genteel summer pastime as well as the crack of Croquet balls, this civilized game was originally a French invention. Migrating to England in the nineteenth century, it gained a reputation as a game for the aristocracy, but has widened its appeal and is now played all over the world.

Similarly popular is Badminton, seen by many people as a poor relation to Lawn Tennis. Played on a smaller court, the feathered shuttlecocks give a false impression of a game lacking in strength but in fact propelling the light shuttlecocks at high speed requires force, finesse and precision. With little equipment needed and simple rules, Badminton is an ideal game to play both indoors and out.

On a more basic level, Marbles has many variations and has been a constant favorite with children, not least because of the interesting terminology involved. Dodge Ball simply requires some open space and a ball. To avoid tears, it is usually best to find one as soft as possible to use.

All the games mentioned so far have one thing in common – equipment. But there are games that require only one commodity in order to have a good time – people. Statues, for example, is popular at parties and just requires someone to take the part of Grandma. Hide and Seek is an old standby which provides endless opportunities for surprise and hilarity. Simon Says requires nothing more than the desire to give the orders – and have them obeyed. Hopscotch, a quintessential childhood game for many, calls only for a piece of chalk and some small stones. Simplicity is the byword here so relax and enjoy!

HORSESHOE PITCHING

Related to Quoits, Horseshoe Pitching is little known outside North America. It is extremely popular here, however, with clubs holding regular competitions under a codified set of rules. It can also be enjoyed less formally, in a park or playground.

Players: *two, or four playing as pairs*
Euipment: *played on a court with horseshoes*
Difficulty: *success only comes with much practice*
Duration: *half an hour*

Court and equipment

Horseshoe Pitching is played on a rectangular court 1.8m (6ft) wide and no less than 14m (46ft) long. This is known as the "pitching court" or the "pitch." At each end of the pitch, a 1.8m (6ft) square is marked out: this is the "pitcher's box." This encloses an inner rectangle called the "pit," which measures 107–180cm (43–72in) by 77–90cm (31–36in). The two pits are dug out and filled with sand, soil, or anything that will absorb the impact of the horseshoes. Each pit is completed by hammering a metal stake into the center – the two stakes are 12.19m (40ft) apart and inclined towards each other by about 7.5cm (3in) from the vertical. The stakes are 2.5cm (1in) in diameter and about 90cm (3ft) long – 35–37.5cm (14–15in) protrudes above the surface.

The areas of the pitcher's box that are not taken up by the pit are known as the "pitching platforms," one being to the left of the pit and one to the right. These must be at least 1.82m (6ft) long. However, it is common (though not essential) to extend them further towards the opposite stake, to allow those who are less strong to pitch the horseshoes from a shorter distance. A "foul line" is marked at the front of the unextended pitcher's platforms, 11.28m (37ft) from

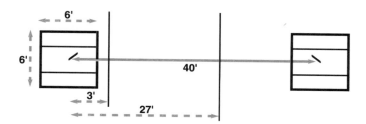

Diagram 1 A Horseshoe pitch

the opposite stake. Another foul line is drawn on the extended platforms, 8.23m (27ft) from the stake.

It is important to consider safety when laying out a pitch, because a heavy iron horseshoe can cause considerable damage when it is thrown. Competition pitches are surrounded by protective wire barriers and backboards are placed behind the stakes, but such measures may be impractical at home. However, it is essential that all games are supervised by an adult, and that no spectator or player is allowed to stand in a position where they might be at risk from an ill-aimed throw.

Each player throws two horseshoes in each round (an "inning") at the stake in the opposite pit so that they land either on the stake or fall as near to it as possible. At home, any horseshoes will do, but in competitions they must conform to precise weights and shapes.

The scoring

A throw that results in the horseshoe encircling the stake, so that a straight edge does not touch the stake when held against the ends of the horseshoe, is called a "ringer" and is awarded three points. A horseshoe that lands with any part of it within 15cm (6in) of the stake is said to be a "shoe in count" and is awarded one point. If a shoe comes to rest leaning on the stake, it is called a "leaner" and is scored as a shoe in count. Any horseshoe that does not satisfy either of these criteria is called a "shoe out of count" and fails to score.

There are two methods of scoring horseshoe pitching: "cancellation" and "count-all." Which

Diagram 2 Cancellation scoring: in this case, the ringer scores three points, but the leaner does not score anything

method is to be used is decided by the players before the game starts. In cancellation scoring only one player can score in each inning: a ringer scored by one player can be canceled by a ringer thrown by the other player, and no points are scored by either player. If this happens, or if neither player throws a ringer, the closest shoe in count scores one point. If there is an uncanceled ringer, it still scores three points, and if the same player has the closest shoe in count a further point is awarded; if the other player has the closest shoe in count he or she is not awarded points. Two uncanceled ringers score six points.

In count-all scoring, all scores made during an inning are recorded and ringers do not cancel each other out.

There are also two ways of determining the winner and, again, which one is to be used is

agreed before the game starts. In the first, the winner is the first player to reach an agreed number of points – 40 is the usual number. In the second, the winner is the player with the highest number of points after an agreed number of innings.

Playing the game

A coin is tossed to decide which player or team will pitch first. In a singles game, the first pitcher throws two horseshoes to the opposite pit, one after the other; then the second player throws two horseshoes to the same pit. Both players then walk to the opposite pit, agree the points that are to be awarded for the inning and then throw back to the pit from which they originally threw, with the player who pitched second during the previous inning pitching first this time. In doubles, one member of each team occupies each end for the whole game — though for safety reasons they must move well away from the target stake before any throw is made. The two players in each pit each pitch two shoes, and their scores are marked by the players at the opposite end. The horseshoes are then thrown back from the other end.

To make a fair pitch, the player throwing must not allow any part of the foot to touch or cross the foul line at 11.28m (37ft). It is usual, however, to allow children and those who do not have the physical strength needed to pitch the full distance comfortably to pitch from behind the foul line at 8.23m (27ft). In addition, one of the pitcher's feet must be in contact with the pitching platform. Any horseshoe that bounces off another surface, such as a backboard, before coming to rest in a scoring position is disqualified.

Hints and tips

Pitching a ringer is far from easy, but as in all games of skill practice is the key to success. The aim is to pitch the horseshoe so that it flies flat and spins horizontally — ideally, turning just enough so that its open end faces the stake when it arrives there. If you start with the horseshoe

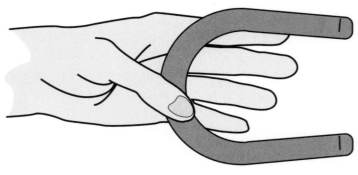

Diagram 3 The grip

Diagram 4 Pitching a horseshoe

open to the left, it should make one-and-a-quarter turns before reaching the stake; if it is held open to the right, it should make one-and-three-quarter turns.

LAWN BOWLS

A game with many thousands of years of history, Bowls is often thought of as a game for the elderly. Nothing could be further from the truth, as an ever younger rollcall of international champions testifies.

Players: for singles, pairs, triples, or teams
Equipment: a set of bowls, a jack, and a mat
Difficulty: simple in essence, but considerable skill and experience is needed at the higher levels
Duration: about 15 minutes for one "end"

The aim of the game

To position your bowls as close as possible to the jack, and to prevent your opponent from doing so by blocking the path to the jack, moving the jack or dislodging your opponent's bowls.

Equipment and the green

Each player uses a set of bowls that consists of four matched balls, which may be made of a rubber composite, plastic or lignum vitae (a hard wood from the West Indies). A bowl must measure 117–133mm (4⅝–5¼in) in diameter and weigh no more than 1.59kg (3½lb). The "crown," or running surface, of one side of each bowl is raised slightly (so that the bowl is not a true sphere) in order to give it bias – as momentum reduces and the bowl starts to slow down it curves or "draws" in an attempt to find its balance. Each bowl in a set carries a distinguishing mark of the same color for ease of recognition.

The bowls are aimed at the jack. This is a smaller ball made of plastic and colored either white or yellow, measuring 63mm (2½in) in diameter and weighing 225–285g (8–10oz). The only other piece of equipment needed to play bowls is a mat, 600mm (2ft 11⅝in) by 360mm (1ft 2¹⁄₁₆in).

Lawn Bowls is played on a rectangle of grass called a "green." The green as a whole must be 37–40m (121ft 4¼in–131ft 2½in) long, and it is subdivided into individual playing areas, called "rinks". Each rink must be 5.5–5.8m (18–19ft) wide. The green is bordered by a ditch, behind which is a grassy bank that rises above the playing surface. The center line of each rink is marked out for a distance of 4m (13ft) from the ditch, and the boundaries of each rink are indicated by the position of markers on the bank.

The condition of the grass that forms the

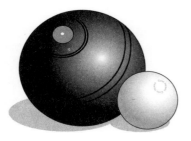

Diagram 5 A bowl and a jack

playing surface has a considerable effect on play: the length of the grass, its density and how much it has been watered and rolled all play a part. Confusingly, a green on which the bowl travels fast – around 12 seconds to run 27m (88ft 6in) – is said to be 'slow', or 'heavy'. This is because there is less time available for the bias of the bowl to become apparent in a curve. A bowl takes around 17 seconds to cover the same distance on a 'fast' green.

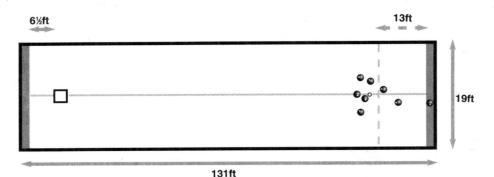

Diagram 6 *A bowls rink, one of several on a green*

Playing the singles game

It is usual for the players to play a trial end – that is, to bowl a set of four bowls each at a jack – before a game begins, so that they can judge the speed of the green. A coin is tossed to see who will play first. The first to play positions the mat on the centre line of the rink, with its back edge 2m (6ft 6in) from the ditch. The player then bowls the jack ('delivers' it), keeping the whole of one foot within the edges of the mat – to fail to do so is a foul shot (as it is when bowling any bowl). The jack must travel at least 21m (68ft 10½ in) from the mat, must stay within the boundaries of the rink and must not come to rest in the ditch, otherwise it is a foul shot. When the bowl has come to rest, it is positioned on the centre line at the length at which it stopped; if this is within 2m (6ft 6in) of the ditch, it is replaced on the centre line 2m (6ft 6in) from the ditch. However, if the jack was delivered with a

foul shot, the opposing player is given the chance to position it, though the original player still bowls the first bowl.

When the jack has been positioned, the first bowl is bowled from the mat. The players bowl in turn, keeping the mat in the same position for each shot. A bowl is said to be a 'live bowl' and can take part in the play as long as it comes to rest within the boundaries of the rink and travels at least 14m (45ft 11in); any bowl that fails to do this is said to be 'dead' and plays no further part in the end. The first bowl in an end to touch the jack, or fall over onto the jack within 30 seconds of coming to rest, is known as a 'toucher', marked with chalk and counted as a live bowl. It is permissible to hit an opponent's ball off the rink, in which case it becomes dead, unless it is the toucher, in which case it is still considered live. However, if the jack is hit off the rink the jack is said to be dead: the end comes to a halt and is replayed.

When all eight bowls have been delivered, the end is over and the players walk to the jack to determine the score. A point is awarded to the player whose bowl is closest to the jack for each bowl that is closer to the jack than the opponent's closest bowl — as a result, only one player scores after each end. The winner of the end is then allowed to reposition the mat at the end of the rink to which the last set of bowls have been delivered. The mat can be placed wherever the player likes for all ends except the first of a game, as long as it is on the centre line of the rink and has its back edge no less than 2m (6ft 6in) from the ditch and its front edge no less than 23m (75ft 5¼in) from the opposite ditch. The winner delivers the jack, and the end proceeds. The game continues until either one player wins by reaching 21 points, or until a previously agreed number of ends have been played.

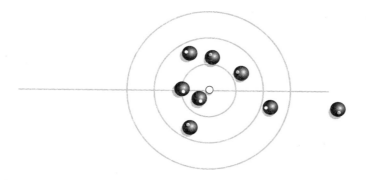

Diagram 7 *Scoring: in this case, A has won two points and B none*

In many championship matches the game is over when 25 shots have been played, the winner being the player with the most points at this time.

Multi-player Bowls

The same basic rules apply, with differences in the order of play. In Pairs Bowls, the players at one end bowl four bowls each, delivering the bowls alternately. They score, and then their team-mates at the other end bowl back all eight, also scoring. Pairs games are normally played to 21 ends. Triples are also played, with three players in each team and each player delivering either two or three bowls and in turn; triples games are usually played to 18 ends. Fours Bowls are played by two teams of four players, with each player delivering two bowls in turn; such games normally run to 21 ends.

Hints and tips

There are various different shots that can be made, all with a specific use. A shot that curves the bowl in close to the jack is called a "draw," while a bowl aimed to protect an existing draw or block an opponent"s route to the jack is known as a "guard." A "trail" bowl attempts to carry the jack towards a bowl or group of bowls behind it, while a "yard-on" is a bowl delivered straight and with some force that is intended to break up a "head" – that is, a group of opponent"s bowls around the jack. Which shot to choose depends on skill, experience and an awareness of the strategy of the game.

CROQUET

Invented hundreds of years ago in France, where it was known as Paillie Maille, Croquet travelled to England in the early nineteenth century, originally under the name of Pall Mall. Over the last few decades it has become increasingly popular and versions of the game are played all around the world.

Players: *two to six*
Equipment: *six Croquet balls and wickets, mallets, nine hoops and two stakes*
Difficulty: *some skill required*
Duration: *about one and a half hours*

The game

Backyard Croquet is the simplest version of croquet and is ideal for family games. It is played over nine hoops, or "wickets." More serious Croquet players prefer the added subtleties of one or other of the two six-wicket versions of the game: American Rules Six-Wicket Croquet, sponsored by the United States Croquet Association (UCSA); and Association, or International Rules croquet, as played in most countries outside the United States and Canada. Full rules of all three games can be obtained in various publications about the sport, many of which are obtainable from UCSA.

The court

Ideally, Backyard Croquet should be played on a rectangular court 30.5m (100ft) by 15.25m (50ft), but it can be played in a smaller space if necessary. The nine wickets are laid out as in diagram 8. The two stakes are put at opposite heads of the two diamonds formed by the wickets: the "turning stake" after the seventh wicket and the "finishing stake" after the fourteenth. Ideally, the boundaries of the court should be marked, but if this is not possible it is sensible to agree beforehand where the boundaries are and any natural features that might mark them.

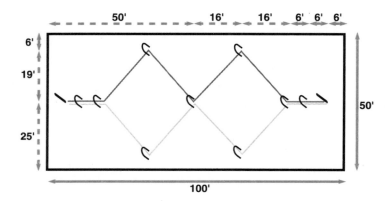

Diagram 8 A Backyard Croquet court

The aim of the game

To be the first side to pass all its balls through all the wickets and hit both the turning stake and the finishing stake at the appropriate time with all balls. It is possible to call a halt to a game before this happens if time is running short – in this case the winning side is decided by awarding one point for each wicket that a ball has passed through and one point for each stake that has been hit.

Playing the game

Each Croquet ball carries a different color, and the balls are divided into two sides: "hot colors" are red, yellow, and orange; "cool colors" are blue, black, and green. If six people are playing, all the balls will be used, but with two or four it may be preferable to play with only four balls – blue and black playing red and green. If an odd number of players are taking part, the number of players on that side will have to play the balls alternately, choosing which ball to play.

A coin is tossed to see which side starts and which colors they will play. The blue ball is always played first, and the other balls are played according to the order of colors marked on the stakes: blue, red, black, yellow, green, and orange. (After the first round, any ball can be played.) For the first shot a ball is placed the length of one mallet head from the first wicket.

The balls must all pass through the wickets in the strict sequence shown in diagram 8. As each ball passes through a wicket a wicket clip of the same color as the ball is placed on the next wicket that it must pass through.

Only one shot is allowed with each ball during that ball's turn, but bonus shots or "continuation shots" can be won in a variety of ways: first, by passing through the correct wicket successfully; second, by striking the turning stake after the seventh wicket; third, by passing through two wickets with one shot or passing through a wicket and hitting the turning stake in one shot (in both cases two continuation shots are won); fourth, by hitting, or making a "roquet" on, one of the other side's balls. A roquet wins two bonus strokes, but the same ball can only be roqueted once during any one turn, unless the ball that is roqueting passes through a wicket or hits the turning stake in the same turn, in which case the original ball can be roqueted once more.

The first of the two bonus shots arising from a roquet can be used to make a "Croquet stroke": the striker's ball is either placed alongside the roqueted ball and in contact with it, or a mallet's head away from it. The original ball is then struck so that both balls move if required. However, the striker is allowed to place a foot on their ball in order that it does not move while the roqueted ball is dismissed to some other part of the court. (If a ball goes outside the boundaries during the course of play it is replaced on the boundary and played from there.) The second bonus shot can then be played. If the roqueted ball is passed through a wicket as the result of a croquet shot, it is considered to have passed through the wicket fairly but does not win a continuation shot for doing so. Continuation shots only last for one turn and cannot be carried on to another turn. In fact, the only continuation shot that can be played is the last one that has been won – if, for example, a striker's ball roquets another ball straight from the Croquet shot, the striker only has two continuation shots, not three.

When a ball has passed through all the wickets but has not yet struck the winning stake it is said to be a "rover." There is no obligation for a rover to be played at the finishing stake, and there is considerable advantage in using it to roquet opponents' balls – the same rules apply as for ordinary balls. However, it can be struck against the finishing stake by any player at any time in the game – at which point it has completed the game and lost its ability to roquet another ball.

Playing a shot

There are a variety of ways in which the mallet can be held when addressing the ball, and three conventional ones are shown in diagrams 9, 10 and 11. Bear in mind that you are only allowed to strike the ball with the face of the mallet. The mallet is not allowed to touch any ball other than that of the striker, nor to touch a wicket or a stake, nor to be in contact with a ball that is itself in contact with a wicket or a stake. However, the penalties for playing a foul stroke are hardly severe in

Backyard Croquet: the balls are simply returned to their original position and the shot is replayed.

VARIATIONS
American Rules Six-wicket Croquet

This more complex version of Croquet is played in North American clubs and tournaments. Only four balls are used, with one side having blue and black and the other red and yellow. In singles the players play both balls; in doubles each player plays the same ball throughout the game. If three players are taking part, one side has two players, each playing their own balls, and the third player plays both balls.

Club courts and tournament courts are 32m (105ft) by 26m (85ft), and six hoops are laid out in the positions shown in diagram 12, with a single finishing stake in the center of the court. However, UCSA recommends that a smaller court 15.25m (50ft) by 12.20m (40ft) is used to

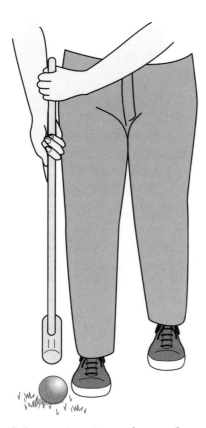

Diagram 9 Some Croquet grips and stances

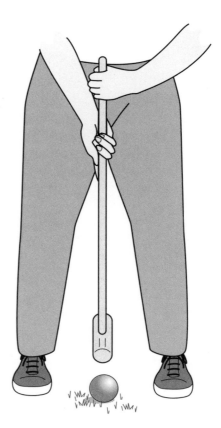

Diagram 10 Some Croquet grips and stances

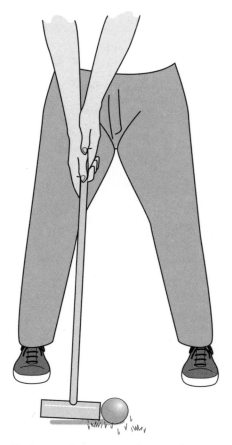

Diagram 11 Some Croquet grips and stances

learn how to play the game. Whichever size is used, the boundaries of the court should be marked by string and a deadness board should be prominently displayed.

As in Backyard Croquet, a coin is tossed at the start of the game, but the winner can decide either to go first, selecting the blue and black ball, or to go second, selecting the red and yellow balls. The sequence in which the balls are played is as on the stake: blue, red, black, and yellow.

The basic rules of play are as for Backyard Croquet, but with a few differences that significantly affect the character of the game. First, you are not allowed to place either a hand or a foot on the ball being struck during a Croquet shot to immobilize it: whether your ball moves, or how much it moves, depends on the skill with which the shot is played. Second, Six-wicket Croquet employs the concept of a ball being either

"dead" or "alive." This is a fairly complex concept to master, and it is even harder to keep track of an individual ball's state of deadness – which is why a "deadness board" is displayed beside the court. This arrangement of colored flaps is updated at the end of every turn. Your ball is considered to be "dead" on a ball once that ball has been roqueted by your ball and cannot hit that ball again while your ball is dead on it. This means that you are not allowed to hit it again until you have come "alive" on the ball: this happens when you pass through a wicket. The only other way of making one of your balls come alive is to keep a check on when your opponent passes through the seventh wicket: you can clear the deadness of a ball simply by declaring the fact before your turn begins, but you must specify the color of the ball that is being cleared.

The concept of dead and alive also applies to rover balls, but in a different way. A rover can only roquet a ball once in a turn, but can clear itself of deadness first by roqueting two balls and then by passing through any wicket, in any direction. However, a rover cannot at any time roquet the same ball twice in succession. In Six-wicket Croquet a rover can be struck against the

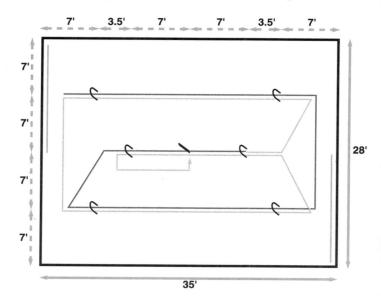

Diagram 12 A Six-wicket Croquet court

stake to finish its part of the game or can be hit against it by a Croquet shot from another rover.

There are also a number of differences between Backyard Croquet and Six-wicket Croquet in the rules covering boundaries and penalties. A ball is said to be "out of bounds" if half the ball is over the boundary line and the player's turn ends immediately. The ball is replaced the length of a mallet's head inside the boundary at the point at which it left the court — the exception is when the striker's ball goes out of bounds after a roquet but the roqueted ball is still in play, in which case it is put back in contact with the roqueted ball wherever it may be. The striker's turn ends if a ball is roqueted out of bounds, but the striker's ball is not considered to be dead on that ball; the striker's turn also ends if a ball is played out of bounds by a croquet shot, and any bonus shot is lost.

Some foul shots do not incur a penalty, and the balls are repositioned and play resumes. These occur when a ball is played out of turn or from the wrong position, or when the wrong ball is played. In other cases, the balls are returned to their previous positions but the offender's turn ends immediately. These fouls include: roqueting a ball on which your ball is dead; failing to move a roqueted ball when playing a croquet shot; touching a ball with a mallet when it is in contact with a wicket (this is known as a "crush"); and hitting the ball incorrectly with the mallet.

Whole books have been written about the tactics and strategy of Six-wicket Croquet. The most important thing to remember is that you must try to stop your opponent from making progress just as much as you try to make progress yourself. The key is to find the correct balance between offense and defense to cope with the level of skill and experience of your opponent

Association (International) Rules Croquet

This form of Six-wicket Croquet is played in countries outside North America – Britain, Australia, New Zealand, South Africa, France, and Japan. It is a simpler version of American Rules Croquet – closer to Backyard Croquet in some ways – with different technical expressions and no concept of "deadness."

The equipment used is identical (with the exception of the "deadness board") to that specified in American Rules Croquet. The Association court is the same as the American version except for balk lines at either end of the rectangle: the first shot of each ball must be taken from behind either balk line rather than the length of a mallet's head from the first "wicket," as in American Rules. (The wicket is named a "hoop" in Association practice, and it is not "passed" but "run.") Games involving three people are not generally played, though there is no reason why they should not be. The black and blue balls still play the red and yellow balls and must be played in order for the first turn only.

The rules for roquet and croquet are the same as in Backyard Croquet, though the striker may not place a hand or foot on their ball while playing a croquet shot; nevertheless, the croqueted ball must move or shake as a result of the strike – the striker's turn ends and the balls are replaced as they were before the roquet if it does so. Since the first shot of each ball is taken from the balk line there is no guarantee that a ball will run a hoop on this shot. Remember that a ball can be roqueted before it runs its first hoop.

BADMINTON

This game originated in the Far East some 2000 years ago and has been popular ever since. Its rules were laid down by British officers in India in the last century – some years before Lawn Tennis was invented.

Players: two or four
Equipment: racquets, some shuttlecocks, a net, and a suitable area to use as a court
Difficulty: skillful and athletic
Duration: about 20 minutes for one game

The court, rackets and shuttlecock

A Badminton court is laid out as shown below in diagram 13. Serious players always play the game on an indoor court, because the flight of the shuttlecock can be be affected considerably by even the slightest gust of wind. Nevertheless, amateurs can play Badminton perfectly well out of doors, in the garden or in a park. In this case, the only parts of the court that it is important to lay out accurately are the posts and net. The posts must be 1.55m (5ft 1in) high, and the net, which should be made of a mesh sufficiently fine that a shuttlecock cannot pass through it, should be 760mm (2ft 6in) deep and hung 2.5cm (1in) below the top of the posts.

Badminton racquets are smaller than Tennis racquets and a little larger than Squash racquets. They are available from most good sports shops – but check that they conform with the International Badminton Federation (IBF) standards if you intend to play seriously. Shuttlecocks, also known as the "birdies" or "birds," were originally made of 16 feathers stuck into a base of leather-covered cork weighted with lead, but nowadays synthetic substitutes are more widely available. The weight of shuttlecocks approved by the IBF varies from 4.74g (0.17oz) to 5.5g (0.19oz), and it is wise to buy the heaviest grade if you intend to play outside in order to minimize wind interference.

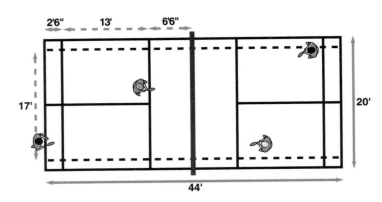

Diagram 13 A Badminton court

The scoring

A point is awarded when the player receiving serve commits a foul or fails to return a shot in bounds. Should the server commit a foul or fail to return, no point is awarded but serve immediately passes to their opponent. According to LBF rules, doubles and men's singles games are won by the first player or side to reach 15 points, while women's singles are won by the first player to reach 11 points. A match is generally decided over three games, though occasionally it is agreed that the winner is the first player to reach 21 points in one game only. At home, you can decide to play up to as many points as you like.

Towards the end of a game of Badminton the "setting" rule comes into force. If the score becomes tied at either of the two scores below the winning post, the player or side that first reached the number of points on which the score is tied has the option of setting the game; this option must be taken or ignored as soon as the scores are tied and before the next serve is made. Setting means that the points so far scored are discarded, the scores are reset to love-all and the first side to reach three points when play resumes wins the game.

So if the game is a men's singles being played to 15 points, and the score stands at 13-12 to player A, player A has the option to set the game if player B wins first the serve and then the next point, making the score 13-13. The same rule applies if the score reaches 14-14. (In women's singles, the relevant scores are 9-9 and 10-10.)

Playing the singles game

A coin is tossed at the start of a game and the winner chooses either at to play at a particular end or to serve first. The server stands in the right-hand service court, with the receiver also in their right-hand court; no part of either player's feet may touch the boundary lines of the service court or be outside them. To start the serve, the server holds the racquet so that it is

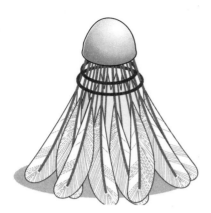

Diagram 14 *A shuttlecock*

pointing down and holds the shuttlecock above waist height in the other hand. The shuttlecock is then dropped and must be hit below the waist with the racquet still pointing downwards. The serve is good if it crosses the net and falls between the long and the short service line for singles (see diagram 13) in the receiver's service court; no "lets" are called during a service. If the server commits a foul while serving, by touching a boundary line or failing to serve into the required area – the serve passes to the receiver.

The receiver loses the point automatically if a foul is committed while receiving service. Otherwise, the receiving player has to return the shuttlecock to the server. It must only be hit once, and must fall within or on the boundary lines for singles (a shuttlecock is only out if it comes to rest completely over a line). No "let" – in which the rally stops and the point is replayed – is called if the shuttlecock hits the top of the net and falls over into the other side. A let is called, however, if a shuttlecock disintegrates during play, as happens occasionally. (By tradition, though, amateur players offer each other lets if an error is made by mischance.) The receiver wins the rally and takes the next serve if the original server fails to return the ball correctly – clear over the net with one hit and into or onto the boundary lines of the opposite court. Any player who touches the net with racquet or body, or allows either racquet or body to pass into the opponents' side of the court, whether

under or over the net, commits a foul and loses the rally.

When each rally has finished, the player who is making the next serve crosses to the other service court, as does the receiver. If three games are being played to decide a match, the players change ends at the end of the first two games. Different rules apply if only one game is being played, however, and also during the third game of a match of three games. If the game is being played to 11 points, the players change ends after one player has reached 6 points; if the game is to 15 points, the change comes when one player has reached 8 points; and if the game is to 21, ends are changed when a player reaches 11 points.

Doubles play

Play starts from the right-hand service court in doubles, as in singles, but only the player in the receiving court may play the shuttlecock. After the serve, either player may play any shuttlecock. On the serve, the shuttlecock must fall within the short service line and the long service line for doubles, and in the receiver's court; as before, on the line is in. Which pair the next serve goes to depends on who wins the rally. However, should the receiving side be next to serve, it is the receiver who serves next, then the receiver's partner after that, should the next point be won. When the original serving side regains the serve, the serve is taken by the original server's partner and so on, alternately.

Hints and tips

It is difficult to master the peculiarities of a shuttlecock in flight, and practice is the only way to perfect technique. One problem is that though the shuttlecock moves with some speed just after being hit, it falls fairly slowly. Unless a shot is played with some skill, therefore, an opponent has plenty of time to line up a return shot. There are four basic badminton shots: the lob, in which a player sends the shuttlecock in a high arc to the back of the opposing player's court – especially when that player is near the net; the drop shot, in which the aim is to make the shuttlecock drop to the ground as soon as it has crossed the net; the drive, in which the shuttlecock is hit so that it passes horizontally over the net; and the smash, in which a lob or high shuttlecock is hit as hard as possible towards the ground.

STATUES

Also known as Grandmother's Footsteps, this game is a staple of children's parties and is guaranteed to make even the most miserable and tearful child cheer up and join in the fun.

Players: one person to be "grandmother" and as many children as you like, given the space
Equipment: none
Difficulty: as hard as "grandmother" chooses to make it; best for under-sevens
Duration: 20 minutes, or until the children become bored

Starting the game

An adult or older child takes the part of the "grandmother" and stands facing a wall or some recognizable point in the garden. All the children line behind the grandmother some distance away –15m (50ft) is ideal, but anything less will do.

Playing the game

Grandmother starts the game when everyone is ready, and the children have to creep up behind her as quietly as possible, taking whatever route they choose. Every so often, grandmother turns round suddenly. Immediately the children see her start to turn, they must stop moving and freeze into "statues." If she spots anybody moving, she points out the child and that child is out of the game. It is worth announcing beforehand that grandmother's decision is final, especially if she is trying to make a particular child win in order to give him or her a prize. The first child to

Diagram 15 A game of Statues

touch grandmother, or the last child left in the game, wins and is awarded a prize. (In some versions of the game, the child who wins takes over as grandmother, but experience shows that this can lead to disaster and is thus best avoided.) Another round then starts.

TAG

There are a variety of tag games, any of which is a wonderful way of burning off children's excess energy. There is a danger, though, that the children may become over-excited and over-tired, so it is best to alternate Tag with quieter games.

Players: six to 20
Equipment: none
Difficulty: easy; suitable for six- to 10-year-olds
Duration: 20 minutes is usually enough

Exchange Tag

The children form a circle about 8m (26ft) across and sit on the ground. One child, the chaser, stands in the middle of the circle. The chaser calls out the names of two children, who have to run across the circle and exchange places with each other. Each has to reach their new position and sit down without being touched, or "tagged," by the chaser. If the chaser succeeds in touching a child, that child becomes the chaser for the new round. It is wise to have an adult or older child on hand to adjudicate in the event of any disputes and to ensure that all the children have their names called at some point.

Bulldog

A playing field is chosen that has two boundaries 50ft apart; the boundaries chosen should not be walls, otherwise there will be risk of injury to the players. All the children line up behind one boundary, with one child left in the middle of the playing field as a catcher – it is usual for an adult to be the first catcher and to give way as catcher to the first child who is caught. At a signal, all the children run to the other boundary, during which time the catcher tries to catch as many of them as possible. Any child that has been caught stays in the middle of the playing field and turns into a catcher. The signal is given once more, and all the children attempt to run back to the original boundary. The last child remaining free is the winner – the bulldog – and becomes the first catcher in the next round. This game can become very boisterous – in fact, it is often used to train children learning to play soccer – so have an adult in attendance to ensure that things do not get out of hand.

Red Rover

This game is a variation on Bulldog, and starts in exactly the same way. In Red Rover, however, the catcher – known as the "caller" in this game – shouts: "Red rover, red rover, send Tom (for example) over." The child called Tom then tries to run to the opposite boundary line without being tagged. If Tom is unsuccessful, he has to go to the "rover's den," which is an area off the field of play. The caller then repeats the formula, asking for another child, and if successful in making a tag sends them to the rover's den. The next time, the call is "Red rover, red rover, send them all over." All the children try to reach the opposite boundary without being tagged. Any who fail join the children in the rover's den and are counted: the number of children tagged is the caller's score. The game continues until every child has had a go at being the rover, at which point the scores are compared and the child with the highest score is the winner.

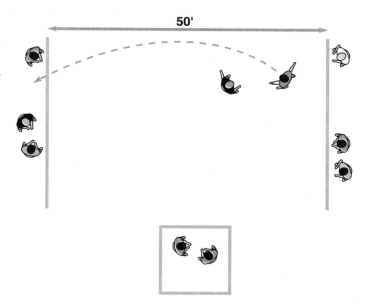

Diagram 16 A game of Red Rover

HIDE & SEEK

This game is an old favorite, and there is a good reason why it retains its popularity: it can be tremendous fun, and even older children enjoy it.

Players: *four to 20, depending on the number of possible hiding places*
Equipment: *none*
Difficulty: *as hard as the children make it*
Duration: *about 15 minutes*

Playing the game

One child is chosen to be the seeker, and stands still with eyes closed for a count of 20 while the other children run off to find hiding places. When the count is up, the seeker shouts: "Here I come, ready or not!," and starts to search out the hiders. The first child to be found becomes the new seeker, but not until the original seeker has found all the hidden children. It is a good idea to put a time limit on each round, after which all the hiders have to reveal themselves – otherwise there is a risk that the children who have already been found will become bored when one player has found a particularly ingenious hiding place.

SIMON SAYS

Also known as Simple Simon Says or O'Grady, this is an old-established follow-my-leader game that still goes down extremely well at parties.

Players: *four to 10*
Equipment: *none*
Difficulty: *harder than you might think, especially if played at speed*
Duration: *about 15 minutes*

Starting the game
One child is selected to start off as "Simon," and the other children form up in front of Simon in a line. (With very young children it is often wise for an adult to take the part of Simon.)

Playing the game
Simon tells the children to perform a certain action – "clap your hands" or "jump up and down" – and performs the action at the same time. If the command is preceded with the phrase "Simon says," the children must carry out the action immediately and any child who fails to do so is eliminated. But if Simon misses the phrase "Simon says" out, the children must not copy the action and any child who does so is out. The winner is the child who is the last left in, and takes Simon's place.

HOPSCOTCH

This classic hopping and jumping game is a test of balance and agility that has helped while away time in school playgrounds and quiet streets for generations.

Players: *from two to 10*
Equipment: *chalk and a small stone*
Difficulty: *difficult at first, but becomes much easier with practice; best for seven- to 10-year-olds*
Duration: *up to half an hour, depending on the skill of the players*

Starting the game
Once an appropriate site has been chosen – it should be level and either paved or covered with tarmac – one of the players draws a grid on the ground in chalk (see diagram 17). The grid should be about 1.25m (4ft) wide and 3m (10ft) long, though it is not important to be precise. It is worth noting that this is only one type of hopscotch grid and there are innumerable variations on it, and on the rules. It is quite common for one form of Hopscotch to be played on one street and a different version on a neighboring street.

Playing the game
The first child to play throws a pebble, "the puck," into the area marked "1" and hops into it, landing on one foot. The child has to stay on one foot, pick up the pebble and hop back to behind the starting line, without allowing the other foot to touch the ground – though it is permissible to hop from foot to foot. If this has been achieved successfully, the child then throws the pebble into the area marked "2," and hops into it, if necessary using area 1 as a stepping stone.

The first player continues until a foul is committed: this may be done either by throwing to the wrong area, or missing the correct one; by hopping onto a line; or by losing balance and allowing both feet to touch the ground at the same time. When this happens the player's turn is over and the next child starts to play. When each player has made an attempt, the first player has another go, throwing the pebble into the area in which they failed last time. The first player to reach "out" and return to the

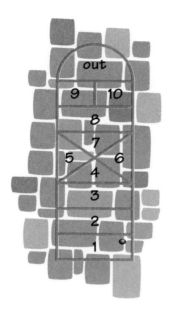

Diagram 17 *A Hopscotch grid*

start line, hopping from area to area with only one foot on the ground, is the winner.

MARBLES

Children's crazes come and go, but Marbles games have been a constant source of entertainment. There are many different Marbles games, all of which have their adherents.

Players: two to six
Equipment: five marbles and a "shooter" per player, chalk
Difficulty: requires a fair degree of skill
Duration: 10 to 20 minutes, depending on the variation being played

The marbles

Marbles are hard balls, made from plastic or glass, measuring about 15mm (½in) across. For many games each player also needs a "shooter," or "taw," which is a larger marble about 20mm (¾in) in diameter. It is one of the traditions of the game that the marbles themselves can be won or lost permanently, with the exception of the shooter. It is as well to make it clear before a game starts whether this rule is going to apply or whether any marbles captured will be returned once the game is over.

Shooting the ring

The players select a reasonably level area of ground and draw in chalk, or otherwise mark out, a circle about 2.5m (8ft) in diameter. Each player them places one marble on the perimeter of the circle, making sure that the spaces between the marbles are roughly equal. A line is drawn about 1.8m (6ft) from the edge of the ring. This forms the shooting line.

First, each player takes their shooter and rolls it to the center of the circle to determine the order of play: the player whose shooter comes to rest nearest the circle's center starts the game; the player whose shooter is next closest goes second; and so on. The first player kneels behind the shooting line – knees must be kept behind the line, but the torso and arms may cross over it.

The aim is to hit one of the marbles on the circle's edge with sufficient force that both the target marble and the shooter end up outside the circle. If this happens, the player captures the marble that was hit and has another go. If the shot is unsuccessful – if the target marble is missed or the marble is hit but ends up inside the circle – the turn ends and one of the player's own marbles must be placed on the edge of the circle. However, the player retains the shooter. The game ends when there are no more marbles left on the circle's rim, and the winner is the player who has captured the most marbles.

Ring taw

As for shooting the ring, a 2.5m (8ft) circle is marked out on level ground, but then a smaller circle, about 30cm (1ft) across is drawn inside it. Each player rolls a single marble to the center of the inner circle to decide the order of play, and each places two marbles in the inner circle. The first player attempts to dislodge a marble from

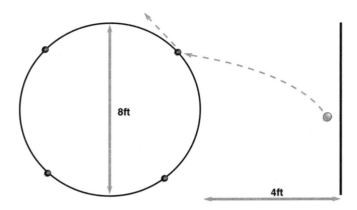

Diagram 18 Shooting the ring

the inner circle, shooting from any point outside the outer circle. If successful, the marble is captured, the shooter is reclaimed and another shot is taken from the place where it lay; if unsuccessful, the shooter stays where it is and the player's turn ends. The next player can either attempt to dislodge a marble from the inner circle, as before, or try to hit the first player's shooter. If the attempt to hit a shooter is successful, the shooter's owner must pay a marble. If the shot fails, whatever its target, the shooter stays

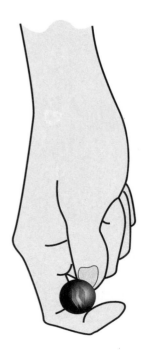

Diagram 19 Knuckling down

where it lies. Each player must take their first shot from any point outside the outer circle, but subsequent shots must be taken from wherever that player's shooter lies. The game ends when there are no more marbles in the inner circle and the winner is the player who has captured the most marbles.

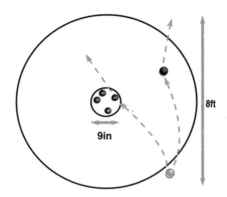

Diagram 20 Ring taw

DODGE BALL

If you are looking for a fast-moving, exciting, open-air game try Dodge Ball. There are many versions of the game, but in all of them the aim is the same — to hit an opponent below the waist with a soft ball.

Players: eight to 20
Equipment: a soft rubber ball about 20cm (8in) in diameter, such as a volleyball
Difficulty: speed, agility and a good aim are needed; suitable for eight- to 10-year-olds
Duration: 10 minutes is probably long enough per game

Free Zone Dodge Ball

The players mark out a rectangular pitch about 14m (46ft) long and 8m (26ft) wide, using chalk if possible, or piles of clothes to denote two goal lines and a centre line (see diagram 21). There are two free zones, one between the center line and each goal line; the areas behind the two goal lines are the end zones.

The players divide themselves into two teams and take their positions in the free zones. The teams toss a coin to decide which one will have the ball first, then play begins. The aim of the game is to get as many of the opposition players into the end zone behind your free zone as possible. Players are allowed to throw the ball to other members of their team, and when a player judges that the moment is right, they throw the ball over the center line with the object of hitting an opposing player below the waist. Any player who is hit must go to the thrower's end zone, and the ball is returned to the thrower's team for play to restart. (A referee of some sort is a good idea for judging near-misses.) However, if the ball is caught before it bounces, the original thrower must go to the opponent's end zone. If the ball misses, it can be picked up by a member of the opposing team, who can attempt to make a hit on any member of the thrower's team. Players in an end zone can still play the ball, which can either be passed to them by a member of their own team by throwing it over the heads of the opposing team or can be retrieved by them if the opposing team misses the ball completely. They cannot move any further forward than the goal line, however.

The game ends automatically if all the members of one team are in an end zone, with the other team winning. Otherwise, the game ends when 10 minutes are up and the winning team is the one that has the most opposition players in its end zone.

Train Dodge Ball

This version of Dodge Ball is more suitable for younger children. All the children except four form a circle about 7m (23ft) in diameter. The four children chosen go into the middle of the circle and form a line, putting their hands around the waist of the child in front: the first player in the line is the engine of the train; the

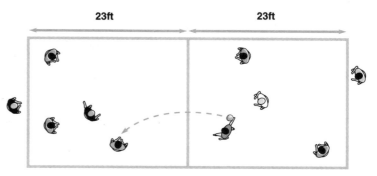

Diagram 21 Free Zone Dodge Ball

second and third are carriages; and the last is the caboose. The players in the circle throw the ball from one to the other, looking for an opportunity to make a hit below the waist on the caboose. The engine tries to kick the ball away or hand it off, or swings the train round to try to avoid it – the carriages are not allowed to fend the ball off. If the caboose is hit, the player who threw the ball joins the front of the line of four and becomes the engine, while the player who was the second carriage becomes the caboose. The original caboose joins the circle of other players. The game continues until each player has had a go at being the engine, and the winner is the engine who keeps the caboose safe for the longest period of time.

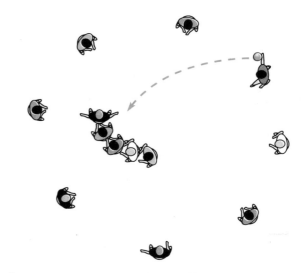

Diagram 22 Train Dodge Ball

RESOURCES & REFERENCES

GAMES ASSOCIATIONS

American Checker Federation
Gene Lindsay
131 Embassy Drive
Morristown
TN 37814
USA

American Contract Bridge League
The Secretary
2990 Airways Boulevard
Memphis
TN 38116-3847
USA

American Cribbage Society
Mr. Jeff Monroe
Membership Chairman
PO Box 10486
Napa
CA 94581
USA

American Go Association
P.O. Box 397
Old Chelsea Station
New York
NY 10113
USA

US Chess Federation
3054 NYS Route 9W
New Windsor
NY 12553
USA

British Chess Federation
9a Grand Parade
St Leonards-on-Sea
East Sussex TN38 0DD
UK

Scottish Chess Association
26/5 Causewayside
Edinburgh EH9 1QB
Scotland

English Draughts Association
Ian Caws
54 Mayfield Road
Ryde
Isle of Wight PO33 3PR
UK

Irish Draughts Association
Sean Phillips
Cullinagh
Newcastle West
Co Limerick
Ireland

Scottish Draughts Association
Donald Oliphant
11 Raeburn Place
Rosemount

Aberdeen AB1 1PQ
Scotland

Welsh Draughts Association
Gwyn Pritchard
15 Awelfryn
Amlwch
Gwynedd LL68 9DG
UK

English Bridge Union
Ken Rowe
Wynford
Awliscombe
Honiton
EX14 0NT
UK

British Go Association
11 Briarview Court
Handsworth Avenue
Highams Park
London E4 9PQ
UK

British Othello Federation
c/o David Haigh
62 Romsey Road
Winchester SO22 5PH
UK

RPGA
The Role-Playing Games Association supports players of all role-playing games.
Contact: RPGA
P.O. Box 61
Maidenhead
Berks SL6 1FX
UK

European Go Federation
Sidlerstr. 5
CH 3012 Bern
Switzerland

AHIKS Europe
European postal gaming society. Offers game-matching service for face-to-face, postal and e-mail play of all board games.
Contact: Colin Smith
14 Dukes Rd
Braintree
Essex CM7 5UE
UK

READING LIST

101 Instant Games
Harlow, E., Macdonald 1977.

Abbott's New Card Games
Abbott, Muller 1963.

Antique Playing Cards
Dover Press, 1995.

Baseball Games
Cooper, Schiffer 1995.

Battlegame Armada
Sutherland, J., Purnell 1990.

Battlegame Book: Fighting Ships
McNeil, A., Usborne 1974.

Battlegame Book: Galactic War
McNeil, A., Usborne 1974.

Battlegame Book: Knights at War
McNeil, A., Usborne 1974.

Battlegame Book: Wild West
McNeil, A., Usborne 1974.

Battlegame Book: WW11
McNeil, A., Usborne 1974.

Best American Card Games
Duncan, D., Foulsham 1989.

The Best Games People Play
Sharpe, R., Ward Lock 1978.

Board and Table Games,
Bell, R.C., Dover 1960.

The Book of Classic Board Games
Klutz Press 1993.

Bridge for Dummies
IDG 1997.

Can You Win the Pennant?
Gelman, M., Archway 1983.

Card Games for Dummies
IDG 1997.

Card Games for Everyone
Parlett, D., Hodder & Stoughton 1983.

The Collector's Guide to Games & Puzzles
Goodfellow, C., Apple Press 1993.

The Complete Book of Mah Jong
Millington, A., Arthur Barker 1987.

The Complete Hoyle's Games
Dawson, F., Wordsworth 1994.

Dice Games: New & Old
Tredd, W., Oleander 1981.

Diplomacy Games & Variants
Pulsipher, L., Strategy Games 1975.

Discovering Dice and Dominoes
Bell, R.C., Shire Publications 1980.

Fifty Years of Flicking Football
Payne, R., Yore 1996.

Five Minute Games
Pritchard, D., Bell & Hyman 1984.

Gambler's Handbooks
Figgis, E.L., Hamlyn 1976.

Game Design Vol 1: Theory & Practice
Jackson, S., Steve Jackson Games 1979.

The Game of Diplomacy
Sharpe, R., Arthur Barker 1975.

Gameplan
Peek, S., Betterway 1993.

Games in Geography
Walford, R., Longman 1969.

Games Playing with Computers
Bell, A.G., Allen & Unwin 1972.

Games Programming
Solomon, E., Cambridge University Press 1984.

Games to Play
Bell, R.C., Michael Joseph 1985.

A Gamut of Games
Sackson, S., Hutchinson 1978.

The Greatest Games of all Time
Costello, M., Wiley 1991.

Go for Beginners
Iwamoto, K., Penguin 1972.

Hanafuda: The Flower Card Game
Nichibo Shuppan, Japan Publications 1970.

How to Play a Good Game of Bridge
Reese, T., Pan 1969.

How to Win at Scrabble
Orleans, Hodder & Stoughton, 1985.

An Introduction to Go
Davies, J., Ishi Press 1984.

Karom Reflections
Chatlani, R., Karom Press 1995.

The Magic of Go
Chikun, C., Ishi Press 1988.

Magic: Official Encyclopaedia
Moursund, B., Carlton 1997.

Modern Board Games
Pritchard, D., William Luscombe 1975.

Neue Taktikspiele mit Wurfeln und Karten
Knizia, R., Hugendubel 1990.

New Eleusis
Abbott, R., Abbott 1980.

New Games in Old Rome
Knizia, R., Reaching Moon Megacorp 1995.

New Rules for Classic Games
Schmittberger, W., Wiley 1994.

The Oxford Guide to Card Games
Parlett, D., Oxford Publishing Co. 1990.

The Oxford Guide to Board Games
Parlett, D., Oxford Publishing Co. 1998.

The Pan Book of Card Games
Phillips, H., Pan 1953.

Play the Game
Love, B., Guild Publishing 1978.

Play Your Cards!
Kaplan, S., U.S. Games Systems 1996.

The Pocket Book of Board Games
Astrop, J., Kestrel 1975.

The Pocket Book of Card Games
Bavin, W., House of Marbles 1993.

The Pocket Book of Marbles
Bavin, W., House of Marbles 1993.

The Pocket Book of Card Tricks
Bavin, W., House of Marbles 1993.

The Pocket Book of Dice Games
Bavin, W., House of Marbles 1993.

The Scrabble Book
Brandreth, G., Treasure Press 1992.

The Second Book of Go
Bozulich, R., Ishi Press 1987.

Spiel des Jahres
Spiel des Jahres Jury, Hugendubel 1994.

Spielecollection 1: Schatzinsel
Wittig, R., Hugendubel 1990.

Spin Again
Polizzi, R., Chronicle Books 1991.

State of Emergency
Guerrier, M., Penguin 1969.

The Treasures of Childhood
Opie, C., Pavilion 1900.

Twelve Tarot Games
Dummett, M., Duckworth 1980.

The Way to Play,
The Diagram Group, Corgi 1975.

What's Your Game?
Parr & Cornelius, CUP 1991.

Winning Ways, Volumes 1 & 2
Conway, R., Academic Press 1986.

INDEX

Page numbers in *italics* refer to diagrams or illustrations

In the UK, Checkers is known as Draughts; a number of entries refer to UK-based Draughts associations

Abbott, Scott, Trivial Pursuit® 110–11
ace, value of 11
Aces in the Pot 200
Aces-or-Better 40–41
Acrostics 222
Agnes
    laying out *19*, 20
    playing 20–21, *20*
AHIKS Europe (postal gaming) 291
Albert, Prince, popularization of Solitaire 12
All Fives
    aim 184
    playing 184, *184*
    scoring 184
    strategies 185
All Sevens *see* Matador
Alphabet Race 226, *226*
Alquerque
    aim 176
    history 175
    playing 175–6, *175*
American
    Checker Federation 290
    Contract Bridge League 291
    Cribbage Society 291
    Go Association 291
American Rules Six-wicket Croquet 279–81, *280*
Anagrams 230, *230*
Analogies 235–6
Animal, Vegetable, Mineral *see* Twenty Questions
Apple Ducking 205, *205*
Arches 259, *259*
Association 244
Australian Five Hundred 88–9, *89*

Baccarat 32–3

Baccarat-Chemin de Fer 33
Backgammon
    aim 119, 122, *122*
    boards 118–19, *119*
    doubling 123–4
    history 112, 118
    playing 119–28
    sample game 119–28, *119*, *120*, *121*, *122*, *123*, *124*, *125*, *126*, *127*
    scoring 123
    strategies 124–7
Badminton
    doubles 283
    equipment 282, *282*, 283
    scoring 282
    singles 282–3
Battleships 227–8, *227*, *228*
    Salvo 228
    Starships 228
Beetle 205–6, *205*
Beggar My Neighbor 94, *94*
Belle Lucie *see* Lovely Lucy
Bergen
    aim 186–7
    playing 186, *187*
    scoring 186–7
    strategies 187
    betting
    history 30
    legality 30
Billiards *see* Carom Billiards
Bingo *see* Lotto
Black Lady Hearts 76
Black Maria 76, *76*
Blackjack
    bank 35
    playing 35–6
Blank Option Scrabble® 110
    Gibson, David 110
Blind Hughie
    aim 188
    playing 188, *188*
Blind Man's Buff 217
    Circle 217
    Seated 217
    Staff 217
Block & Draw Dominoes
    aim 181
    playing 181, *181*
    scoring 181
    strategies 181–2
Block Dominoes 182
board games

chance 101
conquest 101
educational 101, 102
family 102
history 7, 101
Internet 8
race 112
Roman 7
strategy 101
Botticelli 242–4
Bowls *see* Lawn Bowls
Box, The *see* Botticelli
Boxes 224–5, *225*
    variations 225
Bridge *see* Contract Bridge
Bridge the Word 253
British
    Chess Federation 290
    Go Association 291
    Othello® Federation 291
Brunot, Jim, Scrabble® 108
Bulldog Tag 285
Butts, Alfred, Scrabble® 108

Canadian Checkers
    aim 158
    playing 158, *159*
Canasta
    aim 53
    origins 46
    playing 54–6, *55*
    scoring 53–4, *53*, 56
cards *see* playing cards
Carom Billiards
    aim 265
    equipment 265, *265*
    history 256
    One-cushion 267
    playing 265–7, *266*, *267*
    Three-cushion 267
    UK Carom Club 291
Casino
    aim 57
    origins 46, 57
    playing 57–9, *57*, *58*, *59*
    scoring 59
casinos 30
Categories 249–50
    variations 250
Charades 212–14
conventions *213*
Cheat 97–8
Checkers

aim 151
American Checker Federation 290
boards 150, *151*
Canadian 158-9, *159*
Dama 130
Damanspiel 130
Eleven-man-Ballot 155
English Draughts Association 290
German 157
Go as you Please 154
history 130, 150
Irish Draughts Association 290
Italian 155-6, *156*
Jeu de Dames 130
Losing 155
playing 151-3, *151, 152, 153, 154*
Polish 158
Russian 157
Scottish Draughts Association 290
Spanish 156-7, *156*
strategies 153-4, *154*
Three-move-Ballot 155
Turkish 159, *159*
Welsh Draughts Association 290
Chemin de Fer
aim 31
Baccarat 32-3
Baccarat-Chemin de Fer 33
banker 31, 32
betting 31-2
dealing 32
scoring 32
Chess
aim 136-7, 143
board 132-3, *132*
British Chess Federation 290
check 136-7, *136*
checkmate 137, *137*
Chinese/Xiangqi 148-50, *148, 149*
clocks 143-4
history 130, 131
Japanese/Shogi 8, 146-8, *146, 147*
Kasparov, Gary vs IBM Deep Blue 8, 131
Kriegspiel 145-6
moves of pieces 133-6, *133, 134, 135, 136*
notation 139-40, *139, 140*
players' employment 9, 130

prize money 9
Professional Chess Association (PCA) 132
Progressive 144
Random 144-5
Russian domination 131
Scottish Chess Association 290
Shogi/Japanese 146-8
strategies 141-3
symbols 140
unusual moves 137-9, *137, 138, 139*
US Chess Federation 290
values of pieces 140-41
World Champions 131
World Championship 131, 132
World Chess Federation (FIDE) 132
Xiangqi/Chinese 148-50, *148, 149*
Chicken, Egg & Bacon *see* Association
children's games, developmental 90, 203
Chinese Checkers
aim 118
history 112, 117
playing 118, *118*
Chinese Chess *see* Xiangqi
Chuckstones *see* Jacks(1)
Cincinnati 45
Circular Blind Man's Buff 217
Clock Patience
laying out 13, *13*
playing 13, *14*
Watch 13
Clue ® (Cluedo®)
aim 106, 107
history 106
playing 106-7
Pratt, Anthony 106
strategies 107
Coffee Pot 247
variation 247
computer gaming
hyperspace 170
Kasparov, Gary vs IBM Deep Blue, Chess 8, 131
Concentration (Pelmanism) 98-9, *99*
Consequences 232
history 222
Picture 232, *232*

Contract Bridge 8
American Contract Bridge League 291
Bermuda Bowl 1991 7-8
bidding 66-70, *66, 67, 68*
Culbertson, Ely 8, 65
English Bridge Union 291
evaluating hand 66-7
history 65
Lenz, Sidney 8
outline 66
playing 70-72, *71, 72*
points 66, 67
sample game 73-5
scoring 72-3
systems 62
Cow & Leopards
aim 115
playing 114-15, *115*
Crack the Eggs 260
Craps
playing 195
scoring 195-6, *195*
Cribbage 46
American Cribbage Society 291
boards 46, *47*
history 47
playing 47-9
scoring 48-9, *48*
three- and four-handed 49
Cricket, Darts 269
Croquet
aim 278
American Rules Six-wicket 279-81, *280*
Association Rules 281
court 277, *278*
playing 278-9, *279*
Cross Dominoes 182, *182*
Crossword 231, *231*
Team 231
crosswords, history 222
Culbertson, Ely, Contract Bridge 8, 65
Cyprus Dominoes 183-4, *183*

Dabs *see* Jacks(1)
Dama see Checkers
Damanspiel see Checkers
Darrow, Charles, Monopoly® 103
Darts 301/501, 269
Cricket 269
equipment 267-8, *268*

playing 268-9
Dibs *see* Jacks (1)
dice
  games 194
  history 179
  probability 194
Dice (game)
  Indian 197
  Liar 197-8
  Poker 196-7, *197*
  variations 194
Dictionary Game 237
  sample game 237-8
Dodge Ball
  Free Zone 288-9, *289*
  Train 289, *289*
Dominoes 179, 180
  Bergen 186-7, *187*
  Blind Hughie 188, *188*
  Block 182
  Block & Draw 181-2, *181*
  Cross 182, *182*
  Cyprus 183-4, *183*
  Double Cross 182, *182*
  Double Nine Cross 183, *183*
  Five Up 185-6, *186*
  Maltese Cross 182-3, *183*
  Matador 187-8, *188*
  Muggins 184-5, *184*
Donkey 94-5, *95*
  Pig 95
Double Cross Dominoes 182, *182*
Double Nine Cross Dominoes 183, *183*
Double or Quits *see* Monte Carlo
Draw Poker
  Aces-or-Better 40-41
  Jacks-or-Better 40-41
  Low-Ball 37, 41
  Misère 37, 41
  playing 39
  sample game 39-40, *40*
  Wild Cards 41
Drop Dead 201
Dumb Crambo 208-9
Duplicate Scrabble® 110
  Wouters, Hippolite 110

Eleven-man-Ballot Draughts 155
Elves, Gnomes & Giants 214-15
English
  Bridge Union 291
  Draughts Association 290

Euchre
  aim 77
  origins 62, 77
  playing 77-9, *77*, *78*, *79*
  scoring 77
European Go Federation 291
Exchange Tag 284

family games, history 203
FIDE *see* World Chess Federation
Five Game *see* Muggins
Five Hundred
  aim 86
  Five-handed 89
  Four-handed/Australian 88-9, *89*
  playing 86, 87-8, *87*
  scoring 87
  Six-handed 89
Five Up
  aim 185, 186
  playing 185, *186*
  scoring 185-6
  strategies 186
Five-handed Five Hundred 89
Fivestones 257-8, *257*
  Arches 259, *259*
  Jacks(2) 259-60
  Magic 258
  Magic Flycatchers 258
  Pecks, Bushels, & Claws 258-9, *258*
Four Corners
  laying out 21, *21*
  playing 21-23, *22*
Four Field Kono
  aim 174-5
  playing 174, *175*
Four Winds *see* Four Corners
Four-handed Five Hundred 88-9, *89*
Fox & Geese
  aim 114
  history 112
  playing 113-14, *113*
Fox & Geese Solitaire
  aim 114
  playing 114, *114*
Free Zone Dodge Ball 288-9, *289*

gambling 30
  see also betting
Game, The

conventions 210-11
playing 209-10
sample game 211
see also Pictures
games
  board 7, 8, 101, 102, 112
  card 11
  children's 90, 203
  computer 8, 131, 170
  crosswords 222
  dice 194
  history 7-8
  media coverage 7-8
  Nash Equilibrium 9
  outdoor 272
  parlor 204
  skill 255, 256
  strategies 9
  territorial 160
  theory 9
  war 130
  word 234
  written 248
General 199
German Checkers
  aim 157
  playing 157
Ghosts 238-9
  variation 239
Gibson, David, Blank Option Scrabble® 110
Gin Rummy
  aim 50
  Hollywood 52-3
  origins 46, 50
  Partnership 52
  playing 50-51
  scoring 51-2
Go
  aim 162
  American Go Association 291
  boards 161, *161*
  British Go Association 291
  European Go Federation 291
  history 160, 161
  playing 162-6, *162*, *163*, *164*, *165*, *166*
  rule of Ko 166, *166*
  stones *161*, 162
  strategies 167, *167*
Go as you Please Checkers 154
Go Boom 96-7, *97*
Go Fish 95-6, *96*

Going Blank 219
Good Morning Madam 219–20
Goose 112
Grandfather's Clock
  laying out 14–15, *14*
  playing 16–17, *16*
Grandmother's Footsteps
  see Statues
Guggenheim 229–30, *229*
Halma
  aim 117
  history 112, 116
  playing 116–17, *116*, *117*
  strategies 117
Hangman 223–4, *223*, *224*
  Team 224
Hanley, Chris, Trivial Pursuit®
  110–11
Hazard *see* Craps
Headlines 250–51
Hearts
  aim 75
  Black Lady Hearts 76
  Black Maria 76, *76*
  playing 75–6, *75*
  Spot Hearts *76*, 77
Hearts Due 200–201
Hein, Piet, Hex 170
Help Your Neighbor 201
Hex
  aim 171
  Hein, Piet 170
  history 160
  playing *170*, 171
Hide & Seek 285–6
  history 203
Hollywood Gin 52–3
Homeward Bound *see* Ludo
Hop Ching Checkers *see* Chinese
  Checkers
Hopscotch 286–7, *287*
Horseshoe
  aim 167–8
  playing 167, *167*, *168*
Horseshoe Pitching
  equipment 273, *273*
  playing 274–5, *274*, *275*
  scoring 273–4, *274*
Housey-Housey *see* Lotto

I Doubt It (Cheat) 97–8
I Have Never 218–19
I Love My Love 235

I Packed My Bag 236
  variation 236–7
I Spy 240
  variation 240
Iceland, Contract Bridge World
  Champions 1991 7–8
In the Manner of the Word 216,
  216
Indian Dice 197
Internet, board games 8
Irish Draughts Association 290
Italian Checkers
  aim 156
  playing 155–6, 156

Jacks (1)
  Fivestones 257–8, *257*
  history 257
Jacks (2) 259–60
  Crack the Eggs 260
  Pigs over the Fence 260
  Pigs in the Pen 260
Jacks-or-Better 40–41
Jackstones *see* Jacks(1)
Japan, Shogi professionals 8
Japanese Chess *see* Shogi
Jeu de Dames see Checkers
Joker Klondike 20

Kasparov, Gary vs IBM Deep Blue,
  Chess 8, 131
Klondike
  Agnes 19–21, *19*, *20*
  Joker 20
  laying out 17, *17*
  origins 12, 17
  playing 17–19, *18*, *19*
  two or more players 19–20
  variations 19–21
Knucklebones *see* Jacks(1)
Kono *see* Four Field Kono
Kriegspiel
  aim 146
  playing 145–6

Lamorisse, Albert, Risk(R) 105
Landlord's Game 103
Lawn Bowls
  aim 275
  equipment 275–6, *275*, *276*
  pairs 277
  singles 276–7
  triples 277

Legs 249
Liar Dice 197
  variation 197–8
License Plates 239
  variation 240
Likes & Dislikes 220
Losing Draughts
  aim 155
  playing 155
Lotto 233
Lovely Lucy
  laying out 23, *23*
  origins 12
  playing 23–7, *24*, *25*, *26*
  variations 27
Low-Ball 37, 41
Ludo
  aim 128
  history 112, 128
  playing 128, *128*

Magic 258
Magic Flycatchers 258
Mah-Jongg
  aim 189
  Flowers & Seasons 193
  Hand from Earth 193
  Hand from Heaven 193
  history 179
  limit hands 193
  Lucky Thirteen 193
  playing 190–92, *191*
  preparation 189–90
  scoring 192–3
  Seven Twins 193
  Snake 193
  strategies 193
  Thirteen Hidden Orphans 193
  Three Great Scolars 193
  tiles 189, *190*
Maltese Cross Dominoes 182–3,
  183
Mancala 101, 160, 176
Marbles
  equipment 287
  Ring Taw 287–8, *288*
  Shooting the Ring 287, *288*
Matador
  aim 187–8
  playing 187–8, *188*
  scoring 188
Matchbox Race 206, *206*
  horse or current bun 206

media coverage 7–8
Mexican Flip 43–4
Misère 37, 41
Moksha-Patamu 112, 129
Monopoly®
  aim 105
  Darrow, Charles 103
  foreign editions 104
  history 103–4
  playing 104–5
  strategies 105
Monte Carlo
  laying out 27, *28*
  playing 27
Murder in the Dark 212

Nash Equilibrium, Nash, John 9
Nash, John, Nash Equilibrium 9
Nine Men's Morris
  aim 170
  history 160, 168, 203
  playing 168, *168*, *169*, 170
Ninety-One
  laying out 28, *29*
  playing 28–9, *29*
  history 203

Omaha 45
One-cushion Carom 267
Othello® *see* Reversi
outdoor games 272
Owari
  aim 177
  history 176
  playing 176–7, *176*
  strategies 177

Pachisi 112, 128
Pairs (Pelmanism) 98–9, *99*
paper & pencil games 222
Parcheesi *see* Ludo
parlour games 204
Partnership Gin Rummy 52
Pass the Orange 207, *207*
  variation 207
Patchesi *see* Ludo
Pecks, Bushels & Claws 258–9, *258*
Pelmanism 98–9, *99*
Pepys, Samuel, on parlor games 204
Pick-up-sticks 260–61, *261*, *262*
Picture Consequences 232, *232*
Pictures 252

Pig (1) 95
Pig (2) 199–200
Pigs over the Fence 260
Pigs in the Pen 260
Ping-pong *see* Table Tennis
Pinochle
  aim 79–80
  playing 80–82, *81*
  popularity in USA 62
  scoring 79–80, 81
Piquet
  aim 82
  history 62
  playing 82–3, *83*, 84–6
  scoring 83–4, *83*, *84*, *85*
playing cards
  development 11
  early European 11
  German 11
  Oriental 11
  Spanish 11
  Tarot 11
  value of ace 11
Poetry Game 228–9
Poker
  aim 36
  betting 37–9
  dealing 37, *37*
  Draw 39–41, *40*
  hand values 36–7
  history 36
  status in USA 30
  Stud 41–5, *42*, *43*, *44*
Poker Dice
  playing 196
  scoring 196, *197*
Polish Checkers
  aim 158
  playing 158
Pontoon
  aim 33
  Blackjack 35–6
  five card tricks 35
  playing 33–4, *34*
  scoring 33, 35
  splitting 35
postal gaming *see* AHIKS
Pratt, Anthony, Clue® (Cluedo®) 106
probability 194
Professional Chess Association (PCA) 132
Progressive Chess

aim 144
  playing 144
Proverbs 246
  variation 246–7

Quizzes 251, *251*

Random Chess
  aim 145
  playing 145
Red Rover Tag 285, *285*
Reversi (Othello®)
  aim 174
  British Othello Federation 291
  history 160, 171
  Japanese domination 171–2
  playing 172–3, *172*, *173*
  strategies 173–4
  World Champions 171–2
Ring Taw 287–8, *288*
Risk®
  aim 105, 106
  history 105
  Lamorisse, Albert 105
  playing 106
  strategies 106
Round Dozen *see* Shut the Box
RPGA (Role–Playing Games Association) 291
Rubik's Cube 220–21
Rummy *see* Gin Rummy
Russian Dominoes *see* Matador
Russian Checkers
  aim 157
  playing 157

Salvo 228
Sardines 211–12
Scissors, Paper, & Stone 214, *214*
Scopa
  aim 60
  playing 60–61, *60*
scoring 61
Scottish Chess Association 290
Scottish Draughts Association 290
Scrabble®
  aim 110
  Blank Option 110
  Brunot, Jim 108
  Butts, Alfred 108
  Duplicate 110
  history 108
  playing 108–10

Solitaire 110
strategies 108–10
Seated Blind Man's Buff 217
Seven Card High-Low 44–5
Shamrocks 27
Shantranj 130
Shogi (Japanese Chess)
  aim 148
  history 130
  pieces 146, *146*
  playing 146–8, *147*
  professionals 8
Shooting the Ring 287, *288*
Short Stories 233
Shut the Box 199, *199*
Simon Says 286
Six-handed Five Hundred 89
skill games 255, 256
Slapjack 91–2, *92*
Snakes & Ladders
  aim 129
  history 112, 129
  playing 129, *129*
  Snap 91, *91*
  Solitaire
  Clock 13–14, *13*, *14*
  Four Corners 21–3, *21*, *22*
  Grandfather's Clock 14–17, *14*,
    16
  Klondike 17–21, *17*, *18*, *19*
  Lovely Lucy 23–7, *23*, *24*, *25*, *26*
  Monte Carlo 27–8, *28*
  Ninety-One 28–9, *29*
  origins 12
  Watch 13
Solitaire Scrabble® 110
Spanish Checkers
  aim 157
  playing 156–7, *156*
Spelling Round 244–5
  variations 245
Spit 92–3, *93*
Spit in the Ocean 45
Spoof 215–16, *215*
Spot Hearts *76*, 77
Sprouts 225–6, *225*
Stairway 252
Starships 228
Statues 284
Stud Poker
  Mexican Flip 43–4
  playing 41–2
  sample game 42–43, *42*, *43*, *44*

Seven Card High-Low 44–5
Texas Hold 'em 45

Table Tennis
  doubles 271
  equipment 269–70, *269*, *270*
  scoring 270–71
  singles 270–71
Taboo 245–6
Tag
  Bulldog 285
  Exchange 284
  Red Rover 285, *285*
Tarot cards 11
Tea Kettle *see* Coffee Pot
Team Crossword 231
Team Hangman 224
Texas Hold 'em 45
  Cincinnati 45
  Omaha 45
  Spit in the Ocean 45
Three-cushion Carom 267
Three-move-Ballot Checkers 155
Tic-tac-toe 223, *223*
Tiddlywinks
  aim 262
  equipment 262
  history 261–2
  International Federation of
    Associations 262
  playing 263–5, *263*, *264*, *265*
  scoring 263
Train Dodge Ball 289, *289*
Transformation 253
Trefoil 27
Trivial Pursuit®
  Abbott, Scott 110–11
  aim 111
  Hanley, Chris 110–11
  history 110–11
  playing 111
Turkish Checkers
  aim 159
  playing 159, *159*
Twenty One *see* Blackjack
Twenty Questions 240–41
  sample game 241
  variation 241

UK Carom Club 291
US Chess Federation 290

Vingt-et-Un *see* Pontoon

Watch Solitaire 13
Weddings *see* Monte Carlo
Weichi 101
Welsh Draughts Association 290
Whist
  aims 63
  origins 62, 63
  playing 63–5, *63*, *64*
  scoring 63–4, *64*
Who Am I? 241–2
Wild Cards 41
Winking 207–8, *208*
  strategies 208
Wolf & Goats
  aim 116
  playing 115–16, *115*
word games, history 234
World Chess Federation (FIDE)
  132
Wouters, Hippolite, Duplicate
  Scrabble® 110
written games 248

Xiangqi (Chinese Chess)
  aim 150
  pieces 148–9, *148*
  playing 148–50, *149*

Yacht 198
Yahtzee® *see* Yacht

GAMES FOR ONE PERSON

Fox & Geese Solitaire 114

Solitaire
Agnes 20–21
Clock 13–14
Four Corners, The 21–23
Grandfather's Clock 14–17
Klondike 17–19
Lovely Lucy 23–7
Monte Carlo 27–8
Ninety-One 28–9
Shamrocks 27
Trefoil 27
Watch 13

Rubik's Cube 220–21

GAMES FOR TWO PEOPLE

All Fives 184–5
Alphabet Race 226
Alquerque 175–6
Anagrams 230–31
Apple Ducking 205
Arches 259

Backgammon 118–28
Badminton 281–4
Battleships 227–8
Beetle 205–6
Beggar My Neighbor 94
Bergen 186–7
Billiards, Carom 265–7
Blind Hughie 188
Block & Draw Dominoes 181–2
Block Dominoes 182
Bowls, Lawn 275–7
Boxes 224–5
Buzz 218
Buzz-Fizz 218

Canadian Checkers 158–9

Carom Billiards 265–7
Casino 57–9
Chess 131–44
Chinese (Xiangqi) 148–50
Japanese (Shogi) 146–8
Progressive 144
Random 144–5
Chinese Checkers 117–18
Chinese Chess (Xiangqi) 148–50
Concentration (Pelmanism) 98–9
Consequences 232
Cow & Leopards 114–15
Crack the Eggs 260
Craps 195–6
Cribbage 47–9
Cricket (Darts) 269
Croquet 277–81
Cross Dominoes 182–3
Crossword 231
Cyprus 183–4

Checkers 150–54
Canadian 158–9
German 157
Italian 155–6
Losing 155
Polish 158
Russian 157
Spanish 156–7
Turkish 159
Darts 267–9
Cricket 269
Dominoes
Bergen 186–7
Blind Hughie 188
Block 182
Block & Draw 181–2
Cross 182–3
Cyprus 183–4
Matador 187
Muggins 184–5

Five Hundred 86–9
Fivestones 257–8
Arches 259
Jacks 259–60
Magic 258
Magic Flycatchers 258
Pecks, Bushels, & Claws 258–9
Four Field Kono 174–5
Fox & Geese 113–14

German Checkers 157

Go 161–7
Go Boom 96–7
Go Fishing 95–6
Guggenheim 229–30

Halma 116–17
Hangman 223–4
Hearts Due 200–1
Help Your Neighbor 201
Hex 170–71
Hopscotch 286–7
Horseshoe 167–8
Horseshoe Pitching 273–5

I Packed My Bag 236–7
I Spy 240
Italian Checkers 155–6

Jacks 259–60
Crack the Eggs 260
Pigs Over the Fence 260
Pigs in the Pen 260

Lawn Bowls 275–7
Liar Dice 197–8
License Plates 239–40
Losing Checkers 155

Magic 258
Magic Flycatchers 258
Marbles 287–8
Matador 187
Monopoly® 103–5

Nine Men's Morris (Mill) 168–70

Othello® (Reversi) 171–4
Owari 176–7

Pairs (Pelmanism) 98–9
Patience, Klondike 19–20
Pecks, Bushels, & Claws 258–9
Pelmanism 98–99
Pig 199–200
Pigs Over the Fence 260
Pigs in the Pen 260
Pinochle 79–82
Ping-Pong 269–71
Piquet 82–6
Poker Dice 196–7
Polish Checkers 158
Pontoon 33–5
Progressive Chess 144

Random Chess 144–5
Reversi (Othello®) 171–4
Risk® 105–6
Rummy, Gin 50–52
Russian Draughts 157

Salvo 228
Scissors, Paper & Stone 214
Scopa 59–61
Scrabble® 107–10
Shogi (Japanese Chess) 146–8
Short Stories 233
Shut the Box 199
Slapjack 91–3
Snakes & Ladders 128–9
Snap 91
Spanish Checkers 156–7
Spoof 215–16
Sprouts 225–6
Stairway 251–2
Starships 228

Tiddlywinks 261–5
Trivial Pursuit® 110–11
Turkish Checkers 159

Wolf & Goats 115–16

Xiangqi (Chinese Chess)148–50

GAMES FOR EIGHT OR MORE

Aces in the Pot 200

Baccarat 32–3
Beetle 205–6
Blackjack 35–6

Charades 212–14
Chemin de Fer 31–2
Coffee Pot 247
Craps 195–6

Dodge Ball 288–9
Drop Dead 201

Dumb Crambo 208–9

Elves, Gnomes, & Giants 214–15

Ghosts 238–9

Hangman 223–4
Hearts Due 200–1
Hide & Seek 285–6
Hopscotch 286–7

Legs 249
Likes & Dislikes 220

Matchbox Race 206
Mexican Flip 43–4
Murder in the Dark 212–13

Pass the Orange 207
Poetry Game, The 228–9
Poker
   Mexican Flip 43–4
   Seven Card High-Low 44–5
   Stud 41–3
Pontoon 33–5

Seven Card High-Low 44–5
Simon Says 286
Spelling Round 244–5
Statues 284
Stud Poker 41–3

Tag 284–5

GAMES FOR CHILDREN

Alphabet Race 226
Apple Ducking 205

Battleships 227–8
Beetle 205–6
Beggar My Neighbor 94
Blind Hughie 188
Blind Man's Buff 217
Block & Draw Dominoes 181–2
Block Dominoes 182
Boxes 224–5
Bulldog 285

Buzz 218
Buzz-Fizz 218

Casino 57–9
Charades 212–14
Cheat 97–8
Checkers 150–55
   Losing 155
Clock Patience 13–14
Concentration (Pelmanism) 98–9
Consequences 232
Cross Dominoes 182
Crossword 231

Dodge Ball 288–9
Dominoes
   Blind Hughie 188
   Block 182
   Block & Draw 181–2
   Cross 182
Donkey 94–5
Drop Dead 201
Dumb Crambo 208–9

Elves, Gnomes, & Giants 214–15

Fivestones 257–60

Game, The 209–11
Go Boom 96–7
Go Fish 95–6
Good Morning Madam 219–20
Grandfather's Clock 14–17
Guggenheim 229–30
Hangman 223–4
Hearts Due 200–1
Hide & Seek 285–6
Hopscotch 286–7
Housey-Housey (Lotto) 233

I Packed My Bag 236
I Spy 240
In the Manner of the Word 216

Legs 249
Liar Dice 197–8
License Plates 239–40
Lotto 233

Marbles 287–8
Matchbox Race 206
Monopoly® 103–5
Murder in the Dark 212

Pairs (Pelmanism) 98–9
Pass the Orange 207
Pelmanism 98–9
Pick-up-Sticks 260–61
Pictures 252–3
Pig 199–200
Ping Pong 269–71
Pontoon 33–5

Quizzes 251

Rubik's Cube 220–21

Sardines 211–12
Scissors, Paper & Stone 214
Scopa 59–61
Scrabble® 107–110
Short Stories 233
Shut the Box 199
Simon Says 286
Slapjack 91–2
Snakes and Ladders 128–9
Snap 91, 261–5
Solitaire
　Clock 13–14
　Watch 13
Spit 92–3
Spoof 215–16
Sprouts 225–6
Stairway 251–2
Starships 228
Statues 284
Taboo 245–6
Tag 284–5
Tic-tac-toe 223
Transformation 253

Watch Sol.itaire 13
Who am I? 241–2
Winking 207–8

Yacht 198

GAMES FOR TRAVEL

Alphabet Race 226
Anagrams 230–31
Analogies 235–6
Association 244

Battleships 227–8
Botticelli 242–4
Boxes 224–5
Bridge the Word 253
Buzz 218
Buzz-Fizz 218

Categories 249–50
Coffee Pot 247
Consequences 232
Crossword 231

Going Blank 219
Guggenheim 229–30

Hangman 223–4
Headlines 250–51

I Have Never 218–19
I Love My Love 235
I Packed My Bag 236–7
I Spy 240

Legs 249
License Plates 239–40
Likes & Dislikes 220

Pictures 252–3
Poetry Game, The 228–9
Proverbs 246–7

Quizzes 251

Rubik's Cube 220–21

Salvo 228
Scissors, Paper & Stone 214
Scrabble® (travel version) 107–10
Short Stories 233
Spelling Round 244–5
Sprouts 225–6
Stairway 251–2

Starships 226

Taboo 245–6
Tic-tac-toe 223
Transformation 253
Twenty Questions 240–41

Who A
I? 241–2

GAMES LASTING NOT MORE THAN HALF AN HOUR

Agnes 20–21
Alphabet Race 226
Alquerque 175–6
Apple Ducking 205
Australian/Five Handed Five Hundred 88–9
Australian/Four Handed Five Up 88–9

Backgammon 118–28
Badminton 281–4
Battleships 227–8
Beetle 205–6
Beggar My Neighbor 94
Bergen 186–7
Black Lady 76
Black Maria 76
Blind Hughie 188
Block & Draw Dominoes 181–2
Block Dominoes 182
Boxes 224–5
Bridge the Word 253
Buzz 218
Buzz-Fizz 218

Canasta 53–7
Casino 57–9
Categories 249–50
Cheat 97–8
Checkers 150–55

Losing 155
Chess
  Progressive 144
  Random 144–5
Clock Solitaire 13
Clue® (Cluedo®) 106–7
Coffee Pot 247
Concentration (Pelmanism) 98–9
Consequencies 232
Cows & Leopards 114–15
Craps 195–6
Cribbage 47–9
Cross Dominoes 182–3
Crossword 231
Cyprus 183–4

Darts 267–9
Dictionary Game, The 237–8
Dodge Ball 288–9
Dominoes
  Bergen 186–7
  Blind Hughie 188
  Block 182
  Block & Draw 181–2
  Cross 182–3
  Cyprus 183–4
  Five Up 185–6
  Matador 187–8
  Muggins 184–5
Donkey 94–5

Elves, Gnomes, & Giants 214–15

Five Handed Five up 89
Five Hundred 86–9
  Five Handed 89
  Four Handed/Australian 88–9
  Six Handed 89
Five Up 185–6
Four Corners 21–3
Four Field Kono 174–5
Four Handed/ Australian Five up 88–9
Fox & Geese 113–14
  Solitaire 114

Ghosts 238–9
Gin Rummy 50–53
  Hollywood 52–3
  Partnership 52
Go Boom 96–7
Go Fishing 95–6

Good Morning Madam 219–20
Grandfather's Clock 14–17
Guggenheim 229–30

Hangman 223–4
Headlines 250–51
Hearts 75–7
  Black Lady 76
  Black Maria 76
  Spot 77
Hearts Due 200–1
Hide & Seek 285–6
Hollywood Gin Rummy 52–53
Hopscotch 286–7
Horseshoe 167–8
Horseshoe Pitching 273–5

I Packed My Bag 236–7
I Spy 240

Klondike 17–21
Kriegspiel 145–6

Legs 249
License Plates 239–40
Losing Draughts 155
Lotto (Housey-Housey) 233
Lovely Lucy 23–7
Ludo 128

Marbles 287–8
Matador 187–8
Matchbox Race 206
Monte Carlo 27–8
Muggins 184–5

Nine Men's Morris 168–70
Ninety-One 28–9

Owari 176–7

Pairs (Pelmanism) 98–9
Partnership Gin Rummy 52
Pass the Orange 207
Pelmanism 98–9
Pick–Up–Sticks 260–61
Pig 199–200
Piquet 82–6
Poetry Game, The 228–9
Poker Dice 196–7
Progressive Chess 144
Random Chess 144–5

Salvo 228
Scissors, Paper, & Stone 214
Scopa 59–61
Shamrocks 27
Short Stories 233
Simon Says 286
Six-handed Five-up 89
Slapjack 91–2
Snakes & Ladders 128–9
Snap 91
Solitaire
  Agnes 20–21
  Clock 13
  Four Corners 21–3
  Grandfather's Clock 14–17
  Klondike 17–21
  Lovely Lucy 23–7
  Monte Carlo 27–8
  Ninety-One 28–9
  Shamrocks 27
  Trefoil 27
  Watch 13–14
Solitaire Fox & Geese 114
Spelling Round 244–5
Spit 92–3
Spoof 215–16
Spot 77
Starships 228
Statues 284

Table Tennis 269–71
Taboo 245–6
Tag 284–5
Tic-tac-toe 223
Tiddlywinks 261–5
Transformation 253
Trefoil 27

Watch Draughts 13–14
Who Am I? 241–2
Wolf & Goats 115–16

Yacht 198